BLOODSHED AND VENGEANCE
IN THE PAPUAN MOUNTAINS

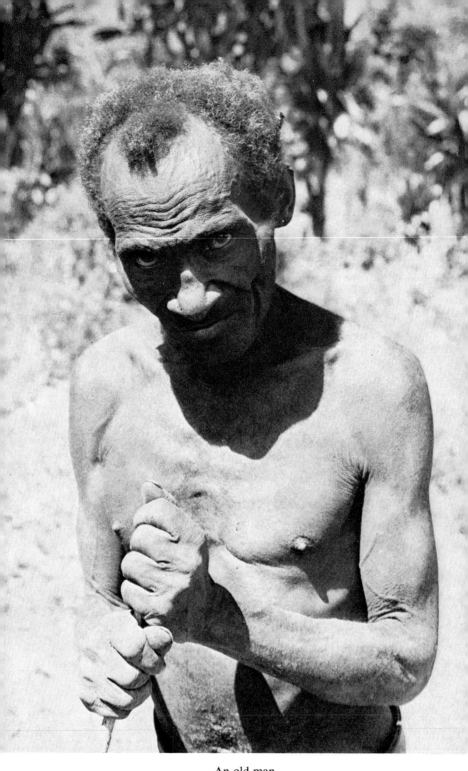

An old man

Bloodshed and Vengeance in the Papuan Mountains

The Generation of Conflict in Tauade Society

C. R. HALLPIKE

OXFORD
AT THE CLARENDON PRESS
1977

Oxford University Press, Walton Street, Oxford, OX2 6DP

OXFORD LONDON GLASGOW NEW YORK
TORONTO MELBOURNE WELLINGTON CAPE TOWN
IBADAN NAIROBI DAR ES SALAAM LUSAKA ADDIS ABABA
KUALA LUMPUR SINGAPORE JAKARTA HONG KONG TOKYO
DELHI BOMBAY CALCUTTA MADRAS KARACHI

© *C. R. Hallpike 1977*

British Library Cataloguing in Publication Data

Hallpike, Christopher Robert
Bloodshed and vengeance in the Papuan mountains:
the generation of conflict in Tauade society.
Bibl.–Index
ISBN 0–19–823192–X
I. Title
301. 6'3'09953 DU740.42
Tauade (Papua–New Guinea people)
Social conflict.

*Printed in Great Britain
at the University Press, Oxford
by Vivian Ridler
Printer to the University*

Preface

IN a well-known paper Professor Barnes (1962) argued some years ago that African models were positively misleading when applied to New Guinea; having had the opportunity of studying societies in both these areas I hope to show that one can only understand many aspects of New Guinea societies (of which the Tauade are fairly typical) by a total and systematic reversal of the principles which govern, for example, African societies such as the Konso (see Hallpike 1972).

It will be suggested that societies like the Konso treat groups and categories as fundamental, and regard behaviour both actual and normative as deriving from the groups and categories of which the agent is a member. For such a society, therefore, 'harmony' will basically consist in the performance by the members of each group and category of those social tasks for which they are essentially fitted and qualified; thus 'right' will be distinct from 'power', and 'order' and 'truth' will be essential aspects of 'right'. The passions will be seen as destructive of order and right, and correspondingly one may expect to find that a basic concern with classification and conceptual boundaries pervades such a culture.

The opposite type of society—and I suggest that the Tauade fall into this category—will be one which regards relationships between individuals as basic, and any existing groups and categories as the precipitate of these relationships—friendship, enmity, revenge, and reciprocity in various forms, co-operation, marriage, competition, and so on. In such a society 'harmony' will consist in the balance of opposing forces, and in this context the passions will not be seen as destructive but, on the contrary, as providing the basis of all interaction, so that the distinction between right and power becomes meaningless. Classification will have little relevance to such a system.

Violence, moreover, will have a very different significance in each of these types of society, but for some reason most ethnographers of New Guinea have paid relatively little attention to violence—relative, that is, to its remarkable pervasiveness and intensity. It would be pointless to speculate on the reasons for what is clearly a dominant academic bias, apart from the reflection that anthropologists have always been concerned to refute popular stereotypes of 'savagery' and are therefore perhaps too easily inclined to dismiss an interest in violence as a concession to vulgar prejudices. But the regulation of violence is a basic sociological problem, and I have therefore made bloodshed and vengeance the central theme of this book and the focus of the contrast between the two types of society already referred to.

It may legitimately be asked why Tauade society and modes of thought should be permeated by the 'Heraclitean' cognitive orientation just referred to. For I am certainly not suggesting that basic cognitive orientations just appear from the recesses of some 'group mind'; the natural, interactive processes of society are constantly generating social phenomena which members of the society then integrate and generalize in the form of value and belief systems and cognitive orientations. In the case of the Tauade it seems likely that Heraclitean modes of thought have been powerfully reinforced by the great dances and pig feasts that periodically require the inhabitants of separate hamlets in each tribe to combine in the building of large dance villages, after which the members of the tribe disperse into new hamlets. These dance villages, and the facilities for creating widely ramifying networks of gift exchange which are provided by the pigs, have clearly been prime factors in the destruction of the original clan organization and in intensifying the atomism of Tauade society. Far from knitting Tauade society together, I believe it can be shown that in this case gift exchange and cross-cutting ties are disintegrating factors and are intimately associated with the high level of violence. The belief that gift exchange and cross-cutting ties (especially marriage) are the cement of human society is then reduced from a universal law to a special case—it only applies where there are stable groups to be cemented, and which can control their members.

This book is therefore also a study of the relations between the ecology, social organization, beliefs, and values of the Tauade. In my first book, on the Konso of Ethiopia, I stressed the central importance of values as principles integrating many of their institutions and modes of behaviour, and the necessity of treating societies as systems of ideas as well as systems of action. But my statement in that book that their values must be taken as given, as similar to the rules of a game, unfortunately gave rise to the belief that I was stating that they were inexplicable and their origins intractable to any sociological analysis. This is a mistaken inference. While basic values are clearly very enduring elements of a society, even they must change; all one can say is that without some historical records the ethnographer has no means of explaining how the values of a non-literate society have in fact changed, and he is thus in the regrettable position of having to treat them as given. Just as I could not explain why the Konso placed such emphasis upon peace or virility, I cannot explain why the Tauade are obsessed with power and aggression, beyond making the rather commonplace observation that this is an obsession shared by many societies in New Guinea for which there is no obvious sociological explanation.

In the final chapter I refer to some confusion between the concepts of 'system' and 'organism' and suggest that while we can give a systematic analysis of Tauade violence, showing how it is related to their ecology, social organization, and basic cognitive orientation and values, it is quite mistaken to construe it as in any way 'functional' or 'adaptive' for their society. Anthropological analyses of conflict have conventionally been concerned to demonstrate the means by which it is regulated. But this is only one side of the coin. In all societies, the means by which conflict is generated are analytically as significant as the means by which it is controlled, and the organization of some societies makes a high level of conflict both permanent and inescapable. It is for these reasons that this book bears the subtitle 'The generation of conflict in Tauade society', rather than 'The control of conflict'.

Acknowledgements

MY principal debt is to various Canadian institutions which made the writing of this book possible: to the Canada Council, which paid for the expenses of two years in the field; to Dalhousie University, Nova Scotia, which appointed me for a second time to a Research Fellowship, thus enabling me to write the first draft of this book free from the distractions of teaching; and to Professor R. F. Salisbury of McGill University, Montreal, who first suggested the Goilala Sub-District to me as a promising area for research.

My debts to the Australian Administration are many. In particular I should like to express my thanks for permission to read patrol reports and other documents pertaining to the Goilala Sub-District. At a more personal level, one of my most pleasant memories of working in the Territory is the unfailingly courteous and genial co-operation with which my requests for assistance were received by a large number of Government Departments in Port Moresby. To Mr. R. Galloway, District Commissioner, Central District, Mr. K. Brown, Deputy District Commissioner, and Mr. D. Fitzer, Deputy District Commissioner, go special thanks in this respect. At Tapini my researches received the full support of Messrs. W. Reid, R. Weber, and W. Cawthorn, Assistant District Commissioners of the Goilala Sub-District. Both they and their patrol officers made me feel at home in the Sub-District office, and their friendly and hospitable attitude did much to make my work a success.

Mr. Ron Holdup, that most ingenious and obliging resurrector of everything on wheels around Tapini, deserves a special mention for willingly giving up his time on so many occasions to keep my motor-bike running. Mr. John Martin gave me much interesting material of an ethnographic nature drawn from his twenty-years' residence in the area, and Mme Yvette Cachard helped to keep up my morale with her excellent French cooking whenever I stayed at her guest-house in Tapini.

I was extremely fortunate in working in an area whose missionaries are the Fathers of the Sacred Heart of Issoudun, based at Yule

Island. It is a great pleasure for me to have the opportunity of thanking, in particular, the Reverend Fathers of Kerau, Fr. C. Guichet, Fr. J. Fridez, Fr. C. Duffey, and Fr. T. Jacob, and Brother J. Delabarre and Sister Mary and the Little Sisters, for looking after me during the two years of my stay. By playing chess on Sunday afternoons and plying me with many a good glass of wine and grog, especially when I came to the mission soaked and exhausted, and above all by their kindly and civilized company, they helped to keep me sane, and by their extensive knowledge of the people which they freely extended to me they were of great assistance in the purely academic aspects of my work. I cannot sufficiently express my gratitude to them. I must also thank the Fathers of Kamulai, Kosipi, Ononghe, and Yule Island for their help and hospitality on many occasions, and I am most grateful to the Father Superior of the mission for allowing me to copy Fr. Fastré's manuscript and to use it in this book.

The New Guinea Research Unit generously allowed me to use its excellent accommodation at Waigani whenever I visited Port Moresby, although I had no connection at all with the Australian National University, their parent body. Whenever I visited Moresby, Dr. and Mrs. Anthony Allen were always most hospitable, and I am very grateful to them for their kindness during my two years' stay. The University of Papua New Guinea liberally made its facilities available to me, and I must thank in particular Dr. D. Froden, of the Department of Botany, for identifying some of the plants mentioned in this book, and Professor D. Drover, of the Chemistry Department, for analysing the soil samples. I am greatly obliged to Mr. Colin Freeman, the Librarian of the New Guinea Collection in the University, for supplying me with much useful bibliographical material, and to Mrs. Sandra Hoath for frequent secretarial assistance. I am also obliged to Professor R. N. H. Bulmer, of the Department of Anthropology and Sociology, for many most interesting ethnographic discussions.

Mr. F. D. Anderson and Mr. R. Galloway, sometime A.D.C.s of the Goilala Sub-District, kindly supplied me with material relating to homicide and other matters in the area from their private papers. I am also grateful to Dr. Margaret McArthur for allowing me to read her thesis on the Kunimaipa, and to quote from it. QASCO Pty. Ltd. of Port Moresby generously produced a contoured map of the Aibala Valley for me at one-third of the commercial price—A$500 instead of A$1500. The revision of the first and final drafts of this book was greatly assisted by the criticisms of the Clarendon Press, and Dr. Rodney Needham was also kind enough to suggest improvements in some chapters of the first draft.

The Papua New Guinea Government has kindly given me permission to quote from numerous court records, patrol reports, and other official matter, but I have deleted all names from accounts of court cases, and from patrol reports which refer to homicide. In addition, I have in many cases deleted names from texts obtained verbally from informants where the persons described are involved in killings, or whose conduct might bring them or their relatives into contempt or ridicule. I have also occasionally suppressed the identities of patrol officers who are still resident in Papua New Guinea or Australia.

C. R. H.

Diptford
South Devon
May 1975

Contents

LIST OF PLATES   xiv

LIST OF FIGURES   xv

LIST OF MAPS   xv

LIST OF TABLES   xvi

ABBREVIATIONS   xviii

I. INTRODUCTION   I

   1. European impact on Tauade society   3

     (a) Pacification   4

     (b) The arrival of the Mission of the Sacred Heart, and the war years   14

     (c) Political and economic change   19

   2. The circumstances of field-work   27

   3. The assessment of sources   33

II. THE AIBALA VALLEY   39

   1. The physical environment   39

   2. The peoples of the Goilala Sub-District   43

   3. Migration, travel, and trade routes   49

   4. The settlement pattern   53

   5. The use of resources   62

   6. Conclusions   75

III. THE ATOMISM OF TAUADE SOCIETY   77

   1. A cognitive model for Tauade social atomism   77

   2. Tribe and clan   83

   3. Land tenure   99

4. Hamlets   108

5. Marriage   122
   (a) Social ties   122
   (b) Control of women   126

6. Conclusions   135

IV. CO-ORDINATION AND CONTROL   137

1. The status of the chiefs   138

2. Ceremonies   162
   (a) The ritual content of ceremonies   162
   (b) Large ceremonies   164
   (c) Small ceremonies   174

3. Compensation and vengeance   188

V. WARFARE   196

1. Small-scale violence   196

2. The pattern of tribal warfare   202

3. Annotated accounts of warfare   211

4. Conclusions   229

VI. TAUADE VALUES   232

1. The status of the passions   234

2. Love and hatred   239

3. Pride and shame   245

4. Heroic and utilitarian societies   249

5. Conclusions   252

VII. THE WILD AND THE TAME   254

1. The culture heroes   256

2. Totems   262

3. Spirits   270

4. Conclusions   273

VIII. SYSTEM AND ORGANISM   275

APPENDICES
I.   Migration rates and hamlet populations   285
II. Sex ratios   291
III. Kinship terminology   292
IV. Homicide statistics   294
V.   Medical statistics   297
VI. Meteorological statistics   298
VII. Soil samples   299

BIBLIOGRAPHY   300

INDEX   307

List of Plates

Frontispiece. An old man

Between pages 76–7

I.   In the high ranges
II.   Goilala seen from Tawuni
III.   Some Goilala people
IV.   Dimanibi, a traditional hamlet

Between pages 172–3

V.   Climbing a pandanus tree
VI.   Disembowelling a pig
VII.   A small feast at Goilala
VIII.   Dawn mists in the Ivane Valley

List of Figures

1. Tapini rainfall 1961–70   42
2. Hamlet layout   55
3. Structure of Larima clan   90
4. Dispersal of agnates among hamlets   92
5. Ancestry of Buluvu Evura   94
6. Relationships of Kire Keruvu and Keru Katemu   95
7. Claimants to Pomutaivi land   103
8. Amo Lume's inheritance of pandanus trees   106
9. Genealogical links between owners of pandanus trees   107
10. Persistence of hamlets over time   110
11. Group structure of Dimanibi hamlet   113
12. Relationship and residence at Dimanibi   114
13. Pattern of marriages between a group of agnates and   125
    surrounding tribes
14. Affinal ties between chiefs   150
15. Genealogy of Tupi clan   152
16. Relatives of Kari who contributed pigs for her funeral   180
17. The generation of conflict   276
18. The maintenance of peace   276
19. Adaptive features of hamlet design and location   278
20. Heraclitean cognitive orientation   281

List of Maps

1. Location of the Goilala Sub-District   xx
2. Goilala Sub-District   44
3. Tauade Dialect distribution   46
4. Settlement pattern   61
5. Hamlet distribution   87

List of Tables

1. Chronology of government and mission influence   27
2. The populations of the three language groups in the   45
   Goilala Sub-District
3. Tribal populations   54
4. Current population of Goilala hamlets   54
5. Population density (Census 1958)   65
6. Garden sizes   66
7. Size of pig herds   73
8. Clan origins of hamlets   88
9. Clan bone caves   89
10. Murders by clan   93
11. The distribution of clans by hamlets   93
12. Effects of migration on tribal membership   98
13. Claimants to Pomutaivi land   102
14. Sample of men occupying successive hamlets together   111
15. Hamlets occupied by Amo Lume in the course of his life   112
16. Cases of relationship between hamlet members   114
17. Garden co-operation and hamlet residence   116
18. Number of diadic relationships according to population   116
19. Relationships of principal disputants in fights at Goilala   117
20. Adultery statistics   117
21. The incidence of crime within and between tribes   119
22. The incidence of homicide at Goilala   120
23. The incidence of homicide in a Kunimaipa tribe   120
24. Marriage alliances between Goilala and other tribes   123
25. Number of marriages of Goilala clans with other tribes   123
26. Marriage links between clans and tribes   124
27. Number of marriages between hamlets and neighbouring   126
    tribes
28. Distribution of wives among adult Goilala males, at one   129
    time
29. Distribution of wives among adult Goilala males,   129
    serially

30. Sex ratios   130
31. Divorce rate in relation to number of wives   131
32. Frequency of divorce (Goilala only)   131
33. Types of relationship between husbands and adulterers   133
34. Social status and government rank   141
35. Recipients of pork at Moripi's pig feast   156
36. Frequency of dances   173
37. Pig-killings at Goilala   175
38. Distribution of pork   176
39. Proportion of pork given to other tribes   177
40. Donors of pigs at Aima Kamo's funeral   180
41. Reasons for donations of pork at Goilala feast   182
42. Donors of pigs at birth feast   183
43. Recipients of pork at birth feast   186
44. Goilala killed by surrounding tribes   202
45. Killing and marriage   203

Abbreviations

The ranks listed below were those of field-officers in the Department of the Administrator at the time of field-work, but the granting of self-government and independence may have produced changes.

D.C.   District Commissioner
D.D.C. Deputy District Commissioner
D.O.   District Officer
A.D.O. Assistant District Officer
A.D.C. Assistant District Commissioner
P.O.   Patrol Officer
C.P.O. Cadet Patrol Officer
A.C.   Armed Constable
V.C.   Village Constable

Papua ceased to be a separate administrative entity in 1942, when the Japanese invasion resulted in the effective amalgamation of Papua with the Mandated Territory of New Guinea, under A.N.G.A.U., the Australian New Guinea Administrative Unit. This union was given final constitutional form in 1949. Under the old Papuan administrative system Districts were known as 'Divisions' and official titles were different in some cases:

R.M.   Resident Magistrate = District Commissioner
A.R.M. Assistant Resident Magistrate = Assistant District Commissioner
C.N.M. Court for Native Matters

Until 1966 cases solely involving natives were tried in these Courts, which have since been replaced by Local and District Courts.

C.M.   Catholic Mission

But one must know that war is universal, and that justice is strife, and that all things happen according to strife and necessity.

Heraclitus, Fragment 80.

What is good? Everything that heightens the feeling of power in man, the will to power, power itself.

What is bad? Everything that is born of weakness.

What is happiness? The feeling that power is *growing*, that resistance is overcome.

Not contentedness but more power; not peace but war; not virtue but fitness . . .

The weak and the failures shall perish . . .

Nietzsche, *The Antichrist*, § 2

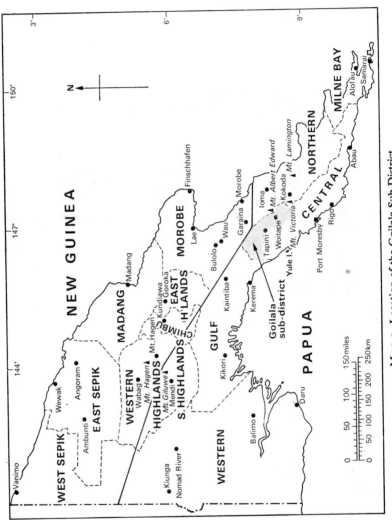

MAP I. Location of the Goilala Sub-District

I

Introduction

THE traveller who directs his steps through the Aibala Valley, where the Tauade have their home, finds at these altitudes a temperate and bracing climate, free from the malaria and debilitating infections of the coast; rain is plentiful and the soil fertile; the forest is rich with useful timber, vines, and barks, as well as birds and small game. The mountainous slopes of the valley can support a wide variety of crops, from yams and bananas in the hot lowlands near the river, to taro, sweet potatoes, and pandanus nuts on the higher ground, and everywhere are streams of cold, pure water. Floods are impossible and droughts are rare, and the people have never multiplied to an extent which would endanger these resources, or one another, by the pressure and competition of numbers.

Yet in this propitious environment the traveller will find no decorative arts, and no pleasure in craftsmanship; everything that is made, even tobacco pipes, and lime gourds and spatulas, is stark and shoddy in appearance. A love of colour and decoration shows itself briefly at great feasts and dances, and imposing men's houses are built for such occasions, but these extravagances are short-lived and are soon deliberately destroyed or left to rot. Ordinary hamlets are clusters of dreary hovels, and despite their ample leisure the Tauade prefer to satisfy the bare necessities of life with the minimum of effort and thought for the future. But in this drab wasteland of meanness and indifference are two founts of relentless energy—pigs and vengeance, the essential elements in the Tauade's endless struggle for glory and prestige. And so it has come to be that this magnificent valley is the setting for a society dominated by pride, bloodshed, and squalor.

The Goilala Sub-District, which includes the speakers of the 'Tauade'[1] group of dialects, covers about four hundred square miles

---

[1] The terms 'Tauade' and 'Goilala' as presently employed are the creations of patrol officers and missionaries, and have no equivalents in indigenous usage.

of the Wharton Range to the north of Port Moresby in the Central District of Papua. To the south, in the lowlands, are the coastal tribes of the Mekeo and Roro; to the east are the Koiari, and to the north, beyond the almost uninhabited forests of the Giumu Valley, are the lands of the Orokaiva. The mountains to the west are inhabited by the Kukukuku, whose reputation as bloodthirsty and intractable exceeds even that of the Goilala.

Tapini, the administrative centre of the Sub-District, is only eighty air miles from Port Moresby and some parts of the area have been under government and mission influence since the first decade of the century, and many Goilala have been accustomed to work in the capital as migrant labourers since the 1950s, but the area remains one of the most economically backward in the Territory.

The Tauade, like all the other inhabitants of the Sub-District, are bush-fallowing cultivators, cutting their gardens from the forests of the high ranges; they also raise large numbers of pigs, which are of vital importance in their social life. While there is great linguistic diversity among the Goilala, their social organization is comparatively homogeneous.

The Tauade are small and wiry, the men having an average height of just over five feet and weighing less than eight stone,[1] though they

----

[1] The following measurements of height and weight were made in the Goilala area by Dr. Kariks and others:

Distribution of heights and weights of some Goilala natives

		Weight (pounds)		Height (inches)	
	Number	Mean	Standard deviation	Mean	Standard deviation
Males	199	111·72	11·34	60·86	2·22
Females	67	93·87	9·40	57·09	1·86

The ponderal index (weight in pounds divided by height in inches) gave values of 1·84 and 1·64 for males and females respectively. The value for males is less than that found by Whyte (1958) amongst young Chimbu natives, but the value for females is approximately the same. Another index obtained by dividing the weight in kilograms by the square of the height in centimetres was 2·12 for males and 2·03 for females. These values are to be compared with 2·33 for young Australian males and 2·28 for male natives of Chimbu (Whyte 1958), and with 2·34 for adult females in Chimbu (Whyte) and 2·28 for Norwegian females (Bøe, Humerfelt, and Wedervang 1957). The same indices calculated for Bougainville natives from figures given earlier (Kariks, Kooptzoff, and Walsh 1957) were 2·32 and 2·22 for males and females respectively. By comparison the Goilala native is therefore under weight for his height. (Kariks *et al*. 1958: 118.)

are muscular and their physique well adapted both to the precipitous mountain tracks and to the cold. They have heavy browridges which tend to give them a scowling and sullen appearance, and they often have large, pendulous noses; the women's faces are masculine and, to European taste, uncommonly ugly.

I. EUROPEAN IMPACT ON TAUADE SOCIETY[1]

The history of European influence on Tauade society reveals much about their attitudes to power and domination, to co-operation, and to material welfare, and is also an essential basis for estimating the distorting influences likely to affect the ethnographer's impression of current conditions.

Since the early years of the century the lives of the Tauade have been increasingly dominated by the activities of the government and the Mission of the Sacred Heart. In this part of Papua the missionaries sometimes advanced into the mountains ahead of the government, and, as in the case of Bishop de Boismenu's heroic journey to Popole, in Fuyughe country, succeeded in establishing good relations with the natives when punitive expeditions had been driven off. But the mission did not establish itself permanently among the Tauade—at Kerau—until more than twenty years after the government had begun regular patrolling in 1917.

There are therefore three main phases in the history of contact between the Tauade and the white man; the first is the period of government patrolling and pacification by force from 1911 to 1939, when the Fathers came to Kerau. At the end of this period the government had established a permanent police camp at Aporota in 1934–5, and the Fathers had begun making exploratory journeys in the area, setting up an out-station at Gane by 1935 and starting to build their main station at Kerau in 1938. The second period is one of predominantly mission activity, especially during the war years, when government control relaxed somewhat, while evangelical activity increased and the Fathers took over responsibility for road building and set up the first school. A common characteristic of these two periods was the acceptance by government and mission of a slow rate of social change; the government was happy to see violence decline, especially as a result of labour migration to Port Moresby, and while economic progress was hoped for little was

---

[1] I am grateful to Dr. Martin Brett for his suggestions on the presentation of historical material in this chapter.

accomplished. In the final phase traditional violence has been largely eliminated and the government, under United Nations pressure, has attempted to promote 'democratic' institutions, such as Local Government Councils, and has introduced universal suffrage with proportional representation, while the well-tried institution of the village constable has been abolished. There have been many attempts to encourage stock-breeding and the raising of cash crops, which have not been particularly successful, while the people have become noticeably more disillusioned with both government and mission. We will now study these phases in detail.

(a) *Pacification*

The pacification of the area was undertaken piecemeal, and patrols from different posts operated in the area for some time. The Aibala Valley was first entered from the Northern District (the Mambare Division, as it was then called, with its headquarters at Ioma) in 1911. But after this patrols were also sent from Kambisi and Mondo police camps in the Central Division (District) as well as from Ioma. Eventually[1] patrols from the northern side of the range ceased altogether and for many years were directed from Kairuku on Yule Island. The establishment of the police camp at Aporota in 1934–5, and the creation of another post at Tapini in 1938, marked the permanent presence of the government in the area.

The first reactions of the Tauade to the white man, both in the Giumu and at Sopu, were timid and evasive. These encounters are vividly described by Mr. J. F. Keelan, P.O., in his report. He was the first officer to penetrate into the Aibala Valley, and on this occasion the purpose of the patrol was purely exploratory, and not punitive. From Ioma he arrived at the Giumu (known to the government as the 'small Goilala') with ten policemen and some carriers on 1 November 1911.

He passed over the range and reached Sopu on 7 December. On 10 December he attempted to take a census, and records the following experience:

I had told Givi Kitoa [the Sopu chief] yesterday to get all the people to come in and that I would put their names in a book so that the government would know its children, i.e. census them. They came all right but

---

[1] In 1919 it was decided that all future patrols into the Aibala were to be the responsibility of the Central Division via Mafulu. See Papuan Annual Report for 1918–19, p. 50 (E. R. Oldham, A.R.M.).

they were so nervy and jumpy that you could do nothing with them. A man would force himself to come up to you, but fear of the book and pencil had bereft him of the powers of speech and he would 'mouth' like a man choking. He would then look at his beloved hills and shouting a name which the interpreter more or less apprehended would dash off as if a fiend pursued. The women were much better, but still very frightened. When I had satisfied myself that it was impossible to get a census I broke a couple of pounds of beads into a dish and gave each woman who had stopped a spoonful of them as a reward for her hardihood. (J. F. Keelan, P.O., Ioma 23/10/11–22/1/12.)

A comment by Lewis Lett, who had many years' experience in Papua, is appropriate here:

. . . it has been a frequent experience in Papua that the first visitors to a new district get through without difficulty where the next comers meet with determined opposition. It would appear that the first sight of white men rouses only curiosity, and that it is not until they have passed on that the natives realise what opportunities they have missed. Probably, too, they find that the amount of food that they have sold to the travellers has depleted their supply, and they are unwilling to be tempted into too generous trading. (Lett 1935: 61.)

There were, however, later government visitors to the Giumu who seem to have aroused no hostility. As long as patrol officers and other Europeans were merely passing through the country, the Tauade seem to have displayed no animosity, but once the government became involved in the suppression of raiding and killing, relations changed dramatically.

Being divided among themselves, the Tauade initially welcomed the Government as a potential ally in their perpetual warfare with one another, but because warfare was endemic any administration attempting to pacify such a region was inevitably drawn into tribal conflicts, as the groups with whom the patrol officers first came into contact complained of having had men killed by other tribes, against whom the government was then bound to take hostile measures.

In 1917 the Giumu were raided by the Lova-Loleava, under the leadership of Kivi-Ketawa, living at Lova; a man and a woman were killed and mutilated, gardens destroyed, and pigs slaughtered (see below, pp. 138–9 for a detailed account of these events). When L. J. Wilson, P.O., crossed the range and entered Lova territory to arrest the killers he met with fierce resistance. In the ensuing skirmishes six natives were shot. Wilson was forced to retreat through

lack of ammunition, an action on which Sir Hubert Murray com-
mented to his superiors in Australia 'I can remember no other case,
since I have been in the Territory, when the armed constabulary
have retired before an armed force' (Letter from the Lieutenant-
Governor of 18 January 1918). Lett remarks however, that Wilson
was a temporary officer appointed during the war, and was inexperi-
enced in this kind of work (Lett 1935: 144).

A month later another, much stronger force of three patrol
officers (Grist, Storry, and Wilson) with thirty policemen as opposed
to ten, went back to Lova-Loleava. In the intervening month these
people had again raided the Giumu, destroying gardens and threatening the people with reprisals for leading the government to Lova-
Loleava. Grist, Storry, and Wilson spent more than five months
continuously in the area, but at the end of this time they were no
nearer to subduing the Sopu and Lova-Loleava than they had been
at the beginning. Their withdrawal seems to have been due to the
exhaustion of their stores. Wilson was speared in the hand, a constable was killed and eaten, another shot himself deliberately through
the thigh with his rifle and died of the wound before the end of the
patrol, and three constables were wounded by spears. About eight
Tauade were reported to have been shot in various skirmishes
during the five months, though the real total was probably higher.

While on a few occasions some of the people were persuaded to
come in to the government camp it was not possible to establish any
meaningful relations with them. In most cases the people deserted
their villages and shouted defiance and abuse from the bush when
the patrol approached. The Fuyughe, too, were formidable fighters
when aroused, and Dupeyrat quotes the account of their resistance
to a punitive expedition in 1899:

Then the whole tribe rose up, relates Bishop de Boismenu. For ten days
they bravely stood up to the soldiers' fire and never gave way, despite the
devastating effects of the dum-dum bullets. The leader of the expedition
told us on his return that he had never found in New Guinea a tribe so
valiant [they were the Sivu] in the face of gunfire. Nightly, they lit huge
fires over against their enemies' bivouacs, and, to prepare themselves for
the morrow's battle, they danced their great war-dances to the sound of
their battle-songs, violent and heart-thrilling as no other. (Dupeyrat
1948: 74-5.)

The spirited resistance of the Lova-Loleava on a later occasion
(described below p. 8) is further clear testimony to the tenacious

fighting quality of the Tauade on occasion. But the Tauade, like the Fuyughe, fought not only in defence of their hamlet or tribe, caught up in an endless round of retaliation that could only be broken by outside intervention, but they killed, and still do kill for the pleasure of killing, though when they learned something of the power of the ·303 Martini–Enfield rifle they became more cautious in opposing the government. As B. W. Faithorn, A.R.M., observed after a patrol in July 1930:

These trips into the Goilala convinced me that the Goilala tribes have no wish to fight . . . They are out to *kill*, not fight. It is the unarmed carrier that they feast their eyes upon and seek the opportunity to waylay. The Goilala natives are often seen walking about unarmed but it should never be forgotten that their spears are always lying handy. A favourite hiding place is the long grass around their villages. Individuals make a practice of preceding a government party moving down to a river and there beside the track or near a crossing conceal their weapons. The natives will then stand about and try to direct one, by signs, where to cross the river. This may be interpreted as a friendly gesture but often it is done to throw dust in our eyes and with a feeling in their hearts that they are glad to see the back of us.

It is at this moment that the foolish carrier, seeing them unarmed, becomes incautious, wanders away from the fold and so gives the ever watchful Goilala the opportunity to seize his concealed spear to attack him. (B. W. Faithorn, A.R.M., Mondo 1/7/30–31/7/30.)

Not all peoples in New Guinea resisted pacification so vigorously, as the following description of the Fore makes plain:

The most obvious immediate effect of the arrival of Australian patrols in the Fore region was pacification. Fighting ceased almost spontaneously throughout the entire region. Most Fore groups did not wait to be told to cease fighting by the new administration, but stopped on their own— almost as if they had only been awaiting an excuse to give it up. A few, such as some of the Kamira people, maintained a warlike stance a bit longer than the others, but without serious raiding. The Fore said among themselves that the *kiap* (government officer) was coming, so that it was time to stop the fighting. They looked to his arrival as the beginning of a new era rather than an invasion. Disputes which could not be settled by the Fore themselves were eagerly put into the hands of the patrol officers for arbitration, and an anti-fighting ethic quickly spread throughout the region. (Sorenson 1972: 362.)

The Tauade, on the other hand, did not see the government at first as a new kind of authority, as the Fore seem to have done, but rather as just another, even if very strange, fighting force, actuated by motives beyond the grasp of ordinary mortals. This incomprehension led to profound difficulties as time went by; much to the bewilderment of the people, the same patrol officer who in one year had 'helped' them against their hated enemies over the river, on his next visit would turn on his old friends, even if they had presented him with a good fat pig, and arrest the chiefs and take them to the malarial gaols of the coast where they died of a strange sickness they had not seen before—malaria—simply because they had carried on the good work, and killed a few more of their enemies in his absence. It took many years before they understood that the government was trying to be impartial and maintain peace equally throughout the area, showing favour to none.

Far from realizing that the patrol officers were acting from the most altruistic motives the Tauade could only have believed that they were fickle and treacherous, as the following incident shows. On 19 January 1929 a patrol to Lova-Loleava encountered hostilities when making arrests:

It was unfortunate that we encountered hostilities at Loleava. These people gave us a great welcome on arrival here, but though I tried quietly to get the wanted men I was unsuccessful, and this was due to V.C. Lipo warning them when I made enquiries. It was then that they turned hostile. As we have to start somewhere in stopping murder I made the first arrest here, as these people have been visited more often and have V.C.'s. The time is past from merely telling them that they are to cease 'paying-back'.

It is only the second time that arrests have been attempted here. On both occasions they have shown what determined fighters they are, and it was a revelation to see the Loleava attacking us time after time in spite of a number of them having been killed by rifle fire.

In the course of this engagement 106 rounds (including ten 'duds') were fired by the constabulary in volleys, and nine men were definitely hit and presumably killed. The actual total seems likely to have been higher.

The administration was in the predicament which faces all those who would do good by force. If they had simply embarked on a course of conquest their motives would have been quite comprehensible to the Tauade, for whom force has always been the ultimate arbiter. If, instead of the small bodies of armed constabulary, often not more than a dozen, and which by their *apparent* weakness excited ridicule and invited attack, a more powerful contingent had been assembled, which had then campaigned through the area, enforcing submission, the same results would have been obtained far more swiftly, causing no more ill will and probably no more bloodshed. For while the policies of the government under the highly civilized leadership of Sir Hubert Murray were Christian and humane, their actual enforcement was very different from the 'peaceful penetration' described in official literature. I have counted in the patrol reports from 1917 to 1932, for the Aibala Valley alone, thirty-three cases of natives who were shot by the government and most of whom, in the nature of things, are likely to have died. Moreover, since patrol officers were well aware of Murray's dislike of bloodshed it was in their interest to minimize these figures. Indications from the reports themselves and from native informants suggest that between 1917 and 1938, merely in the Aibala Valley, it would not be implausible to estimate that between 75 and 100 persons were killed, either by the police, or by other Tauade acting in concert with them.

While the people understood force, most of the policies of their rulers remained mysterious to them. Apart from suppressing violence, the patrol officer's first task was to take a census, an entirely mysterious procedure for the people, but an essential foundation, of course, for any sound administration. The requirement for all pacified villages to build a rest house for the government was more comprehensible—a visible token by which the people expressed their loyalty to the government, and a means of showing hospitality. The distribution of uniforms and handcuffs to village constables was extremely popular and a distinction which was eagerly sought after. The obligation to carry the baggage of patrols—essential in a rugged country without pack-animals or tracks which they could negotiate— was very much less eagerly sought for, as was the obligation to work on the construction of bridle tracks. Mr. Speedie began the first 'road' from Speedie's Gap to the police camp at Aporota in about 1936, but by 1940 the supervision of roadwork in the area had been taken over by the mission, which has subsequently pegged and supervised the construction of a graded track encircling the whole of the valley, as well as two tracks to Tapini. These tracks were originally designed for the use of pack-animals, but are now normally traversed by motorbikes, and form essential arteries of communication for government and mission in the area. Since the physique of the natives is ideally adapted to their precipitous paths, which take the most direct route

down a spur, they have been slow to appreciate the advantages of
these roads, which they regard as for the benefit of the white man,
and they take every opportunity to avoid working on them, and, in
remoter areas, like to fence them off from pigs and incorporate them
in their gardens. In 1972 I was obliged to hack down a garden fence
built across the main route from Kerau to Tapini. The track from
Kerau down to the bridges across the Aibala has been largely
ruined by the people's practice of running streams down it for long
distances, which they use for cutting ditches around their gardens.

The building of 'house-lines'—compact and stable villages close
to the graded tracks—was strongly encouraged by patrol officers,
but such villages are often only inhabited for the visits of officials,
usually for the annual census, after which the people scatter to their
true homes.

As government control strengthened in the 1930s, patrol officers
began enforcing various sanitary policies; these placed special
emphasis upon the burial of corpses instead of exposing them to rot
on platforms, the digging of latrines, the building of special pig-
houses instead of the pigs living with the women and children, and
general cleanliness of water-supplies, houses, and villages. Exposure
of bodies on a platform continued until as late as 1952 in some cases,
and while the people today recall how unpleasant it was to have
rotting corpses in close proximity for a few weeks, their continued
devotion to the relics of their dead suggests that in the absence of
government control they would revert to the custom of exhuming
the bones of the dead, even if they would no longer expose them on
platforms. Government policy with respect to inhumation, which has
had the full support of the mission, has meant that traditional
burial customs are no longer practised, however, and the initiation
of boys, which was closely associated with the bull-roarer enclosure
built for the death of a chief, has also disappeared.

Latrines are probably the least controversial of the government's
innovations. The Tauade feel a great disgust for faeces in any case,
so here no violation of traditional attitudes was involved. Sorcery
and adultery are punishable under the law of Papua, and the people
are sometimes prepared to use the courts in these matters. Here
again, compensation for adultery was the traditional means of
settlement, so perhaps less innovation has been made here than might
be supposed. Not only did it require many years of struggle by the
government to impose its policies, but even when the people had at

length acquiesced in their performance they were as far as ever from understanding their spirit. Sir Hubert Murray was a lawyer, and held the position of Chief Judicial Officer as well as being the Lieutenant-Governor. It was natural for him to regard the British system of law, transplanted to Papua in the form of the Queensland Criminal Code (Adopted), as one of the highest manifestations of social morality. He may well have been correct in this belief, but since the Papuans did not understand these principles of legality their enforcement merely produced bewilderment and demoralization that have persisted to this day.

The clearest example of this opposition between native custom and British legal precepts is in their respective ideas of individual responsibility. The Tauade realize that acts are the work of individuals but are not concerned, when exacting vengeance, that it should fall on the head of the guilty party. They are satisfied if anyone from the group concerned is made to suffer. This attitude does not derive from any concept of 'group responsibility'—quite the opposite, in fact. For, as we shall see, the group, especially the tribe, does not exercise that degree of control over its members which would make such a notion of collective responsibility meaningful. It is rather a question of group 'irresponsibility'—any member will do to gratify the impulse of vengeance. Moreover, while individuals are sometimes indicated as guilty to injured parties seeking vengeance, this is often because no one is willing to risk life and limb in their defence or because these scapegoats are willing to take the blame for a more influential person; the following description by a cadet patrol officer of the arrest of a murderer at Zhamora, in the Pilitu Census District, illustrates this:

They [the people of the village] realised that some form of restitution for the alleged killing would be pressed upon them, but could not understand that the person responsible for the crime was the one on whom the punishment should fall. Three successive times I was presented with 'substitutes' (all insignificant gaol-fodder in the tribal hierarchy) and when these were sent away after an explanatory talk, I was presented with *two* men, said now to be the joint killers. Later, a sum of £10 was added as an extra inducement. (A. N. Flowers, C.P.O., Pilitu, 23/11/61–29/11/61.) [Note the recent date of this report.]

The Government attitude, on the other hand, was that the guilty person, and only he, was to be arrested. This was of course quite incomprehensible to the people. If they produced a 'culprit' why could not the white man be satisfied, instead of asking all sorts of absurd questions about who had really committed the act? After all, since the Tauade had no conception of any 'law' that had been broken by homicide they were bound to see government attempts to arrest killers as a new kind of vengeance, to be placated by yielding up an insignificant member of the group. By sternly setting its face against any kind of corporate retribution the government in many ways made its task not only more difficult, but more odious to the people.

The idea that a group as powerful as the white men obviously were, would not use this power to their own advantage was unthinkable to the Tauade, and I believe that it still mystifies them. The suggestion that men of power would go to considerable personal trouble to come to an alien land, 'to serve their captives' need', and impose all sorts of irksome restrictions on its inhabitants *for their own good*, must seem utterly preposterous to the Tauade.

In view of the government's liberal attitudes it is significant that the only two government officers in the Goilala Sub-District who since the war have been dismissed from the service and imprisoned for unlawful punishments of natives, are the two held in the greatest respect by the people. 'They were strong,' they say, 'we listened to their voice.' Of one of them they say 'Yes, he was bad; he burned our houses, and killed our pigs and beat us. But he was good—he was like us, he understood our fashion.' This officer, who still lives in the Territory, has no difficulty in recruiting labourers from the Goilala, and, indeed, I am told that he has more applicants than he can find room for. The other officer is also remembered with respect, and in 1972 gained the overwhelming support of the Goilala voters in his attempt to win the Central District Regional seat in the House of Assembly elections.

In my experience a display of strength and domination not only gets the best results from the Tauade but makes them more amiable into the bargain. Three of my pleasantest days were spent supervising the cutting of a motor-bike track from my house to the plateau above the hamlets where I lived. Far from resenting my stream of shouts and orders, the men and women working under my direction seemed to be put into the best of spirits by them. This kind of response is not confined to the Tauade. In far more dramatic form, Hides encountered it during his Purari–Strickland patrol. Having been attacked by the Waga Furari, Hides's party repelled them by rifle fire, inflicting a number of casualties. The people's attitude, hitherto one of utter contempt on account of the apparent weakness of the patrol, changed dramatically, not into fear, but *friendliness*:

The thunder of the rifles had brought silence in the country around us, and we walked out of the timber into cultivation again.

Our attackers came to meet us with presents of food. They stood and offered the bunches of bananas and bundles of spinach: but the food was thrown back at them, and I explained that we did not take presents from people who had tried to murder us; and further, that when we were ready for food, we would take it.

Later, he accepted the food and made camp:

The attitude of these people was extraordinary. Within an hour or so of the attack, fully three hundred men, all of them genuinely friendly, were sitting around the party; and it would have been indelicate, I thought, to have even suggested to them that only a short time before we had been fighting with them. (Hides 1936: 122–3.)

Far from regarding the imprisonment, as opposed to the execution, of murderers, as a liberal and humane policy, the Tauade consider it an exasperating and inexcusable weakness. The A.D.C. at Tapini in 1955 summarized the people's attitude on this matter in a report as follows:

The following line of thought is common throughout the District, particularly in the Tau'ade:—'If we kill a man, the government comes along, arrests us and puts us in prison to await the Judge. The Judge comes, hears all the talk, and then commits us to prison for a number of years. We go to Bomana prison. There we are well-fed, well-clothed; we live in good houses and don't have to work too hard. The government looks after us well, and when our time is finished, the government sends us back to our village. We have lost only a few years, and on return to our village we can say to our people: "See, the government did not kill us, we have come back to you." Gaol is nothing; we are not frightened of gaol.'

As a counter to this manifestly contemptuous attitude to the law, more and more natives are showing signs of exasperation and saying—

'The government has been in Goilala for a long time. Ever since the government came here people have been killing one another and the government has been putting the murderers in gaol. But still the people continue to kill one another, and it is obvious that a few years in gaol is not acting as a deterrent. The people are not frightened of gaol, for they know that they can murder, suffer a temporary absence from their village, then return as big men. Why does not the government do something about it? If the government acted strongly, the people would soon be frightened and abandon this wicked custom.' (A. D. C. Tapini to District Commissioner, Central District, File 11/213, 11/3/55.)[1]

(b) *The arrival of the Mission of the Sacred Heart, and the war years*

In 1940 the government considered abandoning the Sub-District and declaring it an uncontrolled area, and invited the mission to withdraw. The Fathers resisted this suggestion, which seems to have been prompted by fears of staff shortage, and in the end nothing came of it. This part of Papua was untouched by the war against the Japanese, however. Tapini airstrip was completed in 1938 and an officer resided there throughout the war, and Aporota police camp was also maintained in use. But even if this period did not see any withdrawal of government control, warfare was a long way from being stamped out. The Fathers, established at Kerau since 1939, record sporadic fighting throughout the valley, and assaults, murders, arson, ravaging of gardens, and killings of pigs were commonplace. For example, in 1944, within the space of a month, the Kileipi went to Ilai, burned the houses, killed the pigs, destroyed the gardens, and killed one man. The Gane people also went over to Ilai and killed ten pigs, so the Ilai in revenge killed a Gane man and wounded some others. On the morning when the magistrate left Kerau to investigate these incidents two hamlets of Ilai could be seen in flames. It was only in the late 1940s and early 1950s that comparative peace was finally imposed on the valley, and this was followed by the migration of men to Port Moresby to work as labourers. This was encouraged by the government as a means of educating the people:

Sending some of the younger men from the Goilala area to Moresby as labourers will have a beneficial effect on the future behaviour of the people, in my opinion. There is insufficient work in the village to keep them occupied all the time, and their minds turn to illegal acts. A spell of work will sophisticate them and give them a broader view of the outside world. Other natives who have been at work at Kokoda are noticeably more helpful to the Government officer than those who have spent all their lives in the village, although woman trouble often crops up when wives are left to their own devices. (W. M. Purdy, P.O., Tapini, April 1951.)

The migration of the younger men to Moresby in ever-increasing numbers (see Appendix I) in subsequent years has clearly been

[1] The average gaol sentences for wilful murder in the Goilala in 1949–55 were about four to five years.

responsible for the marked diminution in violence throughout the Sub-District, though at the expense of transplanting the violent proclivities of the Goilala to Moresby itself (see Appendix IV). It is not obvious that migrant labourers have been more significantly influenced by the disciplines as opposed to the temptations of a modern society as a result of their experience in Port Moresby. Unfortunately, shortage of time and money prevented me from making a study of Tauade migrants in the town.

In some ways the mission has had a greater influence in the area than the government, especially at the personal level. Unlike the government, the mission policy is for its priests to remain in the same area for many years, which allows them eventually to gain a thorough mastery of the language and a good knowledge of the local people and their customs. During my two years' residence in the area there were three A.D.C.s at Tapini; the first of these arrived with me, and if I had waited for two or three months before leaving there would have been a fourth. This rapid turn-over of staff has clearly hindered the administration's comprehension of the people. By contrast, two of the Fathers at Kerau have (1972) been there for twenty-five years, another for about seventeen, and the fourth for about five years.

From the beginning there has been the policy of founding main stations, such as Kerau, as bases from which periodic visits are made to out-stations consisting only of a chapel and a little house for the priest. The area is divided up, with one priest having responsibility for pastoral work in each of these divisions and staying at each out-station for two or three weeks at a time.

The Sacred Heart Mission began extending its influence into the Tauade area from its station at Polomania in the Ambo region, south of the Ivane, during the 1930s; and Dupeyrat's map, published in 1935, shows that an out-station had been established before that date at Gane, while mission records show that Frs. Guivarc'h and Wendling were making extensive expeditions in the area during the late 1930s, having earlier been preceded by Frs. Dubuy, Bachelier, and Sorin. The first mission publication in a Tauade dialect appeared in 1936.

In 1938 Frs. Wendling and Guivarc'h arrived at Sene, where they hoped to make a station. The people, however, were involved in warfare with the Laitate (see below, pp. 220–7) and the government was insisting that the Sene return to the Ivane Valley. For these reasons

the Fathers decided that they would have to found a station elsewhere, and early in 1939 moved to Kerau. Even by this time they had
begun a vigorous programme of conversion, and opened a school
for twenty-five catechists. For some reason they retained their saw-
pit at Sene while building their church and other dwellings at Kerau,
so that the planks had to be carried across the valley. Nearly three
hundred of these disappeared *en route*, stolen, broken, or thrown
into the Aibala. From the beginning the Tauade were not slow to
take advantage of the Fathers if they thought they could get away
with it. The following anecdote is a good example of this. Late in
1941 a man from Kariaritsi came to the mission and, as it was the
Feast of All Saints, was given some food, including that part of the
cake known as the *Part du Pauvre*. Shortly afterwards, during
Benediction, it was discovered that a priest's cape was missing.
Suspecting that the man from Kariaritsi was responsible, the
Fathers followed him over there and asked him if he had stolen it.
'But Father, how can you say such a thing? After you had been so
generous to me, would I repay you by stealing from you?' 'Ah, I
see,' said the Father. Then, after a pause, he said casually, 'By the
way, have you cut up that cape yet?' 'Oh no, I'm going to keep it as
it is' was the unguarded reply, and the game was up.

The mission steadily advanced its work during the war, despite
the violence around them. No Father, Brother, or Little Sister has
ever been molested, however, in the thirty-five years of the mission's
existence. In 1943, for example, the boys from the school went with
the Sisters on a picnic to Kataipa. Their route crossed a battlefield
where the Kunima were fighting; in deference to the Sisters, hostilities were suspended to allow them and their charges to cross in
safety, after which the spears and arrows began to fly as vigorously
as before.

The practical responsibility for roadwork was assumed from the
government at the beginning of the war and, physically speaking,
the graded track which now traverses the whole of the Aibala Valley
is the most impressive achievement of the mission. A dispensary was
also built at this time, and continues to provide basic medical
treatment without charge.[1]

[1] The government's policy of providing medical treatment and other services
without charge has encouraged attitudes of dependence and the belief that the
white man's resources are limitless, without engendering any corresponding sense
of gratitude.

The first educational programme was started for the catechists who, being of relatively mature years, do not seem to have made very satisfactory progress, but children were taken as well and in time a flourishing school grew up. While I was there the school contained about 130 pupils of both sexes up to the sixth grade, but numbers have been in the habit of fluctuating considerably, especially when there has been violence affecting the children. The most serious cases were in 1949, when a boy at school was axed to death inside the compound, and just before I left, when a boy was axed to death by another boy, his uncle, in what appears to have been an accident. Since the school takes boys as boarders from many different tribes, it is particularly vulnerable to the effects of the pay-back system.

The Kerau school is the most important source of education for Tauade children. The government school at Tapini was only started in 1962, and while it takes children from around Tapini it is chiefly used by the families of station personnel and has no boarders. For a time after the war the catechists ran schools at some of the out-stations. These were not a success; the catechists were not qualified teachers, they became involved in disputes with the local people, and there were accidents and even fatalities to the children in their care. The final blow seems to have been the decision, controversial within the mission, that the catechists should no longer be paid but should work for the love of God. Perhaps understandably this did not prove a sufficient incentive, and the system collapsed. At present schools are being revived at Sopu, Kileipi, and in the Pilitu, with qualified teachers supplied by the government, and these may be more successful.

A store was opened in 1954 but it sold relatively little until the completion of the airstrip in 1967, before which time all supplies had to be brought in by horse-caravan from the coast. The store is used to finance the purchase of vegetables to feed the children who board at the school.

The religious impact of the mission is hard to assess, since its attitudes to many customs have been shared by the administration. The most obvious case of this is the opposition to the exposure of the dead on platforms and the burial of human remains within villages. This was forbidden by the Native Regulations, and was also denounced by the mission. Again, the mission has also been opposed to violence, dances, abortions, adultery, and sorcery, which are also punished by the government.

While there has been a diminution in some or all of these practices it does not necessarily follow that this has resulted mainly from fear of punishment by the government. For one must not underestimate the influence which missionaries can have, built up over many years' acquaintance with the people and expressed through the local language by frequent personal intercourse. While the powers wielded by the patrol officers were much greater they were correspondingly seldom invoked, since until about 1960 two or three years might elapse between patrols to some areas.

In spite of the length of time for which the mission has been established at Kerau, it has not so far had what might be called a great success in religious terms. For example, at Goilala,[1] out of 155 residents only thirty-five had been baptized, and the great majority of these were young people or infants. Many of these, moreover, had imbibed their Christianity from the school at Kerau as part of the religious instruction included in the curriculum. While Goilala is an example of the familiar phenomenon of people who are close to a mission often being the most hostile or indifferent, I do not think that the level of Christianity in the rest of the valley was much higher.

Religious faith is not, of course, open to scrutiny and evaluation by the ethnographer. A man may tell us that he believes in God, and that Christ is his Saviour, and for statistical purposes we may record that man as a Christian. But to estimate the sincerity and motivation of his faith, motivations which may be obscure even to the believer himself, is a task for which the ethnographer has no competence. The Fathers are well aware that for many of their converts Christianity is very superficial, though they assure me that in some cases the faith of individuals is extremely deep and sincere.

But while a few persons may be able to transcend the limitations of their culture, it is an obvious fact that Roman Catholicism today is the product of two thousand years of European history. For the Tauade to be able to grasp in the space of a few years the basic implications of so profound and complex a religion would be as extraordinary as their displaying an understanding of the principles of British justice and representative government. The point can well be illustrated by an anecdote. I remarked earlier that the Tauade found the idea that men of power would be prepared to rule others for their own good, without benefit to themselves, quite incompre-

[1] The name of the small Tauade tribe with whom I lived. It has no connection with the name of the Goilala Sub-District.

hensible. Similarly, moving from the sphere of government to that of religion, they found the idea of the Son of God dying for men equally hard to understand. A Father at Yule Island told me of how the mission had been showing a film of the Life of Christ to a group of coastal people, who are considerably more sophisticated than the Tauade. When the scene was shown of Christ being beaten and humiliated by the Roman soldiers, the audience was convulsed with derisive laughter, and was clearly on the side of the Roman army, since anyone who allowed himself to be beaten up like that was obviously a 'rubbish-man'.

Some of the Fathers, especially perhaps those of an earlier generation, would reject what I am saying on the grounds that, as Fr. Dupeyrat expressed it (1948: 108), ' . . . the Christian religion is quite independent of any form of civilisation' and that therefore, for example, 'The Fuyughes are deeply, to the core of their being, Catholics' (106). I do not think that this is borne out by the facts and, indeed, not all his colleagues by any means would agree with him. As one Father in particular was fond of saying 'First, a thousand years of the Old Testament, then we can start on the New!' It was perhaps under the influence of beliefs such as Fr. Dupeyrat's in the immediate transmissibility of religion that many incautious baptisms were given in earlier days—'with a hosepipe', as one Brother described it to me. Certainly today great emphasis is placed upon the understanding and sincerity of potential converts, and the idea that the 'success' of the mission is reflected in a steady rise of baptisms and communions as shown by a line on a chart is something of the past.

It should be noted that a small Lutheran Mission exists at Kuputaivi, led by native catechists from the Northern District. This mission seems to have arrived in about 1955, but its impact has been slight and its converts are mainly found at Kuputaivi and Moingili.

(c) Political and economic change

Both mission and government have always regarded large dances and pig feasts as the main obstacle to economic progress, after warfare itself, and in recent years these occasions have therefore been the focus of the most prolonged antagonism between the natives and those who seek to change their way of life. The cessation of violence has made it much easier to organize such ceremonies and this has resulted not only in their being held much more often, but also in a decline in the standards of etiquette and oratory which formerly distinguished them. The government and mission have both been concerned with the effects of the dances, which result in the destruction of gardens by pigs, because herds are always allowed to increase to the largest size possible before the ceremonial slaughter; the corresponding destruction of gardens by the pigs in the areas which have been temporarily abandoned by people invited to a dance held by another tribe; the depletion of food resources by the large numbers of the guests, as many as a thousand, who may stay with the hosts for two or three months; the danger to health posed by such large gatherings during epidemics; and the frequent violence which accompanies them, not to mention the numerous cases of adultery. The attempts by the government to regulate the frequency and duration of dances by issuing permits is a long-standing source of friction between the administration and the people. For a period of about ten years during the 1960s the mission was able to forbid Christians to attend dances, which effectively prevented any dances being held in areas with substantial numbers of converts, but the Bishop enjoined a relaxation of this prohibition with the result that the dances began again even more vigorously than before. As everyone in the government and mission realizes, now that the people no longer have the outlet of war, dances are the only form of enjoyment left to them. The government was always aware that once violence had been suppressed something had to be supplied to take its place. As Jack Hides, an outstanding patrol officer who worked in the area in 1933–4, wrote:

As I stood outside my tent that evening, and looked down on the valley of the Loloipa in the glow of sunset, I reflected on these savage people and my experience with them. Just 'civilizing' them, I thought, would be to make still-born children of them, for they would become lifeless. If we interfered with their mode of living, which occupied all their thought and energy we, in effect, broke their lives. In giving them new conditions of life, we must supply them with a reason for living.

As I looked upon this fertile valley for the last time, I visualised its slopes growing coffee, tea, and other useful things; and I tried to see the savages of today as the industrialists of tomorrow, who, in place of their fighting and killing, would be using their energy in cultivating the soil and becoming accomplished artisans. With civilization must come industry—energetic, vitalizing industry; for this alone can be the salvation of these people. When it will come, of course, I do not know. But this I do know: that the Papuan savage, taken quickly after the civilizing effect will stand up to the revolution and will become just as good an industrialist as he is today a cannibal, a fighter, a likeable gentleman when you get to know him. (Hides 1935: 46–7.)

Hides has penetrated to the heart of the matter when he says 'taken quickly after the civilizing effect'. For this was impossible in the Tauade situation. The administration did not have the resources to provide agricultural officers, economic advisers, political education officers, and all the other staff which has since become available to stimulate and assist political, economic, and social development. Communication with the coast by road and potential markets for cash crops were non-existent. This was not, of course, the fault of the administration, which was also labouring under the stringencies of an extremely small budget. The effect, however, was to intensify the lack of understanding between government and people. The native saw the white man as a totally different being, not even human, as he understood the concept, who imposed a series of quixotic restraints upon his traditional way of life which, even if bloody, had been fun. A process, not of mutual understanding, but of mutual accommodation was thus tacitly established, whereby the natives agreed to observe certain basic government laws in return for being allowed to continue with as much as possible of their old way of life. Since the government at that time had nothing more positive to offer, it had no alternative but to agree.

The main physical obstacle to economic development has been the lack of communications with the coast since there are no roads and aircraft capable of transporting large amounts of freight can only use Tapini airstrip. Attempts have been made to encourage the growing of coffee, English potatoes, and other types of European vegetables, but the great distances over which this produce has to be carried on foot makes such projects impractical until roads are sufficiently developed to allow vehicular traffic. The export of vegetables is only possible for those whose gardens are close to an airstrip.

But the attitudes of the Tauade themselves are perhaps more potent in inhibiting economic development, and it is significant that even such enterprises as trade stores, which can be operated on a very small scale, have been few and have invariably failed when owned by natives. The people have not the slightest conception of economic realities and think that all the proceeds from a sale are profits. Thus a man with a few dozen tins of food in his 'store' is promoted in his neighbours' eyes into a man of wealth who is expected to share his good fortune with his friends and relatives by giving away much of his stock for nothing. Alternatively, they may be unwilling to buy from a fellow native for fear of being cheated.

Even where a project has been started under European management and has brought considerable benefits to the people, they have abandoned it. Mr. John Martin, who knows the people well, having originally been a lay brother at C.M. Kamulai, operated a farm at Erume in the Loloipa Valley, on the border between the Tauade and Kunimaipa. Beginning in about 1961, by 1965–6 he was purchasing more than 200,000 lb. of vegetables a year, as well as paying local labour. Since only the people of Erume and their immediate neighbours were involved, the income for this small area was considerable. In the seven years during which the project operated more than A$36,000 was paid out in wages and the purchase of vegetables, an average yearly sum of A$5,200. The business eventually came to an end because the people became dissatisfied with the money which they were receiving for their produce. Some of them had visited Moresby and had seen that vegetables commanded a price there which was several times greater than that which they were getting. Having no comprehension of economics, they could not understand that freight and handling costs had to be paid, as well as the distributor's profits. Mr. Martin told me that after the collapse of the project some men at Erume, with potatoes to sell, refused his price per pound, and preferred to hire a tractor to carry them to Tapini, where they had been offered a higher price. Since they had not taken the cost of transportation into account they eventually earned less money by selling the potatoes in Tapini, at a higher price, than if they had accepted Mr. Martin's offer. Again, through their lack of any concept of numbers beyond 2, the people are incapable of calculating the relationship between weekly and daily wages. For example, a daily wage of A$0·30 might be rejected, but wages for a seven-day period of A$2·00 might be accepted as 'big money'.

Moreover, even when they have money, they fritter most of it away on trivial purchases. At Erume the people spent about 85 per cent of their income from the project in the store—established at their insistence—and it seems that the pattern of their spending there was similar to what I observed at the mission store at Kerau. Brilliantine, chewing gum and 'lolly-water' (soft drinks), baby-powder to make their skins shine, rice and bully beef, vast quantities of soap, fancy clothes that soon become sordid and tattered, and trade tobacco are their commonest purchases. The mission was puzzled for some time to explain what the people could do with all the soap which they bought, and Fr. Guichet finally solved the mystery when one day an old man took him into his confidence and opened his box of 'riches' to show him. Inside were dozens upon dozens of bars of soap which the old man was hoarding, as dogs' teeth were hoarded in the past.

Very little of their money is spent on tools or other useful and durable goods such as fencing wire for their cattle. In part this disparity of expenditure can be explained by the fact that spades last much longer than chewing gum, and after so long a period of contact the people are by now reasonably well supplied with tools and gardening implements. But it also reflects their very scant interest in taking practical steps to improve their physical environment.

The relative failure of cattle projects which have been attempted in the last dozen years among the Tauade exemplifies in a number of ways the people's inaptitude for economic ventures. The earliest patrol officers, noting the wide expanses of grassland in the Aibala Valley, foresaw a great future for cattle-raising in the area. In fact, on closer examination the seemingly lush grass proves to be thin, and each beast requires a very much larger area of land than it would in England or Australia. But cattle have the great advantage of being able to take themselves to market, and there is, after all, a great deal of grass in the Aibala Valley. Yet the Tauade have not taken readily to keeping cattle. They regard them, like pigs, as a source of prestige, not as a capital investment, and, provided they can see them roaming around and can kill one now and then for a feast, they expect to derive no more from them. They have been persistently instructed in cattle-raising by the mission, which took the initiative in supplying the first stock in the area, and by the patrol officers and the agricultural officer, who makes regular patrols from Tapini to examine and treat the stock. But the people cannot be bothered to purchase and erect wire for paddocks, which are essential to separate the young heifers from the mature bulls. In addition, envy towards those who own cattle, and quarrels over pasturing rights, have also impeded the construction of paddocks. Nor will they buy salt for their cattle, although they know it is necessary, or attempt to apply the simple medications which are supplied free by the government. Nor are they much interested in sending them to market, though it has been possible for some time to drive cattle to the coast.

It might be concluded from all that has been said so far that the

Tauade are not interested in material wealth of the Western variety, but only in pursuing their traditional way of life, unhindered by all the troublesome adjustments which are necessary for economic development. But this would be a profound misunderstanding of the Tauade. When the Fathers first came to Kerau, with some experience of other parts of Papua, they were struck by the extraordinary envy of the people for their material possessions, which were poor enough in those days. I frequently experienced the same phenomenon myself as I sat on my veranda and watched a group of Tauade peering, mesmerized and motionless, into my squalid hut, as if it were Aladdin's cave. Far from being content with a few trinkets and mirrors, the Tauade have an intense craving for the white man's goods, but, paradoxically, are not prepared to do anything to change their condition themselves. They envy the beautiful kitchen-garden at the mission, and are always ready to help themselves to a few vegetables as they pass through, but display no interest in growing those same vegetables in their own gardens, apart from a few leeks, onions, and English potatoes. Yet they will willingly bring 15 lb. of sweet potatoes to purchase 1 lb. of rice, which they like because it makes them feel bloated. They envy the sawn-timber dwellings which the mission has built at Kerau and many other out-stations. The Fathers have offered to cut up into planks any trees which the people bring to the saw-mill, on the basis of a 50–50 sharing of the timber, but no one has ever taken advantage of this.

As we shall see, envy is a typical feature of an atomistic society such as the Tauade, and it is this mutual envy which inhibits initiative; all the norms and constraints of their society work against the accumulation of property by one man.

The Tauade have found modern political institutions even harder to grasp than business operations; the establishment of the Local Government Council in the Tapini area in 1963 propelled them into the wonderland of 'democratic' politics, although village constables continued to exist in villages outside the Council area. The imposition of the Council was determined by the administration in Port Moresby, under the influence of the United Nations, as a policy for the whole Territory irrespective of the wishes of the local people or the level of their political understanding, which in the Goilala Sub-District is minimal:

In one case, the people of Perumeva, Erumelavava, and Koilolavava had the idea that the elected councillors would be the rulers, not only of the people, but also of the ground within the electorate boundaries. They also thought that the boundary marks were to be clearly defined and no one from one electorate was to own land in another. It appeared they considered that each electorate was to be a self-contained unit and no aid was to be sought from another. (P. R. Hunter, C.P.O., Loloipa, 18/4/63–9/5/63.)

Three years later a patrol officer summed up the effectiveness of the Council as follows:

... It must be admitted, painful though it may be, that co-operation, progress, self-assistance, cleanliness and spirit in those villages under the control of the village policemen far excels that of the villages in the Council area. (P. Briggs, P.O., Aiwara, 23/8/66–9/9/66.)

It was evident during my stay in the area that the people had never understood the reasons for, or the operation of, the Council and regarded it merely as an additional tax burden, which it was.

In 1964, within a year of the imposition of the Council, the inhabitants of the Sub-District were required to vote for two members in the national House of Assembly, by a polling system more complicated than that of Great Britain. Since the House of Assembly has been totally irrelevant to the lives of the people, however, we need waste no further time upon it.

It will have become clear that, while the Tauade wish to obtain the material goods of the white men, they have no grasp of the institutional means by which economic and political development of the type demonstrated to them by the white men can be produced. Fr. Fastré[1] wrote very perceptively:

As opposed to the white man, the Papuans do not believe in the perfectibility of Man. For them, Man is as unchangeable as the animals; the behaviour of each is based on different instincts and must necessarily remain what it is. They believe that they have always been what they are, and that the whites also have always been what they are. No, they do not believe in unlimited improvement! This simple-minded attitude is partly responsible for the small effect of the white man's example on the black. (Quoted in Dupeyrat 1935: 473.)

The Tauade are aware that left to their own devices they drift inevitably into violence and bloodshed, and, equally inevitably, that any attempt to better themselves economically is doomed from the start. I believe that they have a deeply rooted contempt for themselves,

[1] See below, p. 28.

in spite of the pride and self-assertion they display. It is clear
from their legends that they do not believe themselves capable of
creating any new institution or custom, whether social or material;
all their institutions were created by the culture heroes, to whom they
liken the white man. Their legends are also full of violent fantasies of
power, of culture heroes massacring whole villages and flinging the
houses into the river, tearing up the gardens, killing the pigs, defeca-
ting and urinating on ordinary mortals, and overturning villages like
carpets and burying their inhabitants beneath them, of death and
destruction sweeping the valley until only stinking bones were left
for the dogs to gnaw on. These tales seem to betray a feeling of rage
and frustration at their own impotence.

It is clearly their belief that only when they become like the white
man in *essence* can they hope to change their ways and have all that
they envy of his life. There was an outbreak of cargo-cult in 1952,
apparently set off by the eruption of Mt. Lamington in 1951 and the
destruction of the government station nearby, and in 1971, as in
other parts of the Territory, there was a resurgence of 'cargo'
beliefs. I was told that, among other things, the patrol officers, the
Fathers, and I would all die, and be born again with black skins, and
that the Tauade would all die and be born again with white skins,
and huge quantities of cargo would be delivered to them.

It is possible that many of them thought that Christianity was a
means of achieving this change of essence, and the Fathers tell me
that the adoption of clothes in particular was a spontaneous movement by the people in the late 1940s, and was not enforced or
enjoined by the mission. Ironically, far from making themselves
more acceptable in the sight of Europeans by wearing clothes, they
turned themselves into replicas of Victorian slum-dwellers.

It is the inability of the Tauade to believe that they are of the same
clay as the white man and that, if they *organize* themselves differently,
they can emulate his ways, which lies at the root of their relationship
with the government and mission. For them, a man's behaviour
derives from within himself and from his ties with close relatives and
friends; they have great difficulty in grasping the idea that behaviour
can be modified by purely organizational groups, categories, and
rules.

In order that the reader may better appreciate the course of events
in the Tauade area, I give here a brief chronology of the spread of
government and mission influence:

TABLE I. *Chronology of government and mission influence*

1901   Some men from the Aibala visit the Kuni area to carry for Pratt's expedition.

1905   Fr. Egidi, M.S.C., and Fr. Chabot visit the area.

1911   Patrol Officer Keelan from Ioma makes the first visit by the government to the Aibala Valley—to Sopu.

1917   First fighting between the government and the Tauade occurs in the Lova-Loleava area.

1918 onwards   Patrols into the Tauade area become regular. Steel is becoming common. Warfare and fighting with the government continue until the late 1940s.

1932   First visit by the government to Goilala. (Not the Sub-District, but the name of the tribe with whom I lived.)

1934–5   Establishment of the police camp at Aporota. By this date a mission out-station had also been established at Gane.

1938   The Tapini airstrip becomes operational. Tapini and Aporota are manned throughout the war.

1938–9   Frs. Wendling and Guivarc'h, M.S.C., come to Sene and then go to Kerau and establish the mission.

1940   School starts at Kerau.

1948   Aporota closed.

1950   Labour migration out of the Sub-District begins with very small numbers.

1952   Aporota reopened temporarily. Labour migration continues to increase during the 1950s, and violence decreases.

1963   The Local Government Council is established at Tapini: it covers most of the Tauade area except the Pilitu. Village constables continue to operate.

1964   First Papua and New Guinea House of Assembly elections held.

1967   Kerau airstrip completed.

1975   Independence.

2. THE CIRCUMSTANCES OF FIELD-WORK

My attention was first drawn to the Tauade because they live in one of the least-studied areas of Papua New Guinea, despite its proximity to Port Moresby. Most anthropologists have concentrated upon the Highlands, the coastal peoples, and the islands surrounding the mainland, while this area of mountain Papua has been much neglected, partly perhaps because of the discouraging disposition of the people, and also partly because of their relatively long period of subordination to government control and mission influence. In addition, the material culture is starkly barren with none of the artistic profusion of other areas.

The Goilala Sub-District comprises three linguistic groups—the Tauade, the Fuyughe, and the Katé or Kunimaipa. I am the first anthropologist to study the Tauade. In 1912 R. W. Williamson published a monograph on the Fuyughe—*The Mafulu Mountain*

People of British New Guinea—based on a few months' residence at
Popole in 1910. This is, however, much inferior to Fr. Paul Fastré's
'Mœurs et coutumes foujoughèses' (unpublished ms. 1937–9). Dr.
Margaret McArthur studied the Kunimaipa during the years 1953–7,
when they had only recently been brought under effective government control, and presented her material in the form of a doctoral
thesis, 'The Kunimaipa. The Social Structure of a Papuan People',
at the Australian National University, Canberra. These are the only
important accounts of the principal groups in the Sub-District.

On a less serious level, the area has been given fame by the works
of Fr. André Dupeyrat, but for the purposes of ethnography their
value is diminished by the uncertain provenance of many of the
stories, and by the author's concentration upon the sensational and
the macabre, to the neglect of the more normal aspects of native
society and daily life. But the basic reason for giving little space to
Dupeyrat is that it is not he, but Fr. Fastré who is the real authority
on the Fuyughe. Indeed, 'Mœurs et coutumes foujoughèses' was
written especially for Dupeyrat's benefit. One can only hope that
Fastré's work will in due course be published and receive the recognition which it deserves.

Fr. Fastré was the first priest of the Sacred Heart Mission to work
in the Goilala, and he established the mission at Popole (Mafulu) at
the invitation of the famous chief Baïva in 1905. Fastré was clearly
a very intelligent man with a delightful sense of humour who expressed himself in a vigorous prose. While he admits that he is not
a sociologist he nevertheless describes the general nature of Fuyughe
society and the character of the people vividly and provides rich
material especially on their supernatural beliefs and related subjects
from a period when social change was still slight.

McArthur's study of the Kunimaipa is sociologically speaking,
more thorough and specialized than that of Fastré, though it is not
concerned with their cosmology; on most matters points of comparison can be established with Tauade society.

I arrived in the Sub-District on 14 May 1970, and finally left on
14 June 1972. Of these twenty-five months, twenty-two were spent
in the field, and three in Port Moresby studying government records.
Not all that time in the field was spent in the village, and I made visits
to C.M. Ononghe, C.M. Kosipi, and C.M. Kamulai, as well as
spending some time at Tapini. After spending a couple of weeks at
the Kerau mission, I moved into the new house which had been

built on the old hamlet site of Pomutu, in the Goilala tribal area, about three and a half miles from the mission. (The name 'Goilala' applied to the tribe with whom I lived has no connection with that of the Sub-District, and is purely co-incidental.[1])

The people were very willing for me to come and live with them, since it is generally believed in the area that white men bring wealth. Some people asked me to open a store, but the only articles which I regularly sold to them were tobacco, newspaper, matches, sugar, and rice. As I soon discovered, to have sold more articles than this would not have made the people more forthcoming and would merely have been extremely tiresome for me. People who came to buy were usually not interested in staying to talk, but made off fairly quickly after getting what they wanted. They would certainly not have been motivated by gratitude to come and give me information.

It is difficult to know if they were disappointed in terms of material satisfaction by my stay among them. In one sense, since their basic expectations of Europeans are the limitless fantasies of 'cargo', they must always be disappointed by such contacts. But at a more mundane level they received plenty of money—for the house which they built for me, for firewood and water, for making a track for my motor bike, and for various artefacts which they brought. Informants were also well paid for their work, and regular informants, such as Amo Lume, received substantial sums for texts and other information, or for accompanying me around the area. I also often distributed tobacco—for they are passionate smokers—to those sitting on my veranda when we were having a good discussion, and at all feasts, where I distributed tobacco to those present.

When I arrived it was made clear through Francis Pelai, the Councillor, who could speak a little English, that I had not come to set up a business, or to teach, or as a missionary, but to learn their language, and this they clearly understood. They seem to have no difficulty in recognizing that Europeans have different jobs and functions, and show no tendency to classify them all as missionaries or government officers. For example, I was on a tour of the Aibala Valley with the A.D.C. who called the people together at every major centre of population and upbraided them in caustic terms for their laziness and indifference to economic progress. They listened to this

[1] I chose this place to live because it had, by Tauade standards, a fairly large population, was conveniently close to the mission without being on its doorstep, and had a magnificent view.

with at least outward respect, but had no hesitation in coming up to me and speaking in a perfectly normal and friendly way, realizing of course that I had nothing to do with the government, and that although I was with the A.D.C. this was just because it was natural for white men to travel together.

But the people of Goilala clearly thought that I knew about *them*, in particular, and even about where I would finally live before ever coming to the area. This fact emerged from some speeches in which my putative progress to Goilala was described. According to this theory, I had first lived on the New Guinea side, then at Samarai,[1] and later at Port Moresby. There I said 'I will go to Goilala' (not the Sub-District), so I came by plane to Tapini, and asked where the Goilala were. The *kiap* told me 'Up there', so I said 'I will go there'. As it stands, this account of my intention to come to a specific spot of which I must have known beforehand is quite intelligible—but this apparently straightforward attempt to explain why I had chosen to live at Goilala, not derived from any information which I had given, has deeper implications about the way in which the Tauade categorize the white man.

Precisely the same notion is found in a text which explains why the celebrated Fr. Dubuy, of C.M. Ononghe, decided to found a mission there. According to this story there was an animal long ago at Ononghe called Dioro—whether this was its generic or personal name is obscure. After being hunted by various humans and biting them or raiding their gardens, and escaping by jumping into the rivers, it came out on the Papuan coast and swam across the sea to France. There it was dark, and the ancestors of Fr. Dubuy grabbed it to kill it, but it turned into a man—brown, not white. They asked him if he was a man, and he said he was. They gave him tobacco, tea, bread, sugar, and rice, which he ate. Then they asked him 'Are you an *agoteve*?' (a culture hero, who preceded the real humans who live in Papua now). He said that he was a real human, which was a lie, because he was an *agoteve*. 'Where is your country?' they asked him. He told them 'Goilala' (meaning the Sub-District). 'Where is Goilala' they asked. 'My country is Ononghe.' he said. They wrote the names of these places on a piece of paper. Then they begot Pé Tupu (Fr. Dubuy) and showed him the piece of paper, so that he would know these places. He came to Port Moresby and then made his way by sea to Kairuku—on Yule Island—and then went to Kubuna,

[1] I had never, in fact, visited either Samarai or the Mandated Territory.

Opapa (ObaOba), and Popole. Then he looked at the paper and said 'Where is Ononghe and Woitape?' The people told him. He arrived there. Eluletamei was the place where he built his house. He did not know where he was. An Ononghe man came to him and told him that he was at Ononghe.

Apart from the notion that Fr. Dubuy already knew about Ononghe before he ever came to Papua, there is the further idea that there was some previous connection between the place and him—the 'animal' which swam to France. In the same way I discovered that the people believed that I was really Apava Tulava, the deceased eldest son of Avui Apava, a chief, who had returned from the dead. I was given this name about ten months after my arrival, during a feast, without any explanation at the time, except that I was now one of them and should stay there, or if I left send one of my brothers to live there in my place. That I was an Englishman was apparently no impediment to this belief, since someone who had come back from the dead could hardly be expected to look normal. But the Fathers told me that someone said to them that it was strange, that I was taller than Apava Tulava had been, and that I had no scar on my left leg, as he had had! Later I discovered that there was indeed a good reason for this choice of identity. While looking for a site for my house I had chosen one where the old government rest-house had been before it was burnt down. The people then suggested a different one, which included the abandoned site of the hamlet of Pomutu. It was in fact a much better spot, fenced and still possessing the two lines of elaivi (Cordyline terminalis) that are always planted as wind-breaks. At the lower end of this plot of land there was a magnificent view down the whole valley of the Ungabunga River (St. Joseph) to the coast, and in order to make the most of this I told them to build the house in that place, scarcely noticing a clump of bushes and some stones just beside it. This was in fact where the bones of Apava Tulava had been deposited, so I had obviously come to Pomutu and had my house built where I did because I wanted to be near the bones which had been mine in a previous existence. The problem for them was solved. They forgot, of course, that it was they who had suggested the site of Pomutu in the first place, but the principle was clear—no one just wanders about aimlessly on the face of the earth. If he goes somewhere there must be a reason, and what better reason than an antecedent relationship? Their belief that I was one of their own returned from the dead also showed that they realized I was attempting a closer rapport with them than any European they had ever known.

This belief was certainly not translated into any practical assimilation into their lives, although the very kindly disposition which my putative father, Avui Apava, always displayed to me may have been connected with this belief. For, even if I had been Apava Tulava in a previous life, I was now something very different, not the same person over again.

It might be asked, did they not treat you as if you were a spiritual being? If one means by 'spiritual being' something ethereal and insubstantial, without bodily functions, then they did not. But they certainly regarded me as being of dubious ontological status. As I remarked earlier, I went on a patrol of the Aibala Valley with the A.D.C. in February 1971, by which time I had acquired some knowledge of their language and customs, and spoke to many people. Some time after this, Fr. Guichet told me that a girl, I think from Kiolivi, was at Kerau, and said to him 'That Mr. Hallpike, is he a man or a spirit?' 'Why should he be a spirit?' replied Fr. Guichet, with some astonishment. 'Ah, well, you see, he knows our language and about our customs.' Later, in June 1971, I returned from Moresby to find that there were strong rumours of cargo-cult. Among these was the belief that I had made the 'riches' which were in my house out of my insides. Such a belief was perhaps understandable in the case of people who did not know me, but when I asked Moise Apava and Apava Oiabue, my informants, if the people at Goilala also thought this, they assured me that some of them did—even though they had helped, or seen others help, to carry my goods from the mission or the airstrip to my house.

There is a school of thought among liberal-minded anthropologists which holds that the ethnographer should behave as much like the natives as possible—sleeping on the floor in filth, eating their food, allowing them to examine his person, and to come into his house at all hours of the day and night. One even hears of female ethnographers parading themselves bare-breasted. The people are not, of course, deceived by such foolishness and, far from taking this kind of person to their hearts, regard them with bewilderment or contempt. They do not expect us to behave as they do, and an ethnographer who tries to mimic their way of life will not be regarded as a true Tauade, but simply as a mad white man. To live alone for two years among people such as the Tauade one must establish some standards of privacy and some line beyond which they know one cannot be exploited. One can best display 'sympathy' by reacting with ordinary human emotions, including anger, in the appropriate situations.

I cannot pretend that I liked the Tauade as a people, especially after having worked with the Konso in Ethiopia. The Konso were straightforward and blunt, ready to reprove me if I offended against their code of behaviour, and rather suspicious of me when I first came to live among them, but when they decided that I was not a threat to their way of life, they proved very friendly and good-humoured, and were also thoroughly honest and trustworthy. The Tauade, while outwardly more compliant—even, in some cases, obsequious—were basically much more reserved and secretive, as well as being sly and dishonest. Again, while the Konso never begged and never asked for anything except cigarettes, the Tauade, on the other hand, were greedy for material possessions, and their limitless rapacity drove me to distraction. While the Konso would come and sit with me purely to be sociable, and no doubt to be entertained by the novelty of the strange anthropologist, most of the Tauade would usually only visit me when they wanted to buy something, usually tobacco and newspaper, and when they had obtained them would drift away quickly.

Obviously, there is an element of personal bias in these assessments of the Konso and the Tauade. As Margaret Mead (1968: 19) says, 'When one views any event or situation, one will adopt a point of view towards it that is congruent with one's own temperament and character formation.' I must admit to preferring plain-speaking, honest, brave, and good-humoured people to sly, deceitful, and secretive people who avoid antagonizing the strong and instead prey mercilessly on the weak and defenceless. I recognize, however, that there are other anthropologists with different preferences who would find these Tauade characteristics congenial and sympathetic, and would, for this reason, have achieved a closer rapport with them than I was able to do.

3. THE ASSESSMENT OF SOURCES

Social anthropology might be defined as the study of the lies that natives tell to anthropologists, especially anthropologists who work with people like the Tauade. Truthfulness for its own sake is not a virtue which is recognized by the Tauade, and while it is insulting to tell a man that he is lying, the insult consists in saying it to his face;

as in the case of theft or adultery, the real shame lies in being caught, not in the act itself.

But while a great deal of one's information is potentially untrustworthy, it is none the less possible to discern types of information which are more reliable than other types, circumstances in which the informants are more likely to be lying than telling the truth, and informants who are more trustworthy than others.

The most reliable types of information which one can obtain from the people are about language, especially botanical names, and names of natural features of the environment, genealogies, and related matters of marriages and where people are living, and details of daily pursuits, such as the making of gardens and the preparation of food.

Their powers of quantification, however, are extremely poor, and they are prone to exaggeration, so that a man may be said to have 'five hundred' pigs, when in reality he has ten. Since their traditional system of counting does not extend beyond 2, with the use of the fingers and toes up to 20, I doubt if they have any real idea of what '100' means in any case. Similarly, they have no units of time except for day, *lariata*, so their attempts to estimate dates in the past can also be wildly inaccurate. (They have a word for the moon, *oné*, but I do not believe that they ever used the lunar cycle to calculate time.) This inability to quantify units of time naturally makes any investigation of the time spans of land utilization, or residence patterns, extremely difficult to accomplish with any accuracy.

In general, their answers to questions are designed to please the hearer, and truth is a secondary consideration. Their propensity to lie in any instance depends on whether they think that the questioner more or less knows the answer to the question anyway, and on whether or not they have some personal interest, usually money, in giving one answer rather than another. Thus inquiries into land tenure where eventual purchase is involved, such as the Kerau airstrip, are inevitably obscured by a dense cloud of claim and counter-claim, because everyone has an interest in demanding compensation and all know that it is almost impossible for an outsider, without exact genealogical knowledge, to adjudicate between rival claims, with the result that a man with a false claim may stand as good a chance of getting some money as a man with a genuine claim. Nor is interest confined to matters of money. On one occasion I asked someone why he was killing pigs, and he replied that it was because of some blood he had lost from some injuries on his hand. Now, loss of blood is taken very seriously by the Tauade, and may be the occasion for killing pigs, and so his answer had some plausibility. It was in fact quite false, and the pigs were being killed to mark his expulsion of a man from the area, and because of his adultery with this man's wife, and he wished to conceal these facts from me. However, while they are fluent and ready liars in matters of day-to-day relations and practical affairs when it suits their purpose, in more recondite matters, such as legends or spiritual beliefs, they find it easier to pretend ignorance if they do not wish to divulge information.

In any community, even where experience is as homogeneous as in a New Guinea[1] village, there are some people who are strikingly more capable of articulating that experience than others. The community in which I lived had only about fifteen men who were old enough to have experience of the days when government control was slight and most of the old customs were flourishing, but not so old as to be senile, and of these some lived too far away to make daily conversations practical, and others either had no interest in talking to me or would have been of no use even if they had. So while I was able to use a number of informants for obtaining basic information, especially about genealogies, as my inquiries advanced I was eventually left with only one regular informant, Amo Lume, a man of exceptional intelligence and knowledge, upon whom I could rely.

It would obviously have been preferable to have been able to draw on a wider range of information than this. It has been supplemented, however, by the use of copious government records—mainly patrol reports, court records, and census data—the information supplied by the Fathers at Kerau, Kamulai, Kosipi, and Ononghe, the work of McArthur, Fastré, Williamson, and others, and some excellent material from a middle-aged catechist, Casimiro Kog, born at Sene, with whom I had the pleasure of working for a couple of weeks at C.M. Kosipi.

In the case of court records it might be argued, in view of what has been said about the propensity of the Tauade to lie when it suits their interests to do so, that these must be the most unreliable of all sources of information. It cannot be denied that the people use the

[1] I use 'New Guinea' here in the ethnographic sense. 'Papua' and 'the Mandated Territory' will be used to refer to the two political areas of the country.

courts fraudulently to revenge themselves. For example, Mr. W. J. S. Graham, A.D.O., recounts the following incident:

A councillor reported two men for failing to maintain roads, and for keeping pigs in the village. They were charged and fined. A week later, the two men presented themselves with four other witnesses to say that the councillor had been cross with them, and that from a distance they had seen the councillor set fire to their houses. The witnesses were close relatives. The councillor was later proved to have been in another village. (Patrol Report, Tapini, 16/6/69–27/6/69.)

But some basic characteristics of their society will still be evident from a sufficient number of cases, even if the witnesses are often lying, since even false evidence will conform to the pattern of behaviour with which they are familiar. For example, in many cases of adultery brought before the courts the man will plead—truly or falsely—that the woman forced herself upon him, and that he had no choice. Now, if it were unknown or highly eccentric among the Tauade for a woman to make sexual advances to a man, such behaviour would not be cited so frequently by witnesses who, having no experience of any other way of life but their own, must necessarily give a reasonably accurate picture of the only way of life which they do know. To take a counter-example, male homosexuality is unknown in traditional Tauade society and understandably does not appear in any court evidence.

A similar mode of reasoning can be used to assess the credibility of the stories of battles in the past. One recognizes that such narratives may contain some confusion of time and place, names may be forgotten or wrongly included, and there may be some tendency to exaggerate the gruesomeness of the details. But an uneducated Tauade, who has spent almost the whole of his life in his remote valley, has no other pattern of behaviour to draw upon but that of his own culture, and it is therefore reasonable to conclude that even if, to make a very extreme supposition, every name and event in a story were false, the general picture of the society contained in it would still be fairly true to life. In the same way, one can learn a great deal about Victorian England by reading novels of the period, which in a sense are quite 'untrue'. However, there is no indication that the accounts of warfare and other practices which are now defunct are seriously inaccurate. Two of the stories of battles told me by Amo Lume can be corroborated by contemporary patrol reports; the later events in the long text on the warfare between the Sene and

Laitate tribes given to me by Casimiro can be confirmed by government and mission records, and the general picture of warfare in this text, and in those from Amo, conforms closely to those in patrol reports.

We are fortunately moving out of an era of unthinking prejudice against oral tradition as a respectable historical source. Fox (1971) has shown, for example, that the orally transmitted political traditions of the Rotinese of Indonesia can be substantiated over a period of *three centuries* from Dutch colonial records. It should not therefore surprise us if the Tauade are capable of remembering the details of battles which they saw forty or fifty years ago as young men, or which were described to them by their fathers or grandfathers.

The Tauade language is one of those known by linguists as Papuan or Non-Austronesian, and like many of these languages is unusually difficult for Europeans to learn—it was at least a year before I was able to converse easily in it and make it an effective instrument of my inquiries. Pidgin[1] and Police-Motu are spoken by some of the Tauade, but I preferred to work entirely in the vernacular, since it was the language used by everyone, especially the older men, and there was ample time at my disposal to learn it.

The linguistic difficulties, the poverty of symbolism, the small number of informants, the lack of clear group organization, and the general vagueness and fluidity of their society made ethnographic research extraordinarily difficult. There are no elegant structural forms to be elucidated, such as one finds in societies with age-grading systems or dual organization, and even the names of individuals seem liable to the prevailing imprecision, since a person may be known by several different names simultaneously, and a single name may refer to a number of persons. One can only hope to grasp the processes of such a society by accumulating large quantities of data to discern general tendencies, and by collecting illuminating anecdotes of behaviour and attitudes, and basing this material on wide genealogical foundations. (My Goilala genealogies, for a community of 155 members, contain about 1,000 names.) The first draft of this book has been reduced by one-third in the course of revision, and evidence presented in support of statements is designed only to be representative, not conclusive.

[1] The ludicrous term 'Neo-Melanesian', for whose adoption some academics once campaigned, has now sunk into the oblivion which it deserves.

A further problem for the ethnographer is to assess the effects of the last fifty years upon Tauade society. Since this monograph is not about social change, data from government records have been used to illustrate what can be shown to have been important features of their society, and while I have also relied on my informants' memories of warfare and other defunct customs and institutions, I am therefore only interested in the present as a means of assessing the past and illuminating those features of their society that are of enduring significance.

II

The Aibala¹ Valley

I. THE PHYSICAL ENVIRONMENT

THE island of New Guinea is divided down the centre by a chain of great mountain ranges, which rise at their highest points to 15,000 and 16,000 feet. That section of the chain which runs through the Goilala Sub-District is called the Wharton Range² and is dominated by the triple peaks of the great Mt. Albert Edward (13,040 feet). To the north west lie the summits of Mts. Chamberlain, Nelson, and St. Mary, from whose sides a network of torrents carry the water from the rains into the great rivers which run through mile-deep valleys to the Coral Sea.

At the highest altitudes the forests give way to rolling plateaux of Alpine grasses and tundra pitted with icy lakes, over which the bitter wind ceaselessly sweeps, wracking the lungs, and where, for the natives, it is death by paralysing cold to be caught in the drenching rain of these heights.

The great ranges, unvaryingly green, endlessly repeating the simple themes of razor-back ridge and river gorge, spur and re-entrant, in fold after fold to all horizons, depress the spirits, since their very grandeur ultimately becomes monotonous. Yet, when the sun is shining with that special intensity only experienced at high altitude, and the air is still fresh and cold, and the dead leaves diffuse an autumnal scent, it is hard not to feel the exhilaration of the high ranges. The valleys are full of the murmurous rushing of distant torrents, born faintly but insistently on the ear. As the climber slowly toils up some impossible mountainside, dripping with sweat and cursing the day he came to Papua, he may come upon one of these streams, splashing in white foam over mossy rocks in some

¹ Also written, in official records, as 'Aiwara'.
² Not the Owen Stanley Range, of which it is an extension, and with which it is often confused.

shaded hollow, with a sandy floor, where he can plunge his face
and drink deeply.

After midday the clouds which have been forming on the ridges
and peaks begin to fill the valleys; under the bright sun, in the clear
air, the valleys seem small and intimate, but as the clouds pour down
the slopes and divide the ridges, and allow only fitful glimpses of the
great peaks, the whole scene acquires a cavernous immensity.
Familiar landscapes are transmuted out of recognition and take on a
mythopoeic grandeur. A single tree on some high ridge stands out
alone above the surging clouds; the sun, setting behind the great
Mount Kutumu, turns the drifting evening mists into gold; the full
moon shines on the valley of the Aibala, and on the low clouds which
fill it, a scene of astonishing quietness and peace.

The months of June to September tend to be the driest, though
September is often noticeably wetter than the other three. Heavier
rain can be expected in October, though November is again frequently rather dry. The rainy season begins in earnest from the beginning of December and lasts until the end of May. Especially in
January, February, and March the clouds often blanket the mountains and valleys for days on end, so that one wakes up every morning to the sound of the ceaseless drip of rain from the surrounding
trees and bushes and from the roof of one's house, and visibility is
often only a hundred yards; the dank fogs, interspersed with thin,
drizzling rain, penetrate everything. It is this weather which is
known to the missionaries as the *fidi*—the people themselves give it
no special name.

The paths are always narrow, and usually steep, and made of
unpleasant clay that rapidly acquires a coating of loathsome slime
when it is wet. In the rainy season movement even from one hamlet
to another becomes a tiresome ordeal of sliding and slithering, the
only alternative to the clay being ankle-deep mud.

During the later part of the rainy season the rain begins earlier in
the day than usual, often before noon, while in the dry season it may
not begin until late afternoon, if it rains at all. Rain does not fall as
thundershowers, and while it can be very heavy, especially under the
mountains, in other places its intensity would not be remarkable in
England. In the inhabited valleys thunderstorms are rare, though
sometimes in the evenings and after dark one can hear the thunder
booming in the high ranges.

Winds can be very violent, especially in February, and on many

occasions I have been woken in the night by my hut quivering in the
blasts sweeping up from the valley below. On such occasions one lies
apprehensive, waiting almost as though for a tidal wave, as the roar
of the wind through the pandanus forest draws nearer, wondering
whether the next shock will tear off the roof and leave one exposed
to the lashing rain. The people are very familiar with these fierce
winds, and it is not uncommon for houses in exposed areas to have
their roofs blown off. The first church at Kerau was blown down by
the wind, and the Fathers' and Sisters' houses lost their roofs several
times before the new houses with iron roofs were constructed. It is
Tauade custom to plant *elaivi* and a number of other species of trees
in parallel lines to give shelter to their hamlets, and in time these
wind-breaks may grow over 20 feet high, surviving long after the
houses themselves have disappeared.

In the dry season when the new gardens are prepared, the bush
burnt, fences cut, and the ground dug over, no rain may fall for as
long as two weeks, and when it does it is usually in the late afternoon
or evening, leaving the mornings fresh and brilliant. At these altitudes the sun's radiation is fierce and burns the unaccustomed skin,
but the air is always cool and in the shade one will quickly shiver.
At night the skies are clear and the air often becomes bitterly cold,
with occasional ground frosts in some places. The lowest tempera-
tures are usually recorded at this time of year.

The average rainfall for the Goilala Sub-District is 103 in. per
annum. This figure is based upon the average rainfalls of Tapini,
Woitape, Guari,[1] and C.M.s Fane, Kerau,[1] Kamulai,[1] Ononghe, and
Kosipi. The spur on which I lived was drier than average, since it is
largely treeless, and some way from the 10,000-foot peak of Kutumu
(Mt. Eyssautier). In the only twelve-month period for which I have
unbroken records rainfall was 59·92 in. In the corresponding period
Tapini rainfall was 74·53 in. (average for the last twenty years
77·01 in.). As one might expect in such country, rainfall is very
variable, Woitape and Kosipi receiving 125 in. and 120 in. respectively, while Tapini and Ononghe only receive 77 in. and 81 in. per
annum. This variability seems to depend partly on the general
locality, and partly on special features of the terrain, such as proximity to high peaks, prevailing wind directions, and degree of afforesta-
tion. Kataipa and Oropoa, for example, were obviously affected by
the rain generated on Kutumu, and I often looked over the valley at

[1] For a few years only. See Appendix VI.

midday and saw the rain lashing down upon these areas under the
mountain, while Goilala was bathed in brilliant sunshine. The higher
end of the valley in the Kuputaivi area which too, is very heavily
forested was also extremely wet, and would often be blanketed in

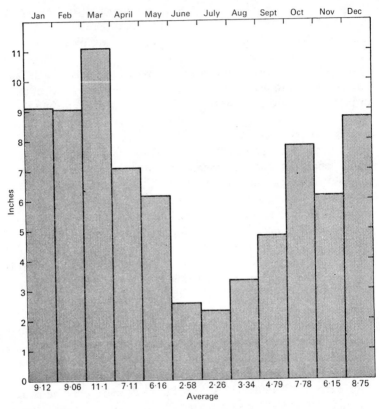

FIG. I. Tapini rainfall 1961–70

rain and mist while Kerau was dry and clear. The yearly pattern of
rainfall can be seen in the histogram, Fig. I.

   In some years, however, there may be drought in certain regions.
In 1965 total rainfall at Tapini was only 48·22 in., and in the eight
months from April through November only 19·86 in. fell as opposed
to the average for the period of 40 in. This was the lowest rainfall
recorded at Tapini in the period 1950–71, but since I left another

drought has been reported. In 1901 there was a drought during Pratt's visit, of which he records:

Lycopodium [a type of moss] were dropping off the trees, and often we could see, in the lower grounds, great forest fires, which consumed the undergrowth throughout large tracts of country, miles and miles being left blackened and burnt up. (Pratt 1906: 127.)

The humidity is high, seldom falling below 75 per cent and often rising in the afternoon or evening to well over 90 per cent—higher than on the coast, which is not often realized. It is presumably an important factor in inhibiting evaporation of moisture from the soil. During the year there is remarkably little variation in temperature; at Goilala the highest maximum recorded was 76·0 °F., the lowest minimum 44·0 °F. The yearly average was 65·0 °F.

2. THE PEOPLES OF THE GOILALA SUB-DISTRICT

The Tauade speakers, of whom this book treats, are one of the three linguistic and cultural groups of the Goilala Sub-District. The Kunimaipa or Katé inhabit the valley of the Kunimaipa River and the Karuama Valley to the south of Mt. Yule. In relatively recent times the Kunimaipa have penetrated the Loloipa Valley by a peaceful process of intermarriage with the Tauade speakers there, so that now the only purely Tauade-speaking villages in this valley are on the eastern side of the valley from Poruava to Tatupiti. There are also important marriage-links between the Kunimaipa and the Tauade at the head of the Aibala River, in the Kuputaivi area.

The Tauade speakers are to be found in the Aibala and Ivane Valleys and in the area south of Tapini known as Pilitu. In more recent years some have crossed the range to Kosipe and have settled as far as Woitape.

The Fuyughe, the third main group, dwell more scattered in the valleys of the Chirima, Vanapa, and Dilava rivers. The relative populations of these groups are given in Table 2 on p. 45.

It is clear from the accounts of McArthur on the Kunimaipa, and Fastré and Williamson on the Fuyughe, that both these groups are similar to the Tauade in values, customs, and social organization, though there are some differences. But while a basic similarity exists, relatively little contact between the valleys over long periods of time has produced great linguistic differences. Thus from linguistic data provided by C.M. Kamulai on the Kunimaipa language, I found that using a modified version of Swadesh's 200-word list there were 7·3 per cent cognates with Tauade.[1] From data on the Fuyughe language supplied by C.M. Ononghe it appeared that there were 9·5 per cent of cognates with Tauade. These figures are very low and indicate, as might be expected, that these languages are mutually quite unintelligible. It does not follow from this, however, that any

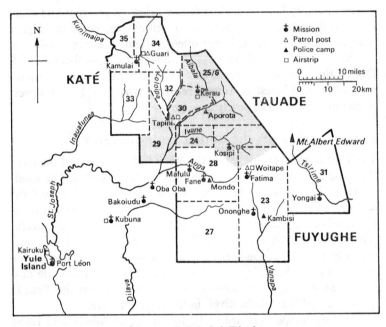

MAP 2. Goilala Sub-District

of these groups conceives itself as a political or cultural unit, or that difference of language or custom on the border between two groups appears to produce any more hostility than is normal for this area.

Since the nature of group definition will be of fundamental importance in our understanding of Tauade society, I shall go into the

[1] Steinkraus and Pence in their study *Languages of the Goilala Sub-District* (1964) conclude that there are 44 per cent of cognates between Tauade and Kunimaipa. This extraordinary result seems due to their method of reckoning cognates, by which they allot points for phonemic resemblance, four points for resemblance between all pairs of phonemes, three points for pairs of words with one different phoneme, and so on. But since two words are either cognates—that is, derived from a common root—or they are not, such a procedure seems quite inadmissible.

matter of collective designations at some length here. The Tauade divide themselves into dialect areas, of which the word *Tauade* is in fact one—*Tauata*. These areas are as follows:

In the Aibala Valley, the tribes on the west bank beneath Mt. Kutumu, the Goilala, Diolivi, and Kunima, and, on the east bank,

TABLE 2. *The populations of the three language groups in the Goilala Sub-District*

Census district	Population	Total
TAUADE		
25/26 Aiwara	4,208	
30 Kataipa	1,930	
24 Ivane	1,002	
29 Pilitu	1,521	8,661
KUNIMAIPA		
34 Upper Kunimaipa	2,270	
35 Lower Kunimaipa	1,465	
33 Karuama	1,108	
32 Loloipa	1,203	6,046
FUYUGHE		
23 Vetapu	5,816	
27 Dilava	1,623	
28 Auga	4,600	
31 Chirima	2,014	14,053
Sub-District total		28,760

Source: Village Directory, Department of District Administration, 1968. Based on the Census of 1966.

the Elava-Tapina, to Gane, Malava, and Kileipi, are all Tauatama. (The suffix -*ma* is merely a plural form meaning here 'people'.) Down the west bank of the Aibala from Kuputaivi to Kurumutu (Kerau) are the Aibala speakers—Kuputaivi-Deelamani, Omoritu, Poneyala-vava, Kopurilavava, Lamanaipi, Tupuru-Doulava, Karom, and Kuru-mutu. Along the southern bank of the Aibala after its junction with the Kileipi and Lova rivers, all the Garipa, Watagoipa, Amuganiawa, Maini, Ita, Onia-Sene, Iveyava, Karoava (Sopu), and Lova-Loleava are Purama speakers. The Lamanaipa, between the Lova-Loleava and the Kileipi are Kuvalema, or Kuvalema-Tauatama. The Kemava, Oropoa, Kataipa, Tawuni, and the tribes over the range in the Loloipa

Valley, are Pioroma. The Amiapa, Lavavai, and Tatupiti or Kapatea-Vaviogoa, are the Iguvai, and the Pilitu are Moinama. The Ivane inhabitants are Ivanima—the Ivane dialect is also called Apekove. The Fuyughe are Puyogama, and the Kunimaipa are the Katema.

MAP 3. Tauade Dialect distribution

The distinctions between the dialects here designated are often quite small, unless substantial distances are involved. Often, it is some distinctive expression, common in one area, which becomes, for outsiders, characteristic of the whole dialect. For example, the Pioroma, of Tawuni, Kataipa, and Oropoa, are renowned among the Tauatama for saying *meila!* instead of *oi kona!*—'come here!'

The first time that the word *Tauata* appears in either learned or official use is in an article by Fr. V. M. Egidi, D.D., M.S.C., in

Anthropos, 1907. He seems to have been the first visitor to Tauade country and probably went from the mission station of Bakoiudu in the Kuni area up the Aibala River to some point in the Aibala Valley, though exactly where is obscure. He writes:

A journey of exploration has taken me into the heart of the Tauata, or Tauatape, tribe, and has allowed me to make some observations which I hope may be of some interest to the readers of *Anthropos*. The tribe comprises all those villages which speak the language known here at Kuni as Afoá, (Ambové to the Fuyughe) and is almost entirely contained in a parallelogram of 30 km. (18½ miles) from North to South, and 20 km. (12½ miles) from East to West. The 147° meridian cuts it a few miles [in] from the West side, while the South side is almost exactly situated on the 8° 30′ parallel.

The name *Tauatape* (*Tauata* for short in ordinary usage) which the people use to describe themselves, here at *Kuni* becomes *Kauaka*, and *Tauatade* among the Fuyughes. I still do not know if the name Afoá, which here at Kuni denotes the language which they speak, has a corresponding name in their language. I will attempt to provide some notes on the language later. For the moment I confine myself to comments on the life and customs of the natives of the sub-tribe of the Aivale, which I have visited. (Egidi 1907: 675.)

While it may be the case that the Tauade understand what is meant by the 'Tauade' *language*, the primary sense of *Tauade* is the *people* and, as Egidi says, the use of the term to describe the Tauade speakers, rather than the language, itself comes from the Fuyughe. For the people themselves seldom use the word *Tauata* to describe their speech, but prefer to use instead the name of their tribe. For example, men of my own tribe, when recommending a particular word or usage to me, would never say *Tauata kato*, 'good Tauata', but *Goilala kato*, 'good Goilala'. The mission took over the use of the name *Tauade*, but the government had from the beginning used the term *Goilala* for the Tauade speakers. The name *Goilala* was first supplied to Europeans by the inhabitants of the Giumu to describe themselves—to the patrol officer who visited them in 1911. In fact, they referred to themselves as the 'Small Goilala'—in numbers, that is—as opposed to the Big Goilala over the range in the Lova-Loleava area. The first patrol officers therefore supposed that everyone in the Aibala was a Goilala, and it was not until 1928–9 that Mr. Ivan Champion discovered that the true Goilala were the people living on the spur where I eventually lived. This has usually been known, incorrectly, as Ororogaivara—also Orogaivarara, and Ororogaiva.

This is in fact the name of a hamlet which was probably a dance village when Patrol Officer Middleton first visited it in 1932, and is now almost deserted. The true name of this tribe is Goilala, but they claim that they have no special ancestral connection with the people of the Giumu. So why the latter should have referred to themselves as *Goilala* is obscure. There is the possibility that it is an instance of two tribes having the same name. For example, there is a Lamanaipi tribe adjoining the Karom tribe, near Kerau, and another Lamanaipi beyond Kileipi, adjacent to the Lova-Loleava.

When the government decided to move the police camp to Aporota, this camp also became known as the 'Goilala' police camp, since the name Goilala was now too well established to be given up, even though it was now known to be erroneous. When the Sub-District was finally established as an administrative entity, the name of the most prominent police camp seems to have been chosen for it.

By such a devious route, therefore, the name Goilala became that of the whole Sub-District—now comprising the Fuyughe and the Kunimaipa, as well as the Tauade—and a word to strike terror into the hearts of the more docile inhabitants of Port Moresby, brown and white alike. The Goilala in Port Moresby were for a number of years employed on the dust carts until replaced by the Chimbu. It would not be straying far from the truth to say that the stereotype of the Goilala in Port Moresby was that of stunted, homicidal dustmen.

This account of the origins of the names Tauade and Goilala shows that they did not arise from any consciousness within the group so named of its own distinctiveness; they are provided by outsiders in recognition of some common characteristic, in this case dialect, which they notice.

The name Tauata or Tauade was therefore chosen by the Fuyughe from one of the *dialect* groups, and used to designate all *speakers* of the language. The Fuyughe passed this name on to the missionaries. The government, entering the area from a different direction, learned to use the name Goilala. This name was retained for convenience even when it was known to be incorrect.

Once the Goilala police camp had been established and the name was used for the Goilala Sub-District, a new stage was reached in the process of creating unity in the minds of outsiders, whereas the people themselves were as yet more aware of the lack of unity. For now the Fuyughe, Tauade, and Kunimaipa peoples were somehow lumped together in the eyes of the outside world as a homogeneous people—

the Goilala. But even if the Goilala themselves still felt no bonds of common loyalty, in the context of Port Moresby this has to some extent been forced upon them, since they possess a single name and an associated and very derogatory stereotype. While they therefore feel no loyalty to each other in their own area, once they are facing outsiders they tend to unite against them on familiar segmentary principles. Moreover, their solidarity against outsiders can be extended to people who are not Goilala at all, but with whom some measure of identification is possible. For example, the Roro people, who live on and around Yule Island, the headquarters of the Sacred Heart Mission, have been told by Goilala in Moresby that they will not be harmed because they, like the Goilala, are 'people of the mission'. Again, I was indulging in some horse-play with an Australian in the bar of the Tapini Hotel one evening and pretending to stab him with my sheath knife. I was immediately approached by some Fuyughe, not Tauade, who asked me if I would like them to kill this man for me; other Europeans living in the area have had similar experiences.

3. MIGRATION, TRAVEL, AND TRADE-ROUTES

The Goilala area seems to have been more isolated from the coast than from other parts of the central ranges. Kariks *et al.* (1958) conclude that 'The blood group pattern resembles more closely that of other highland people than it does that of the coastal natives' (p. 122) and 'The Goilala blood group pattern differs markedly from the patterns of both the Central and Northern administrative districts . . .' (p. 121).

Dr. F. W. Clements, who made a medical expedition to the Goilala area in 1935, confirms that as far as medical evidence goes there seems to have been little personal contact with coastal natives:

. . . we found that the disease [yaws] had made but little progress inland; altitude may explain this, but more probably it is the absence of that intimate contact between peoples of the mountain districts and the coast so necessary for the spread of the disease. The coastal native had till recent years always regarded the mountain men with great awe and fear. We were privileged to attend a mountain dance to which coastal natives had been invited for the first time. The dance is an occasion for intimate social contact between visitors and hosts. At the next village along the mountain road several cases of framboesia [yaws] were encountered—all in natives who had recently attended a dance visited by coastal natives. (Clements 1936: 454.)

Clements also confirms that fairly regular social contacts were
maintained across the ranges between the Giumu Valley and the
Aibala:

Several cases of paralysis [poliomyelitis] were seen amongst the coastal
natives, and two cases were found in the depths of the Goilala. This very
interesting finding led to an inquiry into the source of the infection. About
1929 a 'sickness' appeared in a village in the Upper Aiwara. Some of the
natives had been on a trading expedition over the range into the upper
waters of the Waria. This disease spread down the Aiwara to the village
of Ororogaivana [sic]. Two trading expeditions left this village, one to go
to Maini and the other to go along the eastern bank of the Lowa to Sopu.
Cases of infantile paralysis appeared both at Maini and Sopu accompanied
by a number of deaths.
    Whereas the epidemic ceased at Maini on the west, it continued on over
the Kosipe swamps down through Waitape to Ononge on the eastern leg.
Natives informed me that a regular trade route runs right down to Ononge
on the east, but that it ends at Maini on the west, explaining the absence
of the disease in the Ivane valley. The trade is very novel in nature, and is
confined almost exclusively to white cowrie shells used as ornaments.
Records from the Mandated Territory show that an epidemic of infantile
paralysis occurred around the mouth of the Waria during 1929. (Clements
1935: 458.)

So while the linguistic diversity of New Guinea tribes, the fragmented and violent nature of their society, and the separation of
inhabited valleys from one another by high, forested mountain
ranges, might lead one to suppose that migration and trade were
rare and untypical in areas like the Goilala, such a conclusion would
be incorrect. Paths, perhaps originally made by pigs, travel over the
ranges through the virgin forest, and social relations between the
valleys have long been maintained; the populations of these adjacent
valleys invite one another to dances, intermarry, use each other's
territory for refuge when warfare and social friction become too
severe, and, of course, trade with one another for valuables. Some
impression of the kinds of migration that occurred around the Aibala
Valley can be gained from these two accounts by patrol officers:

Ariome, Moigili, Aromaitsi, and Kopukoru people about 30 years ago
crossed to the Ivane valley from the Aiwara area because of continual
friction arising over ownership of katoro [pandanus] groves and pigs in
Goilala. Today these people with the exception of Moigili and Aromaitsi
still garden, collect katoro nuts and run pigs in the Goilala [the Aibala
Valley]. For many months at a time the people desert their villages in the
Ivane valley and move to bush houses, and Ita-Lavavai village in the Goilala

and Kiliai village, en masse, have moved to the Goilala and for approximately 12–18 months will remain there feasting and on a generally extended celebration.

The Moigili and Aromaitsi people do not now move from their present site probably because of adequate and very rich garden areas that are available on the southern bank of the Ivane valley. (R. F. Hearne, P.O., Tapini, November 1953.)

The Sopu want to build a gardening village at Lolopa in the Giumu valley. This has previously been banned by Government officers and of late the Sopus have not been using the area. The reason behind their removal was that the Iarewa people who live further down the valley objected to the presence of Sopus on land which they claimed for the purpose of hunting.

Bottrell visited Sopu and discussed the matter with Iarewa who were dancing there, as to whether it could be arranged for the Sopus to resume gardening operations in the Giumu as their own land is limited for a population of 450.

As a result, he found that the Iarewa have no valid claim to land in the Upper Giumu, as they themselves were originally Goilala people who moved over into the Giumu from the Lowa (Goilala) area, where they still own katoro trees. The making of a village at Lolopa is thought to be advisable by both Bottrell and myself, but the Sopus have been told to await a ruling from a higher level. (W. M. Purdy, P.O., Tapini, March–April 1951.)

Dr. McArthur writes as follows concerning migration from the Kunimaipa Valley:

The biggest concentration of Kunimaipa speakers in the Trust Territory of New Guinea live in the Bubu valley where there are about 800 of them. That is the only area in T.N.G. where the settlement of Kunimaipa speakers is not recent. Migrants from the Kunimaipa and its tributary valleys settled in the Ipi-Biaru valleys, about 2 days' walk from Wau, in the upper Waria valley and in the Ono-Kau creek areas, probably in the 1920s and 1930s. Some of them are still living in each area. Intermarriage between the people at the head of the Kunimaipa valley and their neighbours over the range on the Ono river, who speak a different, but probably related, language, has been going on for generations. Migrants to the other areas settled on unoccupied land.

And in a note on the people living in the Tapala valley, she says:

The Tapala people say that their ancestors moved over into the valley from the lower Kunimaipa only after the arrival of steel axes. That would be in the early years of this century.

Prior to 1914 the upper Akaifu valley was also occupied by Kuefa people from the lower Kunimaipa. They moved back to the Kunimaipa after reprisal action against them following the murder of a prospector. (C. J. Adamson, private communication.)

The moves across the mountains were part of a mass exodus from the valleys of the Kunimaipa and its tributaries during the 1920s and 1930s, in the course of which several parishes were completely deserted and others depleted of up to about half their normal population. In addition to these moves large numbers went from the east bank of the Kunimaipa river to the Bubu, where they had long traded and intermarried. Some are still living there, but the majority returned after the Kunimaipa and adjacent valleys were brought under Government control in the years following 1947. Others went from the west bank of the Kunimaipa river to their hunting grounds in the Timoni and Auraipi valleys where many of them are still living.

People say they moved partly because the incidence of killing rose in the Kunimaipa valley, and partly because they grew tired of fleeing into the bush whenever a patrol passed through.

[The Kunimaipa often attacked patrols, but the old people, the women and children fled into the bush with their pigs and camped there until the patrol passed on.] It was normal practice to retire when the incidence of homicide reached a high level, either to other parishes or, if they were suitable for settlement, to hunting grounds. Most of the areas in T.N.G. to which they went were already under Government control. (Pp. 2–3.)

She further states at p. 5, n. 1:

Many of the people at the top of the Aiwara valley are bilingual, a result of intermarriage and frequent contact with Kunimaipa speakers in the Bubu and Jevi Wataiz valleys.

Thus the large areas of unused land, the relatively safe tracks through the mountain forests, and the low density of population in some of the valleys, allowed fairly substantial migration to take place, often as a result of warfare or social friction. But movement within the valleys was very much more dangerous except for chiefs or large bodies of people going as guests to dances. One such case is recorded by A. E. Pratt, an amiable English naturalist, and his son, who made two expeditions into Kuni and Fuyughe country in 1901. While they observed considerable violence, both corporate and individual, they did not have to defend themselves by force. Being short of carriers at one point, they took advantage of a visit by some Aibala men who came to their camp at Dinawa, near Obaoba, to ask them to come and carry for them at a date to be fixed, and, on the receipt of tobacco, the Aibala agreed, and returned to their country on the slopes of Mt. Saint Mary. When Pratt was almost ready to leave Dinawa, he had a message sent to the Aibala by the traditional means of calling across the intervening valleys:

A few days earlier, in pursuance of the compact the Ibala people had made with me, I had set the telegraph in motion, and told Fa-lo-foida to call up Keakamana, Keakamana to call up Tapua, and so on stage by stage to the distant home of my picturesque mountaineers, to tell them that the time had come to redeem their promise and earn the tobacco advanced on personal security alone. The calling accordingly began, and in less than ten minutes Ibala of the five days' journey had received my summons [both estimates are obviously exaggerated]. During the afternoon the answer arrived. Ibala was willing and would come. Accordingly, close to the time fixed for our departure—September 23rd—we were cheered by the return of our merry friends, who came like the honourable gentlemen they were to discharge their obligation. (Pratt 1906: 163.)

Such ease of travel, however, seems to have been unusual, and the movement of men on a large scale through populated areas only took place when large dances were arranged and the chiefs of the various tribes had managed to negotiate the peaceful passage of guests along the route to and from the dance. Small groups of travellers took their lives in their hands if they travelled through the territory of other tribes.

As a general rule it will be found that in the Goilala proximity generates conflict, and that social relations are most amicable when the groups are separated by mountain ridges and forests, which allow communication, but which are not the source of disputes. It should also be noted that migration has not been the result of land conquest, but of social conflict, especially that generated by quarrels over pandanus trees and pigs. Migration is not one-directional; on the contrary, there seems to be a constant ebb and flow as those who have migrated outstay their welcome in their adopted home, or return to harvest pandanus nuts and make fresh gardens in their old homes.

4. THE SETTLEMENT PATTERN

The characteristic settlement pattern has always been one of relatively discrete, named tribes[1] inhabiting spurs around the main

[1] Following *Notes and Queries on Anthropology* in defining a tribe as 'an autonomous population inhabiting a territory with clearly defined boundaries'. (Royal Anthropological Institute, 6th edition, p. 66.)
I have deliberately avoided the term 'parish' first proposed by Hogbin and Wedgwood (1953) which they define as 'the largest group forming a political unit'. (p. 243.) They reject the use of the *Notes and Queries* definition of 'tribe' for the incomprehensible reason that 'In Melanesia there are no tribes; there are only groups of people who speak the same language (often with differences of dialect)

valleys. Except during the existence of dance villages these tribes do not reside in a common settlement, but are dispersed in clusters of small hamlets. Table 3 gives some tribal populations for 1958.

The current populations of the various Goilala (Ororogaivara) hamlets is given in Table 4. Tribal organization will be discussed in

TABLE 3. *Tribal populations*

Galoa (Sopu)	477
Lova-Loleava	232
Kileipi	130
Malava	145
Gane	168
Ilai & Kiolivi	290
Tapina & Elava	128
Karom	160
Kurumutu	160
Kunima	173
Ororogaivara (Goilala)	164

Mean size: 202

TABLE 4. *Current population of Goilala hamlets*

Hamlet name	Males	Females	Total
Deribi	6	4	10
Dimanibi	20	22	42
Itoveve	6	3	9
Kalava	1	1	2
Kilakilakila	7	5	12
Kiolilama	8	4	12
Moigili	9	4	13
Ororogaivara	1	2	3
Palaileve	12	14	26
Patima	11	15	26
Total	81	74	155

and have a similar culture.' (p. 252.) They seem to imagine that a tribe properly so called must contain at least several thousand people under centralized leadership. The Tauade simply have small tribes.

The English parish is, administratively, the smallest unit in the hierarchy of local government, and ecclesiastically, is that area served by a particular Anglican church for the solemnization of births, marriages, and deaths. It would be hard to find another institution as irrelevant to New Guinea society as this, and one is therefore led to suppose that Hogbin's and Wedgwood's conception of the 'parish' is derived from some local antipodean variant, together with such other monstrosities as 'calf-parishes', 'hearth-groups', 'carpels', and 'galaxies'.

the next chapter. Data on hamlet populations in other parts of the Aibala Valley are given in Appendix I.

The traditional ground plan of a hamlet was, and often still is, that of two lines of huts occupied by the women, with a men's house at the upper end, and, if the population is large enough to warrant it, a second men's house at the lower end; Fig. 2 shows an example of the layout.

This plan is the product of a number of factors—the custom of building hamlets on ridges, the need for a defensive capacity against attack, the small size of the population, and ceremonial requirements.

In mountainous and forested country it is easier to fell trees growing on ridges than elsewhere, the ground is better drained, and the gradient along the crest of a ridge is always the shallowest. For these reasons paths tend to run along these crests, and therefore the habit of building hamlets on ridges also facilitates communication between them. It should be noted, however, that by no means all hamlets, even before pacification, were built on ridges. Some of the oldest settlements at

FIG. 2. Hamlet layout

Goilala were on level areas of ground close to streams. While it is not, of course, now possible to deduce if these settlements were laid out in two lines, it is significant that in the Aibala Valley today there are many examples of the double-line layout in locations where this is not demanded by the terrain.

The defensive advantages of building hamlets on ridges are clear; the sides of a steep ridge are difficult to assault, and the narrow ends of the hamlet relatively easy to defend. The men's house, and its location, seem to have been basically a defensive institution. Situated at the vulnerable ends of the hamlet, they ensured that the men would be grouped together with their weapons during the night, when the settlement was most vulnerable, instead of scattered and leaderless when the enemy struck.

In the old days before pacification settlements were protected with stockades. McCleland writes 'Their [Sopu] villages have single stockades, but the only good stockade I saw was in Givi Getava's village, due probably to a row with the Dapa [Lova-Loleava]. The stockades have openings through which one man at a time can enter.' (McCleland, Kairuku, 14/1/22–10/2/22.) Champion describes a village (Tatupiti) as follows. 'The village consisted of 8 houses built on the ground with narrow doors which a person would have to squeeze through. There were four high stockades dividing the villages into sections and the entrances to these were hardly wider than those of the houses.' (Champion and Smith, Kambisi, 6/12/28–16/1/29.) L. J. Wilson, P.O., records that 'Dapa has 18 large houses, stockades on 3 sides 5 feet high, the fourth side a steep cliff. Every fourth house is fenced with a wall 15 feet high.' (Wilson, Ioma, 13/11/17–7/12/17.) In 1932 Mr. Middleton had occasion to visit Tatupiti and found that a quarter of a mile from the village were

a series of high barricades spaced at 20–50 yard intervals, each 15–20′ high. The only passage through these was by a small hole immediately over the track at the base, barely large enough for a man to squeeze through. Flanking the track on the village side of each barricade were hundreds of needle-pointed sticks and pieces of bamboo placed at such an angle that anyone breaking through or round the barricade would certainly have been impaled. The village, a new one, was protected by a double stockade 20–25 feet high and hundreds of sharp pointed sticks were driven into the ground between the stockades. (S. G. Middleton, Kambisi, 1/12/32–15/12/32.)

Tree houses were constructed in some places, and I have been shown the site of one at Goilala from which spears and rocks could be thrown, but these were probably rare.

Williamson describes Fuyughe fortifications as follows:

The villages are, or were, protected with stockades and with pits outside the stockades, and sometimes with platforms on trees near the stockade boundaries, from which platforms the inhabitants can shoot and hurl stones upon an enemy climbing up the slope. The stockade is made of timber, is about 15–25 feet high, and is generally constructed in three or more parallel rows or lines, each of the lines having openings, but the openings never being opposite to one another. These protections have now, however, been largely, though not entirely, discontinued. It is, or was, also the practice, when expecting an attack, to put into the ground in the approaches to the village caltrop-like arrow-headed objects, with their points projecting upwards. [He is presumably referring to bamboo foot-spears.] (Williamson 1912: 98–9.)

Nowadays men's houses among the Tauade have fallen very much into disuse, except on the occasion of the building of a dance village, when the men's house at the top of the yard is of special importance.

THE SETTLEMENT PATTERN

In ordinary hamlets men nowadays tend to sleep with their wives, and usually only older men, or bachelors and widowers, still sleep together as at Moigili, one of the Goilala hamlets. It does not seem that the Tauade men's houses were conceived as in any way helping to conserve their virility, since the Tauade have sexual intercourse in the bush during the day, making any regulation by nocturnal restraint impossible. It is likely that some men's houses will continue to survive, because of the domestic advantages of widowers and bachelors sleeping together; men's houses are also ideal centres of hospitality for travellers since no more domestic adjustment is necessary to accommodate a stranger than to make room for him beside the long fire that runs down the centre of all such houses.

The traditional plan of the Tauade hamlet, besides having the advantage of defensibility and adaptation to the terrain, is also ideal for social occasions, especially dances and the killing of pigs. The dancers can occupy the long yard, charging down its length with fierce shout and song, brandishing their spears, while the women and children watch in safety from the huts lining each side, and the chiefs can sit on the veranda of the men's house. The yard is also ideal for the pegging-out and killing of long lines of pigs, and the distribution of the food in great heaps, and the erection of ceremonial platforms, and speech-making—everything, in fact, that is Tauade ceremonial. It is perhaps for this reason that the plan is sometimes retained even where the terrain does not demand it. (Model villages laid out at the behest of the government are usually rectangular.) Finally, it is worth noting that the strongly dualistic quality of the plan of the traditional hamlet is not reflected either in the social relationships of the members of each of the lines, nor is it ascribed any cosmological or symbolic significance. This type of ground-plan is not, however, indefinitely extensible beyond about sixty houses, since such hamlets become unmanageably long and difficult to defend.

Hamlets have always tended to be small, containing only a few families; the only exception to this being the dance villages, which may have between about thirty and seventy houses; the largest of such villages can have more than 1,000 guests, who remain there for several months, besides their hosts. Neyland reports 4 villages at Amiapa, and many single huts, 7 at Barua, many small villages up the spur to Maini, and 3 villages on one spur at Lova (Neyland, Kairuku, 2/5/18–10/7/18). McCleland notes some single houses near

his camp, in the vicinity of Loini creek. In the patrol reports from
1917–29 there are fifteen references to the sizes of hamlets by number
of houses, which break down as follows:

1–10	11–20	21–30	31–40	41–50	(50+)
6	3	3	1	0	2

The two villages with more than fifty houses (fifty-seven and fifty-
nine) were both at Sopu, which has the largest population in the
Aibala Valley, and since they were obviously dance villages can be
ignored for our purposes. At Goilala I made a survey of ten earlier
hamlet sites, where the people could remember the actual names of
the owners of the houses and their location. My interest here was in
trying to establish the different groups which had lived together on
particular occasions, and so I ignored the smallest sites. The number
of houses was as follows:

1–10	11–20	21–30	31–40	41–50
1	5	2	1	1

The hamlets numbering 43, 34, 30, 25, and 20 houses were all
built specially for dances. The present distribution of houses at
Goilala is:

1–10	11–20	21–30	31–40	41–50
7	3	0	1*	0

* Being built.

Egidi also notes the preponderance of small hamlets, with the
existence of what are obviously dance villages to serve the whole
hamlet group—essentially the same pattern as can be observed
today.

The excessively mountainous terrain (from 1,000 metres to 2,500 metres
above sea level) [3,280–6,800 feet] does not lend itself to the formation of
large villages; there may be a few here and there but usually a village has
only four or five huts, of which one (*tumúte*) is used by the men, and the
others (*kiaté*) by the women and children . . . The villages of the Tauade
are very numerous, and assembled in groups, each of which, besides having
a distinctive name, almost always has a central village which is used for the
ceremonies of that group. (Egidi 1907: 675.)

Williamson writes of the Fuyughe that 'the average size of their
villages is small. Some of them have only six or eight houses, though
many villages have thirty houses, and some of them have fifty or
sixty or more'. (Williamson 1912:99.) The last were presumably

dance villages. Fastré, however, disagrees with Williamson that the size of traditional Fuyughe villages was small:

Once the villages were much larger, because of the necessity of defending themselves against enemy attacks. For they did not all employ the Sivu technique of defence by dispersion. Epidemics have diminished the population to an enormous extent. To epidemics add peace, which has brought security, and the numerous disputes between villagers, and we have the main causes of the dispersal which has occurred. (Fastré 1937–9: 375.)

It is not my place to decide between Fastré and Williamson as to the original size of Fuyughe villages, although Fastré is obviously the more authoritative source. But with regard to the original size of Tauade villages, however, it is possible to demonstrate that their traditional size was not *much* greater than at present. It is true that we have no evidence for the population of the Aibala Valley in the nineteenth century, before any epidemics resulting from white contact could have reached it. But let us assume that the Tauade population was drastically reduced at the end of the last century, before the arrival of Egidi. Unlike the Fuyughe area there was still no government control in the Aibala and consequently, if Fastré's argument that the Fuyughe lived in large villages 'because of the necessity of defending themselves against enemy attacks' is true of the Tauade also, there would have been nothing to prevent them, however much their population had been reduced, from crowding into one large village for each tribe, while warfare continued. But neither Egidi nor the first patrol officers report any such thing, yet they were writing at a time when warfare was common. The belief that the Tauade have never lived in large villages is supported not only by these considerations, but by the incompatibility of such a form of settlement with their social organization; in particular, the mutual jealousies of the chiefs, the lack of any means of social control for handling large permanent groups, and the tendency to volatile and violent behaviour in disputes.

It should be noted, however, that the propensity of the Tauade to dwell in large, fortified villages seems likely to have been affected by the intensity of warfare at different times. Pratt records the effect of an outbreak of hostilities on the settlement pattern. It should be remembered that even large fortified villages could have been built in a few days.

From Sam we learned further that the Fa-lo-foida people, through fear of the Baw-boi [Boboi] people, had cut the suspension bridge, and that the natives further up the St. Joseph River, on hearing of the tyrant's [a Boboi chief] warlike preparations, had left their villages and had settled on the site of the camp I had just quitted. Their object was, of course, to be near friendly Fa-lo-foida, which would in time of stress be to them as a fenced city. [It was a heavily defended village.] This incident led to the formation of quite a new township, and before I left Dinawa for good my old camp on the St. Joseph had become a considerable village. It was a curious example of the way in which political necessity affected the *locale* of village communities. (Pratt 1906: 139.)

There can be little doubt, therefore, that the preferred settlement pattern of the Tauade has always been that of small hamlets, of between 10 and 20–5 houses, but often smaller, with at least one men's house in each hamlet, and that dance villages were, then as now, built specially, and were not the normal culmination of every hamlet, as seems to have been the case among the Kunimaipa.

Two characteristics of the Tauade settlement pattern therefore require examination: the small size of hamlets, and the clustering of hamlets. We have already established that large hamlets are not a permanently viable form of settlement for the Tauade, and the abolition of warfare was followed by a marked diminution of hamlet size once the need for self-defence disappeared, while the inhabitants of dance villages always disperse once the festivities are over, leaving only a remnant behind. When I asked the Goilala why they preferred the scattered hamlets instead of living together they always replied that if they had to live together they would fight. The Fathers confirmed that at one time they had tried to get the people in one area to form a big village but the ensuing quarrels and violence led to the abandonment of the experiment. Apparently the Lutherans at Kuputaivi had the same experience, and while patrol officers have in some cases in the past enforced the building of large villages—house-lines on the dance village pattern—the people only come and live in these for the annual census. The settlement pattern is shown in Map 4.

Given that the Tauade find small residential units more manageable than large ones, we must further explain the clustered pattern of their dispersal. It might be suggested that the location of hamlets is designed to permit the easiest access to gardens. Within broad limits, of course, this is true, and Map 5 shows how hamlet locations have moved up the mountain to keep pace over time with the gradual erosion of the forest, and are not found in areas unsuited to cultivation. But if one considers the location of hamlets at any specific

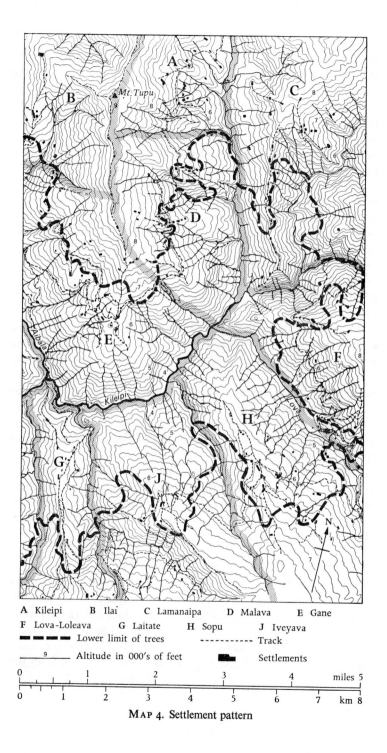

A Kileipi   B Ilai   C Lamanaipa   D Malava   E Gane

F Lova-Loleava   G Laitate   H Sopu   J Iveyava

▬ ▬ ▬ ▬ Lower limit of trees   ---------- Track

_____9_____ Altitude in 000's of feet   Settlements

MAP 4. Settlement pattern

time it is clear that the gardens are not immediately adjacent to them, and that it would be as easy to make the gardens close to the hamlets as it is to move the hamlets, so this cannot explain why in many cases the hamlets are very close to one another. For example, in the cluster comprising the hamlets of Dimanibi, Pomutaivi, Moigili, Amuaeve, and one other at Goilala shown on the aerial photograph of 1957, the average distance of the hamlets from one another is only 320 yards (see Map 5).

Clearly, a single large village would be just as convenient for access to gardens as a cluster of hamlets grouped as closely as these; moreover, it will be shown that men from different hamlets often cultivate the same gardens. One explanation for this proximity derives from the nature of the terrain; for reasons already given the majority of hamlets are built on the ridges of spurs, and since spurs tend to converge at peaks or plateaux, as the hamlet sites follow the receding forest line they will necessarily come to be built closer together.

But there are two other factors responsible for the relatively close clustering and these are both social. The accounts of Egidi and the first patrol officers make it clear that Tauade hamlets were built close together in traditional times when warfare was unchecked. It is obvious that, while fighting occurred between the hamlets, they also had a common interest in being able readily to combine in resisting the assaults of other tribes. The closer the hamlets were situated to one another, within limits, the better they would have been able to co-ordinate their defence.

The second factor is simply the daily need for co-operation; the individuals in each hamlet have friends and relatives in the others whom they see every day, and once the hamlets have been separated it would be pointless to make communication between them more difficult than necessary.

5. THE USE OF RESOURCES

Tauade material culture is, of all aspects of their lives, that which has been most influenced by European contact, principally by the substitution of steel for stone. This process began long before the people had ever actually seen a white man, by the normal processes of trade. For example, Egidi writes of stone adzes, 'these, however, have begun to disappear, and give place to steel axes, imported from the coast, and obtained in exchange for feather ornaments, of which they seem to have an abundance.' (Egidi 1907: 678.) Patrol officers make many references in their reports during the 1920s to steel axes, plane blades, bill hooks, tomahawks, and spears tipped with knife blades, as well as knives.

It does not appear that stone tools were actually made in the Aibala Valley, since while I had no difficulty in obtaining demonstrations of traditional hafting techniques, no one was capable of explaining how the stone blades were made, or how the incisions were cut in the stone bark-cloth beaters. It seems impossible that since stone tools were used within living memory they would have been unable to tell me how they were made, if indeed they had been manufactured in the Aibala Valley. I was often told that the culture heroes had made them. While it seems true that the stone pestles and mortars found in the area were made by people of a different culture, this is certainly not the case with stone axes, or bark cloth beaters, since Fastré gives a long account of the quarrying and manufacture of stone tools.

The solution to this problem was suggested to me by Casimiro, my catechist informant. He told me that stone tools were once made in the Chirima and Fuyughe areas, extending as far as the Ivane, at Minaru, and were then traded with people who did not possess either the stone or the skill to work with it, for dogs' teeth, pork, feathers, and other valuables.

The best account of a traditional material culture which must have resembled that of the Tauade very closely is Miss Blackwood's *The Technology of a Modern Stone Age People in New Guinea*, which describes that of the Kukukuku near Wau and Bulolo in 1936–7, before they were influenced by European tools, and the reader is advised to consult this if he wishes to obtain a detailed picture of a material culture and technology very similar to that of the traditional Tauade.

The Tauade also resemble the Kukukuku in the stark barrenness of their artefacts, artistically speaking. There was a limited amount of wood-carving, chiefly of posts in front of the men's houses in dance villages, and designs on bamboo tobacco pipes, but, as Fastré says, the only art form which they know is the dance, and the self-decoration which accompanies it: '. . . the art of the dance and personal adornment, living painting and sculpture, the sole art-forms to which they seem truly sensitive . . .' (Fastré: 74.)

A thorough professional study of the ecology would have required knowledge and skills which I lack, and would have been a full-time

job in the field. Even the computation of the area of garden cultivated per head is exceedingly complicated. For gardens are not of
equal yield at any one time, since they may be coming into production, be at full production, or be going out of production; one may
require, from its location, many times as much energy to carry its
yield home as another; soil fertility differs markedly from place to
place, and to complicate matters further, one has to take account of
the pig population, as well as the human demographic structure, in
determining the ratio of food supply to human needs. But it is none
the less possible to give a general picture of the use of the natural
environment, without dabbling in matters beyond the competence of
the ethnographer.

Each tribe inhabits a section of mountainside, usually a spur, or
set of spurs, between two torrents, which are designated as boundaries. Their land thus extends down from the forested ridges,
which may reach 10,000 feet, to the river, somewhere between 2,000
and 4,000 feet. These low-lying areas, too hot for sweet potato or
taro, were used in the past for the extensive growing of yams and
bananas, but in more recent years yams seem to have been much less
commonly grown, though bananas are still very common. The
people gave as the reason for the relative discontinuance of yams the
increased ravages of pigs, and claimed that pigs with a 'European'
strain in them tended to be more voracious foragers than the traditional stock. Yam gardens were also of necessity further from the
hamlets than the higher gardens of sweet potatoes, and thus less
readily protected from pigs. McCleland also states that 'They eat
potatoes during the wet and yams during the dry season.' (McCleland, Kairuku, 14/1/22–10/2/22.) If this was the case then the
availability of rice from the mission store in recent years may have
been a factor in the decline of yam production. But to judge from the
large quantities of yams tied to the trunks of trees in the dance yard
at Sopu, before a very large pig-killing there, yams are still grown
abundantly for special occasions. The planting of yams, and also of
taro and sugar-cane, are male occupations, and all these vegetables
have more status as prestations to guests than sweet potatoes, and
also more attendant taboos. Early patrol officers and Egidi refer to
yam houses, but these, if ever common, have now long ceased to
exist.

The normal altitudinal range of the sweet potato appears to be
5,000–8,500 feet, though local peculiarities of terrain, such as

shelter provided by the forest, or cold air flowing down a stream bed, can modify these limits. The people cultivate at least twenty-two varieties of sweet potato, and in any garden several varieties may be represented. This compares with nine varieties of taro and twelve of yams. Gardens are prepared when the rains cease, the work perhaps beginning in May or June, and going on until October or November, depending on the weather. Potatoes (henceforth I shall refer to sweet potatoes simply as 'potatoes') will be ready for eating 6–9 months from the planting of the runners, depending on the amount

TABLE 5. *Population density* (*Census 1958*)

Tribe	Population	Area sq. miles	Area acres	Persons per square mile	Acres per head
Kataipa	118	1·9	1,216	62·1	10·3
Goilala	164	8·39	5,370	19·54	32·74
Karom & Lumioto	160	7·5	4,800	21·3	30·0
Kanitata & Kopuri	155	6·53	4,179	23·74	26·96
Maini	214	7·0	4,467	30·57	20·87
Amuganiawa	68	3·1	1,984	21·94	29·2
Watagoipa	132	6·9	4,422	19·13	33·5
Average	144	5·9	3,777	28·33	26·2
Total	1,011	41·32	..	24·45	..

of rain they receive. The men's job is to cut the fence posts and dig the ditches, if any, erect the fences, and do the heavy work of clearing the ground—chopping and burning trees, uprooting sword-grass, and doing much of the preliminary digging. The women plant the runners, which they bring from their old gardens, and also tend them subsequently and clear the weeds. But there are no prohibitions against men planting potatoes, and bachelors and widowers habitually do so. Tauade society is not remarkable for a rigid demarcation of sexual roles. Men's subsequent agricultural labours are expended in growing bananas, sugar-cane, and tobacco, and a little taro, and in climbing the pandanus trees when the season arrives for harvesting their nuts.

As I have indicated, estimates of land use in relation to population are complex problems, but it is possible to give some gross figures for Tauade land use. Table 5 shows the land available to seven tribes, calculated from an aerial survey.

In 1957 the population at Goilala was cultivating 48·5 acres of garden, that is, of gardens just planted, in full production, and about to be abandoned. (This estimate is based on aerial photographs, and, further, is made of a time before rice and other foodstuffs now purchased in large quantities at the mission had arrived on the scene to distort the nutritional picture.) At this time there were 155 residents, so the total area of garden per head was 0·31 acres. Assuming that the total period of any garden's life, from planting to abandonment, is $2\frac{1}{2}$ years on average, this would mean that the average increment of new gardens planted per head would be 0·125 acres. If we allow a fallow period of thirteen years—some of the gardens shown in the photographs of 1957 had just been abandoned when I came in 1970—this would mean that the Goilala population needs about 250 acres of garden land in order to maintain its present population. This is well within the limits of available land which, even at the higher altitudes, comprises about 1,500 acres. Pressure on land is therefore not a problem for them. Table 6 shows garden sizes in 1970–2.

TABLE 6. *Garden sizes*

Acres	Name	
0·6	Pomutaivi	
0·7	Pomutaivi	
1·1	Dauraupu	
1·6	Kupeava	
1·7	Kovela	*Average:* 3·42 acres
4·2	Poroyava	
5·0	Amuaeve	
5·6	Urumeve	
10·3	Poroyava	

Garden sizes in 1957 were:

0·3	3·1	
0·6	3·2	
0·8	3·4	
1·1	5·3	*Average:* 2·93 acres
1·4	5·5	
1·7	6·2	
2·0	7·1	
2·2	··	

The preferred area for gardens is among the secondary vegetation often close to the primary forest. It can be seen from Map 5 that the vast majority of Tauade hamlets are close to the tree line. The reason which they give for this preference is that the soil is better. In some cases they have cleared land with only a light covering of bush or sword-grass, but actual grass land is seldom chosen for garden sites. It tends to be too far from the hamlets, which have moved up the valley sides with the timber line, the soil is relatively poor, and wood for fences has to be carried a long way. In a few cases they are made, but the justification given for this is that they are sufficiently far from human settlement to be in less danger from domestic pigs. In these cases there is always a convenient stream which can be diverted to carry away the spoil from a ditch which is dug around them.

But one also finds that, albeit in the minority of cases, the people continue to cut down the primary forest—a process which in the past, of course, has been the principal means of destroying the forest cover of the valley. That the forest was cut down mainly for agricultural purposes, rather than for firewood or house building can easily be deduced from the fact that ample firewood can be obtained from picking up dead wood or felling small trees. Hard woods (oaks, beeches, etc.) do not burn easily and are extremely difficult to fell. When they were cut in the old days they were either left to rot, used as rough fences as they lay, or, in the case of smaller trunks, split with stone or wooden wedges and used as fence-posts. The majority of trees, however, were not cut but burned, and the larger trunks were often left standing, almost denuded of foliage and branches. This process can be observed at the present time in the area around C.M. Kosipi where the virgin forest is being felled by fire for new gardens. If anyone doubts that stone tools could have been used to fell large trees, he should study Plate IV(d) in Miss Blackwood's *The Technology of a Modern Stone Age People in New Guinea* which shows a substantial tree felled by a stone adze.

It is claimed by the natives that the traditional pig (*sus scrofa*) was not given to rooting in gardens, so that their ancestors did not have to build the stout pig fences around their gardens which are now necessary. (McArthur was told the same by the Kunimaipa.) It is certainly true that the modern pig, which I shall describe shortly, is ingenious at breaking into and ravaging gardens; the damage which one pig can do in half an hour is amazing, as is their capacity to detect weaknesses in a fence and force up the posts to squeeze through. Consequently the men have to erect tall fences, often over

6 feet high which, being of solid construction, use up vast quantities of timber.

The scarcity of timber in fact makes it a more important commodity than land. In the past the natives gave no thought to the conservation of timber, and old fence-posts were allowed to rot *in situ* and were later used as firewood. Only now, when the primary forest at Goilala has been reduced to about 25 acres, are they trying to conserve fence-posts by uprooting and stacking them for re-use, a practice which I have not seen elsewhere in the Aibala Valley. It should be noted, however, that the Goilala, together with the Kurumutu, Kunima, and Diolivi, are allowed access to the forests on the flanks of Mt. Kutumu nearby. Again, though they are quite familiar with the planting of trees—which is, after all, how they propagate pandanus—and do so when creating wind-breaks around their hamlets, in most areas they have not bothered to replace those trees felled for gardens. However, at Goilala awareness of imminent shortage seems to have produced a change of attitude, and I was shown a number of young trees said to have been planted by various named individuals. Moreover, they habitually burn large tracts of grassland in the lower-lying areas. Originally this had the justification of driving out small edible animals, such as rats, and killing poisonous snakes, but the burning of grass today is largely a symptom of pyromania, not of any desire to hunt or to make gardens. The land used for gardens is only a fraction of the land that is burned every year. There have been many cases of grass-fires becoming uncontrollable, and burning pandanus stands, gardens, villages, and people. The result of this constant burning is that trees never have the chance to re-establish themselves in the affected areas. It would be a mistake, however, to imagine that the grasslands are now useless for agricultural purposes. As can be seen in Appendix VII, where soil samples of the area are analysed, the grasslands are richer in nutrients than might be expected from their constant exposure to the leaching action of the rain. It is likely that the rain washes the ashes, produced by burning, down the mountain sides, so that especially at lower altitudes the soil is enriched. In fact, as we noticed earlier, it is loss of timber, rather than degradation of the soil, which is crucial. Earlier this century the people of Laitate, originally a clan of the Goilala, were forced to move from their land at the confluence of the Aibala and Lova rivers on account of shortage of wood.

The Tauade, like us, treat the bounty of nature as inexhaustible, and squander their resources recklessly until brought up short by the realization that they are nearly bankrupt. I was often driven to reflect on their habit of thinking only of today, when during the rainy season I watched some dim figure out in the mist and driving rain hacking at a soggy tree stump to get kindling for his fire. While the men's houses usually have a supply of dry wood most people only have a few days' wood at hand, if that, and so have to replenish their stock as they go to and from the gardens. But while they know quite well that wood which has been stored for some weeks burns much better than damp wood, they cannot be troubled to lay in a good supply before it is needed. Yet there would be nothing to prevent them co-operating to fetch large quantities of wood and storing it.

The pandanus nut is the other traditional form of vegetable food of the Tauade. There are three varieties of the tree: *kurupu*, which grows from about 5,000 feet upwards; the *kuvepe*, found from about 6,500 feet upwards; and the *taipi*, which is a wild, high-altitude forest variety, smaller and more spindly than the other two. The *kuvepe* differs from the *kurupu* in that its dead leaves remain attached to the trunk instead of falling to the ground as do the leaves of the *kurupu*. These leaves, which are found in profusion on the floor of the pandanus forests, are the sole traditional roofing material used at this altitude. The roots of the leaves can also be used as umbrellas in the rain. The women gather the leaves and trim off the roots, and the spikes which run along the edges, and collect them in bundles which they bring to the site of the house which is being built. The traditional type of house, in which the roof came down to the ground in the form of an 'A', only needed timber for its ends, as well as for the floor in the men's houses. When the Tauade only had stone adzes they probably cut this timber from the bark of pandanus trees, which is easy to strip and makes good planks. The aerial roots are of quite different texture and when stripped into long shreds provide a very tough binding for house-building.

The nuts ripen in the later part of the year, the harvest taking place roughly between September and November. There is a marked tendency for the crop to fluctuate according to a two-year cycle, in the first year being large, and in the second year being much reduced, and so on. The nuts consist of a large number of fibrous husks gathered around a pithy core which holds them together. When this dries in the ordinary course of nature the nuts fall to the ground, scattering the husks. They are therefore cut down before the core has had time to dry, since the pigs would eat them if they fell to the ground, and so that when they fall and strike the ground they do not fragment. The nuts usually grow only on trees which have branched at least once, which means that they hang 50 or 60 feet above the ground in many cases. Since they may weigh between 70 and 90 pounds avoirdupois, the force with which they hit the ground can be imagined, and people who have been unlucky enough to be standing in the wrong place while a man is cutting them, or during a high wind, have been killed in this way. Only men climb the trees, which they do by the use of hand and foot-ropes. There are a few recorded cases of these ropes breaking, or men losing their balance especially when transferring from the main trunk to the branches, when they have to release the ropes for a moment. Falls from such heights naturally result in serious injuries or death. While the cutting-down of the nuts is men's work, the women's job is to carry them to a clearing in the forest, where they are broken up and the core removed. Usually several families will arrange to visit their trees together and make a convivial day's outing of the work, gorging themselves on the fresh nuts as they break them up and prepare them. Nuts destined for immediate consumption are broken into clusters of about the size of two fists, while those for ceremonial use are cut into two halves, to be decorated later with designs cut into the husks. When this work is completed, the women pile the processed nuts into their string bags and set off home, up the steep and slippery mud tracks, often bearing loads of at least 100 pounds. In the old days people sometimes lived for days in the forests, where they smoked the nuts.

The ground beneath the trees is covered with dense undergrowth and vegetation, including masses of rotting leaves. The soil itself is usually extremely wet. *Elaivi* (*Cordyline terminalis*) is planted at strategic points to demarcate plots, usually owned by groups of relatives, but any attempt at making even a sample survey was frustrated by the extremely steep and muddy ground, as well as by the dense vegetation.

The pandanus is deliberately planted, a seedling being first raised from a nut in a seed-bed, and then transplanted to the area of ground where a man is starting a plantation. The absence of any appreciable number of young men in Moresby has left a shortage of men capable and willing to climb the trees, and the Fathers confirm that in many areas at the present time large amounts of nuts are left to fall to the ground where they are eaten by the pigs. But while the trees are less jealously protected than they used to be, so that there is no longer the same strenuous opposition to felling them when a graded track is being made, for example, they are still among the most prized possessions of the Tauade, together with their feathers and their pigs. At Goilala I found many hundreds of newly planted trees, and the distribution of smoked nuts is still of great importance at feasts. In the past the pandanus nut had a significance even greater than its use as a ceremonial prestation, for it was the only food which could be stored, by smoking. When warfare was constant, gardens were often destroyed, so the availability of the smoked nuts was of the greatest importance as a form of emergency rations.

The pig occupies among the Tauade, as it does in many other parts of New Guinea, a position in the esteem and affection of the people which is comparable to that of the cow in parts of East Africa. The traditional breed, as was mentioned earlier, has been modified by stock introduced chiefly by the mission, but to judge by the prevalence of the long snouts and hairiness of the traditional breed the stock is still far from the European type of pig.

The pigs roam in the vicinity of their owner's hamlets by day, returning in the evening an hour or two before dark to be given their meal of raw potatoes by the women. They traditionally sleep inside the women's houses, which are divided longitudinally so that the pigs occupy one side and the woman and her children the other. The pig has its own entrance. (More recently there has been a tendency for the pigs to be given a separate house from that of the woman, if her husband is in the habit of sleeping there.)

The women especially develop great affection for their pigs, and traditionally in some cases would suckle a piglet which had lost its mother, or which had perhaps been obtained from someone else's sow. I never saw such a thing during my own residence there, however, and it seems that the custom may be defunct. Dupeyrat, in *Mitsinari*, pp. 246–50, gives a peculiarly disgusting description of a woman who kills her first-born child and feeds the carcass to the pigs, nursing a piglet in the place of her child. He states that this occurred in the Kunimaipa, within a day's walk of Golopui's village, which was near Givena. Dr. McArthur informs me privately, however, that no such custom existed among the Kunimaipa. Williamson also writes:

I was told by Fr. Chabot, the Father Superior of the Mission, that among the neighbouring Kuni people [no connection with the Kunimaipa] a woman would kill her child for extraordinary reasons; and he furnished an example of this in a woman who killed her child so that she might use her milk for suckling a young pig, which she regarded as being more important. Whether such a thing would occur in Mafulu appears to be doubtful; but it is quite possible, more especially as the Mafulu women do, in fact, suckle pigs. (Williamson 1912: 177.)

(The fact that women suckle pigs does not, of course, necessarily mean that they kill their children in order to do so!) At the end of his manuscript Fastré makes a page-by-page analysis of Williamson's book, but has no comment about page 177. Since he is very ready to point out any errors, one can only take his silence as indicating some measure of agreement. When I asked Amo if the Tauade had ever followed such a custom, he emphatically denied it, however, and said that while abortion had always been common, women never killed their children, unless they were mad. Since Amo had never attempted to conceal the more sanguinary customs of the Tauade from me and, if anything, tended to embellish them, I am inclined to think that the Tauade, at least, did not follow this custom.

It is none the less true that women feel much affection for their pigs, especially when the time comes for them to be killed. When pigs are killed ceremonially they do not weep for them; they seem reconciled to their inevitable death in the dance yard, and this honorific setting perhaps mitigates their sorrow. But it is a different matter if a pig is 'murdered' rather than killed ceremonially. Then they mourn them almost as if they were children. Amo Lume's pig Oropiti ravaged his garden of English potatoes, and when he tried to drag it away it bit his hand, so in a fit of rage he got his spear and transfixed it. For hours his wife's cries of grief were carried up to me through the mist from their house.

The number of pigs which a woman will maintain will depend, among other things, upon the imminence of a large dance. The average maximum is about eight pigs. Table 7 represents a census of pigs which, to ensure the greatest degree of accuracy, I took among people in my immediate vicinity, and whom I knew well.

It will be noticed from the table that men of high status do not have more pigs than other people, and in some cases have less. We shall see later, however, that the size of a man's pig herd is not of great importance; what matters is how many men he can persuade to contribute pigs for a feast. The unmarried men, as might be expected, usually have fewer pigs than anyone else, and those which they do have are looked after by their female relatives, usually sisters or daughters. The high proportion of male to female pigs is striking. This reflects the people's extreme reluctance to kill small pigs. The rational policy for their herd would be to increase the proportion of females, but since they cannot kill the small males— because, by custom, they cannot eat the meat themselves or give it

TABLE 7. *Size of pig herds*

Name	Male	Female	Piglet	Total
Francis Koupa*	1	2	3	6
Koilo Nomai†	1	5	4	10
Bauai Katemu	5	1	1	7
Keru Katemu*	6	4	1	11
Kire Kaita	4	5	3	12
Amo Lume	4	5	3	12
Tuna Tauru	3	3	3	9
Itago†	3	0	0	3
Katai (f)	4	2	2	8
[Avui Maia* (1 wife only)	0	0	2	2]
Kavini Ivei†	1	1	0	2
Mogu Apava†	1	1	0	2
Moise Apava†	?	?	?	3
Anono Apava†	?	?	?	6
Lariava Moripi*	1	3	3	7
Kirau Ivoro	3	1	3	7
[Keru Avui* (1 wife only)	1	2	1	4]
	38	35	29	111

* Man of high status.   † Unmarried man.

away, because there would not be enough—they have to keep them alive until they are reasonably well grown. Indeed, they may keep an old, castrated male for years, watching him grow like a prize marrow —'as big as a house'—for the glory and renown it will bring them to hear their great pig talked of when he is finally killed. Amo Lume's Petsi was a lumbering great brute, obviously with much 'European' blood in him, who was always breaking into my garden and rooting it up. Almost certainly he will be killed at the coming dance at Patima (1972).

Pigs are contributed by women at feasts, especially at funerals, when men may allow their daughters or wives to take pigs for the

death of one of their relations, and there is, I believe, a clear alloca-
tion of pigs between husband and wife, though I was not able to
obtain statistical confirmation of this point. Some pigs are reserved
for particular occasions, while others are killed according to *ad hoc*
demands, such as compensation for adultery, which cannot be
predicted in advance.

A pig which has died, even if the meat is several days old, will
still be ceremonially distributed. Maia Laiam's pig was bitten by a
snake (*kotou*) perhaps three days before it was cut up. I did not
partake of the meat, but those who did told me that it stank. Fr.
Sicot, M.S.C., of C.M. Kosipi told me that he sometimes had trouble
with cows that had died of disease and been buried, because the
natives would come at night and dig up the carcasses again. In 1942
the mission at Kerau recorded that one of their schoolboys from
Lamana, who had been given rotten pork by his mother, had died of
eating it, as had his cousin in the village. The pig had apparently died
on a Tuesday and not been cooked until Friday.

I have not found that the actual killing of pigs today is carried out
in the ferocious manner described by Fastré, Hides, and Dupeyrat.
I give their accounts of pig-killing in the section on ceremonies. The
years of government and mission influence have undoubtedly
moderated the people's natural exuberance in this respect. Today
the killing of pigs is effected with a nonchalant air as a purely utilitarian act. They are, on the other hand, not particularly solicitous
about the degree of suffering endured by the pigs, so that on several
occasions I have seen them put the pigs over the flames to singe off
the hair while they are still alive. Another, for a change, was shot
in the face with a shotgun, instead of being clubbed to death. This
was not very effective, as the man's aim was poor, and the animal
rushed blinded and shrieking into the bush, where it had to be caught
and beaten to death with choppers.

It is because of the affection with which they regard their pigs—
'they are like our children'—that they say that they, the husband and
wife, will not eat their own pigs, though the children may be given
some of the pork if they are small. Relatives and neighbours, however, are under no such prohibition. A man is obliged to distribute
the meat of his pig not only because of the prohibition upon him and
his wife from eating it, but because any good thing which a man
has cannot be consumed in isolation. For a man to go off with a few
friends and eat a pig alone, to avoid giving the meat to other people,

would be most shameful to them. The killing of pigs should always result in a ceremonial division of the meat, accompanied by speeches. The only exception would be when men have killed someone else's pig, and need to eat it clandestinely. This principle applies to tobacco, for example, so that when I gave a stick and some newspaper to someone as a reward for some service, he would, almost invariably, break it up and distribute it.

Demand on a man's resources by those who, temporarily or permanently, are worse off than he is, helps to promote an egalitarian society as far as property is concerned. But the giving of things is recompensed by the prestige which is acquired by so doing. The importunities of the poor are thus not apparently resented by the rich because generosity confers honour on the host or benefactor in proportion to the size of the gift, and the renown for generosity is greatly sought after by individuals and by whole communities. Generosity is the mark of a chiefly man, while meanness is one of the stigma attached to the *malavi*, or rubbish-men. Thus while Tauade society is egalitarian with regard to property, it is far from egalitarian as far as status and reputation are concerned.

6. CONCLUSIONS

Some general characteristics of the environment in the Aibala Valley, and the people's use of it, can now be reviewed.

Land of the necessary fertility to meet the demands of the existing population is plentiful, even allowing for the large areas which have been reduced to permanent grassland by persistent burning. The introduction of steel tools has clearly accelerated the destruction of the primary forest over the last fifty years, but the shortage of timber has not yet had any significant impact on the Tauade way of life, except in the case of the Laitate tribe (see p. 68).

Bird life, especially the white cockatoo, has apparently been greatly depleted by the introduction of shotguns, while the hunting of small game in the forests, which used to be conducted with dogs and nets, seems to have ceased entirely, nor are the grasslands hunted for rats as they used to be. The reasons for this are obscure, but it is likely that hunting was stimulated by food shortages caused by warfare, and nowadays meat and rice can be purchased from the mission store.

The mode of agriculture permits a great deal of leisure to the people, especially the men, since the bulk of garden work is performed by women; it will become apparent that abundance of leisure for the men was a significant contributing factor to warfare.

The availability of land permits men and their families to move easily to other tribes where they wish to take up residence for a time, either to cement relationships with relatives there or to escape from hostilities generated in the tribe they have left. Moreover, houses of the type inhabited by women and children can be built quickly with little labour, which is another factor facilitating mobility of population.

The custom of building large dance villages is made possible by the expansive potential of the agricultural system, and the relative ease of house building from materials provided by the forest.

Pigs, slaughtered by the hundred at these dances, are well able to care for themselves without human attention, and since they are agriculturally useless, neither providing manure nor being used for draught, and contributing no by-products such as milk, herds can be almost entirely wiped out on these occasions without causing any inconvenience to the human population.

It should be noted, moreover, that pigs become veritable parasites since they are kept in larger numbers than would permit them to be stied and hand fed, so that as their numbers increase they are continually breaking into gardens. The people prefer to tolerate the loss of food to pigs caused by destruction of gardens, the labour of growing the extra food necessary to hand feed the pigs, and also the social disruption and violence caused by the depredations of the animals, and the theft and killing of wandering beasts. The pig is not kept for reasons of utility, but for reasons of status; the mass slaughter of pigs is one of the best examples of a fundamental Tauade value, which seeks to transform material wealth into prestige.

I. In the high ranges

II. Goilala seen from Tawuni

Amo Gomisi

Mōgu Apava

Kamo, Koitepe and Aito

III. Some Goilala people

IV. Dimanibi, a traditional hamlet

III

The Atomism of Tauade Society

I. A COGNITIVE MODEL FOR TAUADE SOCIAL ATOMISM[1]

THE violence of Tauade society cannot be understood without a preliminary analysis of its atomistic quality. As will become apparent, this atomism is also accompanied by an indifference to categories, rules, and the symbolic potential of the natural world. Moreover, the passions of individuals are not seen as destructive of the social order but as the very stuff out of which social processes are generated. This consistency of cognitive orientations and institutions led me to contrast them with those of the Konso of Ethiopia, among whom my previous field-work was conducted: it rapidly became clear that Konso institutions, beliefs, and values were opposed to those of the Tauade in a regular and consistent manner. The systematic nature of the contrast suggested the hypothesis that these two societies are ordered by two very different cognitive orientations, which I distinguish as 'Aristotelian' and 'Heraclitean'. One of the basic features of Aristotle's metaphysics was its distinction between Form and Matter, such that each individual thing is the manifestation of its Form. 'Matter then is simply the element of possibility, of changeableness in things. Form is the stable, permanent, knowable, scientifically definable element in things.' (Armstrong 1965: 79.) For Heraclitus, on the other hand, reality is a world of perpetual change and conflict, 'a world in which all things are subject to the law of perpetual change, and die continually into each other's life, and in which the only possible harmony is a delicate and precarious tension of opposing stresses . . .' (Armstrong 1965: 11.) The distinction between these two philosophical systems can perhaps be expressed in a different way, by saying that the world consists of various kinds of entities,

[1] A version of this section was first published in *Ethos* vol. 2, spring 1974, pp. 69–76. I am grateful to Professors J. A. Barnes and Andrew Strathern for their comments on an earlier draft of this section.

D

and of relations (interactions, that is) between those entities, Aristotle holding that it is types of entity which are fundamental, while
Heraclitus believes that relationships are.

Those societies which conceive actions and relationships between
individuals as basic, and for which groups, in so far as they exist,
are the product or precipitate of actions and relationships, I call
Heraclitean. Those societies, on the other hand, which treat groups
and categories as primary realities, and actions and relationships as
deriving from the nature of these groups and categories, I call
Aristotelian.

Perhaps I should emphasize that the distinction between Aristotelian and Heraclitean societies is not simply one of social organization but also of cognitive orientation. For example, in reading such
descriptions as those of Strathern and Meggitt of Highland New
Guinea (Strathern 1971, 1972, and Meggitt 1965) one has the strong
impression that the elaborate segmentation of corporate groups in
these societies is not derived from an Aristotelian cognitive orientation, like Konso society, but is the product of circumstances, such
as population pressure on land. It is therefore possible to have a
superficial appearance of Aristotelian structure, but where the basic
mentality of the people is Heraclitean.

In the same way, the Sarakatsani shepherds of Greece, described
by Campbell (1964), clearly have an atomistic society, but are not,
as far as one can tell, Heraclitean, since they are Christians and
possess a complex set of social categories and role models.

Truly Aristotelian or Heraclitean societies are those which not
only possess the appropriate cognitive orientation, but whose social
organization is also ordered in terms of it. Societies may be atomistic
or corporate for many other reasons besides their cognitive orientation.

But I was fortified in my belief that such a distinction between
societies is meaningful and important by the discovery that the
linguist Capell, in *A Survey of New Guinea Languages*, makes a similar one. He distinguishes languages in terms of whether they are
'object-dominated' or 'event-dominated'. In making this distinction
he refers to an interesting observation by Kaplan:

One of the basic divisions that is made among explicit philosophies, and
I would suppose it expresses a basic division also among thought worlds or
conceptual categories that people themselves employ, is ... between ...
those for whom the world is fundamentally a matter of processes and events

and happenings, and those for whom the world is fundamentally a matter of objects or things or substances. (In *Language and Culture*, ed. Hoijer 1954, p. 207.)

The Konso are a good example of an Aristotelian society. They live in walled towns, which are divided into dual sections, and these in turn are subdivided into wards. Descent is organized on the basis of patrilineal, exogamous clans, but for practical purposes the descent group is the lineage, which is united around the person of the lineage priest, whose office descends by strict primogeniture. Yet another type of group is the working-party, based on friendship and co-operation in agriculture. Wards, lineages, and working-parties all have leaders, ceremonial or festive occasions when they meet together, and appropriate norms of behaviour and duties to one another. There is, moreover, a complex form of generation-grading system whose principal effect is to divide the male population into the categories of boys, warriors, and elders. Again, in Konso society a sharp conceptual distinction is drawn between men and women. Men are seen as providing the moral framework of society through the patrilineal basis of its institutions, by the transmission of the ancestral precepts at the hands of the elders, and by their monopoly of counsel and blessing. Women are seen as fluid and irresponsible elements in society, physically necessary to it for their fertility and labour in fields and kitchen, but requiring the social discipline of men. Yet a further social distinction is that between craftsmen and cultivators. The craftsmen form a despised class and are not permitted to intermarry with cultivators because they are held to be quarrelsome, and trade is considered to destroy the bonds of society.

Among the Konso, personal relationships are therefore differentiated according to sex, residence, descent, co-operation in work, generational seniority, and occupation, in terms of the cultivator/craftsman distinction. Where relationships are differentiated in this manner bounded groups are necessarily formed, and behaviour towards members of the various groups and categories to which a person belongs will be conducted in terms of clearly defined norms, appropriate to each group and category.

We may therefore summarize the concerns of Konso society as 'the social order' in general, and in particular as boundaries both spatial and social, complementary solidarities, the specialization of social function, elaborate ritual and symbolism, and time-reckoning and quantification.

The Tauade have a totally different society which will be briefly summarized here, to emphasize its contrast with that of the Konso. The Tauade are divided into named tribes numbering on average about 200 people, inhabiting fairly clearly demarcated areas whose boundaries are usually mountain torrents separating spurs and ridges. Tribes are split into a number of small hamlets, each of which coheres around one or two chiefs. While there is an ideology of the inheritance of chiefly power in the male line, in practice it is clear that the personal qualities of the chiefs are also essential for their recognition. Named clans exist, with vague territorial areas within the tribal land, but though the clans can be said to have a patrilineal appearance there is no concept of lineality as such, and it is possible for people, especially chiefs, to change clans by exercising their cognatic ties. The clans tell us nothing about people's residence, marriage, migration, garden co-operation, or any other aspects of social relations.

The membership of hamlets is not based on patrilineal kinship except for that between fathers and sons or a group of brothers. Cognates, affines, and friends are all to be found in the same hamlet. Hamlets are constantly changing in the composition of their membership, and hamlets themselves often break up and new ones are formed somewhere else. A man may live in more than twelve hamlets in the course of fifty or sixty years. While hamlet members may make gardens together, it is also common for members of different hamlets to co-operate in this respect and for members of the same hamlet to make gardens in different places. Groups of relatives in each tribe have numerous relatives in other tribes, and there will be much social intercourse between them. There are, in any tribe at any one time, many temporary residents from other tribes living with their cognates, affines, or friends, and similarly many of the natal members of the tribe will be living elsewhere, even though they usually return after a few years.

In this society, then, relationships are undifferentiated in terms of descent, residence, and co-operation, age is not the basis of any special respect, and there is little polarization of society in terms of sexual stereotypes even though the Tauade, like the Konso, have men's houses. Individuals are thus constantly obliged to maintain a network of personal ties, dominated by reciprocity in the form of gift exchange, compensation, vengeance, and sister exchange as the ideal form of marriage. The relations between individuals are emotionally highly loaded, and the Tauade are notable for pride, self-assertion, envy, and for a capacity both for tearful sentimentality and homicidal rage.

One of the most striking characteristics of Tauade society is the absence of social stereotypes in the minds of the people themselves. It was impossible to obtain any clear characterization of, say, women's behaviour as opposed to men's, of old men's as opposed to young men's, and so on. They express, it is true, stereotypes of chiefs and *malavi*, or rubbish-men, but these turn out to be very complex and in some ways contradictory. For the Tauade the individual, the particular, is significant; the general, the categorical, elicits no attention or interest. Thus we find a great indifference to boundaries, social, spatial, and conceptual; virtually no time-reckoning, not even commonly used words for the seasons or months; no quantification to speak of since they have no words for quantities larger than two; no symbolism, and a very poorly developed sense of ritual. Unlike the Konso, who are vitally concerned with peace, the Tauade have no word for this concept, and display no awareness of a social order which is ruptured by violence. While they approve of a man who is ready to accept compensation for an injury, they also respect a man who resorts to violence when provoked. Both types of behaviour are normal for them. (At times I had the strange sensation that I was living in a curious parody of American society, individualistic, mobile, dominated by the love of money, sex, and violence, but without American technology!)

The principal features of the Konso and Tauade societies thus display a fundamental and systematic opposition that can be analysed in the following general terms:

ARISTOTELIAN	HERACLITEAN
Social harmony is the result of a correct structuring of social categories and groups	Social harmony is the result of a balance of forces
Emotions are a threat to the social order	Emotions are integral to the operation of society
Bounded groups and clearly defined categories	Lack of stable and clearly defined groups: social categories poorly defined
Differentiated relationships	Undifferentiated relationships
Stereotyped modes of behaviour	Very varied behaviour patterns; a considerable range of responses will all be accepted as normal

And therefore there is a propensity for the following more specific social characteristics to develop in the Konso and Tauade societies:

KONSO	TAUADE
Relatively little emotional content in personal interaction	Personal interaction tends to have high emotional content
The restraint of overt self-assertion	Much personal pride and self-assertion
Relatively little emphasis on reciprocity, at least in the form of gift exchange and vengeance	Much emphasis on reciprocity in terms of gift exchange and vengeance

I am not suggesting, however, that these variables are always correlated in the same way, and it should be specially emphasized that the themes of personal domination and hostility which pervade Tauade society are not inherent in all atomistic societies. They can obviously occur in societies based on corporate groups, and it is possible for atomistic societies to avoid hostility by a different value system which forbids personal competition, and for such competition and hostility as occur to be resolved by the withdrawal of the competing parties from social contact. Examples of such societies are those of Tristan da Cunha (Munch 1971, 1974) and the Majangir of Ethiopia (Stauder 1972). In the first there is a powerful ethic forbidding men to assert themselves, and the society has been able to resist the attempt of at least one aggressive clique to establish its domination. While information on personal hostilities is scanty it seems that the rejection of leadership prevents the emergence of factions and that hostilities are probably inhibited by the lack of mobility, since a person who makes himself too objectionable to his neighbours will either be shunned or have to leave the island altogether. For the Tauade, of course, mobility is one of the prime factors in allowing men to escape the social consequences of their actions.

In the case of the Majangir, whose ecology is very similar to that of the Tauade, mobility appears to operate in conjunction with a value system less aggressive than that of the Tauade to mitigate hostility by facilitating the mutual withdrawal of enemies.

We can say therefore that atomistic social organization does not of itself produce violence; the extra ingredient of an aggressive ethos is required, and where, as in the case of the Tauade, mobility is also high, the society will have a large amount of violence. Pride, self-assertion, and vengeance will therefore be the most variable features of the distinction between atomistic and corporate societies, but personal conflict and animosity will be more easily generated in atomistic societies, and once a pattern of violence has been established these societies will have greater problems than corporate or Aristotelian societies in controlling it.

Just why the Tauade should have this particular cognitive orientation is far from obvious, but I am not claiming that it was whisked out of the depths of some collective unconscious for reasons unrelated to social and environmental circumstances. It seems likely, for example, that where population densities are very low the variability between individuals will be more striking than the resemblances, and relations between individuals will assume a significance and importance that they will not possess in larger and denser populations where the claims of groups on the conduct of their members will be greater. (Though it should be noted that many societies with low population densities are Aristotelian.) Mobility of residence will perhaps accentuate this effect in a situation of low population density, as will the network of pork exchange. But the point of cognitive orientations of the Heraclitean/Aristotelian sort is that, whatever their origins, they permeate *all* the collective representations of the culture, such as symbolism and forms of classification, time-reckoning and quantification, and are not confined to social relations.

Modes of thought are not self-generating, but having come into existence they order people's conception of reality with a rigour and consistency that cannot be attributed to the natural processes of society alone. The susceptibility of primitive societies to ordering in terms of simple conceptual structures will be further discussed in Chapter VIII.

This chapter will be concerned with the atomistic character of Tauade social institutions, in the course of which we will examine the constitution of such groups as exist—tribe, clan, and hamlet—and the nature of land tenure, and it will be shown how conflict is further engendered by the relations between the sexes, as men seek to control women.

2. TRIBE AND CLAN

I have stated that for the Heraclitean mentality it is types of relationship that precipitate groups, and this is born out most clearly in the nature of the tribe and clan as the Tauade perceive them.

It would be misleading to describe tribes and clans in their society as based either on a cognatic or an agnatic ideology, since the Tauade have no 'ideology' of descent at all; rather they are aware of many kinds of bonds between persons which are indeed connected with descent but which cannot be reduced to any abstract principle by which rights to group membership can be effectively defined.

The bonds which they recognize are those of blood; upbringing in the same family or hamlet; possession of rights of use of land and pandanus trees; co-operation in gardening; common residence and the mutual support in disputes which that implies; the bonds between men created in the men's house; and the inheritance of influence by sons from their fathers. It would, however, radically distort their view of their society to give special emphasis to any of these ties.

Consequently, there is no word in the Tauade language by which categories of kin may be distinguished, as the following examples show:

pila relative, friend (especially used in the One-Sene area)
ki relative, friend (especially in the Goilala area)
valavala relative, friend (Motu loan-word, though its similarity to *vala*, tame, should be noted)
lagimi relative, friend (another Motu loan-word, not used much at Goilala)
etsiva used especially of siblings, and their immediate descendants, but seems to have no lineal connotations. In the discussions which I had with informants on this word, it was included with *ki, valavala*, and *pila* to mean *nan'ili'koneama*, 'we are of one blood', thus implying that some distinction was made between agnates and cognates, on the one hand, and affines and friends, on the other, but in practical usage no such distinction was made. Further details of the kinship terminology are given in Appendix III.

Although the tribe is divided into clans, we shall see that these clans have no real existence as groups; the effective social unit within the tribe is the hamlet, which is recruited in terms of all the forms of personal relationship listed above. But the hamlet is also comparatively short-lived, and during its life its membership is constantly changing; it therefore deprives the clan and tribe of any effective form of coherence around a simple principle of lineality.

Tribes fought with a considerable degree of unity in battle, and their land is divided by established boundaries of streams or ridges from that of adjacent tribes, but there is no word for 'tribe' or 'clan', and while there is a clear idea that people are linked by blood, *nan'ili'koneama*, 'we are of one blood', blood relationships have no lineal characteristics and ramify among individual members of surrounding tribes to include cognates as well as agnates.

There is also a vaguer term which expresses not only some sort of common descent but a tradition of close social co-operation; this is *nan'kuru'konetsuema*. The mission dictionary gives the meaning of *kuru* as 'clan', but the people themselves said that it was an abbreviation of *kurupu*, 'pandanus', and that the expression meant that such people were closely related, literally, 'we are people of one (lot) of pandanus, people who share the same pandanus trees'. Since their trees are the most enduring form of real property which they possess and inherit, surviving for perhaps five generations or so, and planted in plots which are shared by a number of people, and whose nuts are usually harvested by several families in co-operation, the trees do represent a continuity not found in other aspects of their lives. It is therefore appropriate to conceive the pandanus groves as representing the continuity and unity of the tribe more clearly than anything else except blood.

When they say therefore that 'we are people of one pandanus', they do not mean that people who are normally resident members of other tribes may not *also* be *kuru'konetsuema* with them as well. Thus while the concept defines the totality of people who have hereditary rights to live in the tribal area, some of these people will not normally do so, having only cognatic claims. Conversely, it is quite possible for a man to say that he is *kuru'konetsuema* with two or three tribes. What he means is that he 'shares pandanus' with *some* members of each of these tribes. (The concept of sharing pandanus is in the last resort an ideal one, since a few groups have no pandanus. This was true of the Laitate before they crossed the Aibala River because their land was at too low an altitude, and as far as I know the Tatupiti, near Tapini, have none either.)

They would describe people who are neither of the same blood, nor of the same pandanus as *karima*, strangers. The word also means 'guests', as at a dance, the clear implication being that only strangers can be guests, though it does not imply, of course, that one cannot invite one's relatives and friends in other tribes to dances and feasts.

Members of a tribe have an ambivalent attitude to neighbouring tribes; they recognize the distinction between their own personal ties with some of that tribe's members, and the ties of the majority of their tribe with the other tribe. Thus when my informants were talking of the relationships between their own tribe, Goilala, and the surrounding tribes, Amo Lume, for example, would still define the Tawuni as 'our enemies' even though he had close connections with some of the Tawuni by birth and marriage; and Moise Apava, whose mother was from Kerau, included them in his list of tribes who were 'our enemies', and, making sucking noises, he added 'our meat, like pork', and grinned. So by saying that 'Tribe X are our enemies' they mean that this is the relationship existing between the groups as wholes, even though related groups of kin in each group would not, of course, be each other's enemies.

Men who had relatives in another tribe would avoid fighting with or killing them in warfare, and would certainly not eat any of their flesh if their bodies were brought back for a feast. But they might, of course, eat the flesh of non-related people in other tribes even if they had relatives in these tribes. Victims of homicide committed by fellow tribesmen were not eaten by other members of the tribe, even by those unrelated to the dead person.

Membership of a tribe does not therefore depend on descent alone, but upon which of a multiplicity of possible ties a person chooses to emphasize—these include descent through women (especially the mother) as well as men, rights to the use of land and pandanus trees, previous residence in a place, and friendship with the men, especially the chiefs, of the tribe.

The existence of the clans, however, shows that the tribe is not simply the vaguely defined and shifting agglomeration of individuals suggested so far, but is conceived as having some inner corporate articulation. The clans are as follows:

Karuai (the dominant clan)	Deribalavavai
Kovete	Darolavavai
Larima	Tupi

It might be suggested in view of the indeterminacy of the tribe's membership that the clans themselves cannot properly be said to form subordinate groups within the tribe, but overlap tribal boundaries by including members of other tribes. In the first place, however, the native model conceives the clans as owning roughly de-marcated areas of land entirely within, and only within, the Goilala boundaries (see Map 5), an ownership originally created by the clan ancestors who first cleared the primary forest in these areas. More-over, a number of old hamlet sites are traditionally associated with

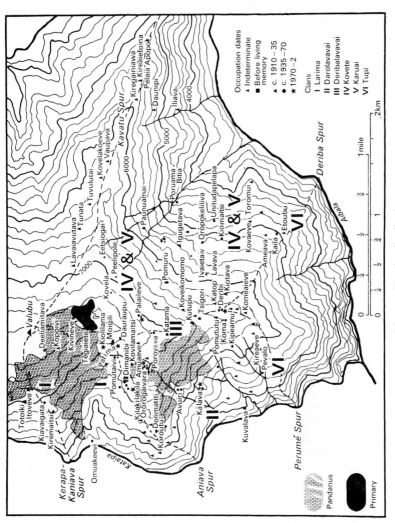

MAP 5. Hamlet distribution

THE ATOMISM OF TAUADE SOCIETY

TABLE 8. *Clan origins of hamlets*

Hamlet	Founding clan
Kaila	TUPI
Kilamalumi	
Kiomaitsi	KOVETE
Unitu dapelapa	
Oropokeliliva	
Toromu	
Koroutu	DELIBALAVAVAI
Kutupu	
Katama	
Koma	
Poragoto	
Amuaeve	
Deribi	
Kalava	
Kilakila	
Ororogaivara	
Poroyava	
Porukelapava	
Tsigori	
Kurulamanata	
Kumikiava	LARIMA
Manaluava	
Omuakeevi	
Oupoun	
Tipotaeve	
Aveveadouloubu	
Dimanibi	
Pomutu	
Itoveve	
Kiawaigata	
Kiremaitsi	
Moigili	
Patima	
Pevalo	DAROLAVAVAI
Avuiri	
Poroyava	KARUAI
Kumutagapoubu	
Poruamabitia	
Vilomepe	
Amapureu	
Variatsi	
Vaupava	
Doupu	
Kenea notovo (on Karuaiava spur)	
Palaileve	

the clans, as given in Table 8, and this association would be sufficient to justify a member of a particular clan in asserting his right to dwell on the site.

There are also a number of caves which are situated on land of the various clans and which are used as ossuaries for the ancestral dead. The details of these caves are given in Table 9.

I visited Duruai orava with Amo, but an apparently recent earth tremor had loosened the massive boulders which comprised the cave,

TABLE 9. *Clan bone caves*

Clan	Name of Cave	Location
Karuai	Duruai orava	Poruamabitia
?	Kaila puputu	Kaila
Larima & Kovete	Dopoadoepe	?
Tupi	Korimai Korope maia	Some *ila bionitsi* (wild bamboo) grows nearby
Deribalavavai	Pipitovoi orava	Near Kaila. There is a cliff and a big tree called Apilata apila dananata by the cave
Deribalavavai	Papakaila tumutu	
Darolavavai	Motomete (a big cave)	

and we were not able to find any bones. Amo shortly after went down to another cave and brought me back the skull and tibia of his grandfather. The dryness and excellent state of preservation of these bones made it obvious that they had indeed been preserved in a cave.

The existence of the clans is thus closely associated with land in a manner that entitles us to conclude that they are conceived as component groups of the tribe. This clan land is also fundamental to the status of the chiefs. These men are said to 'protect' the land of their clan and are conceived, genealogically speaking, as the inheritors of the power and fertility of the clan's chiefly ancestors. But I shall discuss the complicated matter of land tenure and the status of chiefs in later sections exclusively devoted to these topics; at this point in the analysis it will be more illuminating to consider the solidarity of the clan as a group.

The genealogical structure of the clans is ascertainable, and that of Larima is given as an example (Fig. 3). It will be seen that the genealogical depth of Larima extends over no more than five generations with any pretence at accuracy, and that no precise links can be traced between 'groups' A, B, and C, which for convenience I shall

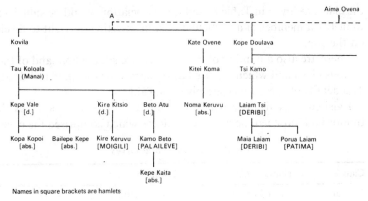

FIG. 3.

call 'sub-clans', though no corresponding term exists, of course, in the vernacular. Kovete is broken up into three such sub-clans as well, as is Darolavavai, but the surviving members of Karuai descend from a single man, Koupa Karoama, the father of a generation that had two living members at the time of my residence there. For practical purposes, then, the great-grandfather is the remotest ancestor whose brothers are likely to be known, and this produces the fragmentation of the clan into groups of second, and even third, cousins.

The Tauade do not for the most part think of their clans as descended from a single ancestor, but from a group of ancestors. The fact that in genealogies of clans such as Larima only one ancestor, such as Aima Ovena, is recalled is simply an accident of recollection and has no general significance, since other clans can trace no genealogical links between the sub-clans. Strathern writes of Melpa clans, however: 'It is important, in fact to stress that it is primarily the assertion of descent from a common ancestor and the use of this assertion to construct symbols of group unity and plurality that one wishes to label in saying that Highlanders 'have' dogmas of descent.' (Strathern 1972: 214.)

It seems to me that the significance of the ancestors for the Tauade is not as 'symbols of group unity and plurality' but as transmitters of fertility and power, of which the chiefs are the inheritors. Williamson (1912: 92) also stresses that among the Fuyughe the chiefs have their status through being the heads of the clans: 'At the head of each clan is the *amidi*, or chief of the clan.' Such unity as the Tauade clan possesses, therefore, derives not from common descent from

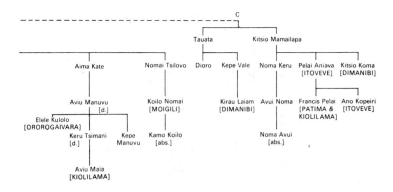

Structure of Larima clan

a founding ancestor, but from the living presence of their chief. Clan members wish to perpetuate their clan (as Avui Maia made clear in his speech at Palaileve—see pp. 184-5). And it is for this reason that murders within the clan are very unusual and disapproved of—I was unable to discover a single clear case of intra-clan murder, as opposed to nineteen intra-tribal killings—see Table 10, from which the killing of the woman Teopo by Ita Kogotsi has been omitted, since he is not a true Goilala.

But this rather vague degree of solidarity vanishes as soon as one tries to draw any concrete conclusions about residence, hamlet populations, marriage, garden co-operation, and other aspects of social relations from the genealogies. Fig. 3 shows that even members of sub-clans commonly inhabit different hamlets, and Fig. 4 illustrates the dispersal of agnates among hamlets in greater detail. This dispersal is even more apparent in the case of the clans themselves, as can be observed in Table 11 which shows the distribution of clans between hamlets.

For while the clans, like the tribes, tend in practice to be patrilineal, this is not really a rigid defining principle of membership at all but simply a result of the fact that influence and co-operation tend to be organized in terms of male relationships. Cognatic ties are also important and allow the blurring of the boundaries between the clans in the following ways.

In giving the clan membership of different people, my informants often coupled two clan names together, e.g. Kovete-Karuai, Karuai-Larima, or even Oropoa-Larima, when they wished to indicate that

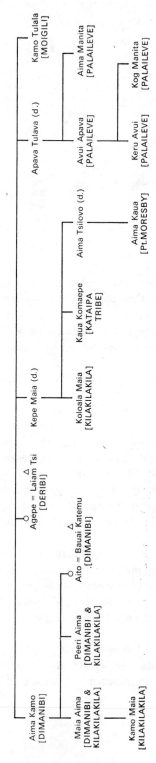

Fig. 4. Dispersal of agnates among hamlets

TABLE 10. *Murders by clan*

Murderer	Clan	Victim	Clan
K— Ka—	Kovete	K— Ko—	Larima
K— A—	Deliba-Lav.	A— T—	?Lavavai
Aima Kamo	Karuai	A— La—(f)	Kovete
Aima Kamo	Karuai	K— T—	Larima
Aima Kamo	Karuai	A— K—	Kovete
Aima Kamo*	Karuai	G— K—	Deliba-Lav.
A— A—	Kovete	T— N—	Deliba-Lav.
Ka— Ka—	Kovete	Ko— E—	Daro-Lav.
P— Ko—	Daro-Lav.	Al— & Va—	?Deliba-Lav.
A— V—	Kovete	A— O—	?Lavavai
M— V—	Larima	B— L—	Karuai
K— Ku—	?Lavavai	Ka— Kul—	?Lavavai
T— T— K— Te—	Deliba-Lav. Deliba-Lav.	K— D—	Karuai
Ki— Ma—	Tupi		
A— L—	Deliba-Lav.	N— Ki—	Larima
Av— Ap— Ko— Ki—	Karuai Karuai	Kē— P— (f)	Deliba-Lav.
Pe— Ku—	Deliba-Lav.	I— K—	Daro-Lav.
Ki— O—	Karuai	Ka— Ma—	Larima
To— & Am—	Daro-Lav.	Iv— Ko—	Deliba-Lav.

* Nephew of the 'real' Aima Kamo.

TABLE 11. *The distribution of clans by hamlets*

(Numbers refer to adult males only)

Hamlets	Clans					
	Karuai	Kovete	Larima	Deriba lavavai	Daro lavavai	Tupi
Deribi	..	..	3	..	I	..
Dimanibi	2	I	I	5	4	2
Kilikilakila	5	..	..	..	..	..
Kiolilama	..	..	2	I	..	..
Moigili	..	2	2	I	..	..
Patima	..	..	I	2	I	..
Ororogaivara	..	..	I	..	..	..
Palaileve	5	2	I	..	..	..
Itoveve	..	..	I	..	I	..
Kalava	..	I	..	..	..	..
Total	12	6	12	9	7	2

Note: Bold type indicates that the clan referred to constitutes the majority of the hamlet.

a man could be considered a member of two clans or, as in the case of Ita Kogotsi, a member of the Oropoa tribe and the Larima clan of the Goilala. Thus it was said that the principal chief Kepe Maia (deceased) had been a member of all the clans because he had ancestors in all of them and people in these clans were glad to have him as their chief.

The clearest case of a chief being claimed as a chief of two clans simultaneously is that of Buluvu Evura (Kimani). When I was originally asking about clan membership I was told that Buluvu was

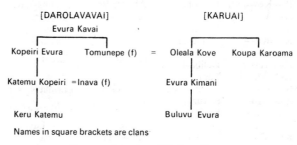

Names in square brackets are clans

FIG. 5. Ancestry of Buluvu Evura

a chief of Darolavavai clan, but further genealogical research showed that his FF[1] had been a brother of Koupa Karoama, the father of Kepe Maia and chief of the Karuai clan (see Fig. 5).

Now Evura Kavai was apparently a big chief of the Darolavavai clan, and it is said that Buluvu has 'taken his place'. This does not imply any exclusive inheritance of a unique office, as we shall see, but rather is a way of saying that Buluvu has claim to status because of this distinguished ancestor. Because Buluvu has another claim to status through his connection with Kepe Maia's line in the Karuai clan, as well as from Evura Kavai, the Darolavavai are pleased to count him as one of their chiefs. As the Karuai have a number of other powerful chiefs, Buluvu perhaps finds it preferable to be a big fish in the smaller pond of the less significant Darolavavai clan.

[1]	M	mother	FF	father's father
	F	father	MF	mother's father
	S	son	SD	son's daughter
	D	daughter		
	B	brother		etc.
	Z	sister		
	H	husband	'e'	as in eS elder
	W	wife	'y'	as in yS younger

Another example of this process can be found in the case of the relationship between the chiefs Keru Katemu (see Fig. 5) and Kire Keruvu, though they are only of middling status; this is shown in Fig. 6.

Tau Manai was a big chief of the Larima clan, as was his son Kire Kitsio (killed by the Kunima, see pp. 212–13). Kire Kitsio's son, Kire Keruvu, has had no children, however, in spite of being married three times. He has not chosen the other alternative of adopting a child. While Kire Keruvu is not the most powerful chief of the

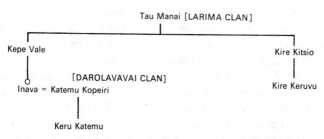

FIG. 6. Relationship of Kire Keruvu and Keru Katemu

Larima he is still a man of influence, and because of his relationship with Keru Katemu through Inava, Kire Keruvu's cousin, it is said that in time Keru Katemu will 'take the place of' Kire Keruvu, and Keru is also said to be a member of the Larima clan.

These examples show clearly that clan membership does not rely on any concept of lineality, but rather upon the tendency of men to place more importance upon their relationships to one another because men are the basis of society, and because there is much greater residential stability of males than females, and because brothers and male cousins tend to form coherent groups. Thus in practice we may call the clans 'patrilineal', but the lineality is not a conscious conceptual or legal principle, but only a general rule of thumb precipitated by actual conduct.[1]

[1] According to Williamson, the Fuyughe also do not make descent the sole criterion of clan membership: 'Moreover, I was told that now, at any rate, the people regard their *imbele* or clan relationship as a social one, as well as one of actual blood, a statement which is illustrated by the fact that, if a member of one clan leaves his village to reside permanently in a village of another clan, he will regard the members of the latter clan, and will himself be regarded by them as being *imbele*, although he does not part with the continuing *imbele* connection between himself and the other members of his original clan.' (Williamson 1912: 91.

It seems clear that Kepe Maia is said to have been a member of all the clans because his status within Karuai as the peacemaker of the tribe made it as advantageous for the other clans to recognize his cognatic ties with them as it was advantageous for him to support his own position by stressing those ties. This does not imply that less important men do not have cognatic ties with some or all of the other clans in the same way, but simply that it is not in these clans' interests to pay so much overt attention to these ties.

One of the most puzzling aspects of Tauade social organization is the existence of these named clans, with roughly bounded territories, pandanus stands, and ancestral hamlets and bone caves, with chiefs clearly representing the clan as a whole. For it is clear that residence, marriage, co-operation, and disputes and actual use of land have no relation to clan structure. In fact, it is impossible to deduce anything about actual social relations from it, except that homicide does not seem to occur between clan members. The clans seem to loom behind social relations like a ghostly remnant of what might have been, but which can never materialize.

It is clear from native tradition that Karuai was the original clan, and that the clans are very old and in a sense basic groups. Assuming that the other clans are descended from later immigrants, as tradition asserts, it is easy to understand when one looks at the map of the earliest settlements that hamlets would have been more dispersed in those days by the large expanse of forest than they are today. One might expect groups of immigrants to have been given collective names and dispersed areas of land to settle on. They would have been the first to clear this land and so would have acquired title to it, as they would to the stands of pandanus which they planted. In their dealings with other clans their chiefs would have played the same role as spokesman that they do today.

We can say, therefore, that the original circumstances in which Goilala land was settled are likely to have produced the clans simply as a result of basic and very familiar migratory and ecological processes. One has therefore to explain why the clans today have ceased to have much impact upon actual social relations. It would have been quite possible for the clan structure to have persisted and, indeed, there are innumerable instances in other societies where precisely this happened. Since the present characteristics of Tauade society have clearly not been produced by contact with government or mission, it is reasonable to suppose that they are the result of indigenous social processes. I suggest that the clans disintegrated for the following reasons.

It seems certain that the original settlers of Goilala lived in hamlets organized on a clan basis; these hamlets would have functioned as co-operative units for agricultural purposes—felling the primary forest and making gardens—whether or not they engaged in warfare. (Williamson also states that Fuyughe hamlets were originally organized on a clan basis, op. cit., pp. 82–92.) While we have no evidence to tell us whether the Goilala clans lived together in single hamlets or if there was an initial propensity for clans to segment at the earliest time of settlement into separate hamlets, it is clear that the giving of great feasts and dances has been the most powerful of all disintegrating factors upon clan organization, as it is upon the hamlets themselves.

In order to give a really impressive feast all the clans of a tribe need to co-operate with pigs and garden produce, and the feast itself has to be held at a single centre, in the building of which every member of the tribe assists. We shall see that the residence pattern of hamlets is completely disrupted by these dance villages, and after the dance village has been abandoned people often live in different hamlets, or construct new ones. Such feasts therefore entail the periodic disruption of hamlets and clans for the duration of the tribe's dance village. The ceremonies themselves, with their emphasis upon display, oratory, and flamboyant dancing, create a competitive atmosphere within the tribe, and the gifts of pork enmesh the individuals in a never-ending sequence of gift exchanges with members of other tribes. The sequences of gift exchanges in turn open up pathways for marriages with members of other tribes and residence there with affines and cognates. The mobility permitted by the ecology is thus reinforced by the network of gift exchange and marriage ties with other tribes and within the tribe itself, thus weakening the clan and tribe still further as co-operative units. As a result the only effective kin groups are those between whom exist the strongest affective ties, such as fathers and sons, or brothers.

I suggest, therefore, that the pig feasts and dances operated together with, and reinforced, the basically Heraclitean mentality of the Tauade, to destroy the clans and hamlets as stable co-operative units. Thus the pigs are not only a source of conflict through their depredations on gardens and their demands on the women who have to feed them but, as the *raison d'être* of the feasts and dances and all that they entail, are a primary factor in the emergence of the atomistic character of Tauade society. This model of 'social disintegration' will be implicit in the remaining analysis of Tauade society throughout the book.

Tauade society is marked by a high degree of mobility between tribes and between hamlets. The stability of membership of a single tribe over time can be judged by the data from Goilala, which covers the period 1959–68 inclusive, given in Table 12. It will be seen that

TABLE 12. *Effects of migration of tribal membership*

1959				1968		
Males	95			Males		
		165	*Total*		*109*	*Total*
Females	70			Females	(66% of 1959 figure)	
Deaths		28		Births	28	
Migration out		27		Migration in	32	
[Male		10]	37%	[Male	12]	37·5%
[Female		17]	63%	[Female	20]	62·5%

Port Moresby migrants are excluded.

after ten years only 66 per cent of the original population was left, and that half of this diminution was due to migration. 'Migration' here refers only to what appears to be permanent removal and does not include absences of less than a year, or even absences of several years where it is said that the person in question intends returning, or absences in Port Moresby.

This degree of mobility, together with the absence of effective lineal descent groups and with low pressure on land is, of course, consistent with Meggitt's hypothesis that

where the members of a homogeneous society of horticulturalists distinguish in any consistent fashion between agnates and other relatives, the degree to which social groups are structured in terms of agnatic descent and patrilocality varies with the pressure on available agrarian resources. (Meggitt 1965: 266.)

Before the social significance of the hamlet as the basic co-operative unit can be fully appreciated it will be illuminating to analyse the system of land tenure and pandanus ownership in some detail, since land tenure plays such an important part in facilitating mobility, and it is, after all, on land that hamlets are built.

3. LAND TENURE

The nature of land tenure among the Tauade can only be understood
when it is realized that as in the constitution of the tribe and clan
a multiplicity of claims and relationships is recognized, and that no
exclusive rights, or clearly bounded plots, exist.

According to McArthur, the Kunimaipa system of land tenure is
one of demarcated plots inherited by a man's eldest son. 'He has the
right to cultivate or to dispose of land (which is rarely done) without
asking anyone's permission. Any person who wishes to cultivate the
land should ask for and receive his permission.' (McArthur 1961: 21.)
It also appears that a man's younger brothers and also his sisters
have residual rights in the inheritance of land, and that men can
inherit the right to land use through their mothers. Any relative can
also ask for the loan of land, and if such land is used a second time
with the tacit consent of the owner, ownership passes to the new
cultivator.

Such a system of land tenure among slash-and-burn cultivators
with these low population densities seems both pointless and full of
contradictions, but since it has been described among a neighbouring
people I feel it necessary to explain at some length why it does not
exist among the Tauade. Indeed, from what has been said so far
about the mode of land use and its relative abundance, together with
the mobility of the population, we could deduce *a priori* that any
system of rigidly demarcated hereditary plots of garden land would
be unworkable. The reasons are as follows:

(*a*) A system of individually owned plots in such an ecological
context would require an extremely complex set of boundary
markers, but none such exists.

(*b*) Moreover, while gardens are divided up by boundaries of small
shrubs and plants while in use, these boundaries are soon overgrown
and lost when the garden reverts to bush, and people say that they
are no longer remembered.

(*c*) As we have seen, gardens are always made in company with
other people, sometimes a dozen or so, and these groups vary in
composition from year to year. If there were a permanent and exclusive division of hereditary plots, it would clearly be impossible to
combine such scattered plots with the requirements of the fallowing
process and with the varying combinations of those who make
gardens together. For a group of people who wished to make their

gardens together might find that none of their hereditary plots were contiguous with those of their companions. It is even more unlikely that having exhausted one set of plots, the same group of people would be able to go elsewhere and find another set of contiguous plots.

(d) In a system of agriculture where land is continuously productive, as well as being in short supply, and where there are capital improvements such as terraces, there is good reason for clearly demarcated hereditary plots. But for the Tauade, any piece of whose land is only used at 12–15-year intervals, if that, and which is in abundant supply, such clearly demarcated hereditary plots would be pointless. The only capital investment is in the fences, which decay irreparably after four or five years.

(e) Pandanus trees, on the other hand, which endure for generations and represent an important source of wealth, are very clearly demarcated into plots, which are shared by a well-defined set of people.

(f) It is clear in fact that the same piece of ground is used successively by quite different people, and that in many cases these people are no longer resident in the area.

(g) Finally, in contrast to pandanus plots, thefts from which can produce severe brawls, I have never heard of a fight within Goilala over land itself, which is further confirmation that there is no system of bounded plots.

Tauade land tenure is governed by the following principles:

(1) The initial clearing of primary forest gives perpetual rights of use to the men concerned and their descendants; this seems the basis of the clans' ownership of land. (But it should be noted that hunting rights may be claimed in some areas even where no clearance has taken place.)

(2) Permission to use land can be given by its original clearers to non-clan members, e.g. to cognates, affines, and neighbours.

(3) Close ties of blood to someone in groups (1) and (2) are also recognized grounds for use of land.

(4) Descent from someone in groups (2) and (3) is a valid principle of land use inheritance.

(5) It is necessary to maintain rights under groups (3) and (4) by exercising them from time to time and, if the land is in the territory of another tribe, by social contact with those in groups (1) and (2).

Clans are said to own roughly demarcated areas of land, and my informants told me that the men who first cleared the primary forest thereby established their ownership of the land, and that these rights had been transmitted to their descendants. The effective disposition of this ownership is in the hands of the chiefs, who 'protect' the land, but the operation of factors (2), (3), and (4) means that in practice nothing can be deduced about actual land use from clan membership. This is because the mode of agriculture and the mobility of the population causes the use of land to reflect a multiplicity of social relationships between cognates, affines, friends, neighbours, and migrants.

When a migrant like myself arrives, however, the power of the clan chief to dispose of the land seems to outweigh that of all other claimants, since I had no pre-existing claims at all to land rights.

I obtained direct confirmation of the chief's power over land in which his clan has traditional rights soon after my arrival at Goilala. The deserted village of Pomutu, where my house and garden were situated, lies in what I later learned was Larima land, and the question of the rent of this ground naturally arose soon after I had settled in. It was originally my intention to grow sweet potatoes on the land which was enclosed by a fence (0·6 acres), and a patrol officer came over to assess the rent which was customarily paid by Europeans to natives, A$2·0 per acre being the usual figure. The principle chief of the Larima is Avui Maia, and there were, including him, seven claimants for the rent. I continue from my diary:

The day got off to a good start with a row over the rent for the land. The young chief (a thoroughly nasty bit of work I have noticed for some time without knowing who he was) demanded $2·0 for *each* of the 7 claimants to the land! I absolutely refused, so he said that I could live here for nothing, but was not to plant anything on the land. Moise and the old chief [Avui Apava] were rather embarrassed by this, and Moise suggested that I get the Fathers to draw up a contract. I shall go over and see them tomorrow to ask for mediation. I will up the rent to $5, for the fence and *elaivi*[1] [i.e. take their value as improvements into consideration] and try to isolate the chief by making the money too attractive to the others. (13 July 1970.)

On the following Saturday Fr. Guichet came back with me to Goilala and put my case. Later the councillor, Francis, came and told me that the claimants wanted to accept the money, but Avui Maia was

_____
[1] The wind-break which survived from the old hamlet.

opposed. I let it be known that I would pay $1 and a stick of tobacco to each claimant, and on 19 August Francis told me that the men wanted to accept it. But Avui Maia did not allow this, and no one ever approached me to claim his share. Since in the normal way the Tauade are eager for money, this is good evidence for the degree of power exercised by the chief in matters of land.

As it turned out, and as I should have realized, the land was an old garden and the yield would have been very poor in any case. So I lived there for the rest of my time without paying rent, and without planting potatoes.

Let us consider the identities of the claimants; these are given in Table 13.

TABLE 13. *Claimants to Pomutaivi land*

Name	Hamlet	Clan
Avui Maia	Patima	Larima
Elele Kulolo	Patima	Larima
Kire Keruvu	Moigili	Larima
Porua Laiam	Patima	Larima
Kepe Mana	Dimanibi	Darolavavai
Keru Katemu	Patima	Darolavavai
Maia Aima	Dimanibi	Karuai

The genealogies listed in Fig. 7 show how these men's claims are justified by virtue of their descent from three Larima chiefs.

Comparisons of these genealogies with the fuller genealogy of the Larima clan (Fig. 3) shows that a number of Larima men are not claimants, while there are two claimants from Darolavavai and one from Karuai. Some Larima men are absent from Goilala, but there are current residents—Kamo Beto, from A sub-clan, Kepe Manuvu and Koilo Nomai from B, and all resident members of C—who have also been excluded. Some of these men, such as Koilo Nomai, are *malavi* (rubbish-men), but Francis Pelai is the councillor; this suggests that not all branches of a clan have rights over all the clan's lands but only to those areas originally cultivated by their ancestors, and also that the less significant members of the clan have simply been ignored. In addition, significant members of other clans, such as Kamo Maia and Keru Katemu, who have cognatic links with the clan, will also be recognized as having a claim. The clearest fact to emerge, however, is that Avui Maia decided who the claimants were,

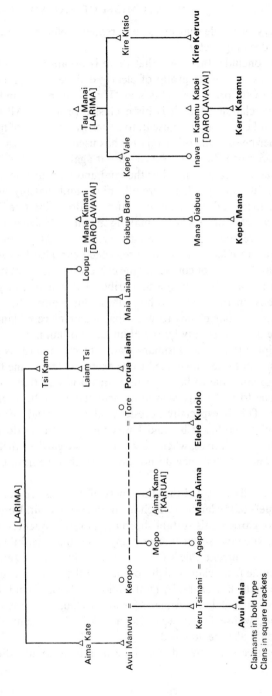

Fig. 7. Claimants to Pomutaivi land

Claimants in bold type
Clans in square brackets

and it is very probable that his own personal preferences were ultimately the deciding factor.

We may conclude, therefore, that there is no absolute ownership
of land by a determinate group of clearly defined people, and that
when a man with prior use rights says 'This is all my ground', he is
certainly not claiming that it is his exclusive property. All that he
means is that he has a right to use it, together with the rest of his clan,
or that either he or some other relative has used it before, thus establishing a precedent by which he can use it again.

It was therefore said to me that the land and trees at Pomutu, the
site of my house and garden, were all 'mine', and that my brothers
could come there and make gardens, and cut down the trees and so
on. But they were not, of course, making me an exclusive gift of this
land; they were stating the customary principle that for them use
establishes a precedent for further use, which can also be extended
to one's relatives. It is, of course, by the exercise of these ties through
his wife or mother, born in another tribe, that a man can go and
make gardens on the land of other tribes. But many other people
will also have similar claims to use a particular piece of land, and
disputes are avoided simply by the abundance of land.

As principle (4) states, customary claims to make gardens on the
land of a clan not one's own need to be exercised from time to time
if they are to continue to be respected; thus it is said that a certain
man has gone to make a garden in a particular place 'to look after
his ground'. This is especially necessary when the land lies within
the territory of another tribe, and I was told that 'If we do not go
and live with our relatives, when we want to make gardens there they
will refuse, and say that they do not know us, that we have become
strangers'.

It should finally be noted that the chiefs of hamlets are not necessarily the chiefs of the land on which the hamlets are built. Residence,
like the use of gardens, also establishes a right of subsequent residence
on the same site, and so we find in many cases that the fathers and
grandfathers of current chiefs of hamlets also lived there, and that
they often come from clans which do not own the land on which the
hamlets are built. For example, Dimanibi is on Larima land, but its
chiefs are Maia and Peeri Aima, of Karuai clan, in succession to
Aima Kamo, whose father was also a chief there; many similar
examples could also be adduced.

Pandanus trees are owned and inherited in a totally different

manner from land. Here we may talk of ownership as opposed to
rights of use, and the model of hereditary, clearly demarcated plots
can be applied quite realistically. The pandanus forests are composed
of at least two dozen named areas, and within these areas are the
plots of the owners. While the named areas are demarcated by natural
features the plots themselves are distinguished by *elaivi* planted at
strategic intervals. After a number of visits to these forests it was
clear that these markers were quite adequate, and that everyone
knew where one plot ended and another began. People have trees in
many different scattered plots.

It seems that originally these areas of pandanus were more closely
associated with the clans than they are now. It is said that the large
expanse of pandanus in the region of Avuiri and Kalava all used to
belong to the Tupi clan, who planted it, until their virtual extermina-
tion in the last century by other Goilala. The Darolavavai planted
the remainder of the pandanus in this area, while the larger expanse
to the north was planted by the Larima. Deribalavavai and Kovete
do not seem to have planted much, if any, in the early stages, and it
is said that the Karuai had none.

My informants claimed as an explanation of the lack of pandanus
trees on Karuai land that the pandanus trees were introduced by
migrants, and that the Karuai had had none originally. This seems
implausible. In the first place, Karuai land is clearly unsuited to the
pandanus tree anyway and, secondly, it is surely more likely that the
small number of original inhabitants would have been content to
gather the nuts of trees that seeded themselves in the forest, and that
only with the influx of migrants did the Goilala start felling the
forest to make room for pandanus plantations. For it is evident that
the large areas of pandanus trees could not have been established at
their present size until the primary forest had been cleared. Nevertheless, it is clear that the Karuai clan did not claim the primary
forest where the pandanus stands grow today, and that these stands
were originally planted by the clans already referred to. As time
passed, however, the ownership of the trees has become thoroughly
diffused throughout the Goilala population.

It is interesting to examine in detail one plot of trees in an area
called Tepuramata, in Larima ground, which lies close to Pomutu,
as can be seen on Map 4. The first trees on this land were apparently
planted by Lavea and Tauama, of the Larima clan. But since the
pandanus tree has a life of not more than about 130 years, it is clear

that these trees are long since dead and have been succeeded by later generations of trees. Amo Lume's inheritance of trees is represented in Fig. 8.

According to Amo, the very oldest trees in his plot were planted by Papaitsi, and some were planted by Kovo Ilituvu and his younger brother Kaita Tseema, which are also still bearing fruit. Assuming that Amo was born in about 1920, and allowing twenty-five years to a generation, Papaitsi would have been born in about 1820. He would not have planted trees before he was married in about 1840–5,

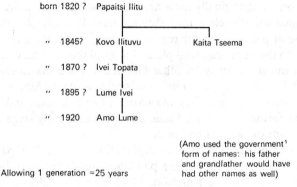

FIG. 8. Amo Lume's inheritance of pandanus trees

and would probably not have delayed beyond the age of 40, in about 1860. It seems certain, therefore, that the surviving trees which he planted are at least 100, and perhaps as much as 130, years old. Whatever their age, I was shown trees which are now owned by a man who is in the fifth lineal generation from the original planter. Naturally, such trees are now very few, and usually have proper names by which the owner treasures them. (See the text describing the felling of pandanus trees, below, p. 189.)

But it is important to realise that the ownership of the land is distinguished from that of the trees themselves. Thus men who have some claim to kinship may use the land on which their kinsmen have trees for planting trees of their own, unless, I think, relations between them and existing occupiers are unusually bad. Amo told me that

---

[1] In which the son takes as his second name his father's first name. The Tauade have taken to this usage quite readily, and it achieves, for census purposes, a degree of order in the otherwise chaotic pattern of their names.

Peeri Aima had planted trees on the same ground as his own, because
Peeri's mother (wife of Aima Kamo) had been the daughter of Kaita
Kaga, a chief of Delibalavavai, Amo's clan. Another Delibalavavai
man, Manautu Kope, also planted trees on this ground. Amo's
father, Lume Ivei, married Manautu's brother's wife, after her
husband Tuna was killed by Apava Aginei. When Manautu died,
Amo killed two pigs for his funeral and was given these trees as
compensation. He and Manautu were very good friends. Again,
Bailepe Kepe, of Larima clan, planted trees on this ground, and when

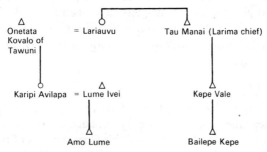

FIG. 9. Genealogical links between owners of pandanus trees

he died Amo gave a shirt and trousers for him to be buried in, and
was given these trees, too, in compensation. There is a rather tenuous
link between Bailepe and Amo, as shown in Fig. 9.

It seems possible, therefore, for people who are relatives or friends
to use the same plot of ground for planting pandanus, but to what
extent relatives, however distant, have a prescriptive right to plant
trees, or have to ask permission, is difficult to say. It seems that if one
has no claim by kinship and one wishes to plant trees on land already
occupied by someone else's, one is expected to pay compensation.
For example, I was told that Kaita Kitai had planted his trees on
ground stolen from Kire Keruvu and Keru Katemu. He should have
paid compensation but did not. While it is correct according to
native ideas to distinguish land from pandanus trees, the fact that the
trees have boundaries around their plots inevitably means that the
land itself is divided into plots, and the distinction between land and
trees becomes blurred.

Thus every plot of trees is owned by a group of men—those
descended in the male line from a common ancestor who planted the
trees originally, and whose descendants have been planting in the

same area subsequently, and by those men who have planted trees in the plot on the basis of wider kin ties and sometimes friendship. Usually trees seem to be inherited in the male line only, though men may inherit use rights through their mothers, but if a man has no sons his trees may be inherited by a daughter. Kilemu Apava had recently planted many trees for the sake of his daughter's son; she was married to Kog Manita and was Kilemu's only child. He will never live to see the trees bear fruit himself. It is also possible to acquire trees by gift, not inheritance, and men give their trees in compensation for favours received, or injuries committed. This capacity to give trees away suggests that when a group of relatives inherit trees they split them up among themselves and do not take fruit from the whole block of trees indiscriminately, at least not without asking.

4. HAMLETS

When the first settlers arrived at Goilala they apparently found that the land near the Aibala was already denuded of trees, and reduced to permanent grassland. We can tell this from the sites of the earliest hamlets—Pevalo, Kaila, Toromui, and Poruamabītīa, which are situated a long way above the river and the people themselves say that there was quite a large expanse of grassland when their ancestors first came, and that for this reason the first hamlets were not built closer to the river. As can be seen from Map 4, the subsequent trend of settlement was up the spurs on the eastern flank of Deriba spur, as the forest was steadily burned and cut down for the preparation of gardens. Most of this land is now covered in grass, though as we can see from Plate II the western slope of Deriba is quite thickly covered in secondary vegetation. It is likely that settlement was more dispersed in the beginning than now, for simple topographical reasons, and has become more concentrated as the hamlets have been drawn closer together at the top of the mountain. The land between the Perume and Deriba spurs is extremely precipitous, and it is not surprising that it has never been used for settlement.

One should not suppose, however, that all the oldest settlements were at the lowest altitudes, and that in consequence topographical height corresponds closely to relative antiquity, the most recent hamlets occupying the highest points. For some hamlets which are situated quite high up the mountain are none the less of considerable antiquity, for example, Dimanibi, Ororogaivara, Avuiri, Kalava, Deribi,

Pomuru, and Amapureu, and perhaps others. The most likely reason for this seems to be connected with the requirements of the pandanus trees. Since the pandanus will not grow below about 5,500 feet there would have been some advantage for those who had many trees in dwelling in close proximity to them.

Whatever may have been the exact reasons, there is no doubt that some of the older hamlets, or at least their sites, have been in repeated use for at least forty years (Middleton mentions Ororogaivara in 1932, for example) and, since some hamlets such as Dimanibi are said to have been lived in by such people as Koupa Karoama, Aima Kamo's father, 100 years does not seem an excessive estimate for the sporadic use of some hamlet sites. Clearly, the populations of such hamlets have waxed and waned, especially as the result of large dances being held in them, and at some points in their history they have certainly been deserted.

Figure 10 shows how hamlets have persisted over time, based on data for 1932, 1942, 1952, 1957, and 1970–2. Data for 1932 is very incomplete, and it is likely that 1942 and 1952 sources (mission and government respectively) have listed only the more important hamlets. As the asterisks indicate, the list for 1957 (taken from an aerial photograph) includes a number of very small hamlets, some with only one or two houses.

One hamlet, Ororogaivara, has persisted for 40 years, another, Moigili, for 30 years, while three have lasted for 20 years, and two for 15 years. It is known from patrol reports that between 1946 and 1952 Goilala was partially or totally abandoned, due to internal killings in the tribe.

There are clearly two categories of hamlet—the larger and more important ones, which have long histories of intermittent occupation, periodically becoming dance villages, and garden hamlets, with only a few houses, small and ephemeral, though large hamlets may periodically shrink to the size of garden hamlets.

We may sum up the general trends of land use for settlement as a slow upward movement, with the gardens being made close to the retreating forest line, and hamlets keeping pace in order to be near not only the gardens but also the supplies of timber provided by the forest for house-building, fences for gardens, and firewood. It is specifically said that many hamlets were abandoned because of the increasing distance necessary to reach the forest. Some hamlets 'leap-frogged' others in this process and were built higher up in the

1932	1942	1952	1957	1970–2
Komamavi (Komaeaieve)				
Poroyava				
Ororogaivara ——	Ororogaivara ——	Ororogaivara ——	Ororogaivara ——	Ororogaivara*
	Taratatae″ (Moigili) ————	? ————	Moigili ————	Moigili
	Kutupu			
	Emaburuvu (Daurupu)			
	Porukelapava			
	Amapureu			
			Deribi ————	Deribi
			Tsigori*	
			Katama*	
			Palaileve ————	Palaileve
			Kovoaluata*	
			Dolimatiti*	
	Kalava ————	Kalava ————	Kalava ————	Kalava*
	Avuiri ————	Avuiri*		
	Pomutu ————	Pomutu		
	Itoveve ————	Itoveve ————	Itoveve	
	Dimanibi ————	Dimanibi ————	Dimanibi ————	Dimanibi
	Manaruava			
			Deeliamitava*	
			Kiremaitsi	
			Kiawaigata*	
			Tounatitava*	
				Patima (Fatima)
		* Very small, garden hamlet		Kiolilama*
				Kllakilakila

FIG. 10. Persistence of hamlets over time

forest near the pandanus stands. Land on the lower slopes has frequently been degraded into grass, though this is much less true of the
western slope of the Deriba spur than it is of the east. If one examines
the pattern of vegetation throughout the Aibala Valley it soon
becomes clear that while almost all east-facing slopes have been
denuded of substantial vegetation it is often quite dense on the

TABLE 14. Sample of men occupying successive hamlets together

Persons				HAMLETS					
	KALAVA	KOROUTU	TAWUNI	KALAVA	AVUIRI	DERIBI	ITOVEVE	POMUTU	MOIGILI	DIMANIBI
Amo Lume	"	"	"	"	"	"	"	"	"	"
Tuna Taura	"	"	"	"	"	"	"	"	"	"
Bauai Katemu	"	AVUIRI	?	"	"	"	"	"	"	"
Airi & Kiara Maini	"	?	"	"	"	O/G	"	"	"	"
Kavini Ivei	"	"	"	"	"	O/G	"	"	"	"
Laiam Kepe	"	"	"	"	"	O/G	"	"	"	"
Aima Kate						O/G	"	"	.	"
Oiabue Apava		AVUIRI	"	AVUIRI	....	O/G	"	"	"	"
Aima Kamo		POROYAVA	"	DIMANIBI	....	....	"	"	"	"
Peeri & Maia		POROYAVA	"	DIMANIBI	....	....	"	?	"	"
Kitsio Koma				POMUTU	KUNIMA		....			
Maia Laiam					KUNIMA		AMUAEVE		DERIBI..........	
Laiam Tsi					KUNIMA	....	AMUAEVE		DERIBI	
Oiabue Baro					AVUIRI..........		POMUTU	MOIGILI	PALAILEVE DERIBI	
Buluvu Kimani						O/G	POMUTU	MOIGILI	PALAILEVE O/G......	
Anamara Koupa						O/G	....	POMUTU	PALAILEVE KIOLILAMA	
Ita Kogotsi				OROPOA	ITOVEVE	DIMANIBI	KOPOIVI	POMUTU	MOIGILI	
Avui Maia							TSIGORI	POMUTU	MOIGILI KATAIPA PATIMA	
Francis Koupa				POMUTU	POROYAVA	A/D	....		MOIGILI PATIMA	

? denotes that the hamlet may be the same as that mentioned above

A blank denotes that the hamlet is unknown to the informant

.... denotes that the same hamlet remained that of residence

O/G Ororogaivara hamlet   A/D Aveveadouloubu hamlet

western slopes. In the same way, on the east-facing side of the Aibala Valley the forest line is about 1,000 feet higher than it is on the opposite side of the valley. This is surely due to the fact that east-facing slopes are more exposed to the sun than western slopes and therefore tend to be drier, and their vegetation is the more easily burned off.

Ecologically, therefore, there is no reason why hamlets should not have been continually occupied for several decades by very much larger populations than are normal either now or in traditional times. But the stability of residence is in fact very limited, and most men only live in the same hamlet for a few years, or even less. The various hamlets occupied by Amo Lume, who was born in about 1920, illustrate this, as shown in Table 15.

TABLE 15. *Hamlets occupied by Amo Lume in the course of his life*

1   Deribi   (born there)
2   Kurudamanata
3   Kalava
4   Koroutu
5   Then to Tawuni, where he spent several years in a number of different hamlets. His first wife died there.
6   Kalava   (again)
7   Avuiri
8   Deribi   (again)
9   Itoveve
10 Pomutaivi
11 Moigili
12 Manuarava
13 Dimanibi   (where he is now)

It was possible to obtain the names of some of the men who had accompanied him to live at some of these places, together with the names of men with whom his contact had been more peripheral. The relationships of many of the men listed in Table 14 can be found in Fig. 11 and will be seen to be similar in type to those between hamlet members generally.

This instability of residence is closely linked to the nature of the groups of which hamlets are composed: the only effective groups of agnates are fathers and sons, brothers, and, less often, first cousins, and these groups are 'stitched' together by cognatic and affinal ties. Beyond these tightly knit agnatic groups extends a network of affinal and cognatic ties that need to be vitalized by periods of co-residence.

Figures 11 and 12 illustrate the nature of the groups of which the hamlets are composed. We see that the commonest relationships are those of an agnatic nature, as Table 16 shows. (It should be noted

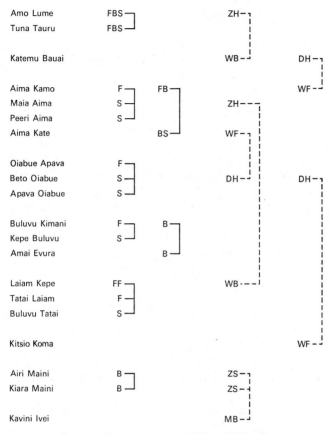

FIG. 11. Group structure of Dimanibi hamlet

that the Table is concerned with the cases of *relationships*, not with the number of individuals. Thus, a relationship of the form

would be entered in the Table as F/S 1, B/B 1.)

TABLE 16. *Cases of relationships between hamlet members*

F/S	13		
B/B	6		
FBS	4		
FB/BS	2		
More distnt.	3	*28*	*Agnatic*
MB/ZS	2		
F/D	1		
B/Z	1	*4*	*Cognatic*
ZH/WB	4		
DH/WF	3		
WZH	1		
BDH/WFB	1	*9*	*Affinal*

Figure 12 shows house positions and the principal relationships between residents. There are apparently four dominant men—Aima Kamo (deceased), Oiabue Apava, Buluvu Kimani, and Amo Lume. These men are said to 'own' the ground between the various boundaries within the hamlet. As in the case of land tenure, they can

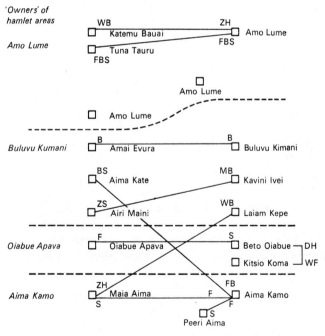

FIG. 12. Relationship and residence at Dimanibi

clearly have no exclusive claim to it; 'ownership' here obviously means 'sphere of influence *vis-à-vis* the persons whose houses lie within the boundary'. In the old days the most prominent chiefs were also said to 'own' the one or two men's houses. We have therefore to distinguish between the current members of a hamlet, whose occupancy will not be permanent, and the clan which owns the land on which the hamlet is built. For I was told

the chiefs of hamlets were those who owned the land on which the hamlet was to be built. They killed pigs and presided over the foundation ceremonies. But they did not live there. They were not responsible for peace-keeping. This was done by the other chiefs, who would get together and order someone who had been a trouble-maker to get out until he had paid a pig—like Lariava Moripi's expulsion of Noma Kitai.

Dimanibi lies on Larima clan land, and is thus in a sense 'owned' by the Larima chiefs, who could, of course, come and live there for this reason (see Table 8 for details of hamlets and founding clans). But Aima Kamo and his relatives also have a claim to live there through repeated occupancy. Aima Kamo's father, Koupa Karoama, lived there, as Aima has done, as well as Aima's two sons, Peeri and Maia. The right to reside in a hamlet is therefore governed by the same principles as those of land use for gardens. There is the right of use according to one's clan membership and also the right derived from one's own, or a relative's, prior occupancy. In practice, however, just as one makes gardens with one's friends, so one chooses a hamlet where one has close ties of friendship or blood. The mere fact of residence in a hamlet, however, does not preclude co-operation with friends and relatives in other hamlets. As can be seen in Table 17, members of the same hamlets often make gardens with friends or relatives in other hamlets.

We will now examine the solidarity of the hamlet in greater detail. Given that hamlets are composed, not of members of a single clan but of heterogeneous groups united under the leadership of one or more chiefs, there seem to be two main reasons why the size of hamlets should be small. The first is that chiefs can only control a limited number of men and therefore the larger the hamlet, the greater the probability of its breaking up into factions led by different chiefs. The second is that the Tauade are a volatile people easily provoked into violence by what in other cultures would be considered trifling incidents. An atomistic society such as theirs will therefore have great difficulty in controlling and co-ordinating personal interaction, since

TABLE 17. *Garden co-operation and hamlet residence*

Garden	Hamlet	Garden	Hamlet
Kepe Manuvu	Ororogaivara	Keru Katemu	Patima
Mogu Apava	Moigili	Avui Maia	Patima
		Amo Lume	Dimanibi
Kire Kaita	Patima		
Kilemu Apava	Moigili	Evete Anamara	Patima
Maia Koma	Palaileve	Francis Koupa	Patima and Kioli-
Kirau Ivoro	Palaileve		lama
Amo Apava	Palaileve		
Noma Koupa	Patima	Maia Koma	Palaileve
Porua Laiam	Patima	Kilemu Apava	Moigili
		Lariava Apava	Palaileve
		Kire Keruvu	Moigili
Laua Kitai	Moigili	Laua Kitai	Moigili
Maia Laiam	Kilakila	Porua Laiam	Patima
Peeri Aima	Kilakila	Anamara Koupa	Kiolilama
		Keru Avui	Palaileve
Keru Katemu	Patima		
Amo Lume	Dimanibi		
Tatai Laiam	Dimanibi		

TABLE 18. *Number of diadic relationships according to population*

Size of population	Number of relationships[1]
10	45
15	105
20	190
25	300
30	435
35	595
40	780
45	990
50	1225
etc.	

[1] The number of diadic relationships in any group of n units is given by the formula $\frac{1}{2}(n^2 - n)$.

the number of diadic relationships in a group increases at a much faster rate than the numbers of the group itself (see Table 18).

Since the number of diadic relationships, and hence of potential quarrels, increases so rapidly, there will thus be a natural tendency for settlement size to be restricted for this reason alone.

Being small, the hamlet therefore provides a basis of effective co-operation, and while many hamlets do not commonly persist for more than about ten years and there is considerable mobility of their populations during that period, they display considerable internal solidarity, while disputes leading to violence are rare. Table 19 shows that fights occur more readily between kinsmen than between members of the same hamlet, though they are not, of course, unknown.

TABLE 19. *Relationships of principal disputants in fights at Goilala*

Total number of fights of which details obtained	24
Number of fights in which disputants from same hamlet	1
Number of fights in which disputants were kinsmen	7

In another case, not included here, Aima Kamo actually killed a member (Korou Tovei) of his own hamlet, but this is distinctly unusual. Table 20 confirms that residence in the same hamlet restrains disputes more effectively than kinship ties. It should be noted that adultery does not necessarily lead to violence and that

TABLE 20. *Adultery statistics*

Total number of recorded cases at Goilala	85	
Cases where adulterer and husband are related	20/76[a]	26%
Cases where the adulterer and the woman he seduced are related	0/76[a]	0%
Cases where adulterer and husband in same hamlet	11/81[b]	13·6%
Cases where adulterer in same hamlet as husband, *and* related to him	4/72[c]	5·5%
(a) Number of cases where insufficient genealogical evidence exists to establish with absolute certainty the existence of a genealogical link	9	
(b) Number of cases where hamlet of one or both parties unknown	4	
(c) Number of cases where genealogical links *and* hamlets could not be traced	13	

compensation may be readily accepted if the men involved are otherwise on friendly terms.

A man's fellow residents will support him if he has a dispute with someone of another hamlet or of a different tribe, and may accompany him if he goes there to get redress from someone who has seduced or run off with his wife, or stolen a pig. But they will also put pressure on him to give compensation if he has injured or offended someone, and they do not feel obliged to risk a fight simply to defend him. For example:

Aima Kamo was at Dimanibi. He came to Pomutu and seduced K— K—'s wives K— and T—, in the same house. K— K— came to the door and looked in and called to his wives 'Who's there?' Aima came out with his axe and hit K— K—, and went back to Dimanibi. K— K— told his *valavala* at Palaileve, Kopoivi, Itoveve, Pomuru, Poroyava, Peelipole, Eetsiogai, and they all came to Dimanibi, so Aima killed pigs as compensation. His *valavala* told him not to speak angrily, and to give compensation.

Persons who steal a pig, for example, may be betrayed by their neighbours, if the owner comes and finds the pig. Men have no hesitation about doing this once they realize that they have been discovered, and see no reason to share the blame with the culprit.

T— (a big thief), O— K—, K— O— (Koupa's father) all went to Laitate and killed a pig of K— K— in the bush, in daylight. They took it away at night and brought it to the Aibala River. They got wood and cooked it where there is a rock-shelter called Dopoaloepe. The next day they dug up the traces and carried the pieces of pork back to Oropo for distribution. K— K— followed the tracks and came first to the rock-shelter where he found the oven [a pile of discarded stones which had been heated in the fire]. He smelt the stones, and the odour of pork. He found a bone, and the *kovelapa* leaves. He came to Oropo and said 'Who stole my pig and killed it down there?' He had a stone from the oven, the bone, and a *kovelapa* leaf. T— said 'I didn't see it.' But Lume Ivei [the father of Amo] said 'It was T—' and he gave away all the other names of the people who had stolen the pig. So T— gave a piglet, O— K— gave a homicide emblem, K— O— gave an axe, and K— K— took them back home with him. He had come to Oropo by himself, but he was a chief, so he was not beaten up. But he was better tempered than Kapa Maugere, who led a raid in revenge. *Malavi* did not go alone like this or they would have been killed.

If the person who had been robbed could not prove who had stolen the pig, even if he was privately sure, there was nothing he could do; for example

K— M— of Tsigori hamlet went and killed A— M—'s pig. [He was from Kunima.] It was out in the bush. He came back and told his men, and those of Kutupu, Deribi, Palaileve, Ororogaivara, Avuiri, and Kalava. At night they went and fetched it and brought it back tied to a pole, to the rock-shelter called Duruai orava. They cooked it there, took it out of the oven, and distributed it and concealed all the traces. A— M— came and said 'Did you kill my pig?' 'No,' they all replied. [They knew that he was only guessing that it was them, as they had left no traces.] So he went away and got nothing. They told him that the Oropo had killed it, but when he went there they denied it.

While there is, therefore, relatively little violence within the hamlet, or between close kin, relationships between members of different hamlets are capable of erupting into violence very easily. They are

TABLE 21. *The incidence of crime within and between tribes*

	Crime	Between tribes	Within tribes	Total

1.	Homicide	15
		
		male/male: 29 cases
		male/female: 5 cases,
		  including 2 killed in
		  accidental grass-fire
		co-wives: 2 cases
			21
			58·3%
				36

2.	Attempted murder	0 male/male: 2 male/female: 1	3	3
3.	Assault	31 male/male: 16 male/female: 10 female/female: 5	87 73·7% male/male: 40 male/female: 40 female/female: 7	118
4.	Fighting and riotous behaviour	21	23 52·3%	44
5.	Indecent assault, rape, attempted rape	4	13 76·5%	17
6.	Threatening and offensive behaviour	12	8 40%	20
7.	Theft	3	4	7
8.	Pig stealing and killing	15	11 42·3%	26
9.	Destruction of property including arson	4	8 66·6%	12

in addition liable to the irritations caused by daily proximity in forest and garden, and by one another's wandering pigs, or wives. One therefore finds that there is a very high degree of violence within the tribe between members of different hamlets. Table 21 shows that violence is often more frequent between members of the same tribe than of different tribes since the tribes are seldom united as wholes against each other, and opportunities for provocation are more frequent within the tribe. Hamlets near the borders of tribes often contain members of each tribe, and thus no special friction exists because of contiguity. (Avevea Doulubu on the boundary of Goilala and Kunima, is a good example of this type of hamlet.)

Homicide naturally has more serious repercussions than any other type of offence, and deserves special notice here. Table 22 shows the

TABLE 22. *The incidence of homicide at Goilala*

During a period of about fifty years—to 1946—there seem to have been forty-eight Goilala residents who were the victims of homicide. The average population during this time would probably have been in the region of 180.

	Intertribal homicide	Intratribal homicide
Males	23	15
Females	6	4
	29 (60%)	19 (40%)

Total for all homicides = 48.
No children were reported killed.

very high level of intratribal homicide at Goilala, confirming the evidence of Table 21. My figures for Goilala are also given general confirmation for the Omu tribe in the Kunimaipa by McArthur. Table 23 gives McArthur's[1] data for the tribe of Omu, in the Kunimaipa area, for a similar period, for a population of about 190.

TABLE 23. *The incidence of homicide in a Kunimaipa tribe*

	Interparish homicide	Intraparish homicide
Male adults	26	4
Female adults	8	4
Male children	4	5
Female children	4	4
	42 (71%)	17 (29%)

Total for all homicides = 59.
The homicide rate per annum: *Goilala* about 1/187.
　　　　　　　　　　　　　　Kunimaipa about 1/162.

[1] McArthur 1961: 321.

Homicide within the tribe naturally produces peculiar problems in the exaction of vengeance. The most striking is the situation in which a member of tribe A kills a member of tribe B. The victim is related to another member of A, who then kills a relation of the murderer, also in A.

A man called K—, of the Oropoa tribe, stole pandanus nuts from A— A—'s trees, and A— A— came and killed K—. He was the kinsman of I— Ko— living at Pomutu. In revenge I— Ko— came and cut off the head of the woman T— with a bush knife. She was the female relative of A— A— and M— L— living at Poroyava.

An example of the way in which homicide may be generated within the tribe follows here:

C.N.M., June 1958.
A fight within a tribe, in which the men A— A— and L— K—, and the boy K— K— are killed.
    B— K—'s evidence. 'On Friday morning I was at Kav— village, and my uncle A— A— who also lives at Kav— was there too. A— A— wanted to kill a pig so that he could obtain a cross from the Mission. [It is very unusual to kill a pig as casually as this for money.] He asked his wife Ki— to round up a pig but she refused to do so. [She probably resented a pig being killed for such a trivial purpose.] A— A— was cross and he took some money and went down to a woman [also] named Ki— and asked her for sexual intercourse. Ki— called out to her husband I— "Come quickly, A— A— wants sexual intercourse with me, make him give us a pig for payment." [i.e. for the insult.] I— called back "It is only talk, he has done nothing, so let it go." A— A— then returned to his house, and after an argument with his wife he struck her [on the back of the neck] with the side of his axe. [She fell down unconscious.] Shortly afterwards, Councillors L— K—, S—, A—, and K— ran past my house towards A— A—'s house. [Clearly to go to the aid of A—A—'s wife Ki—.] All were carrying axes. Shortly after I heard A— A— call out "They have killed me". [They had. He had been axed in the chest by L— K— the Councillor.] I went inside and got my bow and knife-blade arrow and ran up towards A— A—'s house. There I saw A— A— lying on the ground, he was lying on his back, and his feet were kicking wildly. Around him were L— K—, S—, A—, and K—. L— K— saw me and came towards me; as he stepped over the fence I shot him with my knife-bladed arrow in the stomach. L— K— stumbled forward and hit me with his axe on the arm. I ran on . . . later I heard that my brother [not necessarily his true brother] K— K— had also been killed.'
    K— and S— were from Ka—, and A— from L—.

5. MARRIAGE

It will now be clear that while corporate groups do exist in Tauade society their membership is based on a multiplicity of criteria and subject to considerable mobility, and that the most important co-operating groups are small numbers of close relatives, usually agnates, but also affines and cognates within the context of the hamlet.

Marriage will first be examined against this atomistic background to show the nature of the social ties which it generates. Marriage in primitive societies also produces basic problems for men in their control of women, and the second part of this section will deal with this, and with relations in general between the sexes.

(a) Social ties

Men marry to have someone to keep their pigs and to work in their gardens, and, of course, for sexual gratification. But the desire to have large numbers of children seems absent, and some men with several children give one or two of them away to friends and relatives for adoption, or even sell them—Keru Katemu had given away two of his children, one to Amo Lume, for example. A striking number of couples are sterile, and it seems that in some cases this is the result of an overdose of a herbal abortifacient, a species of vine eaten with cinnamon and ginger. McArthur says that the Kunimaipa practised abortion so that sexual relations would not be interrupted, and this seems a very plausible explanation for the Tauade as well, though I did not have her ease of access to female informants on this point.

A man's relations with his wife's relatives are of great importance, and it is customary for the couple to go and live even for several years with her relatives, who are pleased to be reinforced by another man for work in the gardens, warfare, and killing pigs. The land of a man's wife or mother is a valued place of refuge when he needs to escape from his own tribe after a dispute or violence; it is clearly for these reasons that so few marriages take place within the tribe.

I collected the details of 204 Goilala marriages, and of these only 19 per cent were contracted within Goilala, while 81 per cent were between Goilala and other tribes. (Marriage data were collected from the three main living generations, thus minimizing the effects of modern conditions, if any, on the marriage pattern.) Of these other tribes those which were the most frequently involved in marriage alliances are listed in Table 24. The marriages are broken down in

TABLE 24. *Marriage alliances between Goilala and other tribes*

Tawuni	26	12·75%
Watagoipa	22	10·8%
Kerau	18	8·8%
Kataipa	16	7·8%
Maini	14	6·8%
Amuganiawa	14	6·8%
Kunima	10	4·9%

TABLE 25. *Number of marriages of Goilala clans with other tribes*

CLANS	KARUAI	KOVETE	LARIMA	DERIBA	DARO	TUPI	KERAU	KUNIMA	GARIPA	GANE	TAWUNI	WATAGOIPA	OROPOA	MAINI	LAITATE	KAROM	AMIAPA	AMUGANIAWA	KATAIPA	ILAI	MINARU	LOVA	AIBALA	WOITAPE	ELAVA	SENE	SOPU
KARUAI	▨	2	5	2	1	0	5	3	2	4	9	1	1	5	4	0	1	0	5	0	0	1	0	0	0	1	1
KOVETE	2	▨	1	5	3	1	3	0	1	0	4	3	1	3	0	1	0	6	0	0	0	0	0	1	0	0	0
LARIMA	5	1	▨	3	4	1	5	3	2	0	3	8	2	2	1	2	0	6	4	3	0	0	1	0	0	0	0
DERIBALAVAVAI	2	5	3	▨	5	0	5	3	0	1	6	2	2	3	3	0	0	0	5	1	1	0	2	0	1	0	0
DAROLAVAVAI	1	3	4	5	▨	0	0	1	0	0	2	8	1	1	0	0	0	2	2	0	0	0	0	0	0	1	0
TUPI	0	1	1	0	0	▨	0	0	0	0	2	0	0	0	0	0	0	0	0	0	0	0	0	0	0	0	1
							18	10	5	5	26	22	7	14	8	3	1	14	16	4	1	1	3	1	1	2	1

Table 25 to show those made by the members of each clan, both within Goilala and with other tribes. It will be seen that in some cases marriages are contracted within the clans.

If one examines the number of marriages contracted by members of different clans with the surrounding tribes, it appears at first sight as if there are some important clusters of marriage ties between certain clans and specific tribes, as Table 26 indicates. But the impression of special relationships between particular clans and particular tribes given by these figures is illusory. In reality, one finds that

TABLE 26. *Marriage links between clans and tribes*

Clan	Number of marriages	Tribe
Karuai	9	Tawuni
,,	5	Kerau
,,	5	Maini
,,	5	Kataipa
Kovete	6	Amuganiawa
Larima	8	Watagoipa
,,	6	Amuganiawa
Deribalavavai	6	Tawuni
,,	5	Kerau
,,	5	Kataipa
Darolavavai	8	Watagoipa

a group of closely related males, often brothers, in one generation may all marry into the same tribe; the clan as a whole, however, displays no such tendency, and the spread of clan marriages is much more haphazard. Again, while a particular line of males may perpetuate marital links with a single tribe over two or three generations, these marriages are few in comparison with the total number of marriages contracted by this group. The genealogy selected from the Karuai clan illustrates these points clearly (Fig. 13).

Just as links between groups of agnates and any particular tribe are not usually maintained over successive generations, or are not even numerous within any one generation of agnates, so we do not usually find that hamlets have any statistically significant number of marriages with other tribes. The most that can be said is that in a few cases people with marriage ties with certain tribes may live in hamlets closest to those tribes, e.g. Deribi with three marriages with Watagoipa and Garipa, and Dimanibi with ten marriages with

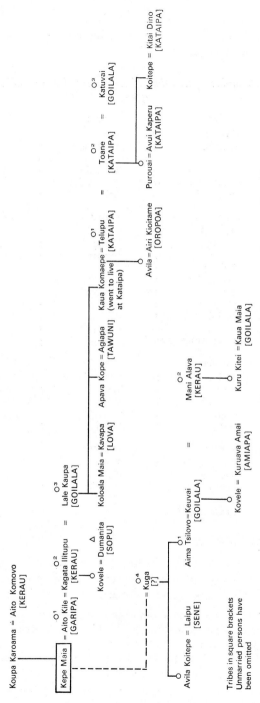

FIG. 13. Pattern of marriages between a group of agnates and surrounding tribes

Tawuni. Table 27 gives some data on the number of marriages in each hamlet with surrounding tribes.

TABLE 27. *Number of marriages between hamlets and neighbouring tribes*

DERIBI		MOIGILI	
Watagoipa	2	Karom	1
Garipa	1	Watagoipa	1
		Kataipa	1
+		Tawuni	1
1 man and wife from		Amuganiawa	1
Watagoipa		Laitate	1
DIMANIBI		PATIMA	
Tawuni	10	Tawuni	3
Kataipa	3	Kerau	2
Kerau	2	Iveyava	1
Laitate	1		
Watagoipa	1		
Elava	1	ITOVEVE	
Oropoa	1	Oropoa	1
Maini	1	Ilai	1
+		Karom	1
1 man from Tawuni		Kunima	1
PALAILEVE			
Maini	2	KILAKILA	
Kerau	2	Tawuni	1
Tawuni	1	Kerau	1
Gane	1	Lova	1
Garipa	1	Maini	1
KIOLILAMA		KALAVA	
Kataipa	3	Amuganiawa	2
Kunima	1	Watagoipa	1
Kerau	1	Tawuni	1
+			
1 man from Oropoa			

(b) The control of women

Marriages, especially between the children of chiefs, were traditionally arranged by the fathers concerned. Casimiro gave me the following description of traditional marriage negotiations:

The father of a boy saw a girl whom he thought would make a good wife for his son. So he would go to the house of the girl's father and say 'Will your daughter one day come to my house and fetch water and give it to me?' This is the form of the question. Later the girl grows bigger, and the boy's father gives presents to the girl's father, and her parents tell her that she will go to that man's house and give him water. They don't tell her that she will be his wife.

The girl knows to whom she will be married, for the other girls talk with her, and tell her that she will be so-and-so's son's wife. If the boy is a bad fellow, the girl says 'Why have my parents given me to that person?' and she is angry. When her father tells her to go to her future husband's place, she does not say anything, but she thinks 'I won't go.' Then she tells her father that the boy is a bad fellow, and he tries to persuade her; if she likes him she will go to his place and marry him, but if she does not like him she may go somewhere else and marry a man she likes.

If she goes to the man whom her parents have chosen, she takes dogs' teeth, feathers, and other riches with her, and when she arrives, the boy's parents kill pigs, and also give a large pig alive to the parents, as repayment for the riches. Long strings of dogs' teeth were also given. The present amount of bridewealth is about A$40. If the marriage does not take place, the boy's parents often demand the return of the riches, initially given as a bond, but not always. In the same way, not all husbands demand the return of bridewealth if their wives run away.

Sometimes the parents of the boy are willing for the marriage to take place, but other relatives such as the mother's brother oppose it. As a compromise they arrange for a pretended abduction to take place, as a result of which bridewealth is paid in the form of compensation for the 'outrage'. In the old days it was forbidden for the children of chiefs and *malavi* to marry. Amo Lume elaborates as follows:

This custom did not apply to the daughters of chiefs; they always gave their daughters, and it was only the *malavi* who stole them. The chiefs would exchange gifts in the infancy of the couple, and this would conclude the arrangement. When the boy and girl had grown up they would marry. The bridewealth of a chief's daughter was 5 pigs, and large quantities of riches, etc. That for a *malavi* would only be 1 pig. The parents of the *malavi* girl would go to the husband's village to get their marriage payment when their tempers had cooled sufficiently after the abduction. In some cases they refused to accept compensation, and took their daughter back again.

Even in the case of the chief's children, the girl went in the night to her husband's village, and slept with her husband there. The next day her parents found her gone, and other people told them that she had gone to her husband in the night. They followed her tracks, and asked those they met if they had seen their daughter. When they came to where she was, her husband paid compensation for her.

Men try to arrange marriages for daughters or sisters for two main ends. The first is to create an alliance with some other esteemed man, and the second is to obtain the sister of the man in question as payment for the woman whom one provides oneself. While the actual incidence of sister exchange is low—since most men do not have suitable sisters for the exchange—it is nevertheless a highly esteemed form of marriage. The attempts of men to arrange marriages for their women folk, and to supervise their sons' and brothers' wives, often leads to violence. Some examples of violence engendered in this way are given below.

An instance of this excitability was very aptly illustrated to the writer while at the Kataipa rest house. A girl was talking to another man who was not her husband. Her husband's father, on seeing this, was under the impression that she was flirting with the man, and as such he did not like it. He rushed into a house and brought out an axe, and was intercepted by the police only just in time. (R. Hill, P.O., Patrol 3/58–9, Tapini.)

Mr. Ridgeway, P.O., told me that while he had been in the Ivane, a man had been trying to get his sister to marry another man so that he could have this man's sister in exchange. His sister was refusing to agree to this, so, in the presence of the Patrol Officer, he seized an axe, and chased her. He made a swing at her head, and, due to the fact that they were both running, missed, though the blade caught her arm, and nearly severed it.

District Court, 25/5/65.
L— I— of S— murdered La— Iv—, also of S—. La— Iv— had been having an adulterous affair with the wife of L—I—'s brother, who was away working in Kokoda. When L— I— had last seen his brother, he had told him about the affair between La— Iv— and his wife. L— I— continues 'My brother said to me "Don't let this upset you too much. When I come back I will fix the thing up." I don't know what my brother intended to do when he came back. I had not thought of killing La— Iv— before [the actual murder]. I had thought that I would wait for my brother to come back from Kokoda and take the matter to court, but my brother did not come back. I did not take the matter to court as my brother is this woman's husband, and it would not have been my place to take this matter to court.'

The event which precipitated the actual murder was the witnessing of sexual intercourse between the couple by L— I—, who had followed them to an isolated garden hut in order to spy on them. 'They had sexual intercourse while I was watching. When they had finished I saw La— Iv— pull up his shorts . . .' L— I— followed La— Iv— through the bush for some hundreds of yards until he reached the graded track. There he made a savage attack upon him with his axe, nearly severing his head from his body.

Only a small percentage of men have more than one wife at any time, as can be seen from Tables 28 and 29.

TABLE 28. *Distribution of wives among adult Goilala males, at one time*

No. of wives	No. of men with	Per cent of men with
0	15	28%
1	32	60%
2	4	8%
3	1	2%
4	1	2%
	53	100%

Number of men who have never married: 3
Number of widowers: 12

TABLE 29. *Distribution of wives among adult Goilala males, serially*

No. of wives	No. of men with	Per cent of men with
0	3	6%
1	21	39%
2	16	30%
3	7	13%
4	3	6%
5	2	4%
6	1	2%
	53	100%

Despite the fact that a percentage of men have more than one wife simultaneously, Table 30 shows that there is a preponderance of men over women at almost all ages in the Sub-District, as in other areas of New Guinea.

Polygamy is in fact possible because these marriages are more unstable than monogamous ones, and there is thus a shifting population of wives who leave one husband and go off with another one. For while women's first marriages are arranged by their fathers or brothers, women are by no means mere pawns in an alliance game:

Superficially the women appear to be regarded as being merely useful for making gardens, looking after pigs, etc. In reporting damage or raids the native almost invariably places pigs first, belongings second, and women last. Actually the women wield a great deal of influence which although invisible is very real. Their partiality for men who have the right to wear the 'paka' [Motu = 'homicide emblem'] is probably the indirect cause of many murders in the past or present.

Women are by no means slaves and have no hesitation in leaving their husbands if ill-treated or dissatisfied.[1] (Annual Report of the Goilala Sub-District 1946/7; reply to Questionnaire TA/62/1.)

TABLE 30. *Sex ratios*

		Children	Adults	Total	Per cent
(a)	McArthur[2]				
	Male	26	72	98	53
	Female	26	62	88	47
		52	134	186	
(b)	Egerton[2]				
	Male	263	484	747	53
	Female	231	420	651	47
		494	904	1398	

A woman leaves her husband in almost every case either from resentment because he has taken another wife, or because the stronger wife has driven her away. (The only customary exception is that of old women who return to their birth place by amicable arrangement with their husbands to die there.) It is for this reason that it is difficult for a man to retain several wives, and we therefore find that the divorce rate is very much higher in polygynous households. The divorce rate for monogamous couples is 4·8 per cent and for polygamous couples 39 per cent, as Table 31 shows:

[1] 'In case of quarrels between husband and wife, their relatives try to make peace. The woman's relatives will kill a pig and give the meat to her husband's relatives if the woman is in the wrong, and the husband's relatives will kill a pig if he is in the wrong and beats her without cause', in the words of one of my informants.

[2] The sources for the calculation of sex ratios are Dr. McArthur's Kunimaipa data as given in her thesis, and Dr. W. S. Egerton (1954) apparently compiled in the area around Tapini. My own data on sex ratios (see Appendix II) is quite consistent with that of Egerton and McArthur. McArthur defines 'children' as those from 0–14, 'adults' as those from 15 upwards, while Egerton uses the ranges 0–15, 16+, and this produces a little discrepancy between their results.

TABLE 31. *Divorce rate in relation to number of wives*

	1 wife	2(+) wives
Marriages	454 (84%)	85 (16%)
Divorces	22	33
	4·8%	39%

(Data taken from sample of 12 tribes in the Census records)

Relations between co-wives are therefore conventionally hostile, sometimes leading to murder, either of one wife by another, or by the enraged husband driven to intervene in the women's quarrels. Table 32 shows the frequency with which all marriages have ended in divorce at Goilala.

TABLE 32. *Frequency of divorce*

	Number of wives	Per cent of total
With husband now	47	46%
Divorced/ran away	26	25½%
Died/murdered	29	28½%
	102	100%

The following cases are good illustrations of quarrels between wives.

C.N.M., April 1954.
At M—, the woman K— was angry with her husband Mo— because he was keeping more company with his other wife O—. K— said to O— 'Let us go and get sweet potato for the pigs.' O— refused and said 'You come and eat pigs' faeces and my husband's semen.' K— hit O— on the head with a stick, and O— hit her back with a knife on the head.

C.N.M., August 1965.
Two co-wives from M— were living at K— near Tapini. They had a quarrel, in which one was killed. The wife responsible says 'we quarrelled over our husband's pouch, and in the course of the quarrel she said to me "Come and eat the pouch's faeces." This is a great insult and caused me shame. We parted and I went into T—'s house and she to K—'s. Whilst I was in the house I was most upset and was thinking about what she had said to me so that I had pain inside and my thinking was not clear. I saw her walk out of the house and I went out taking my axe with me. I did not intend

to kill her but just to cut her with the axe to punish [her] for saying these bad and very insulting words to me. In the Goilala [Sub-District] this is a most shameful and degrading expression for one woman to use to another.' She then struck the other woman on the head, inflicting fatal injuries.

K— K— was at Deribi. His wives O— L— and K— T— were angry with each other. O— L— had a big piece of wood and hit K— T— several times with it, so that she soiled herself. K— K— was angry and came and beat O— L— with another piece of wood. He got O— L— and made her pick up the faeces with her hands and throw them away. Then he hit her hands because they stank. I [Amo Lume, my informant] was a small boy at this time. Then K— K— killed one of O— L—'s pigs and one of K— T—'s. He invited all the Goilala and made an oven and cooked the pigs. He cut a piece of bamboo, and both the women had to say into the opening 'We will not fight with each other again.' Then he took a stopper and blocked up the hole, and said 'I stop up your words. I will not speak again. If you quarrel again I will take out the stopper and kill you.' He dug a hole and put the bamboo in it. Then he put *elaivi* on top of it.

Aima Kamo's wives Ke— Kit— and Ki— Ke— came and were angry with his third wife M— and hit her. M— got up and hit Ki— Ke— and Ke— Kit—. Aima Kamo came and got a big piece of wood and stuck it in the ground and tied all their hands to it. He lit three fires around it, one for each woman, and gave them all a good singeing, and beat them as well. They were running at the eyes, nose and mouth. Aima blew the fires and stuck pandanus leaves in them [they burn very fiercely]. He cut off their g-strings to shame them and burned the strings in the fires. When he was in a better temper he let them go, and put warmed *elaivi* on them to soothe their cuts. He then planted *elaivi* in the ground 'So that there will be no more fighting'.

Emotional reaction to adultery varies from man to man and also depends on the type of offence and the circumstances of its discovery; but since every man is willing to take advantage of sexual opportunities with other men's wives, compensation is often offered and accepted to settle matters in a realistic spirit.

Yet it is common for an adulterer to be hit by a husband who catches him in the act, and if the injuries are not serious it seems that the usual compensation of a pig is expected by the husband. But if a man is speared, or severely injured in some other way, this may prevent compensation. This is one of many areas of Tauade life when men's actions cannot be accurately predicted.

B— K— of Ororogaivara came to Pomutu when M— A— was here and seduced A— his wife. M— A— was in the men's house down below and came and saw what was happening. He got his axe from the men's house and hit B— K— with it. M— A— told the men of Pomutu, Moigili, Palaileve, Deribi, Tsigori. All went to Ororogaivara and got a big pig from B— K— [never a small one in such cases] and brought it here [to Pomutu] and cooked it. M— also beat up his wife.

K— T— of Palaileve hamlet seduced A— K—'s wife K— K— at Kutupu, and took her to Tawuni where his *valavala* were. A— K— searched for her, and then killed two of K—T—'s pigs when he heard what had happened. A— K—'s *valavala* ate them. K— T— heard of this and came back, leaving K— K— at Tawuni. A— K— took a spear and stuck it through K— T—'s legs. A— A— came and chased A— K— to Kutupu and then into the bush. [K— T— is A— A—'s father's brother.] A— A— then came back and took out the spear which was sticking in K— T—, and he recovered. A— K— called K— K— back to Goilala. There was no compensation because K— T— had been speared.

K— M— of Palaileve seduced E— K—'s wife K— Ko— at Poroyava. It was at night, and he crept under the floor with a piece of *kerapata* cane and poked her to wake her up. She asked who it was and when he said 'K— M—' she opened the door and let him in. He copulated with her. E— K— was in Moresby. He saw what happened in a dream. When he came back he said to K— Ko— 'Who came at night and poked you with a stick, and stuffed you?' 'It was K— M—' she said. 'Ah', he said, 'I saw this in a dream.' So he demanded a pig from K— M—.

While the number of cases is too small to be statistically reliable. Table 33 supports the hypothesis that, with the exception of two instances of brothers' wives, the wives of close kin are not commonly seduced, that cousin's wives are more frequently seduced, and that

TABLE 33. *Types of relationship between husbands and adulterers*

Agnatic	Cognatic	Affinal
BW ($\times$2)	FZSW	WBW ($\times$3)
FBSW	MBSW ($\times$2)	ZHW
FFBSSW ($\times$2)		DHW
FFFSSW	3	SWM ($\times$3)
	___	SWFW
6	15%	ZHBSW
___		BWFZSW
30%		
		11
		___
		55%

All these terms are in relation to the *adulterer*.

the commonest category of kin for seduction are affines' wives. Normally, however, there is no relationship at all between the seducer and the cuckold. It is also noteworthy that there are no cases recorded where the seducer is related in any way to the woman.

Women therefore have considerable freedom, not only to reject their father's or brother's choice of husband, but to desert him later, and to drive away any other wives he may acquire, if they are strong enough. Dances were always followed by a rash of desertions by wives who left their husbands to cohabit with guests whose dancing had attracted them, and Fastré records one dance which led to twenty-five killings in this way. Even today dances often have similar consequences, though on a smaller scale.

The men, for their part, are constantly trying to control their women, to make them marry the men with whom they wish to become allied, and to keep their own wives, or kinsmens' wives, from being seduced. At the same time they are themselves always looking for the chance to seduce other men's wives. But while there are many instances of violence in the court records by men upon women (see p. 119) there is no organized or ceremonial hostility between the sexes and, indeed, it was very difficult to obtain any clear statement of how men saw women as a category; the Tauade are not given to making that kind of abstract statement, but prefer to talk in terms of particular cases. But women are certainly seen as having very positive sexual appetites; in cases of adultery, especially where the woman comes from a different tribe from the man charged with seducing her, he will plead in court that she forced herself upon him. The following story is quite a graphic illustration of the way in which women's sexuality is seen as destructive of the man:

There were two *agopalai* [culture heroes] in the olden times [at Kataipa], a man and a woman. The man was called Panai Kavegai, and the woman was called Olala. They were young and married, and copulated and begot children. Then they eventually became old, like Aima Kamo. They stayed at home, and did not go to their gardens, or along the paths. Their children went out and got food and wood for them. Kavegai was in his men's house. Olala was in her house. Olala called to him to come to her. He came to her house and stood in the entrance, and she told him to come in. She said 'Our children have gone to fetch wood and potatoes, so let us copulate.' Kavegai tried to mount her, but his penis was dead and he could not get an erection. Olala got up and straddled him like a man, and she wore out Kavegai so that he died.

Their children brought the potatoes and fire wood, and found that

Kavegai was no longer in his men's house. They called out for him. They asked Olala 'Where has Kavegai gone?' She said 'He came here to get his sweet potato, and copulated with me like we used to do—we were both like youngsters.' She was lying, because she grabbed him first. The children came and saw his body and said 'Why is he lying dead?' She replied, 'He came here and copulated with me, and died. It was your father's fault.'

So they took him out and put him in his men's house. His relatives then came to the funeral and mourned, and killed pigs and made speeches—'Our father, our grandfather, is dead. He copulated with his wife and died', the children said. 'Now we will no longer be *valavala*; we will take each other in marriage and copulate, and when our children are born they will inherit in our place.'

The pride and ambition of the men, for whom women are necessary for social success, and the freedom of the women to desert or humiliate them by impugning their manhood or copulating with other men, frequently conflict, and violence erupts. But although Tauade women, like their pigs, are the cause of much violence, the Tauade do not see them as dangerous to the social order. On the contrary, they are sometimes depicted in the legends as the preservers of culture and social life, as opposed to the destructive force of the men.

6. CONCLUSIONS

Upon closer examination it will have become clear that the atomism of Tauade society needs to be qualified by the reservation that there are also important focuses of co-operation—close relatives, hamlets, and chiefs. It would be impossible for any society, however anarchical, to sustain the war of all against all, and what actually occurs here is the war of some against the rest. The causes of this are (1) that aggression against other members of the society requires the security of support by close relatives and hamlet members, (2) that injury to any member of this group of supporters will be grounds for vengeance, thus broadening the occasions for violence, and (3) that these groups are impermanent, and of small size, making co-ordination and control in the absence of any superordinate authority or wider solidarity very difficult to achieve. It will also be seen that the powers of the chiefs enabling them to co-ordinate ceremonies and warfare, and negotiate peace, also give them the opportunity for despotic behaviour.

It is therefore precisely because there are concentrations of power and co-operation within every tribe that violence is facilitated, in the context of a general ethos of vengeance and power-orientation.

A society which was absolutely atomistic in the sense that there was no co-ordination between individuals would not only be impossible but would have no potential for large-scale violence.

Nevertheless, while Tauade society contains these nuclei of co-operation, group coherence and permanence, and hence control of members, have been thoroughly fragmented by gift exchange, as we shall see in the next chapter, especially in the section dealing with ceremonies. As a result, cross-cutting ties become channels of vengeance, on the one hand, and means by which aggressors may escape from awkward situations, on the other.

Gluckman, who was Dr. McArthur's examiner for her thesis on the Kunimaipa, predictably draws very different conclusions on the social implications of pig feasts and prestations from those advanced here. He refers to the Kunimaipa taboo on eating pork from pigs raised by oneself or any of one's close agnates or those of one's spouse, and continues:

A consequence of this taboo is that you have to pass on your own and relatives' pigs to someone else to eat, while you get a pig from him: and out of this compelled exchange there has developed a widely extended and ramifying set of exchanges which spread over the whole land. Indirectly men and groups of men far apart are involved in this system: directly it involves only neighbouring groups. (Gluckman 1965: 61.)

After referring to the interests of 'big men' in maintaining peace, since their prestige within their own groups depends on their relations with pig-exchange partners, that are disrupted by warfare, Gluckman concludes:

. . . we start here with what seems, as I have already said, to be a rather silly, indeed childish superstition [the taboo on eating one's own, and close relatives', pork] and we end with a widespread system of international trade which contributes to an international peace, in which leaders of each group have the greatest interest, in order that they be able to maintain their own positions among a very irascible and quarrelsome set of people. (Op. cit., p. 62.)

This interpretation of Kunimaipa and, since they are in relevant respects very similar, Tauade pork exchange is based on the fallacious assumption that there is something incompatible between exchanges of pork and endemic warfare, but actually founders on the fact that it is precisely this 'widely extended and ramifying set of exchanges' that provides the social channels which facilitate violence and make effective corporate groups impossible.

IV

Co-ordination and Control

IN Tauade society, with little in the way of corporate restraints beyond the hamlet and no awareness of a general social order, personal force and energy must prevail and social processes come to be directed at every turn by relatively few men of sufficiently masterful character. Indeed, the impulses that encourage conflict also produce the occasions and means of co-operation for the Tauade are a people with a great desire to dominate and preen both as groups and as individuals, and domination is only possible when people are prepared to co-operate to that end. Being collectively ambitious for renown, the Tauade therefore need co-ordination to make their great feasts and dances a social success, and since they are not prepared to fight one another to mutual extinction they need some rough precepts and forms of conciliation for composing their feuds, however grudging and transitory the peace may be.

In this chapter we will therefore examine how the chiefs co-ordinate and control the tribes; the significance of ceremonies in the affirmation of ties; and the means of composing disputes. It will become clear, however, that the chiefs' power is frequently despotic and resented; that ceremonies are pervaded with hostility; and that violence is frequently preferred to the payment of compensation.

Before considering the status of chiefs, however, it is worth noting that age has no claim to respect among the Tauade; they respect the social skills of some old men, especially in such matters as oratory or knowledge of legends, but there is no general sentiment of deference towards older men as such. Indeed, the process of ageing itself is the object of shame and ridicule, and to avoid overt insult men publicly admit to the onset of old age on ceremonial occasions; they traditionally bound their heads in bark cloth and today wear hats to escape the humiliation of being called 'bald heads'. The Tauade are more impressed by the decrepitude and failing powers of age than by its accumulated wisdom.

Nor is there any clear conceptualization of the distinction between the generations. People address one another not by such terms as 'Uncle' or 'Father' but by personal names, and when I asked if a father would be offended if his son addressed him by name, they were much amused—'Why should he be angry? He would hold out his arms to embrace his son and say, "My boy!".' While the elderly have no group status and cannot command obedience, they continue to be loved by their children and grandchildren. Old people are treated kindly, and their families see that they are supplied with food and firewood. But while some older chiefs may retain much of their influence, they have their influence not because they are elderly but because they are chiefs, and there is therefore no place in Tauade society for decision-making by any group of 'elders'.

I. THE STATUS OF THE CHIEFS

In every tribe there is a small number of men who dominate their fellows. They usually have two or more wives, organize dances, negotiate peace and alliances with other tribes, make speeches on public occasions, are conventionally dignified and generous, 'protect the land', as we have seen, are able to move between tribes without fear of assault, are prominent in warfare, and can kill their low-status enemies without fear of reprisal; their death is marked with special ceremonial, including the exposure of their bodies on platforms (unlike the common folk whose bodies are buried). Yet such men are accorded differing degrees of prestige according to a multiplicity of criteria; here, as in every other aspect of Tauade culture, distinctions are not marked by clear boundaries.

An example of a chief of high status is provided by Ketawa of Lova-Loleava, who led the raids on the Giumu in 1917 that resulted in the police action by Patrol Officer Wilson.

Ketawa had a daughter called Notara, and he had originally given her in marriage to a man of Giumu called Rumania. This was when Ketawa was living in the Giumu himself at the hamlet of Nuvia. Gopi of Nonoawu continues (speaking in 1918):

The Giumu people called the Goilala[1] to dance at Giumu. A man K— had a daughter named N— who was married to R—. L—, a Veile man, wanted N— as his wife [the implication being that he saw her at the dance, as is often the case] and N— wanted L—. K— gave N— to L—. R— was angry

[1] The 'Big Goilala', i.e. Sopu, Lova, etc.

with K— and said 'Why do you take my wife N— from me? I have paid a pig to you for her and she is my wife.' K— gave N— to L— and went with the Goilala to Veile. L— took N— to Veile. After the man K— went to Goilala, he told the Veile people to go down to Giumu and kill the people there. K— was angry with the Giumu. K— was wild because R— spoke bad to him because he had taken N— from him and given her to L—. K— called the people of Gomena, Apuawa, Pe-u, Periari, Uniari, Noravu, Veile, Iani-e, Nonoawu, Taupeti, Sopu, Nomagai, Guveviawu and some small villages to Veile.

K— told the people to go and kill all the Giumu people and they heard his talk and went down and killed O— [a woman] and Gi— [a man]. A— G— and Aw— killed the woman and T— killed the man. K— went with the Goilala to Giumu but he did not kill anybody. I went down to Giumu and broke up the gardens; E— went down and helped to smash the gardens and kill the pigs. I did not see the murders done, but was told by the men who did them when they came back from killing them. We burnt the Giumu people's houses and slept in the gardens one night, when we returned to Veile. G—, a brother of K—, killed a pig and gave it to the men who had been to fight the Giumu, and we all made a dance, afterwards going back to our villages. [Grist, Storry, and Wilson (Ioma, 19/1/18–6/8/18) reported that when they had arrived at Giumu the villages of Nuvia and Udulu had disappeared, and were reported to have been raided and burned by the Big Goilala. O— and Gi— were axed and their bodies mutilated.]

After the government retreated (P.O. Wilson's abortive patrol at the end of 1917) the Big Goilala returned to the Giumu, enraged that they had informed the government about the first raid. Gopi continues: 'We saw the government go away from Veile, and watched them for two days. After the government went away, we all went down to Giumu to kill some more of the people, but did not see them, so we tore up their gardens and went back to Goilala.'

People may differ about the status of particular chiefs, and the criteria by which they evaluate status are themselves complex. In such a situation it is very easy for the outsider, whether he be patrol officer, missionary, or anthropologist, to impose upon the fluidities of native life a model of his own, since the ambiguity of the facts may allow two or more contradictory models each to claim support from certain aspects of Tauade society.

The two models of social status which claim our attention are first, the 'chief' model, and second, the 'big-man' model. According to the first, status is well defined and strictly hereditary, usually by primogeniture, and considerable power may be vested in the office's holder.

According to the second model, which currently pervades New Guinea ethnography, status is not inherited, but is achieved by each man according to his display of various talents and characteristics. As de Lepervanche expresses it, 'Leaders are emergent. A big-man reaches his position through his own initiative and in competition with his peers, and during his lifetime he may achieve prominence as a warrior or garden magician or ritual leader, or he may become successful in economic exchanges with others.' (de Lepervanche 1973: 3.)

The first patrol officers believed that there were hereditary chiefs of varying grades, some being chiefs of particular hamlets, others of whole tribes. (It should be noted, however, that Mr. S. G. Middleton, the first patrol officer who spent much time in the area, was familiar with Fr. Fastré's views on the hereditary status of chiefs among the Fuyughe—see Papuan Annual Report 1932–33, p. 20.) The office of village constable was given to men who were considered capable of exercising some control over their people. Middleton wrote:

The clothes [of the village constable] are eagerly sought by all, but are not given out haphazard. To qualify for the honour of wearing the uniform, for to them it is an honour, the Chiefs are told that they must make an effort to bury the hatchet as regards inter-tribal enmities. And to show by constant demonstration their willingness to assist the government in all matters . . . In most cases the man recommended for appointment is selected by the people themselves and is usually a chief, but seldom the principal chief of the tribe. (Goilala Police Camp Annual Report, year ending June 1936, pp. 1–2.)

While for reasons of administrative convenience government officers are inclined to look for 'chiefs' in native societies, it seems clear from Middleton's patrol report that the people themselves put forward candidates for the position of village constable, and that Middleton was well aware of indigenous gradations of rank, since there was no reluctance on the part of the people to identify their chiefs. Mr. Middleton, on the first visit of any government officer to Goilala in 1932, named the chief of Poroyava village as Aima Kamo, which he was, and learnt that the chief of the whole tribe was (Kepe) Maia, to whom in consequence he gave a red *rami* (a kind of cummerbund) and belt, as a sign that he was now Village Constable. It was the unanimous opinion of all my informants that Kepe Maia was indeed chief of all the Goilala. They also confirmed that the village constables of other tribes appointed at this time were chiefs, often principal chiefs. As Table 34 shows, at Goilala village constables were always men of standing, usually major chiefs.

P. Briggs, P.O., conducted the Local Government Council election at Goilala in 1966 (Tapini, 29/4/66–6/5/66). According to his patrol report, the results were as follows

Amo Tume [Lume]   o
Keru Awi [Avui Maia]   56

This shows very clearly the social influence of the chiefs, since Avui Maia is one of the most important chiefs at Goilala. The unanimity of the result is particularly striking.

TABLE 34. *Social Status and government rank*

Village constables	Village councillors ('Two Shilling Councillors')
1. Kepe Maia**	1. Lariava Apava*
2. Mana Kimani**	2. Tuna Tauru
3. Maia Koupa^a	3. Amo Lume
4. Keru Manuvu**	4. Avui Apava**
5. Peeri Aima**	
6. Bulvu Kimani**	
7. Kire Keruvu*	

Local government councillors	Committee members
1. Avui Maia**	1. Amo Lume
2. Francis Koupa*	

Numbers beside each name indicate the order in which the person was appointed.

* Minor chief.
** Major chief.

 [a] I could not identify this man, because his name is not on my files; he is clearly listed under some other name.

Nevertheless, supporters of the view that the Tauade have no hereditary chiefs might argue that all the evidence quoted so far from patrol reports is quite consistent with an interpretation of Tauade 'chiefs' as really 'big-men'. Anthropologists of this persuasion would say that both the government officers and the Fathers were imposing preconceived models on the data, models derived in the patrol officers' case from stereotypes about chiefs in primitive society, and in that of the Fathers from their experience of the culture of the Mekeo and Roro, among whom hereditary chiefs would be conceded to exist.

It seems to me, however, that anthropologists have tended to assume too readily that inheritance plays no part in the status of big-men, whereas a closer scrutiny of their genealogies would probably show in many cases that their fathers, uncles, or grandfathers were also of high status in a larger number of instances than indicated by probability alone. Strathern, for example, shows that among the Hageners major big-men have a 3:1 chance of being the sons of big-men, and that 'for a current big-man whose father was a big-man the chances are > 2:1 that there are or have been other big-men in his small lineage . . . Twelve out of eighteen major big-men among those for whom I have details are said to be descended from fathers and fathers' fathers who were big-men.' (Strathern 1971: 210.) But it is also clear from Strathern's account that the status of big-men at Hagen is far more closely related to wealth and participation in the exchange system—the Rope of Moka—than is the case with the Tauade chiefs.

The Tauade say of a chief that he has 'taken the place of' his father, or father's brother, or grandfather, but it is important to distinguish between the concept of juridical inheritance, proper to a society which has clear notions of lineality and succession to specific office, and the 'inheritance' which the Tauade have in mind when they speak of a chief 'taking the place of' one of his forebears. Lineality as such has no interest for the Tauade. What does concern them is the fact that men exercise power; that some men have stronger personalities and greater capacity to make effective decisions and manipulate their fellows than other men; and that the sons of such men, often the eldest sons, often exhibit these capacities as well. Moreover, as we shall see in the chapter on cosmology, their belief system is based on the idea of the creative 'force' which persists in all species of living things, including man, and which manifests itself in generation after generation. For them, in each clan men arise in every generation who display this undying power which is often transmitted to the sons or near relatives of its possessors. It is this set of observations and beliefs which is the basis of their 'hereditary' model of chiefship.

Neither the 'chief' model, nor that of the 'big-man' can therefore be applied in the strict sense to the Tauade, but I have chosen to call their eminent men 'chiefs' because the hereditary model is such a significant aspect of their status, and because social processes facilitate the acquisition of power by the sons of men who have themselves exercised power. And it is the belief in the transmissibility of 'power' from generation to generation that makes its exercise the more acceptable to the people.

I suggest, therefore, that the simplistic dichotomy between 'ascribed' and 'achieved' status, which seems to underlie the 'big-man' model in current New Guinea ethnography, does not do justice to social reality, either in New Guinea or elsewhere. The popular English conception of a 'gentleman', for example, has some resemblance to that of the Tauade '*ami*'—the gentleman is supposed to display certain personal characteristics, e.g. honesty and good manners, but the capacity to display these characteristics is, or was, also attributed to his 'breeding', a complex notion combining both social and biological inheritance.

The status of the chiefs can only be properly appreciated when their attributes are seen in contrast with those of the rubbish-men, or *malavi*. The two commonest words to designate status are *ami* (or *amiteve*) which I translate as 'chief', and *malavi* (or *malaviteve*) which corresponds to the familiar New Guinea term 'rubbish-man'. The suffix *-teve* simply means 'the one which/who', and can be used of persons or things in conjunction with an adjective, e.g. *koriteve*, 'the bad one'. The word *ami* means 'big', but is seldom in my experience used of anything except social status. The usual word for physical bigness is *karo*, and for unusual physical bigness, *touma*, or occasionally *maro*. An adjective can be given substantival form by the addition of the suffix *-atsi*; thus *amiatsi* could be translated as 'bigness, chiefship, power'.

The word *malavi* is of uncertain etymology, but there is no reason to think that it has been borrowed, as some important words in current usage have been. As in the case of *ami*, it has a number of connotations which overlap in a complex manner. In the dictionary compiled by some of the first Fathers at Kerau its meanings are given as 'orphan; poor creature; abandoned'; and *iva malavipe* is given as 'widow'. The general sense of the word is clear, being that of poverty and dependence, a lack of capacity to control others or defend oneself. The people with whom I discussed the status of the *malavi* were agreed on their poverty—an unmarried man, a *kapuriteve*, with only one or two pigs and no house except the shared quarters of the mens' house would qualify as a *malavi*—'the *kapuri* only sleep on sacks, they have no blankets'. It was for this reason, among others, that it was explained to me that only the *malavi* would come and work for me, because only they needed the money.[1] As well as being poor, the

---

[1] The Tauade also regard working for someone, even a white man, as undignified, and thus not befitting the status of a chief.

malavi are conventionally considered mean. They are *komutuma*, people who do not give; their bellies are bitter, *lat'logivai*, as opposed to the people who give generously, the *alituma*, especially those who give to children and old people. The *malavi*, or those who have their nature, are also greedy, and stuff themselves with food and lick the grease from their hands, and when they have something, such as tobacco, which they should share, take it away to smoke in private. Amo Lume, my chief informant, was always very contemptuous of the way in which Moise Apava would never share out the tobacco which I gave him, as he (Amo) did, but used to put it in his pocket and go off with it. A *malavi* will go and hide in the bush and try to avoid making contributions to feasts in the form of pork or food. It is customary among the Tauade to kill a pig when one has suffered an injury, including the loss of a tooth. When Ita Kogotsi, an old widower, killed a pig some time after he had cut his toe severely with an axe, his generosity was favourably contrasted with the meanness of old Moise, who, when he lost a tooth, failed as usual to come up to scratch, and did nothing about it. In the case of meanness we encounter a quality which can be attributed to individual chiefs as well. Apava Aginei, Moise's father, was a chief of middle rank, and it was said of him that he was an *ami malaviteve, alit'ma iniopu* 'he was a rubbish-chief, he did not give generously'.

The characteristics of meanness and greed, which are applied to the *malavi*, have the additional implication that the *malavi* are worse thieves than men of high status, while theft, on the other hand, is held to be beneath the dignity of the chiefs.

There are two other characteristics commonly attributed to *malavi* which at first sight appear to contradict one another. One of these is feebleness, in the colloquial English sense of 'wet'—*kape, tegere, latu*—and the other is aggressiveness, in that it is supposed to be the *malavi* who liked stirring up trouble, while the chiefs traditionally tried to avert it. The conception of the *malavi* as wet, feeble, and useless, is exemplified by Moise Apava and his two brothers Mogu and Kilemu who were thoroughly characterless and lacking in spirit. This is related in Tauade eyes to sexual inadequacy. It was said of one man that he had never married because he had a small penis— 'If the women saw his penis they ran away!' More generally it was said that women liked fierce men and despised the weak ones.

Opposed to this aspect of the *malavi* character is that of pointless aggression. If we treat this type of aggression as comparable to theft or adultery, that is, a form of social irresponsibility that causes trouble, even though enjoyable to the perpetrators, and oppose it to one of the principal functions of the chiefs—that is, the organization of feasts and dances—we can see why some sort of aggression could be characteristic of *malavi*. The success of a dance or feast depends on the ability of the chiefs to prevent outbreaks of violence; if such occur the chiefs suffer a loss of prestige. The *malavi*, on the contrary, have no special commitment to the success of a social gathering and might take malicious pleasure in seeing one spoilt. It is in this sense that I was told that 'If the chiefs were entertaining people the *malavi* would come to kill them, and would be sent away by the chiefs.'

In assessing the status of the chief, we not only have the problem of the same multiplicity of criteria as those which define the *malavi* but the problem of estimating the effects which pacification has had on the powers of the chief. One of the best indications that chiefly status is something *sui generis* among the Tauade is that the cessation of warfare and the institution of the men's house, and the cheapening of the status of ceremonies, has not led to the disappearance of the chiefs. Of course, the chiefs are not now as powerful as they once were, but there is no doubt that their wishes and opinions are still of paramount importance in Tauade life, and that if law and order break down, as they are likely to do in the future, the chiefs will reassert themselves in traditional style. (I am speaking of the most important chiefs here.) The Tauade clearly feel that a virtue inheres—admittedly to a variable degree—in their chiefs, which is not present in ordinary men.

Peacemaking[1] is a vital function of chiefs both in war and for the organization of dances. Peacemaking is seen as a manifestation of power, not as weak and womanly behaviour. The power of the chiefs to negotiate peace was one of their essential qualities, and a tribe which had lost its principal chief had thereby lost a vital asset. It seems likely that there was always only one clan in any tribe that could produce chiefs with the right to speak for the whole tribe— a clan which could claim to be descended from the original 'owners of the ground'.

A successful dance needs peace, and only a chief can organize such an occasion since some of the guests have usually come from many

---

[1] It is interesting that there is no Tauade word for 'peace'; the word in current usage, *maino*, is a Motu loan-word.

miles away, so that the guests have to pass through the territories of many intervening tribes whose consent and co-operation must be gained. The chiefs have also to maintain the peace during the dance itself and co-ordinate the arrangements for the guests. They decide on the location of the dance village and the house sites within it, on the time for killing pigs, and the harvesting of the pandanus nuts if they are to be used as food for guests at a dance.

Casimiro told me that

A chief would visit other tribes to see his relatives, and when he came back he would speak the names of the various paths leading to the lands of the people he was thinking of inviting, and then people would know that he was planning a dance. The chief would think of all the people he wanted to invite, who would be well received and go away speaking his praises. In the same way, the chiefs gave the order for the erection of the bull-roarer enclosure [*polo piluala*] for the initiation of the children [see below pp. 158–62]. The *polo* was very important, it was not a game. If ordinary people carried out this work of the *polo* the chiefs grew angry, and told other people to kill them, so for this reason the chiefs were the bosses of all this work. In your country, not everyone can make money, only the government; so not everyone could give the word for the *polo*, only the chief.

Once the site of the dance village has been chosen, the chiefs decide where the houses will be built. For example, at Patima where the Goilala were about to build a large dance village, Kaua Komaepe (Francis) came over from Kataipa where he was living and spoke, in virtue of being the grandson of Kepe Maia. He said that the Fathers had put a taboo on the cemetery, so they would build no houses there, and then went round the site saying where houses might be built; Lariava Moripi then allocated the positions for each person's house.

Oratory is an integral part of peacemaking and organizing feasts and dances. The Tauade consider it shameful to give away pork without making a speech to recount the history of the events leading up to the occasion, and so the capacity to speak fluently and persuasively in public is one of the marks of a chief.[1] For example, Lariava Moripi was much in demand to make the speeches at Goilala feasts, even on occasions when he seemed to have little personal connection with the events in question. In the traditional society the ability to use the correct allegorical expressions was

---

[1] The literal translation of *Keegi ta*, to make a speech, is 'to boast'.

necessary for the orator, and it was said in my time that none of the young fellows could make speeches like the old men, which had been full of *manari tsinat*, or allegory. Fastré writes as follows of the use of allegory in Fuyughe speeches:

At the time of a dance, a fellow from Amalala had said to Daniel [Fastré's informant] and his adoptive father, Amo Kau, 'You, who make the rain fall, make your KONO stand straight.' (A KONO is a pillar of a men's house, and here has the meaning—*Enlafe*—of 'dancer'). What he meant in ordinary language was 'You others, who boast about making the rain fall, and producing good weather, just try to have a dance, and dancers, like mine.'

It was a gross insult, it seems, and the wound cut deep into their hearts. At the first GABE [dance] in Amo Kau's village, it would be avenged.

Amo Kau charged Daniel to reply on his behalf.

'I would speak badly', said Daniel, excusing himself.

'Go along with you! You're the Father of the Word. I'll tell you everything which you have to say. If they won't listen to you, I'll see to it that they do.'

'So I stood up, and let out a yell to shut everyone up. Everyone shut up. Without naming the chap [the man who had issued the challenge], who was called Sini, I said, "The things of the dance are not exactly unknown; the *Gutas* are not new; the birds of paradise plumes are not unknown. There is only one type of dance, and one dance is like another. So don't talk to me about unusual ones. Mine and yours are alike".'

'When I had finished, everyone wondered what I had meant. Those who were in the know explained my words, and everyone said "It was well done. He got what was coming to him. Now he will have to keep quiet".'

'Sini took himself off, ashamed. Very likely he is busy looking for the retort to make to me on the next occasion. For one prepares something like that a long time in advance, and one makes a Gabe only for the pleasure of being able to insult (*Kopiamai*) someone.'

I thought that Daniel's story (which I have translated almost word for word) had something odd about it, but I did not say anything. He gave me the explanation as soon as I read him the account which I had transcribed.

'When I said to Amo Kau that I would speak badly, I did not mean that I would be ashamed or afraid to speak in public. I was neither ashamed nor afraid. I knew very well what I wanted to say, but I didn't know how to say it. So Amo told me these formulas, and when I knew them by heart, I went to speak them in the dance-yard in front of the dancers and all the guests. For I don't know all these formulas used at dances. It's a special, hidden, language. As for me, I would have said all that straight out so that everyone could understand it without trouble. When the men speak like that [allegorically] I understand it, I find it pleasing, but I can't talk like that myself. And when I don't understand, I ask someone to explain it to me.' (Fastré: 258.)

Since such mastery of oratorical skills can only be acquired by instruction and the chance to practise them, it is inevitable that chiefs should ensure that these opportunities are given to their sons or younger brothers.[1] Thus at Goilala the ceremonial prestations of pork were usually made by Erico, younger brother of Avui Maia, or by Kamo Maia, son of Peeri Maia. The speeches used to be taken very seriously, and no noise or interruptions were allowed. If a child cried out its parents had to pay a fine, and Mr. Martin recalls one occasion when the speeches were stopped for a couple of hours because this fine was not forthcoming from a particular couple. Dogs which barked were killed, as were pigs whose squeals disrupted the proceedings.

The powers of the chiefs were closely associated with the principal paths running through tribal land, and they had the power of putting a taboo on a particular path, usually for reasons of mourning. It was customary for men from other tribes to pay the chief who controlled a path some present for the use of it, and I was given a number of accounts of men who were killed by angry chiefs because, when visiting relatives with gifts, they did not give the chief anything. The coming of the government has naturally caused this power to fall into abeyance.

Chiefs were traditionally more mobile than the *malavi*. Because the retribution for the killing of chiefs was much greater than for killing men or women of no importance, people of other tribes would hesitate to kill them, and they could go more or less as they pleased, while men of small status took their life in their hands when wandering in the territory of other tribes, as we shall see. Moreover, because polygyny was and is more frequent among the chiefs, a chief can rely on a wider network of kinsmen than could the *malavi*. The power of chiefs to travel widely in the old days, fairly much at will, is compared with the same power of white men.

The material wealth of the chiefs in terms of pigs and wives is greater than that of the *malavi*, but even here it is not the rule that

[1] But it is also true that oratory, and ceremonial skills generally, like qualities of leadership in warfare, do provide opportunities for talented men of relatively humble birth to rise in the social scale by their own efforts. Hides (1935: 62) quotes the case of a dance chief who told him that he acquired his ceremonial skills, and his consequent status, by observation of the chiefs' deportment. This is the same chief whose speech is quoted below, pp. 168–9.

all chiefs have many wives. Some men are too fierce, and frighten the women so that they run away, or refuse to marry the man in the first place. Evura Kimani, Buluvu Kimani's father, was such a man and had only one wife. Similarly, Ita Kogotsi, who only had one wife many years ago, was said only to have been interested in killing, not in love-making. Other chiefs, such as Kire Keruvu, have had several wives, but none of them has borne children, presumably because the man is sterile.

While it is true that a man attracts women sexually by his reputation as a killer, and that chiefs play a significant part in society as war leaders, it still seems to be the case that general social status is more important in acquiring wives than a reputation for mere bloodshed. Aima Kamo, for example, with about two dozen killings to his name, had fewer wives than his brother Kepe Maia, who is not reputed to have killed anyone.

It is difficult even for a chief to have many wives simultaneously, however, in view of the animosity even between the wives of chiefs in many cases. The more wives a man has, the more pigs they can look after, but the relatively small number of chiefs would mean that their herds would still be greatly outnumbered by the pigs of the rest of the tribe.

It is always stressed that the chiefs marry one another's daughters and sisters, which helps to maintain a kind of class solidarity among the leaders. The degree of intermarriage is shown in Figure 14. For reasons of space, many ramifications of affinal ties have been omitted.

There is a general principle that men of high social status can kill *malavi* with relative impunity but are nevertheless expected to pay compensation eventually. Failure to do so may involve an insignificant friend or relative of the chief being killed. My researches into the status of homicide victims showed that in almost every case they were *malavi*. The following story illustrates the almost frivolous killing of a *malavi* by Aima Kamo, who was also living in the same small hamlet with him. Aima, a chief, blames the killing on another member of the hamlet, who is then killed by the dead man's friends and relatives:

K— L— came to Pomutu and seduced O— K—, the wife of V—. V— came with his bow and chased him to Dauraupu. K— L— got his bow and came back and killed V—. Then K— L— ran away to Ilai and stayed there. Mr. Speedie [Miter Beeti as he is called by the Tauade. It is by no means sure that the acts attributed to a particular patrol officer, especially forty years ago,

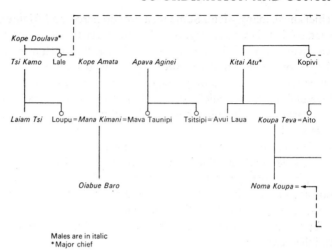

FIG. 14.

were not in fact done by another officer.] asked who had killed V—, and he
was told that it was K— L—. He went and burnt K— L—'s hamlet at Ilai.
K— L— came back and lived at Iguname close to Poroyava. He was there
with K— T— and Aima Kamo. K— T—'s *ene*[1] K— To— had a pig which ate
the sweet potatoes in the garden of Aima Kamo. K— T—, K— L—, and
Aima Kamo went down to the garden near Dimanibi and saw the damage
that the pig had done. Aima Kamo killed the pig. He was laughing.
K— T— said 'Why have you killed my *ene*'s pig?' Aima turned round and
put a spear through him. Peeri Aima [the younger son of Aima] grabbed
K— T—, and they both killed him, and K— L— also speared him. Aima
Kamo pulled out the spear. Aima took his son Peeri away with him and
they both went back to Iguname. T— T—, Ko— Te—, I— Ko—, and others
went to Iguname, and Aima and all the men of Iguname fled to Kutupu.
[Ko— Te— and the others clearly caught up with them here and] Aima
Kamo said 'I did not kill him, it was K— L—', so Ko— Te—, T—
T—, and K— M— all killed K— L— and cut off his hands and threw
them in the bush. A— A— could not get one of these hands which had
been thrown in the bush, but cut off the big toe of his right foot and took
it to Aporota and gave it to Miter Beeti. T— T—, K— M—, Ko— Te—,
and the others all came to Aporota, where they were arrested. Miter Beeti
came to Goilala and wrote his report. When he found out what had
happened he let the matter drop. He gave the *tapùa* [lit. cloth, the uniform of a village constable] and T— T— was Councillor, and told the
people to pay compensation. Then Aima Kamo paid dogs' teeth, a string
stretching from Dimanibi to Moigili [!] to Ko— Te— and the relatives of

[1] Elder brother.

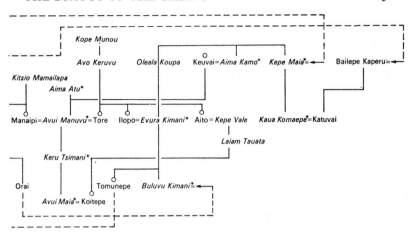

Affinal ties between chiefs

K— T—, and Ko— Te—, and K— M— also gave dogs' teeth to the relatives of K— L—.

The chiefs did not kill each other, only the *ninipima*, the little people. Only Kepe Maia did not kill people. He would send Aima [his younger brother] away when he had killed people.

Aima Kamo also killed A— K— (of Kilamalumī hamlet) because he insulted Aima's sons Peeri and Maia.

He said 'Cut off your sons' penises and eat them'. He said this because they had defecated in his stream and he had come and drunk from it. So he was angry when he saw the faeces in it and insulted them. A— K— had no children. He was speared in the throat by Aima. Tauru Ivei and Lume Ivei came and collected his body. They took him back to Oropo and killed pigs on his body and buried him. He was a *malavi*. After some time Aima killed a pig and gave it with dogs' teeth to Tauru and Lume.

The killing of a chief, on the other hand, was sometimes followed by the massacre of the entire hamlet responsible:

Ivei Koromi [an ancestor of Amo Lume, and apparently a chief] had his yam garden ravaged by a pig. He lived at Deribi. He went to his relatives at Elava, who gave him yams to replace those which he had lost. On his way back he was ambushed by Toto and Amuna and their men from Kalava. He was using their path. They took his body and hid it in the top of a pandanus tree [the leaves are very dense]. Nomai Kilovo came looking for women of Kalava to copulate with, and passed by the tree, where he noticed the body. He recognized a sore on the leg of the corpse, and went back to his hamlet, Deribi. He spread the story of what he had seen, and the men of Oropo, Kililivi, Poruamabitia, Dimanibi, Poroyava, Tsigori, Kutupu, and Pomuru, all took their weapons and came to Kalava and surrounded it. [The hamlet had a stockade around it, and Toto and Amuna and their men were inside it.] So the other Goilala told a lie to trick them. They said, 'Come with us, we are going to kill Tawuni people.' This was

Koupa Kopoi

Kate Kama

Koupa Karoama

Aima Kamo

Together with the Amuganiawa and the Tawuni, the other Goilala exterminated the Tupi. Kavu Kaita was the only survivor e.g.

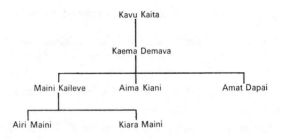

Kavu Kaita

Kaema Demava

Maini Kaileve   Aima Kiani   Amat Dapai

Airi Maini   Kiara Maini

These two men are the only survivors of the Tupi clan

FIG. 15. Genealogy of Tupi clan

to make them come out. So the men came out, and the Goilala killed them, and killed the women, and the children, everybody in Kalava, about '25'.

After this, the Tawuni came in the night and attacked the Goilala, in revenge [because some of their relatives had lived at Kalava]. They killed some Goilala who had moved into Kalava. There was no more killing after this until the Goilala killed a man and his wife at Tanini, in revenge for this raid.

Again, a long time ago Koupa Kopoi, a great chief, and ancestor of Aima Kamo, was killed by the Tupi clan (see Fig. 15).

A chief who is killed may also be swiftly avenged by another chief; there seems to be some solidarity between chiefs in their own defence, as in this story, when Aima Kamo avenges the (accidental) death of Kopeiri Evura by killing Evura's wife, since she was a relative of the killer!

Kire Kitsio of Poragoto hamlet had a plot of pandanus called Ketsia-poluava. Oleala Koupa of Kalava, Kiani Evura of Kalava, and Kope Kapuri, also of Kalava, all came and stole some nuts. Kire Kitsio came with Karo Kavai, also of Poragoto hamlet, and saw that his nuts had been stolen. Kire cut one of the *povo* [the aerial roots] and hit Oleala with his axe, then Kiani Evura, then Kope Kapuri. Then they went back fighting to their hamlets. Oleala, Kope, and Kiani all hit Kire. They eventually got back to Kalava, where they cut off each other's *etapa*.[1] Oleala and Kiani cut Kire's *etapa*. Karo Kavai saw this and picked his spear and flung it and it stuck in the ground. Tau Kemapa was one of Kire's *valavala* at Kalava and he cut Oleala's *etapa*. This was before Karo threw the spear. Karo got another spear (he had four) and K— E—, who was the chief of Kalava saw Kire Kitsio's penis hanging out, and told them to stop fighting. Karo flung the spear at Kope Kapuri, but he ducked and it hit K— E— instead and killed him. Everyone ran off and told what had happened to K— E—. Aima Kamo was at Dimanibi. Apava Aginei was at Deribi. Kitai Komai was at Deribi and Ano Keruvu was also at Deribi. They all went with their *valavala* to Kalava and Aima came and pulled out the spear, and killed K— E—'s wife A— L— with it. She was Karo Kavai's *alupu*.[2] She was dead. He axed her as well. He flung her body on top of K— E—. Aima took Amai, K— E—'s son and Katemu his other son (he later begot Keruvu Katemu) and put them in the men's house and said that they were *taravatu*.[3] Lume Ivei was living in this men's house. Keruvu Kope, Kitai Komai, Apava Aginei all went to Poragoto (Karo Kavai's hamlet) and killed A— T—, Karo's *aluteve* as vengeance for Kopeiri. Kopeiri was a chief so the other chiefs would all go and avenge another chief when one was killed. Then they all went back to their hamlets.

Lume Ivei, Komae Lariava-Evura, Tauru Ivei, Maini Kaemai, Apava Lavava, Aima Kovio, Kilemu Kaita, Pelai Kaita, all came to Kalava and put the bodies of A— L— and K— E— in the same house. The women wept for them. The next day the Oropoa, the Kataipa, the Tawuni, the Kunima, the Watagoi, the Amuganiawa, the Laitate, the Gane all came and the men of Kalava gave pork to them. K— E—'s son Katemu gave pork to the Kataipa and two *kire*, Kilemu Kaita killed another pig and gave to the Oropoa, Pelai Kaita gave pork to the Kunima, Kotou gave pork to the Laitate, Lariava Evura gave pork to the Amuganiawa, Lariava Korou gave pork to the Watagoi. They cooked the pork. They made a big *polo* enclosure there. The boys were put inside a little house which was built inside the *polo* enclosure. The children were Amai Kopeiri, Katemu Kopeiri, Oleala Evura, Kiara Maini, Koma Kinime (Amo Lume's *ene*)

---

[1] Genital coverings of bark cloth.   [2] Younger sister.   [3] Taboo.

Tuna Tauru, Apava Oiabue, Baro Oiabue, Maini Avui, and Avilapa, the daughter of Avui Ivei. Amai Kopeiri killed a pig, and all the children had pigs killed for them by their fathers. The children were washed in the little house, where they stayed three days. They were given plenty of food. The visitors [the Tawuni, Kataipa etc.] had brought dog's teeth, homicide emblems, pork [which they presumably gave to the children, although the text does not mention this fact]. The children came out when the pigs were killed. They mounted the platform, and were given their *etapa*. The bodies had been placed in a *tseetsi*, [a kind of basket of forked branches]. The body of A— T— was placed with the bodies of K— E— and A— L—.

The killing of a chief may also lead to vengeance upon his tribe by relatives in other tribes, and fears of this or of further internal violence may produce the dispersal of the whole tribe into temporary residence with relatives in neighbouring tribes—as at Kanitatalavava in 1969. A sequence of killings in a tribe would also be liable to produce a temporary dispersal:

The people of K— village have all migrated to Kariaritsi, Lumioto, Kopuri, and Kanitata villages since the recent murders there ... A— K—, S— I—, and A— Ko— who were involved in the murder of A— A— of K— were acquitted on a charge of wilful murder at the Supreme Court sittings and have now returned to their villages. As far as the relatives of A— A— are concerned these three killed him [and will be dealt with]. (Cadet Patrol Officer Wadsworth, Tapini, 19/8/58–7/10/58.)

It was also customary for a killer to flee to another tribe for a while, until tempers had cooled sufficiently for friends and relatives of the victim to consider accepting compensation; there are many instances in the genealogical records of men who have sought sanctuary at Goilala in consequence of having killed someone in their natal tribes.

Naturally, a chief will violently resent an assault upon his person, as the following account of a pig-killing held on 4 November 1971 makes clear. The reason for the occasion was that some time previously Moripi had seduced Noma Kitai's wife Lopono, and also possibly his other wife Keuvai. Noma found out and beat Moripi with a piece of wood. Karuvu Koma rescued Moripi, and took away the piece of wood.

Moripi is sitting on the veranda of the men's house at Moigili. He speaks first of Keru Tsimani [a big chief now dead] and of how he used to stop men fighting, and how his son Avui Maia succeeded him, and also maintains peace. He seems to be implying that he is a chief too, and so should not be beaten. He then addresses one of the posts of the veranda, which he says is like his brother [an example of the *manari tsinat* or allegory which the Tauade so enjoy]. Moripi says that after he seduced Noma's wife, Noma beat him as he is beating the post [hitting it with his axe]. Noma is my brother [actually a distant cousin]. He did not cut me with the axe, and there was no scar. We have always fought over women and pandanus. Kitai Ovene is dead, I buried him at Patima [he is Noma Kitai's half-brother] and Utalamapa his wife is my corpse, and when she dies I will bury her at Patima. [He is implying that he is still friends with Noma Kitai's other relatives.] But Noma is *maski* [Motu for 'nothing']. He will go to his wife's country, he will not come back here, either to this hamlet or to that one [where?]. [He is angry because among the Goilala it is the custom for the adulterer not to be beaten by the husband, who only asks for compensation.] If he comes here, they will tell the story of his death. He will not go to the village there [at Patima? This could also mean that even when he dies he will not be buried on Goilala land.] There will be no enemies here. He beat me with a piece of wood, and will become nothing. He will be my big enemy. The woman sitting there who gave birth to me says that he will become her big enemy too. The enemy will become nothing to me. [Saying this he tears off the post from the men's house and flings it on the ground.] Kirau (Pio), Kate Kanitoro, Avui Manuvu (Maia), these men are my friends, and friends do not fight with each other. A different story. Ano Kopeiri, when I seduced his wife, did not beat me, he only spoke to me [asked for compensation], I seduced Avui Noma's wife, and he did not beat me, but only spoke to me. But Noma Taeno (Kitai) came with his friend Tuna and beat me. Karuvu Koma and his wife were sorry for me. [Here he gives a piglet to Karuvu Koma. Then after a short passage, which I do not follow, he says that his speech is ended. Various short addresses follow, more in the nature of a public discussion, and then the pork is distributed, by Erico, the younger brother of Avui Maia.]

Kepe Manuvu, Lariava Moripi, and Kire Keruvu each contributed a pig. Maia Kulolo gave a piglet to Moripi for him to give to Karuvu Koma. The list of recipients of pork (Table 35) shows clearly how prestations cut across hamlet and clan membership.

I have suggested that the Tauade chiefs are not simply big-men because their status is supported by an ideology that credits them with the possession of inherited power, and because this ideology is also based on the realities of Tauade life in which forceful men naturally come to dominate their fellows and have special opportunities for passing on this influence to their sons. Indeed, the existence of the clans, vague entities though they are, provides a conceptual model according to which the clan can be represented by descendants of the founders who have inherited their potency.

We must now examine this cosmological status of the chiefs in greater detail.

In writing of the Fuyughe, Fastré says that they believe every living thing has its *Utame*, which is its archetype, and which lives for ever, in material or spiritual form; if the *Utame* disappeared, the species

TABLE 35. *Recipients of pork at Moripi's pig feast*

Recipient	Clan	Hamlet	Reason for gift
Maia Kulolo			Gave a piglet
Amo Lume	Deliba	Dimanibi	Repayment for earlier gift of pork
Kirau Pio		Palaileve	Repayment for earlier pork
Avui Manuvu		[Kunima]	So that he will spread the news of the feast
Kate Karua		[Diolivi]	Moripi's friend
Ovene Kitai		[Koma]	,,
Karuvu Koma		[Diolivi]	,,
Amo Kopeiri	Larima	Itoveve	,,
Kate Karuai		Avevea	,,
Kirau Laiam		Kiremaitsi	,,
Beto Oiabue	Daro	Dimanibi	,,
Katemu Bauai		Dimanibi	,,
Kepe Manuvu	Larima	Ororogaivara	,,
Anamara Koupa	Deliba	Kiolilama	.,
Pelai Maga		Kiolilama	,,
Amai Evura	Daro	Dimanibi	,,
Avau Tupi		Deribi	,,
Tuna Tauru	Deliba	Dimanibi	,,
Apava Oiabue	Daro	Dimanibi	For bringing sugar-cane, etc.
Keru Katemu	Daro	Patima	,,
Myself			

Where hamlets are enclosed in square brackets the person does not live at Goilala.

would disappear also. So it is with men, except that each tribe is believed to have several chiefs who are its *Utame*. 'A tribe which has no more *Utame* chiefs is finished as a tribe. It is then as if the women were to bear no more children.' (Fastré: 2.)

The Tauade have a concept, *ăgo*, which is very similar to that of *Utame*, and which will be discussed at length in Chapter VII. And while I could not establish that the Goilala thought that the death of their chiefs would cause the sterility and disappearance of their tribe, it was clear that there was a vital association in their minds between the principal chiefs and birds (especially the *tuna*, a bird of prey) and sacred oaks, and height in general. Most striking of all, when a chief died in the old days, a special enclosure was built into which his body was taken, and which was then in many cases used for the initiation of children, especially boys. This seems a clear affirmation of the idea that his vital force is seen as passing into the young. To substantiate these points, it will be necessary to describe funeral ceremonies in some detail.

There are two traditional methods of disposing of the dead. Chiefs were placed on platforms which were situated in the middle of hamlets. The stench from the decaying flesh was naturally appalling, and the people, in recalling it, say 'We could not eat, we were retching because of the smell.' They also say that the maggots from the corpses would come and crawl over them as they slept. Some informants say that the maggots caused *poroto* (leprosy). While chief's bodies were exposed on platforms, it is said that everyone else was buried in the centre of the hamlet, encased in the bark of a pandanus tree. When the flesh had rotted, the relatives dug down and pulled off the head, which was the property of the widow.

The so-called 'platform' was in fact an elevated basket, *tseetsi*. In trying to demonstrate its shape, my informants would hold up a hand, with straight fingers forming an inverted cone. A *tseetsi* is described in a patrol report as follows:

When leaving Tawuni in the Aibala valley, I saw a cage of split-saplings, open at the top and about 6 feet high. Inside was a split log about 5 feet long, hollowed out, with a handle at one end. Inside this 'frying-pan' were 2–3 bones, the remains of a chief's son who died 3–4 years ago. (B. G. Wilson, P.O., Tapini, January 1952.)

Monckton (1922: 34) provides a sketch of what was probably a similar type of platform, seen in a village on the northern slopes of Mt. Albert Edward. Casimiro told me that in his area at least (Sene), the *tseetsi* were lined with *oraitsi, igurulautu* (Umbelliferae, 713[1]), and *lavutata*, all being various types of trees or shrubs. The *tseetsi* itself was built of *dimaniti* and *toio dimanitsi* (a kind of oak). At Sene a long time ago these *tseetsi* were built in the branches of trees, but later they were constructed on the ground, and only bones were placed in trees. The chiefs' children were placed in *tseetsi*. The people cut *avutata* (Schuurmansia, 771[1]) and *kepovo* (Polyscias, 702[1]) as well as

---

[1] This number is from Dr. Froden's Goilala collection of plants in the Department of Botany, U.P.N.G.

the same types of trees as those mentioned above, and placed them around the body. The intention of this was apparently to hasten liquefaction.

If the purpose of exposing the bodies of chiefs had simply been to accelerate putrescence the platforms could have been built in the bush. But it is clear that they were always built inside the hamlets where their presence was thoroughly revolting even to the relatives of the deceased. This suggests that the odour was in some way regarded as important in itself, perhaps as a vehicle of the dead man's vitality, though I must admit that I did not verify this hypothesis in the field.

When a person died and his body had rotted in the *tseetsi* or in the ground, the bones were taken by his relatives and washed in a stream. The skull in particular was washed out with water introduced through the *foramen magnum*, with which the remains of the brain were flushed away. The children of the deceased are said to have drunk this water. Then the skull was put in a string bag with the rest of his bones and dried over a fire. It was customary to keep the bones of the dead until a great dance was held, when they would be brought out and put in string bags and danced with. When the time for this dance came the bones were shared out, the eldest son having the skull, the second the jaw, and the wives and sisters and daughters taking most of the bones. Pigs were killed at this time, and their blood was symbolically, but not really, supposed to fall on the bones. The bones of the dead, if a chief, were put up in the branches of a sacred oak and left there permanently, and if of some lesser person, were deposited in one of the various caves on the tribal land. It is also clear that some bones of chiefs and of ordinary people are buried in the hamlet sites, but the locations of chiefs' bones will be marked by red *elaivi*.

Besides the bones of the dead another important focus of traditional ceremony was the *polo* or bull-roarer. According to Casimiro there are several in each tribe, each in the custody of a certain chief. I was not able to discover if any still existed at Goilala.

The *polo* ceremony is particularly interesting in view of its association with the death of chiefs, and with the initiation of children, in particular of boys. Indeed, the death of a chief could also provide the occasion for an initiation ceremony, almost as if by deliberate choice they were affirming the growth of new vigorous life out of the ruins of mortality.

When a chief died a *polo piluala* (bull-roarer enclosure) was con-structed, within which the bull-roarer was to be swung. It was necess-ary to construct the enclosure as quickly as possible, since if it were built slowly several people might die. The men of the hamlet invited guests to help them in the work. A ring of stakes was placed in the ground and bound together by horizontal strips of wood. While the enclosure was being built the men working on it danced round it inside singing a song of mourning, and as the horizontal strips were added they shook the enclosure—they were cleaning it, *polo kopi enai*. The topmost ring of wood was called the *polo natapa*, and marked the completion of the enclosure. Leaves and branches were hung around the enclosure from the top. Only men could enter it, women being tabooed. Once the work was completed, several large pigs were killed inside the enclosure, and a little hut was also built in-side it. This was for the guests who had helped with the work, and they ate and slept there; the pork of the pigs which had been killed was for the men who had done the work of building the enclosure. But it is clear that the chief object of the enclosure was to provide a sanctuary wherein the bull-roarer could be whirled away from the gaze of the women. The guests in the house came out at night with their pork after the feast, and, making sure that there were no sparks from their torches, went back to their homes, taking care not to be seen on the way. While the *polo* was being built, the chief's body had been in his house, and now was wrapped in a new net bag, which was decorated with feathers, homicide emblems, dogs' teeth, and flowers. This was carried, like a hammock, to the enclosure, and was taken inside through the gate called *amui poana*. When the chief had 'seen' it, he was carried out and 'shown' the lines of pigs waiting to be killed, and was then put back in his house. When the pigs had been killed and eaten, the speeches made, and the guests had returned home, his corpse was put in the *tseetsi*.

The same enclosure was also used for the initiation of boys if suitable numbers were ready for it. The men made the boys live in the little house in the enclosure for three or four months and fed them special food to make them tough. On such occasions chiefs' sons and the sons of *malavi* underwent the same treatment. The leaves of the *kaviolopo* were put in the food to make them fierce and able to kill men in battle. They danced inside the enclosure and were beaten by the men with *lomipi* (Harmsiopanax) and *kamulepe* and *kumopo*, types of nettles, so that they became mad with rage, and did not know

their own relatives; they were filled with undying hatred; after about
four months the men cut a hole in the enclosure (presumably a
formal one, since an informal mode of egress for elementary sanitary
purposes would seem to have been necessary). Guests were then
called to the feast. The boys were given bows and arrows and spears,
and danced inside the enclosure, all the while being beaten by the
men. When they were let out they were berserk and wanted to attack
anyone whom they found, and killed any dogs or pigs which they
came across. Then they went back inside the enclosure, and pigs
were killed and distributed to the guests, and when they had departed
the boys came out normally. Some had their noses pierced at this
time, but others were too angry and had to wait.

Ample confirmation of Casimiro's account can be found in patrol
reports. Sir Hubert Murray wrote:

In his report Mr. Hides mentioned the death of one Govei, Village Constable of Maini, and added that 'his burial platform was encircled by a tall
Pilitu [cf. *piluala*, the term used by Casimiro] about 20 yards in diameter,
a mark of very high respect among these people for their dead'. Asked
what a Pilitu was, the Patrol Officer replied as follows, 'This is a ceremonial enclosure built and used only on the death of a chief. Its correct
name is "Polo"; Pilitu is the name of the fence, or stockade, which is
generally 20 to 25 feet in height and made of tall green trees cut for the
purpose. Inside the enclosure is a house. When a chief dies, the Polo is
quickly made; [cf. Casimiro on the necessity for speed] the chief's body is
placed upon a platform in the open, and all the boys of the tribe who have
not yet reached the age of puberty are placed inside the house and kept
there for two days. At the end of this period the chief's pigs are killed and
eaten, the boys are released from the enclosure, and the dead man is buried.
This practice is supposed to enable boys to reach manhood quickly.' [My
emphasis.] (Papuan Annual Report, 1933–4, p. 22.)

It will be noted that this confirms Casimiro's and Amo Lume's
accounts of initiations in many details, except that it makes no
mention of the bull-roarer and the tormenting of the boys which is
also mentioned by Fastré among the Fuyughe. The period of two
days seems curiously short, but is supported by the account of the
initiation after Kopeiri Evura's death (see above, pp. 153–4). The
length of the boys' seclusion may well have varied according to time
and place.

An account of a similar enclosure is given by W. R. Humphries,
A.R.M. On 7 May 1921 his patrol visited Donapu on the Akaifu
River in the Kunimaipa. He writes as follows:

It was at Donapu that I first saw the Pilita—a name given to two or three miniature houses, encircled by a bamboo fence some twenty feet high. The enclosure does not seem to vary much in size. Those that I saw had a diameter of approximately twenty yards. Into these dog kennels, then, are placed young boys ageing from 5 to 10 years, perhaps. Incarcerated behind these high strong fences, they are fed regularly and 'grow strong' very quickly. Their food is passed to them by their parents, usually the father, and it seems that they are imprisoned thus for upwards of a month. Apparently the sole purpose of the Pilita is to make young boys become strong very quickly. I saw no evidence of the Pilita east of Mount Yule. (Papuan Annual Report, 1920–1, p. 126 and Appendix II. The photograph of the 'Pilita' is exactly like the enclosures described by Hides and Casimiro.)

Putting all these accounts together, a number of general characteristics of these initiation enclosures emerge:

1. The boys are always pre-pubertal.
2. They are secluded from all sight of the outside world. The great height of the fence, referred to in all accounts, is obviously significant as a symbol of seclusion.
3. The boys seem usually to have been fed by men, though Hides does not mention this. Casimiro also says that they were fed special food.
4. The idea is to make the boys 'grow strong', or 'reach manhood quickly', or 'to make them tough'.
5. The presence of the chief's body was an integral element of initiation among the Tauade and Fuyughe, and possibly among the Kunimaipa.

It seems that the basic purpose of such enclosures was to segregate the young boys from their mothers, and women in general, and to place them under the supervision of men, who would take over their nourishment to make them strong and virile. This is, of course, a basic theme in boys' initiation rites generally. The chief's body within the enclosure as a source of 'power' is basically consistent with the general objects of the initiation.

It should be noted, however, that in some cases girls as well as boys might be placed in the enclosure. See, for example, the account of Kopeiri Evura's death above, pp. 153–4; and I was told by other informants that girls could also be initiated in this way. There seem therefore to have been two kinds of initiation, or at least two stages; one short one for girls as well as boys, and another more prolonged one, after the chief's body had been taken away, for boys only that included physical ordeals imposed by the men. The point of including girls was perhaps to impart vitality and fertility to them, consistent with those mystical attributes of chiefs discussed earlier.

2. CEREMONIES

(a) *The ritual content of ceremonies*

I refer to Tauade 'ceremonies' more from want of any other word to denote feasts and dances than to attribute the quality of 'ceremoniousness' or ritual complexity to these occasions. There are clearly two basic reasons for this lack of ritual elaboration. The first is that without a clearly defined set of roles and statuses, and without group boundaries, the actual organization of ritual of any complexity is virtually impossible. The second, equally important factor is that for the Tauade everything is what it is, not another thing. For them, symbolism is a dormant possibility of the mind. Blood is red, but 'redness' does not seem to suggest 'blood' to them in any profounder sense than that of mere resemblance; bones of relatives are treasured, and those of enemies are scattered with relish, but 'bone' as such has no general significance of 'death', conceived in any abstract mode.

From 'symbolism' I exclude magic, of course, and in earlier years the ceremonial killing of pigs seems to have been accompanied by magical rites that have now lapsed. At one dance which Mr. John Martin observed some twenty years ago the pigs (about 150) were laid out in rows, each within a rectangle of canes. Then a man came round with a bamboo knife with which he cut the mouth of each pig. There followed a man who spat herbs on the incisions; then another man who painted the pigs with clay; and then a number of other ritual specialists as well. Before dawn two men covered with blankets and holding bundles of ritual medicines with bones protruding from them had crawled all round the dance yard and touched the pigs with these bundles. Again, as we saw in the last section, the deaths of chiefs and boys' initiations were accompanied by a number of fairly complex ceremonial acts. But such acts seem either magical, as in the treatment of pigs before slaughter or of psychological intent, as in the harassment and infuriation of the boys during initiation; there is very little in any of the ceremonies that is properly speaking symbolic. The only exception seems to be the attention given to height, which is clearly associated with domination and hence with chiefly status: we find that the most important men's house in a dance village is situated at the top of the yard, or the head, as they call it; that chiefs' bodies were exposed in raised baskets, their bones being placed in the branches of sacred oaks; and that for speeches very tall platforms are sometimes built, while in the legends the culture heroes are depicted as alighting in the tops of trees and urinating on human beings.

Despite Tauade inability to develop symbolic systems or elaborate rituals, such ceremonies as they perform have a few constantly recurring themes, depending on their size. These are the dance (the most important being held at night), the killing of pigs, and speech-making. Dances only occur, as a rule, when guests from other tribes are formally invited, and on these occasions it is primarily the guests who dance. For the largest dances special guest houses are built, and the visitors in some cases come from many miles away and spend several months with their hosts. They usually indulge in some licensed destruction of the hosts' dance village.

The killing of pigs and the making of speeches are very closely linked since the Tauade consider it shameful to kill even a single pig without distributing the meat formally, and this requires a speech. On all but the least significant occasions small platforms will be built on which the chief personages of the ceremony will sit during some part of the proceedings, and the speakers may also use it for delivering their harangues, though in my experience they prefer to walk up and down on the grass. Ceremonies are always held in the space between the lines of huts in one of the hamlets.

But while all ceremonies have a number of common elements, there are crucial differences between large and small ceremonies. At large ceremonies guests from other tribes are present and the whole occasion is conducted in a competitive atmosphere in which hospitality itself becomes a taunt to the guests, challenging them to do as well themselves when their turn comes to hold a dance. The guests in turn challenge their hosts by their dancing and their display of stamina and sexual attraction. Large numbers of pigs are killed on such occasions, and this in itself ensures that they are held at infrequent intervals; in the old days it was also difficult for chiefs to negotiate a peaceful route for the guests to reach the dance.

In the case of smaller ceremonies, whose participants are largely drawn from within the tribe, the competitive element is muted and the participants are evidently more concerned with emphasizing their ties with one another. Yet even here the very affirmation of ties may be rebuffed by other members of the community who stay away from the ceremony, or in other ways behave disparagingly.

(b) *Large ceremonies*

The large dances, to which all hamlets of the tribe contribute, have as their ostensible purpose[1] the honouring of the bones of the dead, and by implication their spirits, before they are laid to rest and forgotten. Yet the basic motivations of the large ceremonies are not obviously supernatural at all, but seem to be the desire of the participants to gain renown for generosity, hospitality, wealth, and stamina in dancing. For these occasions special villages are built, requiring many months of preparation; there may be up to seventy or so houses for guests, of which many will be for men only; the chiefs of the host and guest tribes will have a large men's house at the top of the village. The whole emphasis on such occasions is upon the wealth and generosity of the hosts, and to this end great displays of food are tied to pandanus trunks, uprooted and re-erected in the dance yard, or heaped on platforms. Guests may be entertained for months, and pigs killed over this period, but the ceremony culminates in a great dance on the night before the main pig-killing on the following morning. Not all dances last as long as this, and on some occasions the guests only come the day before, dance during the night, and leave next day with their pork, after the speeches.

At the present time the tradition of the big dance, to which the guests proceed through the intervening tribal areas, dancing and killing pigs as they go, has continued, and, for example, at the end of 1971 large dances were held along the right bank of the Aibala to Omoritu, then at Sopu, and finally at Kiolivi.

The following is a description of one such dance at Lamanava in 1947 witnessed by Mr. F. G. Driver, P.O., and one of the Fathers:

A group of visitors with faces painted and heads bedecked with Bird of Paradise, Cassowary and other brilliantly coloured plumes, singing and gesticulating with spears, ran down the slight incline and tore the fence posts away from in front of the village. The village was then open to all visitors to attend the dance. The villagers then danced out to meet all the guests. This is the only time the villagers dance, as it is actually them giving the dance for the visitors. The pigs, food, and all other things pro-

---

[1] Cf. Williamson 1912: 125 on the 'laying' of the chiefs' ghosts as the primary object of the great feasts among the Fuyughe.

vided for the dance are given by the chief of the village; this person just looks on all the time the dance is in progress.

After the first rush all was quiet for a time, then the dancers came in led by a few women. I am told that these women are the wives of the visiting chiefs, and in the case where the wife is too old to dance, the daughter takes her place. The party of dancers, numbering about 50, all carried spears, and danced for about half an hour, then all ceased till darkness, when dancing would again commence, with drums to replace the spears. After dancing had ceased everyone sat and talked and ate the food which had been tied to the posts in the village. This food was yams, taro, and Gatoro [pandanus] nuts.

The night's dancing commenced about 2100 hours. Prior to the commencement of dancing a very small pig was killed and its blood was allowed to flow on the ground. As I was sitting next to one of the Fathers of Kerau Mission I asked him the reason for this. He told me the natives' explanation for this is 'so that the dancers will get the smell of blood in their nostrils'. A short speech by the chief of the village followed, the translation being that the visitors were to broadcast the news far and wide that they had attended a dance at Lamanava village. The dancers had congregated at the eastern end of the compound, which was about 100 yards long, then the 70–odd dancers moved off to their own accompaniment of drum beats and whistle blasts.

The first rank of dancers are all the visiting chiefs. These men lead the dance at night; women do not dance at all during the night.

In the dance itself there seemed to be a basic rhythm, this being 3 beats on the drum, accompanied by 3 whistle blasts, a short pause, and then a further 2 beats and 2 blasts. The dance step itself is a constant 3 skips forward and 3 skips back, then a series ranging from 9 to 12 hops. These 'hops' may vary from a true hop to a sideways movement of the leg in either direction. This is followed by a chant, then the whole procedure is repeated. When the party reaches the end of the compound they turn round and return, the Chiefs always being in front.

This dancing and killing pace is kept up all night, and by morning only the strongest dancers remain, the others slowly dropping out as they become too weary to continue.

Shortly after daybreak the Chief of the village arises and tells the dancers 'You have danced well, go and sleep!' The dancing ceases, then, usually during the afternoon, the pigs are killed and the dance is ended.

Lighting facilities for the dancers are provided by the women of the village; it is their duty to supply light. In this case it was supplied by bundles of burning cane grass carried by the women; about 6 precede the dancers and the same number bring up the rear.

In this case the plumes worn at night were far better than the ones worn during the day. During the afternoon only feathers were worn; during the night high head-dresses were worn, some being fifteen feet long [tall].

These are supported by a framework of cane strapped to the trunk of the dancer. Just above the head is a circle of feathers, some being 3 feet in diameter. These feathers are placed flat and in some cases a pattern is worked into the design. (F. G. Driver, P.O., Tapini, August 1947.)

This description is still applicable to the form of dances at the present time. But before I attended the night dance at Kovokupe I could not understand why the Tauade were so excited by dancing, since those 'dances' which I had hitherto witnessed were pathetic, squalid, and bedraggled affairs. On Thursday, 9 September 1971, I had dinner at the mission and returned to Kovokupe (where I was to sleep the night), at about 20.00 hours. The whole scene had been transformed. The dance yard, so sordid and unappealing in daylight, was now a stage, lit by the glare of torches held by the wives of the hosts to illuminate the footsteps of the dancers.

Great clouds of smoke from these brands swept across the dance yard, blown by the strong wind, and in the lurid and fitful yellow glare could be seen the incredible figures of the dancers themselves. Like moving idols, they were no longer the stunted little men of daylight—they had donned their immense feather head-dresses made of magnificent plumes on cane frames strapped to their heads and torso and were transformed into superhuman monsters 12 feet high. These extraordinarily impressive figures were gathered into a pack of sixty or so fighting men, each man—for only men form the body of night dancers—carrying two raw bamboo poles; these they thumped rhythmically on the ground in unison, producing a sonorous and powerful accompaniment to their songs. As I watched them dancing and singing up and down the yard with tireless energy, they seemed to have taken on the qualities of the *agotevaun*, the culture heroes before the dawn of time, beautiful as birds, with the endurance and virility of giants, melodiously exulting in their strength, and roaring their triumph across the ranges. All through the night they danced, for about ten hours, the weaker dropping out in the course of the night, but the strongest unflagging in the dance until the light of dawn broke over the great valley of the Aibala. At length, in that chill grey light, movement was stilled, and the spell was broken; the yard was again revealed in all its trivial nastiness. But now I understood the meaning of the dance.

The killing of the pigs takes place on the morning after the night's dancing. Fastré gives the following description:

The dawn begins to break . . . a final song. It is the last day of the dance.

Men dash about, grabbing the poles to which the pigs are tied, and putting them in line in the dance-yard, one next to the other. As reinforcement against the clubs and rocks [which will be used to kill the pigs] two stakes are driven into the ground by each pig, and the pigs tied to these stakes are unable to make any movement.

This produces one or two fine rows of victims stretched from one end of the village to the other.

The slaughter is considered to be like a battle, the declaration of war on the pigs, *Ovol'Aje Mame*. The same expressions and the same rites are used for war and for this slaughter.

Then there is the distribution of clubs to those who have none. Plenty of men have brought their own. For it is a passionate business, and no one wants to be left out.

As for the remainder, if there are not enough clubs, there is no need to worry about that. The village fence is close by, and is full of pieces of timber which can be used in the attack.

Each man takes his club on his shoulder, as for a parade, but a parade of crouching men in the middle of the dance yard . . .

You will see, all at once, these crouching men leap into life.

The chief, standing on a pig, looks at the executioners crouching in front of him, and says, in a commanding voice:

'If it is on Olome, let the lightning strike.' No one moves.

'If it is on Kutuna, let the lightning strike.' No one moves.

'If it is on Mapu, let the lightning strike.' No one moves.

'If it is on Manei, let the lightning strike.' Everyone, in unison, without moving their feet, rises and crouches down again with the speed of lightning. The movement has been so rapid that one has hardly noticed it.

'If it is on Ole, let the lightning strike. Hou! Hou! Hou!' In a single bound, everyone leaps up, and screaming, brandishing their clubs, they fling themselves on the pigs.

For several minutes one can hear nothing but screams and howls, the shrieks of the pigs as they kill them, the yells of rage from their assailants, screams of joy and triumph from the spectators in honour of the attackers and their victims, the lamentations of the women who weep for their pigs.

Of everyone gathered there, I am surely the only one who finds the business nauseating.

You have surely understood nothing of the chief's discourse.

I attempted to understand it myself for a long time. The first thing to grasp is that this slaughter is an imitation, an *Evone*, of real war, in every action and in every word.

The pigs are the enemy. In the translation below, the basic assumption is that of warfare. We may say 'the enemy'. The proper names are those of mountains. The speaker first names those which are far away, and then names those which come closer and closer. Finally, when he names the mountain where the pig killers are, they leap up.

We may therefore translate:

'If the enemy is on Olome (Pitsoko), leap like lightning.' The enemy is not there; no one moves.

'If the enemy is on Kutuna, leap like lightning.' The enemy is still not there. No one moves.

'If the enemy is on Mapu, leap like lightning.' It is still too far; no one moves.

'If the enemy is on Manei, leap like lightning.' We burn; we rise and fall with the speed of lightning.

'If the enemy is on Ole, leap like lightning. Hou! Hou! Hou!' We are there. With a bound like a flash, everyone leaps up. (Fastré: 96.)

Hides describes a somewhat similar occasion in the Ivane:

Next morning, before moving on, I witnessed a most interesting spectacle. It was the killing of the pigs, a ceremony that is carried out after a big dance. Some two hundred pigs were tied to pegs and lying in two even rows down the middle of a village nearby, and as I stood waiting, the dance chief, accompanied by fifty or sixty powerful men armed with wooden clubs, entered to commence the ceremony. This dance chief wore long cassowary plumes fastened tightly round his head by a band of Job's tears, and as he came through the entrance into the enclosure of the village, all eyes turned towards him. He was a great showman, this man. Sweeping round, grace and rhythm in his every movement, he charged down the first line of pigs, brandishing in his right hand a beautiful black spear that was tasselled about a foot from the point with 'cuscus' fur, and feathers of a brilliant plumage.

Proceeding up the second line of pigs he halted, stepped on to one of the helpless animals, and then gave voice in the manner of his profession. The audience of visiting dancers waited expectantly.

'See! We are rich in pigs,' he shouted. 'We are the true people. Our plant people gave many pigs to feasts; we are still giving many to-day. We are doing the same thing.'

There were murmurs of applause from the audience at such fine speech, while the fifty or so armed men now became nervous and fidgety, grasping their terrible-looking weapons more securely.

'We have big gardens,' this man continued. 'Plenty pig,' and he allowed this to sink in. 'Our women are strong; our sons are strong; that is why we are strong people.' Then dropping his spear and taking a club from one of the men near by, he yelled something at the top of his voice, at the same time smashing the jaws of the animal upon which he had been standing.

Then began a horrible scene; the armed men fell upon the two hundred helpless pigs and battered them to death. The din that ensued was awful; the men yelled and the dying pigs, whose lower jaws had to be broken in accordance with custom, squealed dreadfully. Blood—brute strength—the squeals of dying animals—the savage was back in his element. (Hides 1935: 60–1.)

The hostility between guests and hosts, permanently simmering since they almost certainly have blood scores to settle, is given ritualized expression in the licence granted to guests to destroy pandanus and other trees, decorations, and gardens. At one of the first dances which I attended, at Dimanibi, the guests, from Kerau, rushed into the hamlet and began furiously hacking down the decorations which surrounded it. When a dance was held at Goilala about ten years previously, guests (from Ilai?) had begun cutting down the sacred oak tree near Dimanibi, and had had to be stopped by the chiefs, who resented this. It is customary for the guests to shoot arrows into the men's house, or even overturn it, and in some cases targets are set up on poles for the guests to shoot at. When I went to a pig-feast at Diolivi, at which there was very little dancing, the visitors cut down a pandanus tree, and the incident of the chief in the Ivane who told his guests to fell some pandanus trees has been recounted elsewhere (p. 235). I was told that it was usual to pay compensation for these outrages—yet it is doubtful if any compensation would be expected for damage to decorations or for the ravaging of gardens; indeed, in the latter case, to accept such impositions is a recognized form of generosity and hospitality. This latent hostility between guests and hosts is well illustrated in this account by a patrol officer:

Laramaite [near Tototo, in the Kataija census district] was recently the scene of a large dance. [For 1,000 people, and 160 pigs were killed.] A tense atmosphere existed as the guests arrived armed with axes, spears and lances. The writer was told that this was quite normal. All spears and the like are placed in honoured positions in the men's house and the axes are used for chopping ornamental trees and firewood . . . Clan chiefs of all villages exerted their influence and remonstrated with the offenders who had brought bows and arrows. The scene, earlier pregnant with suspense, changed and a happy jubilant feast and dance followed. (B. G. Wilson, P.O., Tapini, January 1952.)

The atmosphere of competition is described in more detail by Fastré:

Before the dance, the chief had been challenged.
    'Hey! Look at these fellows. Amo Kau, who wants to be a great man. He thinks he over-tops everyone, when he doesn't even come up to our

ankles. He's inviting a crowd of big men to his Gabe. He's sure they'll come. We're going to have a good laugh—there'll be no one!'

These disagreeable comments have been relayed to him [Amo Kau] and very probably exaggerated. That is quite normal.

If one provokes a person, one does it thoroughly.

No one forgets an injury. It is one of the great pleasures of the Gabe to be able to repay someone in his own coin: injury for injury, humiliation for humiliation.

On the night of the dance itself, the *Gab'u babi* [hosts] congratulate one another on the tremendous success of the occasion. One might suppose oneself transported into the middle of a Mutual Admiration Society.

There comes a point when the chief can stand it no longer. He must declaim his joy, his good fortune, his pride, and also his revenge. He takes his revenge there and then.

'*Tororo ta*' shouts someone. 'Stop' translates Daniel. Hands are poised on the drums, songs stifled in their throats. 'Not a movement, not a sound, in the dance-yard. The women give suck to their babies so that they will not cry, they muzzle the dogs to stop them howling. As for the pigs, there is nothing to bother them; they are asleep in the bush', says Vitale. [Another informant.]

'Listen, all of you. I have something to say to you. You, So-and-So, you have challenged us to get these dancers to come. And to make your words come true, you have visited them, and exhorted them, and even bribed them not to come. Well! Have they come? I will take them by the hand and introduce them to you, so that you can get a good look at them. Do you recognize them? What is this person's name? And what is his village? And what is this one's name, and from what village does he come? And this one, and this one, and again, this one? So take a good look, and see how fine they are. I am a great man, the son and grandson of great men, an *An'Uta*, and everyone respects me. You can go and find other dancers like these, and we will come and see them when it is your turn to give a Gabe.'

In corners, people are whispering 'It is well done. He [the challenger] can say nothing.'

The man thus addressed has to keep quiet for the time being, and go and hide his shame. That is what he does. At day-break, he will disappear, and will not be seen again. He will brood on revenge. For seven years, if necessary, but he will have it. He will not fail to repay it on the night when he has the dancers in the yard of his own village. (Fastré: 257–8.)

After fighting between the Goilala and the Tawuni on one occasion, the Goilala taunted the Tawuni 'You are useless *malavi*, you will not succeed in holding a dance'. So the Tawuni people sent the invitations to the chiefs of the Loloipa and Kunimaipa to show how big they were, by getting these chiefs and their people to come to their dance. One dance village was at Tanini, another at Dalavapila (both Tawuni places).

With regard to the dances which always accompany those pig-killings to which substantial numbers of guests are invited, Rappaport suggests, following Wynne-Edwards, that

Certain information is imparted by the massed dancing of the males. First, it presents to the female spectators larger samples of the males of unfamiliar local groups than they are likely to see assembled at any other time or place. The males, furthermore, signal by their participation in the dance their general interest in the females as a class. [One really might have thought that such interest would be taken for granted.] It would be difficult to conceive a more economical means for communicating information concerning the availability of males than the sample presentation of the dance. (Rappaport 1968: 193.)

Unfortunately for this hypothesis, dancers among the Tauade are almost all married.

Wynne-Edwards suggests that such displays in the animal kingdom are selective mechanisms, since 'such individuals that were undernourished or depressed would presumably have greater difficulty in achieving mating than the dominant and well-fed'. (1962: 251.[1]) (Rappaport 1968: 194.)

But undernourished and depressed individuals would have trouble attracting women in any case, whether or not they danced badly. While sexual display, expressed in the endurance and exuberance of their dancing and the finery of their plumage, is an essential element in Tauade dancing, the fact remains that the dancers are usually married, and excite reciprocal passion in their hosts' wives, as well as in the unmarried girls. So one of the features of the dance has always been the sexual jealousy caused by married women who are tempted to be unfaithful by the sexual allurements of the dancers, and much violence has traditionally been the result, from men who beat their women for admiring the dancers, and from battles between tribes caused by women later leaving their husbands and going to live with men to whom they have first been attracted at a dance. Fastré records that when he was first at Popole, one dance in particular led to twenty-five killings in this way. Thus the sexual element in the male display during dancing is not primarily meant to serve as a means for pairing off the unmarried couples; it is essentially

---

[1] Wynne-Edwards, V.C., *Animal Dispersion in Relation to Social Behaviour*, Oliver & Boyd, Edinburgh and London, 1962.

narcissistic, and the women are there basically as mirrors for male self-esteem.

Again, Rappaport suggests that traditional dances may be 'epideictic' displays.

Epideictic displays are those that impart to the participants information concerning the population's size or density prior to behaviour that may affect that size or density. Included by Wynne-Edwards are the 'dancing of gnats and midges, the milling of whirligig beetles, the manoeuvres of birds and bats at roosting time, the choruses of birds, bats, frogs, insects, and shrimps'. (1962: 16.) (1968: 195.)

Whatever may be the case with gnats, midges, or even whirligig beetles, this form of reasoning is not very persuasive when applied to Tauade dances. For they have a thorough knowledge of the composition of neighbouring tribes, of the people, in short, with whom they are likely to have to fight, and do not require this sort of information to be presented to them in a dance.

Twenty-five years ago when there was much more fighting and it was harder to maintain the large gardens necessary for a dance, ceremonies were held much less frequently, perhaps only once in ten years by any one tribe. Fastré also says 'One could perhaps count from 15 to 20 years from one Gabe [big dance] to the next. There are more now', though I think this is an excessive estimate as far as the Tauade are concerned. McArthur says for the Kunimaipa, however, that even when she was there in the years 1942–52, there were seven dance villages at Omu (population 200) and sixteen in the forty years before that. In earlier years, in the average parish of approximately 100 people, a dance village was built every three to four years. (McArthur: 284–5.) It should be noted, however, that according to McArthur each hamlet in what she terms a parish builds its own dance village. This is in contrast to the Tauade custom whereby a single dance village serves for the whole tribe, and also to the Fuyughe, of whom Williamson writes: 'The feast, though only to be solemnized in one village, is organized and given by the whole community of villages.' (Williamson 1912: 125.)

The consequences of endemic warfare in themselves appear sufficient to explain the relative rarity of large dances in the old days. There is a further possibility, namely that the changes in the genetic characteristics of the pig population have produced an animal which is faster growing and more fertile than the traditional breed, and that this allows the people to raise the same amount of large pigs much

V. Climbing a pandanus tree

VI. Disembowelling a pig

VII. A small feast at Goilala

VIII. Dawn mists in the Ivane Valley

more quickly than they used to be able to. McArthur says that in the Kunimaipa, while pig herds vary with the size of ceremonies, the average herd comprises 2 to 3 sows with litters, and 2 or 3 geldings, that is, about 10 pigs in all. (McArthur: 27.) The average herds at Goilala held by married couples are of similar size—9·1—and litter size also seems to be within the traditional range of litter size, as estimated by Malynicz (n.d.) and Rappaport (1968), who consider that more than four piglets in a litter is rare, and that the average size is about two. Unfortunately I have no data on the growth rate of pigs, but visual acquaintance with Tauade pigs suggested that they

TABLE 36. *Frequency of dances*

	Number of dances					
	1	2	3	4	5	
Number of tribes	27	5	9	2	2	*45* total
	60%	11%	20%	4·5%	4·5%	100%

were closer to the traditional stock than to introduced varieties, and if this is so, their growth rates should perhaps also be closer to those described for the traditional New Guinea pig. These considerations lead us to conclude that it is not so much genetic changes in the constitution of the pigs which has led to the possibility of more pork and hence more dances, but rather that the suppression of warfare has made dances an increasingly desirable form of entertainment and mode of competition, and has at the same time made them easier to organize.

At the present time, by a regulation of the Tapini Local Government Council, the organizers of a dance which is to last for more than a day have to obtain a ticket from the administration. This allows a maximum of fourteen days of celebrations between fixed dates. The system is abused in that not all dances are reported, and those that are may ignore the specified dates. It is possible to obtain some idea of the frequency of dances from Table 36 which represents the number of tickets issued in the period May 1968 (when the ordinance came into existence) to February 1971—thirty-four months in all.

The strains which the necessity of raising large herds of pigs impose are well expressed by one of Fastré's informants:

Because of the Gabe one thinks of nothing but pigs, and nobody thinks of anything else. If the women are dying of over-work—what of that? As long as the pigs get fat. The children are sickly, stealing food because they are dying of hunger. Let it be. As long as the pigs get fat. The pigs multiply to such an extent that people can no longer feed them; starving, they ravage the gardens. Let it be, as long as the pigs get fat. (Fastré: 22.)

And a patrol officer wrote of the ravages of pigs in 1950:

Food is particularly short in most villages throughout the area traversed. The only villages which have an abundance of food are Matsialavava, Kataipa, Kiletu, Kuputaive, and Omoritilavava. However new gardens have been completed in most areas and the shortage should be overcome within the next few months. Pigs seem to be more numerous and destructive than ever and the natives blame them solely for the food shortage. There were many gardens which have been completely destroyed by pigs. People throughout the grassland areas have difficulty in constructing adequate fences due to the lack of timber. Undoubtedly this is a factor underlying much of the ill-feeling in the district. (A. M. Bottrell, P.O., Tapini, August 1950.)

(c) *Small ceremonies*

Pigs, not dances, are the focus of small ceremonies, and it is the personal details of their distribution, not the emotional connotations of their slaughter in large numbers, that will concern us in this section.

In some respects pigs are killed rather as in our society we produce a special bottle of wine or brandy to celebrate some notable occasion. The principal occasions when pigs are killed in a person's life cycle are:

  1. Birth
  2. Assumption of genital coverings
 *3. Piercing of ears
 *4. Piercing of nose
 *5. Giving of drum
  6. Marriage
  7. Announcements for the falling-out of teeth and baldness—old age
  8. Death

*obsolete

Pigs are also killed in compensation for homicide, adultery, and seduction, the loss of blood by injury, for making peace, for the return of relatives who have been away, for the building of a hamlet, the placing of the first fire inside a new men's house, and a number of other occasions. Thus a certain quantity of pigs must inevitably be slaughtered each year, irrespective of any impending large ceremonies. Table 37 gives the occasions and number of pigs killed at Goilala during my stay.

In the period 1 March 1971 to 28 February 1972, twenty-nine pigs were killed, mostly of medium size or larger, while perhaps half a dozen piglets were given away live. If we estimate the number of

TABLE 37. *Pig-killings at Goilala*

	Number	Date	Occasion	Pigs killed
	I	13 July '70	Pigs killed for Kerau guests	3
	2	7 Feb. '71	Ita Kogotsi's toe	I
1 year	3	I Mar. '71	Birth feast	2
	4	28 Mar. '71	Birth Feast	7
	5	16 May '71	Feast at Diolivi	2+ some piglets given away
	6	17–18 July '71	Aima Kamo's funeral	11
	7	4 Nov. '71	Moripi's expulsion of Kaita Kitai	3
	8	9 Feb. '72	Porua Laiam's pig bitten by snake	I
	9	28 Feb. '72	Feast at Patima	3
	10	14 Mar. '72	Kari's funeral	2
	11	20 April '72	Birth feast, my departure feast	4

Goilala pigs during this time as about 400, and the number of pigs killed or given away in the twelve-month period immediately preceding as about thirty-six, this is 9·0 per cent of the total herd—at its present level of development a relatively small amount. If there is a fairly constant rate of 'obligatory' pig-killing in any one year, this in itself would be sufficient in the early years of a herd's development to keep numbers depressed for some time, though it is evident that most occasions for killing pigs can be deferred. Even though local killing of pigs is not primarily undertaken with other communities in mind, a substantial amount of the pork distributed does not go to the community which provided the pigs. As we can see in Tables 38 and 39, 25 per cent of the recipients of pork at the local Goilala feasts were not themselves Goilala. The actual quantities of pork which the latter received, in relation to that distributed among the Goilala, is

TABLE 38. *Distribution of pork*

1. *Ita Kogotsi*

| Goilala | 20 portions |
| Kerau | 2 ,, |

2. *Pork from Ivane*[1]

Goilala	19 portions
Oropoa	1 ,,
Tawuni	1 ,,

3. *Birth feast at Ororogaivara*

Goilala	12 portions
Gane	1 ,,
Kunima	3 ,,

4. *Birth feast at Palaileve*

Goilala	9 portions
Gane	2 ,,
Watagoipa	2 ,,
Kerau	1 ,,
Kunima	3 ,,

5. *May 17 pig distribution at Patima*[2]

Goilala	22 portions
Amuganiawa	4 ,,
Tawuni	1 ,,
Laitate	1 ,,

6. *Aima Kamo's Funeral*

Goilala	27 portions
Amuganiawa	2 ,,
Kerau	3 ,,
Gane	2 ,,
Tawuni	7 ,,
Tanini	2 ,,
Kataipa	4 ,,
Oropoa	3 ,,
Kemava	1 ,,
Watagoipa	2 ,,
Aibala	1 ,,
Kunima	1 ,,

7. *Moripi's feast*

Goilala	16 portions
Kunima	3 ,,
Watagoipa	1 ,,
Diolivi	1 ,,

8. *Patima feast*[1]

Goilala	27 portions
Kerau	1 ,,
Maini	1 ,,

9. *Porua Laiam's pig*

Goilala	27 portions
Tawuni	1 ,,
Gane	1 ,,
Watagoipa	1 ,,
Garipa	1 ,,
Oropoa	1 ,,
Kunima	1 ,,

10. *Feast at Patima 28 Feb. 1972*

Goilala	23 portions
Oropoa	1 ,,
Kunima	3 ,,
Diolivi	2 ,,
Tawuni	1 ,,
Kataipa	1 ,,

11. *Kari's funeral*

Goilala	26 portions
Tawuni	2 ,,
Oropoa	1 ,,
Kataipa	1 ,,
Kunima/Oropoa	1 ,,

12. *Birth feast, and my departure*

Goilala	17 portions
Sopu	4 ,,
Maini	1 ,,
Tawuni	4 ,,
Tanini	1 ,,
Kopoivi	2 ,,

[1] This pork was not killed at Goilala.
[2] The pigs given by Diolivi the previous day killed at Patima.

not, of course, necessarily 25 per cent of the total, but calculation of the weight of pork distributed was impossible in the circumstances. The proportions of pork distributed among the Goilala and other tribes is given in Table 39.

The number of feasts observed was too small to allow a fuller picture of the gift-exchange pattern to emerge, but if the lists of recipients of pork and their tribes are examined, it is clear that Ta-wuni, Kunima, Kataipa, Oropoa, and Kerau are the tribes to which pork is most frequently given. It is interesting that Maini, Amugan-iawa, Watagoipa, and Garipa, on the opposite bank of the Aibala, received very little pork, despite the number of marriages with members of these tribes (see Table 24), but possibly over a longer period this imbalance would be rectified. Chiefs receive more gifts of

TABLE 39. *Proportion of pork given to other tribes*

Feast number	Goilala %	Other tribes %
1	91	9
2	90·4	9·6
3	75	25 (birth)
4	53	47 (birth)
5	78·5	21·5
6	49	51 (funeral)
7	76	24
8	93	7
9	82	18
10	74	26
11	84	16
12	59	41 (birth)

pork than ordinary men, as one might expect, but the number involved is too small to allow firm statistical conclusions to be drawn.

It is clear from Table 37 that there are many prestations of pork to members of other tribes, especially at births and deaths, and it cannot therefore be maintained that the large ceremonies are essential for maintaining the links between tribes. Large ceremonies occur comparatively infrequently, and over several years the number of prestations produced by small ceremonies will certainly be spread over a wider range of tribes than those resulting from a single large ceremony, even though the actual quantity of pork will be less.

The total number of donors of pork at these feasts is thirty-two, and the total number of recipients living at Goilala is 128. It does not appear that any of the donors was himself a recipient of pork from any other donor at any of these feasts. From this it follows that each pig killed ceremonially produced at least four debts within the tribe, and that repayment of these debts is extremely slow and not made at the soonest possible opportunity. In other words, debts will obviously accumulate, and there must of necessity be some chance for 'wiping the slate clean', an occasion which is clearly provided by the great feasts.

Therefore, irrespective of the dominant motives of the Tauade in holding large pig-feasts—the propitiation of the dead, the acquisition of honour, the humiliation of enemies, the relief of boredom—there are certain consequences of the killing of pigs as settlement of debts that can be shown to necessitate large periodic killings, at least within the context of Tauade society. Thus given (1), (2), and (3) below, (4), (5), and (6) will follow:

(1) Pigs are always split up, and not given whole—with a few exceptions to be noted below.

(2) All gifts of pork must be reciprocated at a later date, if shame is to be avoided, but equivalence between gifts is maintained.

(3) Most feasts take place within the local community—the tribe—which absorbs about 75 per cent of the gifts.

(4) Therefore periodically each tribe kills a large percentage of its herd on a single occasion, and invites large numbers of strangers to receive the pork.

(5) At all large pig-feasts money is given for pork, usually by visitors, but men may also contribute a pig in return for payment.

(6) Pigs are given whole at large feasts, usually to chiefs of other tribes, who then take the pig and divide it up on their own account. Small piglets are also given away live, as we have seen.

Giving away pigs as whole units clearly simplifies the network of debt, and the acceptance of an immediate money payment short-circuits the whole system and circumscribes the spread of debt. The invitation of large numbers of outsiders allows a great many pigs to be killed by the host community, to pay off its internal debts, and yet to have the surplus pork absorbed by other tribes, in the form of whole pigs.

The small ceremony is extraordinarily formless and confusing. People drift in during the morning, and sit around a fire, or lie on the grass if the weather is fine, and sometimes a man rises to his feet and harangues the others, often about matters that are quite irrelevant to the business in hand. Other men may be working on the platform, if one is to be built, while women and other men are digging the earth oven. For this stones are heaped on piles of timber which are set on fire, so that clouds of acrid smoke drift across the gathering.

A chief at last gets up and obtains silence, and launches into a rambling oration, often interrupted, and with many asides on matters of current interest in the area. Usually only two or three chiefs speak, apart from the person or persons who are most closely involved in the feast itself. During the speeches the pigs may be clubbed, but no one has any definite responsibility for this. Sometimes when the pigs have been killed the men will rush down to the end of the village and roar in triumph, and their shout will carry across the valley so that their neighbours may know they have killed pigs. This shout is called the *avīava*.

The speeches often fade into general conversation, while the pigs are butchered and put in the ovens, wrapped in *kovelapa* leaves. While they are cooking, some more speeches may be made, unless it starts to rain, when everyone takes shelter in the huts and smokes and gossips. Finally, the pork is distributed ceremonially; a knot of men gather round the pork which is laid out on *kovelapa* leaves. A chief, or a chief's son learning to distribute pork, actually calls out the name of each recipient in a loud voice, shouting 'So-and-so, your share of pork is here!', which is the standard formula, whereupon an assistant carries the piece of pork to the person named. The chief calls out the names given to him by the men actually involved in the prestations, and between each announcement there is a discussion over who should get what piece next. When the pork has been distributed the meeting gradually breaks up as everyone takes his pork away or, usually, gives it to his wife to carry for him.

While people eat roast sweet potatoes or smoked pandanus nuts during the proceedings and the guts of the pigs are cooked in pots and distributed with rice for immediate consumption by all present, pork itself is an honorific food and not eaten as a communal feast, but is taken away by the recipients and eaten privately with their families and close relatives.

A funeral is a singularly appropriate occasion for a wide range of relatives and friends to gather together, and for pork to be distributed (see Table 39), though the numbers of those attending such a meeting will depend on the status of the deceased. In the old days it was the custom for the relatives to bring presents of valuables to the bereaved and be given pork in return, but today money is given instead. In Fig. 16 are shown the principal relatives of the old woman Kari, who died at Goilala on 12 March 1972; her funeral was held the next day at Dimanibi.

Buluvu Kimani provided the pig 'Deliba'. Kamo Maia and Laiam Kepe provided the pig 'Ipili', of which they are co-owners. Buluvu's wife Orai died some years before, and Laiam Kepe killed a pig for her, so on this occasion Buluvu killed a pig for Laiam Kepe's mother.

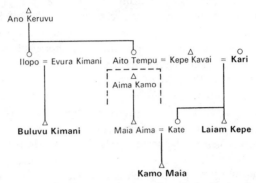

FIG. 16. Relatives of Kari who contributed pigs for her funeral

The meat of these pigs was distributed among those present, in return for gifts of money. At Aima Kamo's funeral a large number of pigs were killed, since he was one of Goilala's most important chiefs (see Table 40).

TABLE 40. *Donors of pigs at Aima Kamo's funeral*

Donors	Number of pigs	Tribe	Relation to deceased
Maia Moimo	1	Tawuni	SWB
Manaip Aima (f)	1	Kataipa	D
Kaita Koupa	1	Kataipa	affine
Damoro Amai	1	Tawuni	SWB
Kuvale Mauru	1	Kunima?	BSS
Kirau Ivoro	1	Goilala	BSDH
Korete (f)	1	Goilala	DD
Kamo and Maia Aima	1	Goilala	SS & S
Peeri Aima	1	Goilala	S
Koloala Maia	1	Goilala	BS
Kinama Maia (f)	1	Goilala	BSW
[Aima Kamo]	1	Goilala	—

Agnates predominate here with other close relatives in the list of contributors. This occasion well illustrates the point made earlier (pp. 72–3) that the size of a man's herd is not really crucial—what matters is the number of relatives and friends who can be persuaded to provide pigs for a feast. Contributors thus have close ties with the organizers of feasts, but the pork is distributed very widely.

Births are the other occasion for the gathering of scattered relatives who might not otherwise meet together except for funerals. The following description of the pig-killing to celebrate the birth of a daughter, Kivo Maria, to Evete Anamara and his wife Keuvai, and to mark my own imminent departure from Goilala, shows the complex network of ties affirmed on such occasions.

Evete and Keuvai live in Amo Lume's section of Dimanibi; Keuvai is the daughter of Mo Kuvari, of Tawuni, and Amo has many ties with that tribe, since his mother came from there. Four pigs were given, as follows:

Donors of pigs	
Amo Lume	1 small
Amai Evura ⎫ Evete Anamara ⎭	1 big
Kirau Ivoro	1 big
Mo Kuvari	1 small
	—
	4

Amo gave the pig because of my speech, and so that all will tell of me and Kivo Maria. Evete gave his pig because he was the father of the baby. Kirau Ivoro gave a pig because he is Amo's friend, and Amo asked him to because I was leaving soon and he wanted to kill one for me and also for the baby. Mo Kuvari (from Tawuni) gave one because he is Keuvai's father—she is the mother of the baby.

Evete gave A$20 for the pigs. Of this A$10 were supplied by Amo; A$16 went to Terupu Aima, who is protected by Kirau Ivoro and who clearly supplied Kirau's pig. Amai Evura's daughter Neavamai received the remaining A$4. No payment was given for Mo Kuvari's pig, as the child was his niece, nor was there any payment for Amo Lume's pig.

The account of the following feast is given in full, to allow the reader to form a proper impression of a small ceremony.

On 28 March 1971 a feast was held at Palaileve for the birth of a son to Kog Manita. Table 42 gives details of the donors of pigs.

On this occasion, unlike the feast at Ororogaivara, a platform was built and was mounted by Korete, daughter of Bauai Katemu, and she was given money on behalf of the child. The following made speeches: Kog Manita, Lariava Moripi, Avui Maia.

Kog Manita begins by referring to the garden of Keru and Lariava at Poroyava, which has been newly made. Amo adds in his commentary that the point of this remark is that the sweet potatoes in the garden will grow big like Kog Manita's son. Then Kog goes on to refer to some smoked

TABLE 41. *Reasons for donations of pork at Goilala feast*

Recipients of pork	Tribe	Reasons for donation
Aita Patovo	Sopu	*Valavala* of Evete Anamara.
Kamo Velikovo	Sopu	,,
Aima Kame	Sopu	,,
Kovei Komitsi	Sopu	,,
Lumani Alano	Sopu	,,
Kate Karita (f)	Maini	She is Amo Lume's sister, living at Maini and visiting Goilala.
Igi Dioro	Tawuni	*Valavala* of Amo Lume. His little daughter gave money to Korete.
Kumo Moimo	Tawuni	Amo's *valavala*.
Kamo Beto	Goilala	
Pelai Kitsio	Goilala	Kitsio gave A$6 for his name to be given to the child.
Kitsio Koma	Goilala	
Beto Oiabue	Goilala	
Kovele Aima (f)	Amiapa	She is Aima Kamo's granddaughter, related to Kirau Ivoro.
Noma Kitai	Goilala	Amo Lume's *valavala*.
Kopa Mauru	Goilala	,,
Kopeiri Kitai	Goilala	,,
Kirau Pio	Goilala	,,
Manua Tovana	Goilala	,,
Kovi Kitei (f)	Tawuni	,,
Ora Moimo (f)	Tawuni	,,
Lariava Moripi	Goilala	Made a speech.
Pelai Maga	Goilala	Amo's friend, gave me a homicide emblem.
Francis Koupa	Goilala	Councillor.
Amai Evura	Goilala	Gave a pig.
Peeri Aima	Goilala	Brought food, gave me dogs' teeth. Amo's friend.
Maia Aima	Goilala	Brought food. Amo's friend.
Laiam Kepe	Goilala	Brought food and tobacco. Amo's friend.
Kioai Pilipo	Tawuni	Brought areca nut. Amo's *valavala*.
Kamau Teresia (f)	Goilala	Wife of Tatai Beto.
Kavai Katuvai (f)	Goilala	Wife of Perai Maga. Both these women are suckling, and it is customary to give women food in this case, as *oruv'ae lok*, compensation for the breast.

pandanus which he, Kog, put in the men's house at Itoveve some years before [he is holding some smoked pandanus, presumably of the same lot of nuts to which he is referring]. Kovele (Kepe Maia's daughter) looked after the smoking of these nuts, and Amo says that she did this because the Goilala were away at Watagoipa attending a dance. While they were away she died, and Avui Apava, her nephew, and his son Kog Manita came back and buried her at Patima. [According to Amo, they put a taboo on the nuts until now, when Kog Manita has lifted it because of the birth of his son.] He concludes by saying that the guests have come today to his hamlet to name the child, and they will be given food.

After this, they distribute the food [pandanus, bananas, sweet potatoes, sugar-cane] into eleven piles, and Kire Kaita says that the food should be eaten first, with speeches afterwards, and Moripi will speak, and Apava [me] will distribute tobacco.

Then Moripi speaks. In the beginning, he says, we were fighting and killing each other, and Miter Beeti [Patrol Officer Speedie] came to Aporota, and Pè Giva [Fr. Guivarc'h] came to Kerau, and made roads and law and clothed people. Miter Hallpike first came to Kairuku and when his work there was finished he went to New Guinea, and when he had

TABLE 42. *Donors of pigs at birth feast*

Kog Manita	1	his son
Kilemu Apava	1	his DS
Oiabue Mana	1	for money (A$6)
Lariava Moripi	1	his WFFBSS. Was given a piglet in return.
Kamo Deego	1	child was named after him
Kirau Ivoro	1	for money (A$4)
Amai Evura	1	for money (A$10)
Katemu Bauai	2 chickens (A$1 for pair?)	

finished writing down their stories he came back to Kerema, and when he had finished his work there he came here to Goilala. He did not come to make a business here. It is a different work. He came to study the language for two years, then when his work is done he will go somewhere else. On Monday we will work on his motor-bike track. [Then there is an abrupt change of thought, in which I am explicitly related to Apava Tulava, whose name I am now given.] The ancestor went away then came back and ...[?] ... Mr. Hallpike then as our ancestor went away and we [?] called him back. Apava Tulava is there at Pomutaivi, a new shoot. I have spoken his name. Your name is Apava Tulava. [Moise explains that my name is a chief's name, 'like a king'—he was Avui Apava's son and Avui is one of the most important chiefs at Goilala. It is highly likely that the occasion of giving a name to Kog's son was felt to be most appropriate to naming me, as a 'new shoot' of the old Apava Tulava.]

Then Moripi's speech becomes more obscure. [The girl Korete is now on the platform with a baby girl called Avia.] This is Avui Laiam's baby, Avia, who went to Moresby with her mother Vata Tau, and stayed there. [Kog Manita will make reference to Avia in his speech later.] Her daughter Avia came here later, and Aito made food for her. She will eat in Goilala, her country. The pandanus is planted in the ground here. This is the story of the tobacco. Eat sweet potatoes, break pandanus nuts, distribute meat, rice, bread, sweet biscuits. Terupu begot a daughter [this is a reference to a third child] the one there, and Otutu took it so that it would not die; Terupu became sick at Tapini, and then came to Kerau, and then came here. Katai Kovele is the girl's name. She will take her food here [she gets a biscuit. Clearly giving food is a rite of incorporation for the Goilala. The reference to Katai Kovele needs explanation. A Watagoipa man, Baro Koupa, and his wife Terupu, came to Kerau after being at Tapini, where the woman was ill. Leaving Kerau they came to Goilala where Terupu gave birth to a baby girl at Palaileve. She stayed in the house of Otutu, wife of Avui Apava. The birth was very painful, and she flung the child away. She was very sick and crazy. Otutu looked after the child but she had no milk, so she took it to Kerau where Sister Mary gave it a bottle. Then Otutu gave it to Keru Avui's wife Kovele Aima, who had milk, to suckle. Kovele asked for the child to be called Katai Kovele.]

Kamo Ligo says 'Give the child [Kog's son] my name. People will quarrel over "Keruvu" or "Maia".' Moripi says 'Give the name "Kamo".' The people say 'Kamo Kavilo'. Moripi says 'You can only give one name.' They seem to be deciding. Then Moripi says 'Take and eat rice, food and meat, potatoes and sweet potatoes' [this is to tell the women to distribute the food.]

Kog Manita then speaks, referring to the naming of his son. 'We will put his name in the [Census] book, and tomorrow we will work on the [motor-bike] road.' Then he refers to the girl Avia. [It is worth noting that Avia's father, Avui Laiam, is the son of Avui Apava, and married to the eZ of Kog Tseepi, of Maini.] Kog says 'It is Kog Tseepi who has planted the *elaivi* at Aporota as a taboo against giving more money to Vata, for the birth of her daughter Avia, because the Goilala have not reciprocated the [earlier?] gift.'

He also seems to suggest that Kog planted *elaivi* at Aporota to invite the Goilala over there to pig-killings when they have finished at Goilala, for the birth of Avia. There is no mention of Moresby. Manita refers to the ancestors, and to the notion of reciprocity.

Avui Maia then rises to speak with a bundle of tobacco. He first refers to the ancestors:

You know well, when our ancestors of Koveta and Larima first came here, they arrived up there, and left again and came back and so on. The ancestors of Lariava (Apava) in the beginning came after the other ancestors, and brought pigs, and taro, and sweet potato, and pandanus, so that we are like guests[?]. For that reason Kovete-Larima are basically not real Goilala (*Loiatsiai, Kovete-Larima aputsua onei namutep mui uopu, mui uama*). He then refers to Kate [his FFF?] and on the other side to his *alu* Beto, Apava Kanitoro (of Kovete) and Lariava Moripi, who has taken his place.

He then goes on to say that Kovete-Larima only beget girls, and they marry men of other places, who come here and inherit land, and one brother brings another, and this brother brings another, so do not give your women to men of other places.

He then talks of the coming of the mission and the government and how they imposed peace, and refers to how [as a result ?] the women of Goilala marry men of many different tribes, e.g. Iveyava, Karoava, and Gane. The implication here seems to be that because of the cessation of warfare there has been an increased tendency for marriages to occur with men of relatively distant tribes. [There is a short passage after this which I cannot hear distinctly.]

He then goes on to say, that you know the law well, and therefore you know why I went to Tapini the other day. [Apparently, according to Amo, a pig belonging to Moise, Kilemu, or Mogu Apava, raided the garden at Poroyava, and Kog Manita, who had married Kate, daughter of Moise, and Atai, daughter of Kilemu, came and found the pig and shot it, as a result of which there was a fight of some sort between Kog and the three brothers, and Amo says that Kog beat his wife Kate. Some of this can be inferred from Avui's speech, and he tells them to pay compensation.]

Then he talks of economic development, and begins by referring to my arrival, and how I had given them tobacco that day at Ororogaivara. He says that they should listen to what Katemu Bauai and Perai Maga say about the Goilala cattle—they are the committee for cattle—and about what Porua Laiam says about the school at Kerau. He then talks of me, and of how I came to live at Pomutaivi. He says that I am called 'Mr. Hallpike' by the government, but that the Goilala call me 'Apava'. 'You gave us tobacco. Do not return to Moresby. Bring your younger brothers, your older brothers, your sisters, your cousins, your 'family' here to live, and tell the government and mission about this. Today is Sunday [it was Monday, in fact!] and people will rest. The day after is Monday, and everyone will work on your road.' The mention of the road leads him to think of the road which Mr. Martin had built to his farm at Erume, and he says that Mr. Martin came to Erume and lived there, and the men distributed tobacco and betel nut, and he made a big business there—an obvious hint to me to do the same.

The distribution of pork by Oiabue Mana then followed.

The list of recipients (Table 43) illustrates yet again the very wide range of ties which is maintained by these distributions of pork.

These occasions are of necessity also pervaded with latent hostility generated in the very process of affirming ties. On the occasion of Aima Kamo's funeral, for example, the proceedings had been going on for some time, and Kamo Maia, Aima's grandson, was making a commemorative speech after the pigs had been killed. At this moment Kinama Maia, an elderly woman and wife of Avui Apava who was one of Aima's sons, arrived and discovered that they had already killed the pigs before she had been able to bring her own.

She flew into a great rage and ran down the centre of the village shrieking with fury to the place where Kamo Maia was sitting on a pile of vegetables, and poked him in the backside with a stick, telling him to eat her faeces. He merely blushed and looked sheepish, while her tirade continued much to the amusement of the spectators. In the end her pig was killed and put in the oven with the others.

TABLE 43. *Recipients of pork at birth feast*

Buluvu Ivoro (Gane)	He will tell the story of Kog Manita's son when he gets back to Gane. He also gave A$2.
Vata (f)	Her daughter is Avia.
Opu Meto (Watagoipa)	
Aia Manumana (,,)	They will tell their people about Kog Manita's son.
Kava Päana (f) (Kerau)	,,
Avui Iotepa (Kunima)	,,
Kamo Deego (Itoveve)	For bringing a pig.
Noma Tomo (Kunima-Goilala)	To tell the story of Kog's boy.
Kopa Ailene	
Airi Maini (Dimanibi)	He brought food for the feast.
Kepe Manuvu (Ororogaivara)	,, ?
Avui Maia (Kiolilama)	For making speech.
Katemu Bauai (Dimanibi)	For chickens.
Tatai Peto (Dimanibi)	
Myself	For my tobacco.
Katai (f) wife of Maia Laiam (Deribi)	For her bananas and taro.
Amai Evura (Dimanibi)	Pandanus and pig.

Fr. Jacob told me that when he was at Gane or thereabouts he saw a man go into a similar fury because the deceased had been put into the coffin (a modern innovation) before he had arrived, so preventing him looking on the face of the departed for the last time. He was a man of magnificent physique and went ramping up and down the dance yard, shouting abuse at those concerned and brandishing his axe. As his rage reached a climax he brought the axe down in a smashing blow on a log where a pregnant woman was sitting. She was so terrified that she soon afterwards suffered a miscarriage.

At the pig-killing to celebrate the birth of a daughter to Evete Anamara, described earlier, Evete, who had come to Goilala from Iveyava some years before as a catechist, spoke with some resentment.

He said that he made his gardens at Goilala with his bush knife called 'Itupi', and then said, 'I came here a long time ago. I taught writing, I taught people in the school. I gave you tobacco, money for smokes, matches, skirts and trousers to men and women. Now my daughter has been born and you have not brought her food [vegetables] for me or for the Kaubada [myself]. Anamara Koupa and Kire Keruvu are not here. They are hiding in the bush.'

On another occasion there was a pig-feast at Patima; this was mainly for the completion of Perai Maga's men's house for the big dance to be held there, and also to mark the return and recovery of Anamara Koupa's wife following her visit to the hospital at Tapini after she had been wounded by an axe at Goilala. In his speech Perai said that his father's country was Kataipa but that his mother Orai was from Goilala; therefore do not speak badly about him (he became very emotional and angry at this point). He would go back to Kataipa after the big dance and after he had killed pigs. He was clearly sensitive to the charge that he was a stranger, and so went out of his way to assert his hereditary right to build his men's house there for the dance, and told them to look well at this house, and not to speak badly about him.

I was myself involved in a display of hostility on this occasion as a result of Anamara's distribution of pork. The background to his pig-killing is of some interest. On the morning of 2 February he brought his wife Keropo to see me. Her arm had been broken with an axe, and was dripping blood. I bound it up and stopped the bleeding, and wrote an account of the matter in a letter which I gave Anamara for the A.D.C. at Tapini. It appeared that she had been injured by Kamo Koilo. Some years before Kamo's wife had run off with a man from Ilai, Avui Medicolo, and abandoned their daughter—Kamau Keropo. Kamo disowned the girl and went away to live at Kariaritsi. Keropo took pity on the child and looked after her for a number of years. At the time of the assault Kamo had returned and demanded his daughter. Keropo refused to hand her over, however, until she had been repaid for the expenses of keeping her. Kamo then took his axe and broke her arm, and dragged his daughter away with him. (He was arrested two days later and jailed.)

In view of my assistance to his wife, by Tauade custom I could reasonably expect a share of pork when Anamara killed a pig to celebrate his wife's recovery and return. As the distribution of the pork proceeded I began to suspect that Anamara did not, in fact, intend giving me any, and so it proved. By this time I was boiling with rage, and could feel my stomach knotting. Seeing my anger, Amo Lume gave me some of his pork. 'But', I said, 'This piece of pork did not have a speech made for it. *You* gave it to me. Who killed the pigs today?' 'Anamara', he replied. So I called Anamara over, and said 'Why did you not give me pork? I wrote a letter to the Kaubada, and gave your wife medicine, and stopped the blood. Why did you not give me pork? I know your customs.' He was silent. Everyone was now gathered round, tensely, without a word, awaiting the result of this confrontation. Again, I said 'Anamara, why did you not give me pork?' and again there was no reply, and he looked down at the ground, ashamed and speechless. For the third time, I said 'Anamara, why did you not give me pork? Shall I tell you why?' 'Yes', he said. Standing only a few feet from him, I glared in his face and roared 'Because you are like a WILD PIG!', and, turning on my heel, I strode down the hill towards the lower end of the village. Pandemonium broke out but I strode resolutely on, looking straight ahead. In a few moments I heard the pattering of bare feet behind me. After a quick glance round to see if the owner of the feet was also wielding an axe, I continued my exit. Then Anamara, waving a $2 note, caught up, with Amo beside him. Anamara asked me to accept the money, to wipe out the insult he had given me. 'No', I said, 'I will not take the money here. You will give it to me in the *kiava* so that all may hear.' Back we went to where the rest were standing. There Amo said that Anamara was giving me $2 for having insulted me, because I had not been given pork. I took the money with a smile, saying 'Enough. It is finished', and then left. Shortly after I had got back to my house, Amo joined me, convulsed with laughter. 'Ah, Apava,' he said, 'You are a real Goilala! Anamara insulted you, your belly was angry, and you made him give you compensation.' And it was true, for in that brief period of time I felt more at home among the Tauade than ever before. I had been insulted, and had responded with spontaneous rage to restore my reputation by humiliating my adversary.

3. COMPENSATION AND VENGEANCE

The basic mode of social control in Tauade society is provided by the opposition of forces—violently in the case of vengeance, and peaceably where compensation is given for an injury. There is no idea of a meeting between disputants and of their case being mediated by some respected arbitrator or council of elders. Reciprocity is a dominant theme of their society, and can be summed up in one expression —'pay-back'.[1] Some people's ideas of reciprocity are very exact, as indicated in the following anecdote:

The defendant in an adultery case, from P—, states 'Yes, I had intercourse with V—. She wanted me to. Previously I had intercourse with her and I paid two pigs compensation. This time the woman came to me and said "You have paid two pigs yet you only had intercourse with me once. Have me again and then you will be square".' (C.N.M., April 1958.)

Compensation and vengeance are both known as *kakit*, 'payment', and their identity is more than purely verbal, having its roots in the basic purpose of 'making the insides good', *kimuv mi kato ena*. Thus it is that an injured party may first take physical vengeance on his enemy, after which each will exchange pork and/or valuables to wipe out the hurt that each has sustained from the original injury and the act of retaliation. The following anecdote illustrates this:

Baro Oiabue of Avuiri hamlet came and stole some pandanus nuts from the trees of Kiara Maini of Komu hamlet. The stand of trees was called Kaemapelamapa. Baro was up in one of the trees when Kiara came. Kiara was very angry when he saw this and said 'Who took my nuts?' 'I did' said Baro. Kiara hit him several times, and grabbed him by the legs and flung him into the Koiava stream. Kiara went back to Komu. Baro drank of the water and revived, and with his axe he chopped down 5 of Kiara's trees. Kiara came and saw this, so in revenge he went to a place near Ororogaivara and cut down Baro's trees, one called Aletuta-malatu, and another one called Dōra, and some younger sisters of these trees. [Pandanus trees which are specially named are old, with many branches, and yield many nuts; they would of course be the specially prized possessions of any man.] Dōra was a very big tree. When Baro found that his trees had been cut down, he hung the husk of one of the nuts of Dōra round his neck, as if it was a *kiokenivi* [the bone of a dead relative]. Baro had cut down the tree 'Koromuvu' of Kiara Maini, so that was why he cut down Dōra of Baro. Kiara also wore the husk of one of the nuts of Koromuvu round his neck. Kiara Maini killed a pig and put the blood on the husk of the nut, before he hung it round his neck, and Baro also killed a pig before he did the same.

After a long time had passed Baro killed another pig, and gave it to Kiara Maini, with dogs' teeth, homicide emblems, piglets, and feathers. Kiara Maini also killed a pig *tamenu* (for putting straight into the oven)

[1] The concept of 'pay-back'—*hani*—permeates Kunimaipa social life and thought. Any reaction which follows at a later date, because of an initial action of the same kind, is said to 'pay back' the first action. (McArthur 1961: 50.)

and gave also two homicide emblems, a piglet, and feathers. They both took their pigs and riches away, and cooked the pigs and gave of them to their *valavala*.

The readiness with which compensation is offered will depend on the temperament of the guilty party, the nature of the offence, the social distance between the parties, and their relative statuses. It is not considered weak or unmanly to accept compensation in the first instance but, on the contrary, is the mark of a dignified man, a chief, who should also be prepared to offer it. But the Tauade also regard rage and a violent reaction as wholly appropriate responses to injury, as in the preceding case. An example of the peaceful offering and acceptance of compensation is given here:

Amai Kopeiri and Kepe Kavai, both of Kalava, killed a pig of Lavava Bailepe, of Tsigori. The pig wandered in the bush near Kalava, and the two men offered it sweet potatoes, and lured it into the village where they killed it. When it was dark they made an oven and cooked it. But the smell wafted up to Tsigori. Bailepe came down and found them cutting up the pig, and confronted them. They were both ashamed. Bailepe said 'Whose pig is that?' 'It is someone's pig', they said. He saw the marks on the ears of the pig and said 'That is my pig'. Kepe and Amai said 'It is your pig. We will repay you.' He said 'Good' and went back to Tsigori and slept. Kepe and Amai cooked the pig and put it aside. The next day they called their *valavala*, also Bailepe and his wife, and others. Amai gave Bailepe a pig, with a homicide emblem and Kepe Kavai gave him another pig and feathers. The other pig was cut up and distributed and eaten.

The status of the parties is highly significant, and a chief who is assaulted may expect compensation on account of the loss of his prestige thereby:

Apava Tulava of Pomuru hamlet stole the nuts of the trees of Tauru Ivei, from the trees called Dimanipi, near Kilakilakila hamlet. He put the nuts on the ground and was cutting them up, when Tauru came and saw this. He said 'Hey, Apava, who cut down my pandanus nuts?' 'I did' said Apava, so Tauru took his club [a *poroto*, wooden club used for killing pigs] and hit him with it a couple of times. Apava lay on the ground. Then he recovered and got up. Lume Ivei [Tauru's brother] came and hit Tauru for Apava. Lume said 'Apava is a chief, you will not hit him. It is forbidden.' Tauru said 'True. I was angry inside.' Tauru and Lume gave Apava some of the nuts, in fact they said he could come and get some more, in compensation for the beating. Now the son of Apava Tulava, Avui Apava, comes and takes nuts from these trees—about five trees in all—which Tauru and Lume gave to his father.

As we saw in the section on chiefs, Lariava Moripi publicly denounced a man who had assaulted him, and forbade his return to
Goilala. In this story a chief kills a *malavi* whom he finds stealing his
nuts, and then goes to live for a while with another tribe until tempers
have cooled. Another chief, Kopeiri Evura, goes to visit him, and is
given pork and an axe to compensate for the death; after a further
delay the killer returns to Kopeiri's hamlet:

K— of Korutu hamlet stole G—'s pandanus nuts at Pelamapa. G— was
living at Kalava, and came and found K— cutting up the nuts. Amo Lume
was a small boy at this time. G— speared him in the heart and killed him,
and then ran off to Tawuni. Kopeiri Ebura came and took the body to
Kalava. K— was a *malavi*—he was born at Kalava. Kopeiri Ebura was its
chief. He killed pigs; G— stayed at Tawuni. Then Kopeiri Ebura went to
Tawuni, and G— killed a pig for K—, and gave the pork and an axe to
Kopeiri. After some time G— rejoined Kopeiri at Kalava. G— was a real
chief, and so was Kopeiri Ebura. Katemu Bauai is his grandson.

If a chief does kill someone and vengeance is taken, it is almost
invariably against an insignificant relative of the killer. An account of
such a case is given above (p. 121), where Ita Kogotsi killed Teopo, an
elderly relative of Avui Apava who had killed a relative of Ita.

When a man of one tribe visits another tribe, or resides with them,
and is killed by them, his relatives in the tribe of the killers may give
compensation to his relatives in his natal tribe, with the implication
that they have failed to protect him:

Kitai Atu killed K—, of Tawuni. K— was a *valavala* of Kovo Ivei. One
day K— came to Deribi; he had come to give betel nut to Kovo Ivei, and
did not give any to Kitai Atu. K— had come along the path called Etupi-
kokurueviava. (Kitai was living at Kutupu.) So Kitai came and said 'The
other day, which path did you come along? Which path did you bring
betel nut along?' 'Your path,' said K—. 'Bring me some betel nut' said
Kitai. 'I have given all the nuts to Ivei' replied K—. So Kitai killed him.
Kovo Ivei killed a pig and gave it to Tawuni. K—'s son Ololi Kuvaitsi
came and got it. Although K— was a small chief, the Tawuni did not
choose to fight over the matter.

The Tauade do not recognize the category of 'accidental homicide',
and exact vengeance and compensation in the usual way:

Two boys, K— of Kutupu, and M— of Deribi, were playing with bows
and arrows, and throwing the canes of *kerapata* [sword-grass]. M— fired
an arrow which hit K— and made him bleed, so K— got a cane and
stabbed M— with it. He stabbed him in the side of his head and it pierced
his brain. He was sick for four days, then he died. His whole face swelled

up. They buried him at Deribi. The Amuganiawa came for gifts of mourning, and so did the Tawuni. The dead boy M— was the younger brother
of Aima Manuvu. The mother of Manuvu and M— came from Tawuni,
and married Aima Kate, the father of Manuvu and M—. Kulolo Elueluvu
was a Tawuni chief, and begot the woman in question. The pork was
given to the Tawuni as compensation for the dead boy because he had died
on Goilala soil. Kate Ovene's boy K— ran away to Kunima and spent
some time there, and then came back and gave compensation, many dogs'
teeth, and a big pig, to Aima Manuvu.

A long time ago there was an Oropoa man called Ku—. He went with his
wife Ka— to their pandanus trees, where they lit a fire. Ku— climbed the
tree and cut down the nuts. A nut fell on his wife as she was blowing the
fire, and killed her. It smashed her head to a pulp. Ku— came down and
found his wife dead. He wept. It was near the river. He went back to his
hamlet, and left his wife's body on the ground. He returned with his men,
and they fetched the body in a big string bag tied to a pole. She was a
Kunima woman. V— and D— were her elder brothers, they were both
chiefs. They all got their weapons. They killed Ku—'s mother A—. Ku—
said *Kato oi*, *kagiti*, 'It is good, it is payment'. They put the two womens'
bodies in the same house. Ku— killed 2 pigs and gave them to V— and
D—, and 5 homicide emblems. The Kataipa came and got 1 pig for their
mourning, and five feathers. They made a *polo* enclosure for the women,
and the children were initiated at this time. Amo Lume's mother was
initiated at this occasion.

Compensation is also one of the means by which support is gained,
since the relatives and neighbours of a man who has been paid compensation receive a great part of it in the form of pork and/or
valuables. They are thus anxious to press him to accept compensation, rather than to fight, and have a basic interest in helping him to
press his claim.

At this stage in the analysis of compensation and vengeance attention has been focused upon the occasions on which they occur and
upon the forms which they take. In the chapter on values we shall see
how reciprocity is justified for the Tauade in terms of their notions of
the human passions and their place in society.

The prestation of things is therefore basic to Tauade social processes, not only as compensation for wrongs but in the affirmation
of ties, and it is appropriate at the conclusion of this chapter to ask
why it should be so prominent in this society yet absent from that
of the Konso.[1]

[1] The remainder of this section is a shortened version of my paper 'Two
types of reciprocity', Hallpike (1975).

It might be supposed that the respective ecologies of the two societies provide the clue to the predominance of gift exchange among the
Tauade and its absence among the Konso. The Konso cannot kill
their stock in anything like the numbers that the Tauade can,
because of the need for the manure. The size of Konso towns makes
any transfer of residence by the whole population of any town for a
period of several months, as is common for Tauade tribes invited to
distant dances, out of the question. The Tauade can expand their
gardens to cater for a much larger temporary population than usual,
while the agricultural system of the Konso is working at nearly full
capacity under normal circumstances. The Konso system of agriculture with its maximal use of available land for agricultural or residential purposes and the consequent difficulty of providing extra
accommodation at short notice makes any construction of dance
villages on the Tauade scale impossible. But while these ecological
factors would prevent the Konso having a system of gift exchange
of the Tauade type, they have no significance in explaining the lack
of *any* kind of gift-exchange system among the Konso. For there
would be nothing to prevent one ward inviting another ward to be
its guests at a yearly feast, or one lineage doing the same for another
lineage. One Konso town cannot leave its stock and depart for several
months to live with another town, but it would be quite possible for
one section of a town to be the guests of another town for a few days.
It would also be quite possible for individuals in the context of Konso
society to exchange gifts of valuables. In the same way, because it is
easy for the Tauade in ecological terms to have their particular type
of gift-exchange system, it does not follow from this that they have
no choice in the matter. The environment may constrain men and
make some types of behaviour more difficult than others, but it does
not dictate behaviour unequivocally.

It seems to me, therefore, that we must look elsewhere for the
explanation for the presence of gift exchange among the Tauade and
its absence among the Konso. To be specific, we must look for it in
the very nature of the reciprocity of actions and things.

Co-operation is only meaningful in a social context wherein the
partners habitually interact, whereas a gift can significantly be given
to a total stranger, requiring for its effectiveness only that it shall have
value for the recipient. In societies such as the Tauade where the
recipients may be people whom the donors hardly ever see, co-operation would be an impossibility, and gifts provide an obvious form of

effective interaction. But it could plausibly be argued that while gift exchange is appropriate for the great pig-killing ceremonies to which distant tribes are invited, communal feasts and norms of co-operation would be perfectly possible within the tribe, since everyone there knows everyone else, and in the course of his life a man may have as neighbours in one hamlet or another almost all the members of the tribe. To answer this perfectly valid objection one must consider the nature of gifts and services more deeply.

It seems to be almost a universally accepted principle that givers of things thereby become superior in status to the receivers; contrarily, a person who performs a service for someone else does not render himself the recipient's superior by doing so but, quite the opposite, his inferior. This aspect of 'service' becomes clearer if we consider the case of a contest of gift exchange where the parties try to shame each other by successively giving larger and larger presents. If this contest were converted into one where not gifts but services were exchanged, so that the victor was he who had performed the most services, such a condition of winning would be indistinguishable from a condition of servitude and social inferiority. Thus to perform a service for anyone makes one's pride vulnerable to shame, since one has put oneself in an inferior position from the start, and if that person for whom one has done the service does not reciprocate, one will be left at a permanent disadvantage. This is quite opposite to the case of gift exchange, since a person who does not reciprocate a gift can be laughed at as a poor fellow, a mean person, and all the resources of pride and shame can be brought against him.

It follows, therefore, that in order for co-operation to be the norm there must be a situation of mutual trust to allay fears that one will be taken advantage of. Gift exchange, on the other hand, can flourish in a situation of open hostility, since the giver of a *thing* has by that very act put himself in a position of superiority to the recipient. The sanction for an effective system of gift exchange is ridicule and the necessary admission by one who reneges upon his debts that he is not man enough to meet them. The satisfaction which this will give to the initial donor is sufficient recompense for the lack of a reciprocal gift.

We may summarize the basic argument of this section as follows:

(1) To give a gift makes the giver superior in status to the receiver, whereas,

(2) to do a service makes the doer inferior in status to the beneficiary; his reputation and pride are therefore vulnerable.

(3) Consequently, we can expect to find that gift exchange will be the norm in societies which are weakly integrated, mobile in group composition, and with ambiguous boundaries between the categories of 'we' and 'they', since loss of reciprocity is no loss to one's pride.

(4) Correspondingly, because of the vulnerable position in which the performance of a service places one's pride, we will expect to find exchange of assistance common only in situations where there is every chance that these acts will be reciprocated. (I leave out of account some ecologically necessary forms of mutual assistance). Mutual assistance will therefore be the norm in societies whose groups are closely knit, stable and enduring in membership, and where the distinction between 'we' and 'they' is unambiguous, in a situation of mutual trust.

More generally, we have seen that while the chiefs are able, in suitable circumstances, to negotiate peace between tribes, their powers of compelling members of their own tribe to pay compensation are limited to their own supporters, if that, and violence often erupts before the chiefs have the chance to intervene. Although dances and pig feasts indeed provide opporrunities for the widening and intensifying of social bonds, and further justify the Tauade's acceptance of chiefly authority, they traditionally occurred too rarely on a large scale to have been an important factor in the restraint of warfare, while the small ceremonies, which only link groups within tribes with groups in other tribes, do nothing but intensify the amorphous quality of Tauade group structure. Compensation for wrongs is essentially an individualistic solution, localized both in time and in its range of social relations, and its very possibility offers offenders a relatively painless escape from the consequences of their anti-social acts.

V
Warfare

BEFORE the arrival of the government, warfare was probably a weekly occurrence somewhere in the Aibala Valley. For example, the Annual Report from Mondo Police Camp for 1931 states that there had been much fighting in the Aibala Valley, and that the Lieutenant-Governor had instructed that no further patrols were to be sent there for the time being. In the Report for 1932 it is said that a visit was paid to the area, and that killing, plundering, and incendiarism were rife. In November 1934, at the time of the establishment of the camp at Aporota, Mr. Middleton writes that there were daily fights between the Maini, Laitate, Amuganiawa, Watagoipa, Garipa, and Oro tribes.

The intensity of intertribal fighting was variable, however, and it seems clear that it was liable to flare up in one area for a number of months, while other areas remained relatively quiet.

I describe fighting between tribes as 'warfare', but this does not imply that the causation of this kind of violence is different in principle from that of violence generated within the tribe. Warfare is not, in its initial stages, a corporate affair involving whole tribes but starts at the level of personal provocation between members of particular hamlets which then progressively involves the rest of the tribes to which the hamlets belong. In some cases the initial violence occurs entirely within a tribe but induces intervention by relatives of those involved from other tribes; this is especially likely to occur when a chief is killed.

I. SMALL-SCALE VIOLENCE

Not all disputes between members of different tribes result in bloodshed, which is often restrained by the means described in the last chapter, as the following case makes clear:

Beto Kioitama, Moise Apava, and Kaga Bailepe, all of Tsigori hamlet, went to a place where the airstrip now is, and killed Vavivi's pig in daylight. [He was a Kerau man.] They tied it up and brought it back to their place. They made an oven at night and cooked it and distributed it. Vavivi followed the trail of blood and [came to Tsigori] and said 'Who has killed my pig?' The people denied seeing it. Then Apava Aginei revealed who had killed it. Vavivi was a chief and he was not angry. 'Good,' he said, 'Give me three piglets' [one from each of the thieves]. The biggest chiefs are not angry, they speak peace.

Even when violence broke out it was often confined to exchanges of arrows and spears, and pigs were soon killed by both parties as compensation. But in some cases, where homicide between tribes occurred, this initiated a long series of killings which might continue for years, without resulting in pitched battles. The Tauade have long memories, and sons may avenge the grievances of their fathers or even of their grandfathers. While this pattern of murder obviously became more common as a result of government pacification, it seems to have been a permanent feature of the traditional society as well.

In 1929 in the course of pay-back killings, the Lole people went to Sopu and killed the woman Kovela, wife of the Village Constable Kove. In retaliation, a Sopu man, T—, caught a woman called N—,[1] wife of a Loleava chief called L—-G—, the woman herself being the daughter of a chief, Givi-Ketava.

In his statement T— says he went to the village of Kariarita which is higher up the valley and belongs to the Small Goilala of the Ioma side. He went looking for Lole men to kill. He found the woman N— there who had had a quarrel with her husband L—-G— of Lole and had run away. T— took hold of her hand and took her to his village of Pe-u where he kept her for the night [for purposes which should be obvious]. In the morning a number of men of Sopu arrived and took the woman outside where they killed her, P— striking the first blow. Then Ko—, Lu—, Ig—, La—, M—, G—, An—, Am— Ta—, Ge— Ga—, Ai— T—, and T— [who had caught her in the first place] took a hand. K—-B—, K—-T—, A— A—, and K— Ka— of Ivei-Ava were called over and helped to cut the body up. [It is not stated if the body was afterwards eaten.] (Ivan Champion and Smith, P.O., Mondo, 4/8/29–7/9/29.)

C.N.M., October 1953.
A— and K— of Ka— murdered L— of Ts—.
The evidence of P—, male child of about 13 years of age: 'I know the defendants A— and K— now before the court. I know the deceased L—. He was my clan brother. I was present when he died. The night before that,

[1] The wife of Lipo Gapa, whose removal from her first husband, Rumania, was the cause of the attacks on the Giumu by the Lova-Loleava described earlier, pp. 138–9.

L— and I slept in Ke—'s house at Ka— and about dawn we went along the road to our own village of K—. As we approached K— we saw the defendants A— and K— following us from the direction of Ka—. I was ahead and ran quickly into the bush and hid in the hole of a hollow tree trunk standing a few yards from the track. L— was about 30 yards behind me, and A— and K— a few yards away from him. Each of the defendants was carrying an axe. They were running. L— made to run up the hill into the bush, saw the defendants were gaining on him and turned right to run in another direction. Then A— came up with L— and struck him a heavy blow on the right side of the back of the head with his axe. The axe was a 3/4 [?] axe . . . Then L— fell down and K— struck him heavily, high up on the spine with his axe. Then the two defendants ran away to the right, towards Aiwarra. When I saw the defendants I ran away to K—. I felt sure my brother was dead, and I was afraid . . .'

A—, defendant, says 'We two have only one thing to say. They killed our sister's husband therefore we killed L—. We did not know our relations had already killed the woman Lu—, or we would not have gone after L—. L— and P— slept in a village higher up. We slept in a village lower down. L— and P— went off to K— earlier. We came along later. We saw them leave the higher village [and go?] across the grass, so we hurried ahead to cut them off by a short cut, and we succeeded in doing so. We hid by the road until they came along. The little boy saw us and ran away. We let him go. We did not want a little boy.'

When a member of one tribe was killed, no attempt was made to retaliate upon the murderer in person, however long a period of time elapsed before vengeance was taken. It was sufficient that any member of the killer's tribe paid with his life, and in some cases the injured tribe was satisfied if their victim came from the general area of the killer's tribe, as in the following case:

On or about the 24th Feb. 1955, a native was killed in a brawl between Goilala natives in Port Moresby. Reports of this killing filtered through to the dead man's relatives at Maini village, near Aporota. The reports were to the effect that K—, a Maini native, was killed during a fight in Port Moresby by a man of Tatupiti.

At 2 p.m. on the 9th inst. [March] a report was received of a killing near Maini village. A party left immediately to investigate, and met a party of natives on the track who were able to give some details of the murder. Sgt. Toro and others continued on to view and recover the body. The body was examined at Tapini, and the wounds showed that the deceased met his death as the result of a particularly vicious and brutal axe assault. The whole of the back from the right shoulder to the front ribs was laid open at least 9″ wide and about 6″ deep, the spine and ribs being completely severed.

Preliminary inquiries have now revealed that the deceased native, A—by name, was a mission helper with Fr. Duffey of the Catholic Mission, Kerau. He was sent by Fr. Duffey early on the 8th inst. from Lavavai village to search for a wandering horse. He had nearly reached Aporota when he met a group of Maini natives travelling towards Tapini. Under questioning, A— said to this group that he belonged to Kariariti, whereupon he was attacked and done to death as a pay-back for the Moresby killing of a few days' earlier. K—, the native killed in Moresby, was a relative of the Maini men, and A— was allegedly a member of the same group responsible for the Moresby killing. So it happened that an innocent native, engaged on a peaceful task, became the latest victim in this vicious custom of pay-back.

This murder has already had its repercussions. From Fr. Besson of Kerau Mission, this report:

'Mr. Kennedy arrived yesterday at Kerau on his way to Tapini. He will tell you how there is big trouble at Kerau since the murder of this week. Our schoolboys are from many different villages and are afraid to be killed as a payback.'

Mr. Kennedy, O.I.C. Ioma, reports that the situation is tense at Kerau, and that it has been necessary to post 2 police there to prevent possible violence. It was in 1949 that a schoolboy was murdered near Kerau, and it is only a few months since peace has been re-established to the extent of children of the former enemy groups mingling together at the mission school. This most recent murder must have the effect of estranging many groups, with the attendant possibility of yet another pay-back murder to 'square' the account. (File 11/213, report dated 14 March 1955, from A.D.C. Goilala Sub-District at Tapini to the District Commissioner, Central District, Port Moresby.)

Where these isolated vendetta killings occur, the perpetrators often attempt to hide the bodies, and throwing them into rivers is a favourite means of disposal. The preceding case illustrates a pervading theme of small-scale violence—the vulnerability of the traveller.

Chiefs had considerable freedom to go where they wished, partly because of the fear of the reprisals which killing them would provoke, and also in some cases because they were good fighters. Ordinary people with relatives in other tribes could usually expect to be able to visit them without fear of attack. But if they offended a chief by not giving him a present for the use of a path which he controlled, or if anyone in the tribe had a score to settle, they risked death, as the following incident at Goilala shows:

O—, of Gane killed K—, Aima Kamo's true younger sister in the following way. O— was her husband. O— had another wife, from Gane, called Ko—. Ko— and K— were quarrelling, and K— came and hit Ko—,

and Ko— hit her back. K— said 'Your wife has "killed" me, so in return
you should "kill" her.' O— was angry, and said 'You will not hit her,
because we will kill each other.' K— then called O— a bald-head, because
he would not beat up Ko—, so O— killed her. Aima Kamo heard about
this; he was at Kutupu, and killed a pig, with Kamo Tulala, Apava Tulava
[his younger brothers] and Avui Apava [his nephew]. Kaita Bolovai of
Gane came and told them. K—'s son, O— I—, also came to Goilala and
told them that the Gane had killed pigs and buried her, at Kopo Ketsiogo,
which was O—'s village at Gane. O— I— brought a pig with him from his
father to Kutupu. Everyone wept for K— and killed pigs, with Kitai
Komai and Aima Manuvu. Then they planted *elaivi* [in her memory] and
gave O— I— a pig, and sent him back to Gane, because he was their
agopi [sister's child]. Time passed.

Then Ku—, of Gane [a relative of O—] and his wife B— [born at
Oropoa] came to Oropoa to see her relatives and get pandanus nuts. They
both spent some time there, and started back to Gane, along the Omua-
keevi path and came to a place near Pomutu—Opealieve village. Aima
Kamo was cutting up pandanus nuts with Kope Kapuri, Apava Tulava,
Kamo Tulala, Aima Kovio, Beto Atu and his son Kamo Beto, they were
all cutting up the nuts with the Goilala women. [I have seen this clearing
in the pandanus forest; it is very dark and gloomy.] B— and her husband
Ku— came up with them, and Aima Kamo saw them and invited them to
sit down. He gave them pandanus nuts to eat, and then told the others to
look after them. He himself went back to Kutupu and got four spears, and
took out the *elaivi*, and then returned to the place where his 'guests' were.
He put the *elaivi* in his teeth, and rushed out of the trees upon them, and
speared Ku—, and then B—, he speared them both twice over. Kope
Kapuri axed Ku— in the head, and Apava Tulava axed B—; Kamo
Koupa axed her as well. Beto bashed them with a stone club. All the
Goilala came and chopped them to bits, then tied them up and took them
along the Urumeva path. Aima Kamo stuck the *elaivi* up B's vagina. Then
they sent along the path Lume Alava, until they came to where the graded
track now is, when they flung the bodies over a cliff there. [This is on the
spur going down to the river opposite Gane.] Aima sang out to O— 'O—,
come down and have a look, so that you may see Ku— and B— copulating',
this was the song that they sang.

O— and his men came down and tied up the bodies and took them back
to Gane (they were chopped up something horrible). The Goilala came
back singing their song of triumph. They did not pay any compensation
for these two. O— had not given any for K— (the pork which he had given
to his son was only a piece of meat, not a whole pig). So because O— had
not given compensation, the Goilala gave none either.

A long time passed. Then Miter Beeti came to Aporota. O—, One
Valitu [the son of Ku—], Kulolo Tetena, Kamo Ilitu, and Kulolo Olioli
all came to Goilala. Aima Kamo was at Poroyava, and he gave them com-

pensation, a string of dogs' teeth for Ku—, and another for B—, and Kope Kapuri also gave dogs' teeth, as did Aima Kovio, Avui Apava, while Kamo Beto gave a piglet, and Kamo Tulala killed a pig. Then O— and his son Ivoro killed 2 pigs as compensation for K— and brought them to Goilala, where he gave them to Aima Kamo, Apava Tulava, and Avui Apava. He also gave them 2 piglets.

Some travellers were killed without even the justification of vengeance:

Kamo Beto was living at Pomutu. Orou Keruvu was at Ororogaivara. Some K— women were at Aporota [Police Camp] with Miter Beeti [Mr. Speedie]. He used to go to Tapini and then to Katé [Kunimaipa] to arrest people, and then he brought them to Aporota, then to Kairuku [Government H.Q. on Yule Island]. Two of the women whom he had arrested escaped, and came through Goilala on their way home. Kamo Beto and Orou Keruvu offered to show the way, and took them down to the Kataipa, where they copulated with them. Then they killed the two women there. E— was killed by Kamo Beto, and Orou killed U—. They buried them in the bank by the river. The river washed the soil away, and the pigs came and ate the bodies. The pigs were seen carrying the bones.

A K— man [name unknown to Amo Lume] was arrested at Aporota, and came through Goilala, [then crossed the Kataipa River] and reached Tanini. Aima Kamo killed him there because he had *keveitsi* (*Tinea imbricata*, a skin disease which produces skin with a shaggy appearance). Kumo Kotsi was with Aima, and everyone came and chopped him up. They dug a hole and buried him. They did not eat him because he had *keveitsi*. They put a big stone on top of him. They killed him because he had *keveitsi*.

A Ku— man was arrested by the *kiap*. His name was Ko—. He was taken to Tapini to work [in the prison] but he did not like the work, so he escaped, and came to Tanini, where he was given food by Kaua Komaepe [the son of Kepe Maia, eldest brother of Aima Kamo]. Aima Kamo said 'You should kill him' so Kaua took an axe and killed him. Beto Aima [of Kataipa] also hit him with another axe. Kumo Kotsi also axed him, and they took him to the Iguam stream, and pushed him in the hole where the water comes out. A Kataipa man came and took him out and cut him up and fed him to his pigs.

It seems, therefore, that the killing of the defenceless stranger, and killing by stealth, perpetrated by members of one tribe against those of another, are patterns of violence that are distinguishable from warfare, which is usually generated by some provocative act, usually theft, witnessed by many and leading quickly to an armed confrontation. If blood was spilt as a result of this, raiding often followed, together with considerable destruction of gardens, killing of pigs, and sometimes loss of life.

2. THE PATTERN OF TRIBAL WARFARE

An examination of the reports of fighting between the years 1918 and 1953 does not disclose any clear patterns of alliance and enmity, beyond the fact that enmity is likely to be aggravated by proximity. Relations between some adjoining tribes, such as Goilala and

TABLE 44. *Goilala killed by surrounding tribes*

Killed by	Number
Sopu	1
Oropoa	3
Amiapa	1
Tawuni	3
Kunima	10
Amuganiawa	1
Laitate	6
Kataipa	1
Gane	1
Watagoipa	1
Maini	1
	29

Kunima, Laitate and Sene, and Sopu and Loleava, have clearly been embittered for this reason.

A more precise idea of intertribal relations can be obtained from the number of Goilala killed by their neighbours, as represented in Table 44. We can see that the degree of intertribal hostility calculated by this method is fairly well correlated with proximity. It is instructive to compare the group of tribes with which hostilities have been greatest with the group with which intermarriage has been most common (Table 45).

The two nearest neighbours of Goilala, Kunima, and Tawuni, appear in both groups, but it can be seen that in general intermarriage tends to be inhibited by a high level of permanent hostility. To this extent the Tauade do not make a point of marrying their enemies. Moreover, even where the Goilala are linked to other tribes by marriage it is only small groups within the tribe which are truly linked in this way. Thus the majority of two tribes can fight each other unin-

hibited by the marriage links between a few of their members. The
Tauade are aware, however, that they frequently fight other tribes
with whom they have numerous marriage links. When I asked Amo
why they married their enemies he replied, 'It is good. We give each
other women to bear sons who will replace those we have killed.' So
while only small groups of relatives within each tribe are regarded
as being linked by marriage, the sons which are the issue of these
marriages are regarded as assets accruing to the whole tribe, and thus
replacing those killed by the tribes from which strange women have
come.

TABLE 45. *Killing and marriage*

Killings (number)		Marriages (%)	
Kunima	10	Tawuni	12·75
Laitate	6	Watagoipa	10·8
Tawuni	3	Kerau	8·8
Oropoa	3	Kataipa	7·8
		Maini	6·8
		Amuganiawa	6·8
		Kunima	4·9

Relations between tribes are greatly influenced by ecological
factors. Tribes on opposite sides of mountains with virgin forest
between them tend to have the friendliest relations, and guests at
large dances are frequently invited from considerable distances. The
primary forest offers few occasions of conflict and forms a natural
barrier which, while not preventing social intercourse, mitigates its
competitive elements. The relations between tribes separated by a
river tend to be less harmonious: while the river is an effective barrier
to pigs, and hence to quarrels caused by their depredations in gardens,
the people used to make yam gardens down by the rivers, and these
were frequently raided by their neighbours on the opposite bank.
For example, on 24 October 1941 fighting broke out between the
Karom (near Kerau) and the Kiolivi, across the Aibala. Two men at
least were injured, and one of these later died. After the killing of pigs
for the death of this man the Karom took vegetables across the river
to their friends at Kiolivi. These fought among themselves over who
would have the most, and ended by destroying the potatoes in the
fighting. The catechist Tumai tried to intervene, but received an
arrow in the thigh. One of his men killed one of the troublemakers.

Sporadic fighting was still going on at the end of November, and in December a man was killed and his body disappeared. In January a Karom man died from wounds received in the earlier fighting.

In August 1950 Patrol Officer Bottrell wrote:

... in the central part of the valley, there is some ill-feeling between Kiolivi on one side, and Elava and Karuma [Karom] on the other. This was caused by the theft of Karuma pigs by some of the Kiolivi villagers. These pigs were killed when they strayed on to Kiolivi gardens, which had been built on Karuma owned land, situated on the Karuma bank of the river. In retaliation for this act, Karuma men, assisted by others from Elava, made an armed demonstration forcing the Kiolivi people to return to their own side of the river and desert their gardens which were subsequently destroyed by the demonstrators. Whilst the patrol was at Elava the Karuma people stole and killed a Kiolivi pig in further retaliation.

The greatest degree and frequency of intertribal violence seems to occur between tribes occupying adjoining territory on the same side of a valley. In such cases there are frequent clashes over the depredations of pigs and the killing of such pigs by the owners of the gardens which they damage, and over the theft of garden produce and pandanus nuts; while the burning of vegetation in the making of gardens sometimes results in the fires getting out of control and destroying pandanus trees, gardens, villages, and people.

Amo Lume said that the Goilala had only been minor enemies with the Laitate since there were no pandanus stands on the old border between the Laitate ground and that of the Goilala before the Laitate moved to Sene land. Moreover, they made their gardens in places different from those used by the Goilala. The Kunima, however, were major enemies with the Goilala, and some of the most vicious and protracted fighting was against this tribe. Again, he said that the Kataipa and Tawuni were one another's major enemies, as were the Amuganiawa and the Watagoipa, since in both cases their borders were adjacent. The following stories are good examples of the ease with which accidental damage by fire, combined with the inflammable nature of the people can produce bloodshed between neighbouring tribes: [This story takes place some time in the 1920s, when the Laitate still had not crossed over into Sene land.]

Aima Kamo, Kitai Komai, Tauru Ivei, Orou Matalivi, Amata Lapai, all had a yam garden at Kavatuvu. The women K— P—, M—, and Mo—, of Laitate were burning grass, and the fire got away and burnt the yam garden of the Goilala men. The women came and dug up the yams and put them in their string bags. Aima Kamo, Kitai and the others came and saw what had happened, with Aima Kovio, Ano Keruvu, and Koma Kovoitsi. Aima Kamo killed K— P— with a spear, and Orou Matalivi also speared her. Ano clubbed her with a stone club. Mo— was killed by Koma Kovoitsi with an arrow, Amata Lapai speared her, Aima Kovio speared her with a piece of sharpened bamboo, and Pelai Kaita axed her. M— was killed by Aima Kamo with a spear, while Avui also speared her, and Beto Atu clubbed her with his stone club, and Avui Ivei axed her. Then they chopped up their bags and yams together, and flung them in the bush, and came back to Kavatuvu, singing a song of triumph. Their husbands at Laitate saw what had happened, and the Goilala sang 'Your wives burnt our yam garden and stole our yams—go there and look'—the Goilala had stuffed yams into the dead women's mouths.

The Laitate took their wives and buried them. After some time, Mana Atu, Kulolo Koporo, Kapa Maugere, Orou Koloala, all of Laitate, came to Deliba lavava and killed T—, wife of A— B— of Pomuru. (She was very old, like Aima Kamo's widow Keuvai.) Mana Atu killed her. They also killed M—, wife of Ts—, son of Kope Munou. She was young. They stuffed yams and sweet potatoes in their mouths as revenge. K— P— had been the wife of Mana Atu. Then the Laitate men went back to their place. Kitai Atu, Tauru Ivei, Aima Kamo, Orou Matalivi, Apava Aginei, Ano Keruvu and Apava Tulava came and got the bodies, and took them to Deribi. They mourned them and killed pigs. Aima Kamo said 'Enough killing' and Kepe Maia came and made peace. The Laitate and Goilala exchanged compensation. Mana Kamaitsi, and Tsivali, came here and got blood-wealth for the three women. Aima Kamo gave dogs' teeth, so did Kitai Atu, and Tauru Ivei killed a pig, Amat Lapai and Aima Kovio both gave homicide emblems, Oleala Koupa an axe, Apava Tulava a piglet, Ano Keruvu dogs' teeth, and Pelai Kaita a homicide emblem. Then the Laitate men went back to their own place. After this the Goilala went in turn to Laitate to get compensation for our two women. Mana Atu, with the Kerau Fathers, killed a big pig, and gave five feathers, 2 piglets, and this was given to Kitai, Aima, Keruvu, Manautu, Tauru as compensation for M— and T—. Then there was peace. The Laitate were given pandanus by the Goilala, in return for which they gave us yams and bananas.

Fr. Guichet told me in a letter after my departure that on 17 September 1972 two of the schoolboys lit a fire at the top of the mission garden, which got out of control. Eventually it burnt a nearby hamlet. The following day the people of this hamlet came to the mission and attacked two of the workers. The Fathers and one of the Papuan teachers eventually pacified them.

The Tauade did not fight because of population pressure on land,

and never permanently occupied land from which the occupants had been driven. The only exception to this is the intrusion of the Laitate into the land of the Sene tribe. This was the result of a complex chain of events which will be described later, in which shortage of timber was far more crucial than land. Land was vacated on occasion because of internal killings and the fear within the tribe of further violence. At other times fighting between tribes became so intense that one of them would disperse temporarily until the rage of its enemies had cooled. On such occasions people went to live with relatives in other tribes, sometimes for two or three years before returning. While the social organization and ecology easily permitted this degree of dispersal, the migrants sometimes made their temporary residences too hot to hold them and had to return home.

For example, at some time between March 1945 and January 1946 most of the Goilala left their spur because of internal killings. It is almost certain that these were those involving Avui Apava and Ita Kogotsi, described above, p. 121. The Goilala lived dispersed among their relatives in various places, including Oropoa and Tanini, until 1950-2, when the friction engendered by their presence forced them to return to their homes:

The raiding at Oropoa in the Kataipa valley had its origin in a dispute about a pig. A pig belonging to an old man Kokosi was missing in the vicinity of Oi'etu hamlet about ½ a mile along the spur above Oropoa. The old man apparently went to get payment from the people he believed responsible for stealing the pig. An argument developed and 2 men, Kaurupu and Kitai, discharged a spear and some arrows and one of the latter pierced Kokosi's leg. [The police who were ordered to arrest the 2 men shot some village pigs at Oi'etu, which enraged the people.] The ire of the people of Oi'etu was then properly aroused and, gathering their relatives from Kataipa and Kariaritsi, they descended on Oropoa. The people of the latter place showed discretion and retired to Orogaivara spur. The raiders then killed approximately 21 pigs. As a result of this most of the Oropoa are now living again in Orogaivara which is their original abode. Only Oropoa with strong family ties in Oi'etu seem willing to remain. It would appear that the undercurrent of hostility is not due to this single affair but is a result of the lack of a definite boundary between the two peoples. In most areas tribes are separated by rivers with deep valleys. In the few areas where this is not so (e.g. Laetata-Sena, Eruma-Karusi) disputes over land rights, wandering pigs, pandanus nut and betel nut groves are more frequent and heated than elsewhere. Payment by Oi'etu raiders to the individuals whose pigs were killed was made. (A. M. Bottrell, P.O., March–April 1950, Tapini.)

Bottrell comments further, in August of the same year:

Kataipa valley.
The disputes over land, pandanus and pigs are continually recurring between the Kataipa and Kame clans living at Oropoa and Tanini on the other [spur?]. It is difficult to arrive at a solution for this long standing friction, already responsible for several woundings, other than suggesting that the people of Tanini and Oropoa should return to their original land on Orogaivara spur. However such a move would be unpopular with them because, although the natives at present living on Orogaivara spur are their own kin, the enmity which caused their original migration may not have been forgotten. This is understandable as this enmity was caused by killings within the clan—a crime not quickly forgotten by these people.

When large-scale fighting impended, no formal challenge was given, and the object was to ambush the enemy, if possible, while they were cutting up pandanus nuts in the forest or cooking a pig in the bush. The party would be surrounded, and then charged, and as many as possible slaughtered.

When the enemy was prepared, and had taken refuge behind the stockade of their hamlet, a few warriors would rush up to the stockade and fire arrows over it, and otherwise provoke the inhabitants into sallying out in pursuit. The band of *provocateurs* would then run away, leading the enemy between two larger parties which would be concealed in creek beds, waiting to surround them. The object was to cripple some of the enemy with arrows and spears, and they would then be cornered and hacked or clubbed to death at close quarters. Clubs were of the stone 'pineapple' or 'disc' varieties, though no doubt wooden pig-killing clubs were also used. Fastré and Williamson describe the use of stone adzes for fighting, and Amo Lume and Casimiro also told me that they had been used, but it seems likely that clubs were the preferred weapon for this sort of purpose. Steel axes were common by the 1930s, and rapidly replaced clubs and stone adzes.

In fact, relatively few men were killed in these engagements, and the Fathers who witnessed some battles in their first years at Kerau tell me that there was a great deal of rushing about, shouting, and firing of arrows, but little physical damage to either side. Some fighting was of course intended more as a threatening display of aggression and virility, and not really intended to endanger the lives of the participants. But it would be a mistake, to judge from accounts, to suppose that all warfare was of this type—it could be extremely bloody on occasion. It does seem, however, that when one party of warriors had succeeded in killing one of their opponents, there was a tendency for them to run away, almost in fear of their enemies' wrath, now fully aroused by the death of their kinsman.

When the people had killed an enemy, they might chop the body in pieces and leave it for his relations to clear up, even going so far as to scatter the internal organs among the bushes to make the task of retrieval so much more distressing. This was done explicitly to cause pain to the relatives of the deceased, as was the singing of derisive songs. It was also common to cut up the bodies of the enemy and take them home and eat them. Allies were also rewarded with human flesh, as a matter of courtesy.

Cannibalism seems basically to have been an expression of rage and contempt for enemies and a means of causing distress to their relatives. A second motive was probably the desire to absorb the strength of the victim, though since women were sometimes eaten this was clearly not an invariable motive. Since the Tauade do not kill pigs except on ceremonial occasions human flesh would obviously have satisfied their desire for meat, but it is very unlikely that human flesh could have made any significant contribution to their protein intake. Each tribe probably partook of the meat of no more than two or three persons in several years, if that, since it appears that only a fraction of those killed in battle were eaten.

The following extract from Hides's account of his Loloipa patrol is the only contemporary statement which we have from the Tauade themselves about cannibalism:

Little Kitai [a near relative of the chief Gopa] told me, when questioned, that he had seen Gopa and all his men return to the village on the day of the raid with the bodies of five strange men. Gopa was greatly excited, and told everyone that he had killed eleven men of the Amula. The five bodies had been cut up and cooked in stone ovens, and men, women and children had eaten the flesh. It was the custom, Kitai said. He did not know why he ate human flesh: he might like it. Perhaps, though, it was because his fathers ate it and he was 'born with the taste in his mouth'.

In the afternoon, while having a look at the prisoners, I asked Gopa why he had killed these people. The exact translation of his reply was as follows.

'You know our fashion. We look at these people; we look at them for a long time. We say they are there: good we kill them. We think of this all the time, and when our bellies get too hot, we go and kill them. No more.'

He admitted that his people ate human flesh. He described, in detail and quite naturally, how he and his party had trapped and slain the Amula; how they had taken some of the bodies of the slain back to the village, where they had been cooked and eaten. Then he told me of the ceremony in which all the private parts of the dead men had been cut off and given to the pregnant women of the village to cook and eat. As regards this custom, he told me that it was practised by these women because it was believed they would give birth to strong sons. (Hides 1935: 46.)

The following incidents related by Pratt show that the Kuni were cannibals too:

It seemed that Ow-Bow's brother [who had just been murdered] had some time before stolen the murderer's wife, and taken her away to his own village and kept her there. After a time it occurred to him that having got her he might as well pay for her, after the native manner, and accordingly he visited the husband in order to settle his account. The husband, however, was not disposed to receive compensation of this sort, and accordingly he killed and ate the other. (Pratt 1906: 224.)

At Madui trouble awaited them [Pratt's son Harry and his party of native carriers.] There had been a native fracas, a man had just been murdered, and the blood-lust was strong in the people, who, on Harry's arrival, demanded that he should give up one of his boys to be killed and eaten. (1906: 229.)

His [the chief of Boboi's] emissaries conveyed to me a most agreeable message, that if we and our followers should honour him with a visit at Mi-Mi, he would kill my men, and have the pleasure of cooking and eating our heads—a compliment, presumably, to the superiority of European brains. (1906: 134.)

The Kunimaipa were cannibals, and Williamson says that the Fuyughe were as well, but Fastré denies this and says that his informants told him that only among the Tauade, 'that home of all abominations', was cannibalism to be found. However, as late as 1931 Fr. Dubuy wrote 'Cannibalism is flourishing a short distance from our station [Ononghe]' (Dubuy 1931: 30). Despite Fastré's statement, therefore, it seems that cannibalism was normal in the area; while it is possible that in some parts, such as around Popole, it was not practised, I find this rather difficult to believe. It seems more likely that, from their respect for Fr. Fastré, his informants did their best to conceal from him a custom of which they were ashamed, and of which they knew he disapproved.

It is an interesting fact that at the very beginning of contact with the government the Tauade were aware that eating human flesh was a custom to be concealed: 'They deny that they eat human flesh, though this my interpreter told me not to believe . . .' (K. C. McCleland, Kairuku, 14/1/22–10/2/22.) This is the only reference to cannibalism which I could find in the patrol reports, apart from the account of the killing and eating of A. C. Gigira—by the same people, the Sopu, who told McCleland that they did not eat human flesh. While the practice of cannibalism is likely to have survived well into the 1940s or even the 1950s, as far as government or mission records are concerned it ceases to exist. It is as though the Tauade themselves were conceding that there was something special about cannibalism which marked it off from murder, exposure of the dead, rape, or adultery, something which cast a unique shadow over their relations with those who had come to survey them for the first time.

Each tribe had a nucleus of redoubtable warriors who provided the cutting edge of their tribe in battle. Aima Kamo was preeminent among the Goilala, and in his younger days seems to have been virtually a homicidal maniac. He was supported by a very tough group, including Kitei Atu, Apava Tsiani, Koupa Teva, Kopeiri Kitai, Ita Kogotsi, and others. Each tribe might be expected to produce now and then such a group of warriors, and Casimiro Kog at Kosipi told me that the Goilala had been renowned as hot, fierce people. There can be no doubt that men like Aima Kamo, who not only had extremely fiery temperaments but were also important chiefs by birth, could significantly affect the relationships of their own tribe with its neighbours for a generation and more. Amo Lume said that once the Goilala had lived in relative peace with the surrounding tribes, but that when Aima grew up and started killing people this changed, and the Goilala became embroiled in battles with everyone.

While chiefs were sometimes killed in battle, it is said that their bodies were not mutilated, out of respect. The role of the chiefs in warfare was not only in the waging of war, but, as we have already seen, in making peace and in sending the *elaivi* to allies to enlist their support in a coming battle. Only a man of honourable standing could send such an official token, and a *malavi* who had presumed to do so would have been laughed at by the potential ally and his conduct violently resented by his own tribe, especially by its chiefs. Just as the chiefs had the responsibility of inviting the guests to the dances and pig-killings and of ensuring that peace treaties were made along the route which the dancers would follow to their hosts' village, so in time of war the recruitment of allies was the chiefs' responsibility, as the spokesmen of their people. Allies were always feasted by their hosts, before or after the fighting, sometimes both, and rewarded with valuables for their participation. If they were lucky they also received human flesh on occasion.

One of the principal factors in the generation of warfare has been the inability of the tribes effectively to control the aggression of their individual members, while at the same time vengeance for their acts is liable to fall on *any* member of their tribe—a state of affairs combining the minimum of social control with the maximum opportunity for extending the network of conflict.

Besides the peacemaking functions of the chief other social processes operated to mitigate the severity of conflict. If those killed were of little status, compensation would be offered and would usually be accepted if the score of bodies was roughly equal, even though it does not appear that an exact reciprocity was ever a strict condition for a truce. Again, such compensation was more likely to be accepted if violence had been suspended for some time, so that tempers had cooled; and further, people eventually sickened of continuous killings. Though it is not mentioned in the texts, it is likely that the persistent destruction of gardens, which was so prominent a feature of Tauade warfare, would also from necessity have imposed a truce of starvation, and perhaps at such times compensation would have been more readily accepted.

In a few cases a tribe was so thoroughly aroused that its opponents thought it wiser to vacate their land temporarily and take refuge with relatives of neighbouring tribes. This happened in the fighting between the Kunima and the Goilala, when the latter's nerve obviously failed them, and they scattered. Such dispersals also occurred when there had been killings within the tribe, as mentioned earlier.

3. ANNOTATED ACCOUNTS OF WARFARE

It will have become evident by now that the full reality of Tauade warfare can only be appreciated when a long sequence of events is described in detail. The basic features of their warfare, already analysed, recur again and again, but its variability will also become apparent.

Text 1

Some Goilala men, including Aima Kamo and Koupa Teva, went

and stole pandanus nuts[1] from trees belonging to Kerau (Kulumutu) and Kunima. In particular they robbed the trees of Ko—, a chief of Kunima. Ko— therefore gave *elaivi* to the Kulumutu, who gave it to the Karom. The Kulumutu chief was A—. They all came with the Kunima to Valubu, and chopped down the pandanus trees of Koupa Teva and Aima Kamo, and also of Aima Manuvu, in the Kopoivi plot. All the Goilala arose and went up there; A— and his men hid, and surrounded the Goilala, among whom were Ku— and Avui Laua. Avui burst out of the ring surrounding him, but Ku— was trapped. He speared Aima Luluai, and then Ko—, chief of Kunima, killed Ku—, with the help of A—. Then the Kunima and Kulumutu and Karom fled, having killed one man.

The Goilala tied up the body of Ku— and took it back to Dauraupu hamlet. There was very heavy rain on this day. They put him in the yard. The women came and wept. The next day they killed five pigs. Their blood fell on him.[2] They made speeches about him. Then they gave pork and *elaivi* to Watagoipa, Amuganiawa, Maini, and Tawuni. These men all brought their weapons to fight. The Kunima and Kulumutu came again to Valubu, and battle raged. Many people were wounded. There was a break in the fighting, then they went at it again. Then K— L— and his younger brother K— of Gane came to join the Kunima, because they were relatives (*valavala*) of Ko—. They came with their men to Kunima and slept there, and were given homicide emblems and dogs' teeth because they were relatives. They went to where the airstrip is, and the Goilala met them there, and battle began. Aima Kamo hit K— L— with a spear, and Aima Manuvu axed K— L— on the head, Koupa Teva speared K—, and Kopeiri axed him on the head. Then the Goilala ran back to their place. The Kunima and Kulumutu tied their two corpses to poles and took them home. The Gane men went home with K— L—'s body. They erected a *polo* in his honour and killed many pigs.

Then the Kunima and Kulumutu came back again to Valubu with bows and spears. The Goilala took their weapons and arose, and went up there and joined battle with them. Then Kire Kitsio was killed by A— by a spear in the liver, and the Goilala ran away.[3] They

---

[1] The theft of pandanus leads to direct retaliation in the form of cutting down the Goilala pandanus trees. Such strict reciprocity is, however, rare.

[2] 'Their blood fell on him.' This expression is metaphorical only. They do not, in reality, scatter the blood of pigs on dead bodies, though they may daub posts and fences.

[3] While the Tauade always stress that chiefs should not be killed, in practice

took his body back to Ororogaivara, and a *polo* was built for him. [Then an initiation ceremony was held for a group of children in connection with the *polo*. This is omitted here for reasons of space.]

While the initiation ceremony was in progress the Gane men made an attack. The Goilala seized their weapons and chased the Gane. There was a big battle. Aima Kamo[1] speared K— K— K—, and Aima Kovio also speared him, and Koupa Teva axed him, as did Orou Keruvu, and Mo Kimani, chief of Watagoipa. Everyone came and chopped him to pieces. The Gane men fled. The Tawuni and Kataipa, *valavala* of the Goilala, were invited to take the bits home to eat. Kolalo Kioketairi [Ketakori?] (who had a twisted lip because he had cut his mouth with a knife while removing human flesh from a bone) cut off K— K— K—'s head and took it to Dimanibi singing a song.

The body of Kire Kitsio was still at Ororogaivara. It was taken to Amuganiawa to escape the Kunima and Kulumutu who were coming to dishonour it. It was placed on a platform at the hamlet of Punepe. The chiefs Kire Keruvu—the son of Kire Kitsio—Aima Kamo, Koupa Teva, Aima Manuvu, and others gave pork to the Tawuni, Kataipa, Amuganiawa, and Watagoipa. These last two tribes took away their pork together with Kire's body, while the Tawuni and Kataipa took away their pork with K— K— K— of Gane's body. They dismembered K— K— K— at the Kovelaiam bridge over the Kataipa River, and made a big oven, in which they cooked the pork and K— K— K— at the same time. Kolalo tied a vine to K— K— K—'s head and held it over the fire to singe off the hair, then cooked it in the oven. When it was taken out, he skinned the face and feasted on the white flesh beneath. After this the Tawuni and Kataipa went back to their places.

The Amuganiawa cut off Kire Kitsio's finger. Kire Kaini did this, and took the finger to the *kaubada* [patrol officer] at Mondo. They told him who had killed Kire, and then brought the finger back, and buried it with *elaivi*.

important chiefs were obviously not always safe. In the course of this fighting K— L— of Gane, Kire Kitsio of Goilala, and Av— of Kunima, all chiefs, were killed, and A— of Kerau was wounded. Kire Kitsio was not a major chief, however.

[1] We note the continued prominence of a small group of Goilala warriors in different battles—Aima Kamo, Koupa Teva, Aima Manuvu, Ita Kogotsi, and Kopeiri Kitai—and that Kepe Maia, responsible for peacemaking, kept out of the fighting.

Then the Goilala went back to raid the Kunima and Kulumutu as revenge for Kire Kitsio. The Kunima and Kulumutu had made a big fire to cook food on the crest of the ridge at a place called Bolovo Teivi. While they were feasting the Goilala crept up and surrounded them. Ita Kogotsi speared Av— of Kunima in the back; he was walking with the spear in him. Elele Kaperu axed him, Kamo Laureni and Beto Motovo also axed him. Av— was a big chief, the elder brother of Ko—. [This was a grave blow to the Kunima.] The Goilala then ran back to their place. They did not mutilate the body but left it for his *valavala* to take and dispose of. When the Goilala returned to Ororogaivara they burned Kire Kitsio's house because his vengeance was now accomplished, and the taboo lifted. The name of the taboo was *lapaua enailata*. They went to Dimanibi and sang and danced. Kepe Maia, who was living at the hamlet of Poroyava, wished to make peace, and caused a big dance village to be built there. They sent *elaivi* to Kataipa, Tawuni, Amiapa-Lavavai, and Kapatea [Tapini]. But no invitations were sent to Kunima or Kulumutu, as they were still enemies. There were great heaps of food in the dance yard.

At this time the Gane men came and stole Kopeiri Kitai's pig, and took it away. They had got to Vaupava on the way back to Gane. Kopeiri was very upset about his pig, which was called Dopu. He and other Goilala, including Aima Kamo, chased the Gane men, who fled at their approach. Kopeiri speared L—. He jumped on the spear to hold L— down, and then axed him to death. Amo Lume claims that he also axed him, as well as Kovelo Tanu [?] and Koupa Teva. They all returned to Poroyava with the dead pig, and left the body of L— there, and the Gane men took it home with them. As the Goilala distributed the pork they made speeches about the killing of L—.

At this time the Patrol Officer came, and was presented with pigs by Kire Keruvu, Kire Kitsio's son, and by Aima Manuvu, and asked to avenge Kire Kitsio. The government party raided the village of Kuruagolavava, and killed five people. Aima Luluai said that Elele Kaperu, Ita Kogotsi, and Kamo [?] Laureni had killed L—, and these men, too, were arrested. [Much of this is confirmed in a report by Middleton, but who claims his party only killed two natives.]

Text 2

Before Amo Lume was born the men of Maini built a dance village at Kapatai-iliti, and invited the Goilala to dance, and the Laitate as spectators. Dūpī was the chief of the Laitate; at this time they had not started to cross the Aibala. Kavai was also a Laitate chief. Now, during the dance, the Laitate stole and killed a Maini pig, called 'Natuvata'. Since the Laitate were not specially friendly with the Goilala at this time they persuaded the Maini that the Goilala were responsible.

Accordingly the Maini were very angry and attacked the Goilala in the dance yard, killing about four of them.[1] Later, in the night, they caught two more Goilala women and killed them. The Laitate seem to have joined in this attack on the Goilala. The two women were cut up and eaten, while the Goilala brought the bodies of the men—Apava Kulolo, Keeto, Tuna Aluagopo, and Kulolo Kamalatu —back to Goilala, to Oropokeliliva, while the Maini and Laitate boasted of the men they had killed.

Evura Kavai, a Goilala chief, Amata Keruvu, Kope Munou, Tuna Koloala, Tau Manai, Koupa Karoama, Goilala Kitsio, Kope Buluvu, and Kaupa Kileuai went [probably with other less important Goilala] to attack the Laitate. In the ensuing fighting the Laitate chiefs D— and K— were both killed and their hands chopped off as a humiliation.[2] A man called L— was also killed. Then the Goilala went to Maini and killed three men and a woman, as vengeance for the two women killed earlier by the Maini. The woman's body was taken back to Oropokeliliva and eaten.

In retaliation the Laitate came to Goilala and killed two women, A— and M—. So after burying these women, and killing pigs for them, the Goilala went again to Laitate and killed three men. Evura Kavai killed O—, Tuna Koloala killed Ku—, and Kope Buluvu killed P— M—. Then the Goilala ran back to their own country. Some years passed, and the sons of these men grew up and heard the story of these doings.[3]

One day A— A—, of Laitate, came to Goilala [with innocent intention] to Deribi. Kope Buluvu, now an old man, took a spear and killed him, and Apava Aginei [father of Moisé] also speared him, and all the Goilala came and chopped up the body. They did

[1] Treacherous attacks on guests seem seldom to have been planned, but violence as a result of some real or imagined provocation was not unknown.
[2] This is just another example of how rules in Tauade society seem to exist only to be broken.
[3] The long delay before further killings in the sequence took place is very striking.

not eat it, however, and allowed the Laitate to come and collect the bits, and take them home and bury them.

A Watagoipa man, K— P—, was living at Katama hamlet nearby [Katama is a little knoll of red clay on the path to Poroyava]. He was a relative of Apava Aginei. Now Aima Kamo was a relative of A— A—, so he was angry with Apava Aginei for killing him, so he came up from Dimanibi and killed K— P—.[1] Aima Kovio, of Ororogaivara, axed the body, as did Oleala Kimani, and Apava Tsiani, also of Ororogaivara. The Watagoipa came and took K— P— back to Watagoipa on a pole.

There was then another Goilala raid on Laitate, in which perhaps three women were killed, and their bodies burnt. Kepe Maia, the chief of Goilala, arranged peace between the Goilala and the Laitate after this. The Laitate came to Goilala for the peacemaking; at Dauraupu. The Goilala, Laitate, Amuganiawa, and Watagoipa, were all present. One of the Goilala chiefs there was Beto Atu—he was living at Amuganiawa, however. When the peace-making was over, Beto set off for Amuganiawa, and the Laitate, with M— A— as their chief, turned aside on their way home, in order to cross his path. They killed him at Amuganiawa, but did not mutilate his body, as he was a chief. The Maini also helped them. As a result Kire Kitsio of Goilala killed O— of Maini, as vengeance for Beto. At this time Kire was living at Amuganiawa at a village called Dunepe, so he could easily go to Maini territory to do the killing. The Watagoipa came and took O—'s body away and ate it. Beto Atu's body was brought back to Ororogaivara and ceremonially disposed of.

When Kire Kitsio had returned to Goilala some time later, another Laitate called A— K— came to the Valubu hill above Goilala, on his way to visit his relatives at Kunima. Kire Kitsio and his elder brother Amai Koburi killed A— K— here, helped by Apava Tsiani. The Laitate came and took A— K—'s body home. Later the Laitate killed Ai— Ka—, father of Aima Manuvu, as revenge for the death of A— K—.[2] [Much later Kire Keruvu of Goilala killed B— Ki— of Laitate and fed his body to the pigs, and on another occasion Apava Tsiani killed a Laitate woman who came and wanted him to take her in marriage.]

[1] This incident is very similar to the killing of Teopo by Ita Kogotsi.
[2] It will be noted in this and other texts that there was usually no attempt to attain any strict equality of deaths on either side.

Text 3

[At some time about 1900] a Kunima chief, A—, stole a pig belonging to Kitai Komai (Atu), a Goilala chief. His hamlet was Kutupu, and Kire Kitsio [?] and Amai Kovuri lived there with him. A— took the pig back to his village at Aineve, and Kitai Komai followed the trail of blood and saw where his pig had gone. He came back and told Kire Kitsio, Amai Kovuri, and many other Goilala. They all went to A—'s village, where Kitai killed him,[1] with the help of Kire Kitsio. Then they came back to their place.

V—, another Kunima chief, and Ku— (a visitor) gave the *elaivi* to the Karom, Kurumutu, Aibala, Elava-Tapina, Lumioto-Doulava, Tupuru-Kaniavai, Ilai, and Gane men. They all came to help the Kunima. They attacked the Goilala and killed many pigs. Kepe Maia was living at Goilala then and Aima Kamo, and Apava Tulava, and they fled too. The Kunima and their allies killed Ee—, who was an old man, and grandfather of Kitai Atu; he had no son. They cut off all his fingers and toes, and put them to cook in the ashes of his fire, among the sweet potatoes. They also killed P—, of Pomututu, and cut off his head, which they placed in the ashes of the men's house. Then they left to return to Kunima. When Kitai Atu came back with his men to Kutupu, he dug in the ashes of the fire for the sweet potatoes, and found Ee—'s fingers and toes. The relatives of P— found his head in the ashes of the men's house at Pomututu, where it had burst with the heat.[2]

On their way back to Kunima, V— and his allies went to the Goilala hamlet of Amuaeve and killed several pigs, and at Variaete-Palaileve they killed more pigs. They took these to Urumeve where they made

[1] It is likely that A— refused to pay compensation for the pig he had stolen. Normally the theft of a pig would not lead to killing, but the refusal of compensation often leads to violence.

[2] The defilements and humiliations customarily perpetrated upon the corpses of their enemies by the Tauade perhaps derive from the release from the apprehension of death, and from a wish to revenge themselves upon their enemies for the fear which they had so lately caused them. After Culloden, for example, the victors mutilated the enemy.

Their officers watched without protest, although one of them wrote with faint nausea of what he saw. 'The moor was covered with blood' he said, 'and our men, what with killing the enemy, dabbling their feet in the blood, and splashing it about one another, looked like so many butchers rather than Christian soldiers. . . ' To the indignity of death the soldiers added profaner, obscener humiliations, unconsciously revenging themselves on the fear they had recently felt.

(*Culloden*, John Prebble, p. 114.)

a fire to cook them. Kitai Atu came up from Kutupu with his men
to chase them. At the same time I— (father of Avui Katemu), K—
L—, and Tauru had returned to Amuaeve, where they found that
their pigs had been killed. They followed the raiders to Dululiaiama,
near Dauraupu, while the raiders were still at Urumeve, cutting up
the meat. Kitai and his men did not come through Dauraupu, however, but came another way. So the Amuaeve men attacked the
raiders independently.[1] The Kunima and their allies surrounded
them, and Ku— and his men killed I—, and stuffed pork into his
mouth, and also killed K— L—. Then they flung the bodies on the
fire and left.

Kitai Komai, Kire Kitsio, Amai Kovuri, Ano Keruvu, Tauru Ivei,
Avui Katemu, Apava Lavava, and others chased them, to where the
airstrip is now.[2] There Kitai Atu, Ano Keruvu, Apava Lavava,
Kire Kitsio, Tauru Ivei, and Avui Ivei killed a Kunima man, K—
Ma—. They cut off his hands and took them home. They also collected the bodies of I— and K— L— and brought them to Kutupu,
where Ee—'s body was. Pigs were killed, and speeches made, and the
bodies of Ee— and P— were taken to Deribi and buried. K— L—
and I— were taken and buried at Oropo.

After some time had passed, Kitai Atu, Ano Keruvu, Tauru Ivei
of Deribi, and many other Goilala went to Kopoivi, their plot of
pandanus trees, to cut down the nuts. V—, Ku—, Aia Lariava, and
their men of Kunima came in a war party and surrounded the
Goilala while they were gathering the nuts. They killed Ai—, and
Iv— K—, his father, and smashed all the nuts. Kitai Atu, Ano
Keruvu, and the others ran away. [Aimo Kamo is said to have been
only adolescent at this time. This seems unlikely, as he must have
been a contemporary of Kire Kitsio.] The Kunima went back to their
place, and the Goilala recovered the bodies of their dead.

A long time passed. Kitai Komai and his men went to Kunima, at
Kupava hamlet. The Kunima were out getting pandanus nuts, and

[1] The defence of Goilala was very badly co-ordinated because of the separate
hamlets, and this caused the men of Amuaeve to attack an obviously larger
force of Kunima, and be defeated, because they did not link up with Kitai Atu
and his men advancing from Kutupu.

[2] After a killing or a successful raid, the 'steam' often seems to go out of the
victors, as we see from the description of how the Kunima were pursued to the
airstrip, losing two men there. This is just an indication of the very emotional
and volatile atmosphere in which raiding was conducted. There is a constant ebb
and flow of morale on each side, as one side is satiated with a killing, and the
losers are correspondingly provoked.

Kitai and his men surrounded them. Kitai speared Ka— Ka—, and Ano Keruvu clubbed him, and the Kunima fled. Kire Kitsio speared U—, and Apava Tsiani and the other Goilala axed him. Then the Goilala returned to Moigili singing a song of triumph. (They were from the hamlets of Kutupu, Deribi, Pomuru, and Oropo.) But they were afraid of what they had done, and some took their valuables and fled to Amuganiawa,[1] while others, including Koupa Karoama, Kepe Maia and Aima Kamo, and Ano Keruvu, fled to Kataipa. The Kunima came down to the Aibala to attack the Goilala and the Amuganiawa, and these, with the Watagoipa, also came down and joined battle with them. The battle was near the bridge called Olulua. While the fighting was going on (in which no one was killed), a Goilala called T— crossed the Aibala by another bridge, Uruapīto, and went up the Dimani spur, and made his way to the Kunima village of Kiawaigata. The Kunima had left their women there unguarded, and although they fled when they saw T—, he killed one of them, A—. Then he came back to Amuganiawa by the Uruapīto bridge, and told them how he had killed A—. So they all sang a song of triumph, telling the Kunima to go and look at their village of Kiawaigata. The Kunima cut the bridge at Olulua, then went back to Kunima, where the other women were mourning at Kiawaigata. They buried A— there.

Then the Kunima were going to kill someone at Kataipa where the chiefs Koupa Karoama, Kepe Maia, and Aima Kamo were living. So they took their valuables and came back to the hamlet of Pevalo at Goilala. The Kunima went down there and surrounded it. Kamo Tulala's younger brother Beto Lovai was killed there by M— and Ku—. Kepe Maia tried to make peace, saying 'we will not kill you'. Maia, Koupa Karoama, and Aima Kamo went to Amuganiawa, and later came back and collected Beto Lovai's body, which they brought to Amuganiawa. He was buried at the hamlet of Kupuavai. His wife Kete Keropo had also been speared in the arm, but she did not die. The Goilala spent a long time at Amuganiawa, and then returned to their own place. When Aima Kamo grew older he killed many Kunima [but the Goilala never avenged the three deaths which they were 'down' in the exchange].

[1] The use of the territory of relatives as a refuge is standard Tauade practice. In this case the Kunima were so infuriated that the Goilala felt safer to retreat to Amuganiawa and Kataipa. This kind of mobility is of great significance in Tauade warfare, since such dispersal to other tribes means that the attackers will have to become involved with many more opponents than hitherto.

Text 4. This is an account of the events leading to prolonged warfare between Laitate and Sene:

The Laitate planted their gourds and yams by the Aibala River, and gave them to the Sene people in exchange for pandanus nut and animals which they hunted in the forest. They were friends with the Sene people at first.

One day some Sene boys were on a ridge (called Orotuiki) above the yam gardens of a Sene chief named P— and his wife K—. The boys had come to Orotuiki with their parents to work in the gardens there. K— arrived after them; the boys saw her and laughed, because there was blood running down her legs, and they thought that she had been copulating with someone.[1] An old man said 'Who are the boys laughing at?' Then he heard that it was P—'s wife K—, and he became angry. They were sitting a little above the garden where she was working. A little bird called *tsivutu* settled on one of the poles for the yam vines. It has a red neck and the wings are white. It was sitting above the woman as she worked. The boys threw a stone at the bird and it missed the bird and hit the woman. She was very angry and shouted out 'Who has hit me? I am not a widow [i.e. a defenceless woman] why have you hit me?' Her husband, P—, came and she told him what had happened.[2]

Her husband became angry, and abused the boys' fathers. Then they all went back to Sene; P—'s village was Ovaritava, and the boys and their parents lived at Sene. They (P— and the men) were quarrelling all the time, and blows were exchanged. Later [probably the same day], the men from Sene village, including A—, his father K— K—, and L— came and surrounded P—'s hamlet. P— and his son Av— [who were both chiefs of the Sene tribe] were in their men's-house, and the Sene men set fire to it.[3] At the same time K— K— put his head inside the house to kill P— and Av—. There was a plank above the entrance, tied with vine, but the fire burnt through the vine, and the plank fell down and hit K— K—. L— was outside in

[1] On later reflection this seemed rather odd. Why should intercourse produce vaginal bleeding? McArthur (1971: 159) may supply the answer when she says of the Kunimaipa 'Women are believed to menstruate only if they are having sexual relations'. This explanation for the onset of women's periods did not occur to me in the field, nor was it suggested by my informants. Dr. McArthur, of course, had better access to female informants than I did. It thus seems quite possible that the Tauade share the Kunimaipa belief in this matter.

[2] We see how very trivial are the occasions of violence, in this case within the tribe.

[3] A typical case of the overwhelming concentration of force.

the yard with the other men when the plank hit K— K—. K— K— called out to L— when the board hit him, and L— thought that Av— and P— had killed him, so he got a spear and killed P—. [He was able to do this because] at this time the leaves had fallen off the side of the house [due to the fire burning through some of the rafters] so he was able to see them both sitting inside. Others got in and killed Av— as well.

The relatives of Av— and P— lived at Maini, Laitate, Ita, Tumi, One, Iveyava, Gane, Karoava, Watagoipa, and Gona in Fuyughe.[1] They wept very much when they heard about the death of Av— and P—. The rest of the Sene were greatly afraid. 'Where shall we go?' they said. 'The Maini will kill us, the Laitate will kill us, the One (their country is called Lamian), and the Iveyava (Sopu) will also kill us, so will the Ita and Tumi and Gona' they thought.[2] So the Sene all went to Karoava, with their chief K— K—, to the village of the Karoava chief An—, at Topom.[3]

He was angry because of the death of Av— and P—. But while his inside was angry, he did not speak his anger, and his lips uttered only kind words [and he welcomed the Sene people].[4] Later, when it was dark, he cut *elaivi*, and sent it to the Iveyava people, saying 'You will come to my village, and surround it, and you will kill the Sene people, as vengeance for the deaths of P— and Av—.' The Iveyava agreed and brought all their weapons and surrounded the village [presumably on some following day]. Before the Iveyava came, An— told some of the Sene men that they would go up the spur and get firewood, but that first they would improve the path as it was slippery, and the bad bits should be dug over. He thought that he would lead the men away from the village and allow it to be defenceless against the Iveyava as only the women and children would be left. So they made the path good, and then went up and got the wood and came back with it. [Meanwhile the Iveyava had arrived, and were killing the women and children.] The Sene men heard the screams of their women and children as the Iveyava slew them, and they became angry. All the men of Sene who had been left behind in the village

[1] The killing of chiefs within the tribe ensures the intervention of other tribes wishing to avenge their kinsmen.

[2] When the exuberance of killing dies down, the Sene people are afraid, realizing that they have gone too far.

[3] In consequence, we see another characteristic feature of the Tauade war-game—the mass withdrawal to the territory of a friendly tribe in order to escape reprisals. [4] The chief An— displays typical treachery.

had been killed, except K— K—, because he was a chief. They had just speared him in the side, and he recovered. An— and the other Sene men came back to the village, when they found their women and children dead. When they saw this they were very angry, and chased the Iveyava men. A man called T— of Sene killed four of the Iveyava, [the rest of] who[m] ran back to their land. In An—'s village they put the bodies on platforms. The people of Loleava heard the story and invited K— K— and the surviving Sene to come and live with them.[1] So the Sene went and stayed there with the Loleava [where they remained for perhaps two or three years]. They made houses and gardens there, and the Loleava looked after them well. Then the Loleava decided to make a big feast, at which the Sene would also be hosts, and the people of the Waria were invited to dance. [This feast was to mark the return of the Sene to their own land.]

The Laitate, Maini, Iveyava, Karoava, Gane, Malava, Kileipi, Lamanaipi, Goilala, Kunima, Kataipa, Tawuni, Kolovo, Watagoi, and Amuganiawa, were all invited as *karuvu* [guests]. They saw the Sene there, and some of the Laitate wept. Some of the Laitate men were relatives of the Sene, and had looked after their gardens and pigs while they were away. They told the Sene how their gardens and pigs were getting on, and they all cried together. The Loleava saw them and said [among themselves] 'Why are they crying?' Amenai Papai, the Loleava chief, also saw them, and said 'What are you about?' because he was angry. He said 'In the past they [the Sene] fought among themselves, and were blown away, as feathers are blown away by a strong wind, and you were not sorry, but now you are weeping with them. Why is this? The killing of Av— and P— was nothing to do with the Loleava, it was the affair of the Sene alone, and we invited K— K— to come and live with us, and they were happy to do this.'

What he thought was that it was not the responsibility of the Loleava to look after the Sene, and that if the Laitate were so sorry for them now, they should have taken care of them then. He was angry because he had looked after the Sene, and now they were being friends with the Laitate, though they had abandoned them in the past.[2]

---

[1] In the case of the Loleava what appears to be real generosity is manifested.
[2] But the attitude of the Loleava chief Amenai Papai is well worth noting. How easily offence is given, in this case because he resents friendship shown

He wanted the Loleava to kill both the Sene and the Laitate, but he decided that they would all dance instead, and his temper recovered. The next day they killed the pigs, then the Sene said to the Laitate 'Who is making smoke in our land?' The Laitate said that A— [a different A— from the one mentioned earlier] and his wife M— were making the smoke. A— and M— were not important people, so the Sene chiefs were angry because two *malavi* had stayed behind, when everyone else had gone to Loleava. So they told the Laitate to go home and eat their pork, and then to kill A— and M—.[1]

The Laitate took their pork home, and when they had eaten it, they took their weapons and their dogs, and came to Orotuiki, where they met A—. The Laitate told him to bring his dog for hunting on the morrow. Then they and A— went back to their respective villages. The next day the Laitate went up to the same place, and pounced on stones in the grass, crying out *nev'ema*, 'my animal' as they did so, to trick A— and his wife into thinking that there was a good hunt. A— and M— hurried to get there, and when they arrived the Laitate men killed both of them with spears. They called out the news to the Sene people who were at Loleava. They heard, and said 'Good, we will go to Sene' and they came back.

A man called Ku— found A— as he lay dying. A— had two *paleala* [shell ornaments] tied to his hair on either side of his head. Ku— said to A— 'Hey, you will die, eh? Look at me.' A— turned his eyes to Ku—, then he died. Ku— cut off the two shells from A—'s hair, so that he could avenge the death of A— in the future. (Ku—'s son now lives at Tanipai.) His spear was called Ilaukura, and he fixed the shells to the point of it. Then he tied up the bodies of A— and his wife and took them back to his village, called Kanapa. (In the time of the culture heroes Kioitame was killed there, at a place called Tumitata, which stands above the village of Sene.)

The killing of A— and M— was known to the Iveyava and Karoava, also to the Loleava. The Loleava had given a piglet, called Toatsikopa, to the Sene to take back to their land with them. When

between the Sene and the Laitate, who have done less for the Sene than have the Lole.

[1] The planned killing of A— and M— illustrates the resentment that insignificant people should remain to 'guard' the land after they have left themselves. It is really the chiefs' function to guard the land. The actual murders seem almost to display a love of treachery for its own sake. It will be noted that at this stage relations between the Sene and the Laitate are still good. The Laitate have looked after the Sene gardens and pigs, and killed A— and M— for them.

they gave the piglet to them, the Loleava told the Sene 'When you get back to your land, do not make big men's-houses, do not parade in feathers or homicide emblems. When you get back, the relatives of Av— and P—, if they see you [showing off] will become angry, and will kill you. If you go back to your land do not do these things, [showing off] but just live there.' The Sene people came back, but they forgot the advice which the Loleava people had given them. They built a men's-house, at a village called Kuvekiava. Then the Ita heard the news of the men's-house and they became angry. 'Why have they killed the chiefs Av— and P—, and built a men's-house on their ground? In our good time we will kill another of their chiefs.'[1]

Then one day another Sene chief called Ket— went to Ita, in order to see an Ita chief named Kam— who was a relative of his. He came to the Ita chief's village, which was called Napata. Before he arrived, Kam— said to his men 'I will ask Ket— in the men's-house if he will pay compensation for Av— and P—. If he agrees, it is well, but if he does not agree, you will kill him.'

Ket— came, and went into the men's-house; then Kam— also went and sat in the men's-house with him. Ket—, however, refused to give compensation for Av— and P—, and Kam— became angry inside. He summoned his men, and the Maini as well as the Ita men came and surrounded the men's-house. Then Ket— got up, and said to the men outside, 'Why have you all come?' They did not say anything. Then Kam— said to him 'You are a chief, they will not kill you. Come, we will go down into the yard.' They descended to the ground, and when they were down Kam— pulled out a spear which he had secreted under the house (the spear was called 'Loluma'), and he drove it into Ket—'s side. Then the Maini and Ita fell on Ket— and killed him. Ket— fell to the ground dying, and as he lay there Kam— said to him 'If you had given compensation for the deaths of P— and Av—, I would not have done this, so it is your fault that the men will kill you.' And saying this the men finished him off. Then they shouted out the news, and Sene heard this, and they were intensely angry, and said 'Another of our chiefs is dead, but it is the fault of our pride'. (Because they had not listened to the warning that the Loleava people had given them. For it was because the Ita chief Kam— heard the story of the Sene's new men's-house that he killed Ket—.)

[1] The Ita are offended by the ostentatious behaviour of the Sene, and their desire for vengeance is revived.

The Ita men took a stone (a *porago*) and made a hole in Ket—, and put the stone inside him.[1] Then the Tumi, the Sene, heard the news, and came to Ita to fetch the body. They did not realize that the stone was inside it. They came to the Loini creek, crossed it and climbed up the other side, and came to a village called Amaina, and said to each other 'Why is it so heavy?' So they cut open his torso with an axe, to see why he was so heavy, and when they found the stone they were utterly astonished, and said 'Why didn't Kam— and his men just kill him, and why did they put a stone inside him in this terrible way?' And they were very angry, and vowed 'In our good time we will kill many chiefs of Ita in vengeance for Ket—'.

Then they took his body on their shoulders again, and carried it to the village of Kipo, where they took out the stone, and placed it in the ground. It was intended as a marker for Ket—, so that they should see his stone, and never stop thinking about Ket—, and then later they would take vengeance for him.

After some time had passed, the Sene massacred the Ita men, women, and children, in a series of raids, in vengeance for Ket—. Finally they killed two Ita chiefs called Tu— and Po—. After this they said 'Enough. That was the vengeance for Ket—. Now we have forgotten him, and we will pay compensation.' [Last five words doubtful.]

Later, the Sene called to the Ita people 'We will give you compensation for Tu— and Po—'. The Ita heard this and agreed. Now Koialolele is the name of some ground by the Loini creek, and that was the place where the compensation was due to be exchanged. When the Sene came with the dogs' teeth, homicide emblems, and feathers, to give to the Ita, an Ita man called Vavini Kotou had already climbed up a tree. When the Sene were going to give the compensation to the Ita, Vavini, who was a chief, shouted 'You will not give the compensation; listen to me. Today I will take this land [which was on the Sene side of the river] as compensation for the two chiefs Tu— and Po—.' The men of Sene then put down the dogs' teeth, and the homicide emblems, and feathers, and said, although they were very angry to lose their land, 'It is what we have deserved. We have killed two Ita chiefs, and they have taken our land. Enough.' They said no more [in fact, knowing the Tauade, they probably

---

[1] The Ita gratuitously insult the Sene by putting the stone in Ket—'s body. It is this kind of provocation which is an important element in embittering and prolonging warfare.

said a great deal more] and went back to their place. It is still Ita land.

Now Ku—, who had cut off the shells from the hair of the dying A— [as told earlier], wanted to kill some of the Laitate in revenge for A—[1] [Ku— was a Sene man]. So Ku— and some other Sene men hid themselves in a yam garden of the Laitate, with spears and bows. The Laitate did not notice them, and came into the garden, whereupon the Sene pounced upon them, and killed two men of Laitate, called P— and La—. After this there was unceasing warfare between the Laitate and Sene peoples. The *kiap* had not yet come to Aporota or Mondo. When there had been many killings, one day the Sene went along a path called Tumitata to collect pandanus nuts. They were cutting up the nuts when the Laitate led by Kulolo Koporo, surrounded them. The Laitate killed I— M—, T— K—, and M— T—, on this occasion. Then the Sene fled to Ita, to a village called Kovai, where they put the bodies of the dead men on platforms. Later, there was another fight between the Sene and the Laitate, in which the Laitate killed another Sene man, named Mo—. The Sene carried his body to the Sene village of Etoroto, because by this time they had left Ita and returned to their own place.

After this, Sene's chief Kire Kamo, the son of A— (not the one who was killed) died suddenly [of natural causes]. So the Sene said 'The chief is dead, who will make peace for us with the Laitate?'[2] And the Laitate said among themselves 'Their big chief Kire Kamo is dead. We will go and kill all the Sene people.' The Sene heard of this talk and were afraid. So they went [over the range] to the Ivane Valley. But there was no food there at this time because it was all bush, and no one lived there. So they all went to Minaru to get food, and then they cut and burnt the bush, and planted sweet potato, taro, sugar-cane, bananas, and maize. While they were waiting for their crops to grow they got their food from Minaru, and from Kona in Fuyughe country.[3] They also went back to Sene and got food from their gardens there.

[1] The killing of A— and M— by the Laitate at the invitation of the Sene now reacts back on the Sene as a whole because of the killing of two Laitate men by Ku— of Sene and some others. General hostilities between Laitate and Sene result.

[2] The crucial role of the chief as peacemaker is shown by the Laitate reaction to the death of Kire Kamo, the principal chief of Sene. The Sene are obviously considered to be greatly weakened by the death of this chief, and the Laitate reaction is to attack them.

[3] When the Sene are driven out of their land they can rely on the generosity of other tribes, e.g. Minaru and Kona.

Then they heard that in their absence the Laitate had raided their land at Sene, burnt the houses, and stolen [killed?] the pigs [those which the Sene had not been able to take with them, presumably because they were in the forest]. They were very angry when they heard this, and took their weapons and went back to Sene. They found that the Laitate had returned [or had never left; this is not clear from the account] and there was much smoke from the burning houses, so that the Laitate did not see the Sene advancing on them. While the Laitate were killing pigs, burning houses, and destroying stores of nuts in the hamlets of Kavie, Kipuratanavai, Lopeamai, and Etoroto, the Sene were surrounding them, and then attacked them. But when the Sene charged they only speared one of the Laitate, named V—, because his cry of pain when the spear went through him gave the alarm to the rest of the Laitate, who fled. Even V— was not killed, and ran away too, with the spear sticking in him. But the Sene surrounded him, and N— grabbed his arms, and Ava— knocked him down with an axe, and other men came up and chopped him to pieces. They were angry because the rest of the Laitate had escaped, so they cut off his genitals and put them on the roots of a pandanus tree, so that the Laitate should see them, and then went back to the Ivane.

Some time after this the government established a post at Aporota, which prompted the Sene people to think that they would now be able to return to their ancestral land. But Kulolo Koporo of Laitate had persuaded the government that the Laitate were the true owners of the Sene land, and that the Sene were the intruders. So when the Sene tried to return the police drove them back to the Ivane again. This policy was maintained for a number of years, but later they were allowed to reoccupy their land.

Casimiro shrewdly pointed out that by forcing the Sene to remain in the Ivane the government was assuring itself of carriers for government patrols on that part of the route between Mondo and Aporota which would have been uninhabited if the Sene had left.

The Tauade are aware that peace is ultimately maintained by a precarious balance of forces, and some of their legends describe occasions when warfare became completely uncontrolled; violence rose to such a crescendo of apocalyptic fury that everyone was exterminated and 'the country belonged only to the animals'. The following story does not seem to be truly about the culture heroes, although

such was asserted by its narrator. It seems likely to be a very old story
of fighting between the Kataipa and Aibala tribes.

A culture-hero chief at Tawuni called Kuve Kalepe had a daughter
called Ata Kotupu. She married a culture-hero chief at Kanitatalavava called Toroy. Her father held a great dance with a bull-roarer
enclosure, and he invited Toroy and the people of Kanitata, and also
the people of Kopurilavava, Lumioto, Kerau, Kunima, and Oropoa
tribes, who all came in their feathers to the dance village at Tawuni.
The story continues,

Pandanus nuts and yams were hung around the yard, and they danced
day and night. The food was taken down and shared out, and the Tawuni
called the pigs from the bush and tied them.

Toroy became very angry because his wife Ata Kotupu was looking at
another man. He hit her in the neck with his axe, and she died. Kuve
Kalepe and his men were very angry at this; they fetched his daughter's
body, and when they saw that she was dead, they flung it down, and took
their spears and axes, and chased Toroy and his men and killed them in
vengeance. The other Aibala, and the chief Lumani, of Kanitata, fled back
to where they had come from. Kuve Kalepe and his men cut up five of the
Aibala men, and cooked and ate them. The men of Kerau, Karom, Kopurilavava, and Kanitatalavava took five of the bodies back with them, to stop
them being chopped up. At Kanitata, Kopuri, Karom, Kerau, and Oropoa
they killed pigs in mourning for the dead men. Then they all took bows and
arrows, spears and axes, and came and burnt the pandanus of Kuve
Kalepe. The pandanus they burned is called Korutu, and was a huge
forest which reached to the precipice, and down towards the Aibala. They
took some of the nuts back to their own places for seed.

Kuve Kalepe went to Nita evivai mana evivai, his hamlet down by the
present Tapini bridge over the Aibala. He called his dog Oburatu with
him. Now two of his pandanus trees which had been burnt down were
called Mulu and Doluapa, and two others were Puti and Tilitupu. Their
fruit rolled down the cliff and into the Aibala, and the water carried them
down to Nita evivai. Kuve Kalepe saw them in the water and wept. His
dog Oburatu saw them and retrieved them from the water. Kuve Kalepe
hung some of the kernels of these nuts around the dog's neck, because he
was sad about the trees, and because the dog had rescued the nuts. He
told the dog to go to Watagoipa, Garipa, Amiapalavavai, and Goilala
and tell the men to come and help Kuve Kalepe kill the Kanitata and their
allies. (At this time dogs had the power of speech, but later a wasp stung
one on the nose, and they lost it.) So the dog did this, and the Watagoipa,
and the Garipa, and the Amiapa all came and they killed pigs, and had
a feast and made speeches. The next day they all arose and went to Kiala
apotapu, on the ridge below the precipice; Kuve Kalepe held Oburatu by
a cord around the neck. Kuve Kalepe's club was called Oitemburiteve.

The chief of the Aibala men, Lumani, said that they would kill Kuve Kalepe, in revenge for Toroy. 'Come and kill me' said Kuve Kalepe. Saying that he loosed the cord around Oburatu's neck, shouting 'Bite, bite, bite!' The dog's tail was wagging furiously, and he was dancing. He dragged down man after man, and savaged them horribly, and killed them. Kuve Kalepe with his club Oitemburiteve was clubbing them furiously at the same time. Lumani had his throat torn out by Oburatu. The Watagoi, the Garipa, the Goilala, the Amiapa were killing them as well. A hundred [sic!] men were up in a big tree, and Oburatu went to the foot of it and bit the trunk, and shook it violently so that all the men were thrown out and dashed to pieces on the ground. They killed 'thousands' of people, and went to Oropoa, Kunima, Kerau, Karom, Lumioto, Kopurilavava, Kanitatalavava, Kuputaivi, Gane, Ilai, who had also been at the dance, and killed them all. The country belonged only to the animals. They were all killed. Only one man and one woman escaped to breed.

The Amiapa-lavavai came and took away corpses to eat, and so did the Gari, the Watagoi, and the Amuganiawa, and the Goilala. Kuve Kalepe and his men made a huge oven at Tawuni, and after washing the faeces out of the bowels of the dead they cut bamboo and put pieces of flesh in them to roast them in the fire. They gave meat to everyone, and then Kuve Kalepe's allies went back to their own places.

4. CONCLUSIONS

The basic factors generating warfare may be summarized as follows:

1. *The propensity to take vengeance on any member of the offending group.* Since retribution seldom fell on the guilty, aggressive men had little reason to fear for their lives, while the relatives of the harmless victims had every reason to retaliate in kind.

2. *The lack of effective sanctions against a man who killed a man from another tribe.* Neither chiefs nor kinsmen nor fellow hamlet residents could prevent homicide by a determined man, as opposed to a war party; the most they could do was apply pressure to enforce payment of compensation.

3. *The multiplicity of cross-cutting ties.* As a result, men in tribes *other* than that of the victim had an interest in avenging him. They might also take vengeance against someone living in their own tribe, simply because he was related to the killer.

4. *Mobility.* This was made possible by the form of the ecology, gift exchange, residence rules, and dispersed kin ties, and was clearly a very significant factor in allowing men to escape from their own tribes to

stay with relatives elsewhere until tempers had cooled and compensation became acceptable.

5. *Compensation.* While compensation put an end to *particular* sequences of vengeance killings, or prevented them starting, it must also have produced a greater *total* incidence of homicide, since a killer knew that he would be able to 'buy off' the relatives of the victim, so that even his kin and neighbours would not have to suffer as a result of his action.

6. *Reciprocity.* The whole ethos of reciprocity, as opposed to mediation, made vengeance an entirely appropriate response to injury.

7. *Men's houses.* The existence of the men's houses within the hamlets clearly accentuated the fissiparous potential of the hamlets within the tribe, and by concentrating men together under the leadership of men whose fighting exploits were admired by all, the men's houses clearly stimulated aggression towards other groups, both within and beyond the tribe.

8. *The ecology and pigs.* The shifting cultivation of sweet potatoes allows the men a great deal of leisure for many months of the year, especially since the women do most of the work in the gardens anyway. In a society organized in the Tauade manner, and with its ethos of revenge, it is clear that prolonged idleness would tend to nourish thoughts of violence, and the settling of old scores. Pigs are the basis of the feasts and dances, and of gift exchange, with all the social consequences these entail; their destruction of gardens is, with adultery, one of the prime causes of violence and conflict.

One thing which above all is clear about Tauade warfare, is that it is not an 'adaptive' feature of their society. Anthropologists habitually spend a great deal of time trying to show that the most unlikely phenomena, like warfare, are socially beneficial, by contributing to the solidarity of the group, or reducing population pressure, or toughening up the young men. Since it is an ill wind that blows nobody good, even warfare can have some of these effects on occasion. But because an institution exists, it does not follow that it had to exist or that no other would have done in its place or that it is the best one possible.

It is clear that Tauade pressure on land is light, and that even where tribes vacate their land, this is always a temporary measure, even in the case of the Sene. Economic scarcity does not produce warfare, but trade—for stone axes, salt grass, pandanus nuts, and so on.

If one asks, moreover, for whom warfare would have been adaptive, one is obliged to define the particular group who so benefited. The Tauade as a group never acted in concert, and there were no stable tribal alliances. While it is true that tribes had to fight for their own safety and self-respect, this was because, given the general society around them, it would have been suicidal not to have done so. They fought because they had to, and to this extent warfare was functional for the individual tribe, or rather, adaptive. But in relation to the wider society the pattern of warfare was simply a vicious circle from which there was no escape. It also penetrated within the tribe itself, where about half the violent deaths were caused by the men of the same tribe. So while it was adaptive for any single tribe to fight others in self-defence, the *total* system so produced was clearly not adapting to anything, but was the product of particular features of Tauade social organization.[1]

[1] For an extended analysis of the 'adaptive' aspects of warfare, see my 'Functionalist interpretations of primitive warfare', *MAN* (N.S.), vol. 8, no. 3, Sept. 1973.

VI

Tauade Values

IT is likely that all societies distinguish between the social and the animal virtues, between the model citizen who attends to his civic duties and deals fairly with his neighbours and the virile man who, whether law-abiding or anti-social, can be admired for his courage, initiative, and qualities of leadership. For the Tauade a 'good' man is one who facilitates co-operation by his powers of co-ordination, and who is prepared both to offer and receive compensation in the settlement of disputes. Such a man is likely also to be a strong man, as we saw in our discussion of the status of the chiefs, and for the Tauade, therefore, strength is the basis of 'goodness' as they conceive the idea. Conversely, weakness, irresponsibility, and anti-social behaviour go together also. To this extent the Tauade are able to reconcile the basic dilemma between the social and animal virtues.

But as we shall see more clearly in Chapter VII on the Wild and the Tame, while they regard the Tame as 'good', and the Wild as destructive, they also conceive the Wild as creative and splendid. Hence men like Aima Kamo who are considered 'bad', 'like a snake, always biting people, never sleeping in his bed at night', are also admired for their courage and ferocity, and for the renown they bring their tribe in battle. So while the 'good' is seen as a manifestation of strength there is a more fundamental opposition between the Wild and the Tame which permeates their culture and is basically unresolvable.

With regard to more specific values, one would single out power, pride, and reciprocity as the most significant, but these are seldom referred to explicitly in the justification or assessment of actions. Power, in social relations, manifests itself in the domination of the weak and the humiliation of adversaries, especially in war and the giving of ceremonies and successful dances, sexual prowess, and wealth in pigs, valuables, and women. Clearly, pride is closely bound up with power, since attacks on a man's or a group's power is also an attack on his pride. But there are many examples of societies which are obsessed with power but which are not atomistic. It is the atomism of Tauade society which makes the individual peculiarly vulnerable, and thus produces those manifestations of self-defence which are commonly designated as pride. Reciprocity is also an integral element of a competitive, atomistic society. For in such a society stability can only be obtained in the form of a balance of forces, by reciprocity, in fact, as opposed to the harmonious integration of social groups and categories in the Konso manner.

Wealth is a means of obtaining power to only a limited extent, since the society has so little permanent capital, and it is primarily desired for the prestige which certain articles confer on their owners, and is thus a secondary element in their scheme of values; it will be treated as such in the section on utilitarian and heroic societies.

Since their society is for them essentially composed of the interaction of forces between individuals, their moral judgements are, perhaps inevitably, more contextual than absolute in their nature. It was extremely difficult to elicit any general value judgements from my Tauade informants, beyond vague categories of good/bad or, more frequently, weak/strong. Read encountered a similar unwillingness among the Gahuku-Gama to make generalized propositions about morality divorced from the social context of the case:

Pressed for an evaluation, their usual reply is a neutral 'I don't know' (*gelemuve*), and it is exceedingly difficult to ascertain whether the act is regarded as right or wrong . . . Nor are the Gahuku-Gama alone among New Guinea peoples in showing this unwillingness to judge. Dr. J. B. Watson of Washington University has told me that he has also come across it among the Agarabe of the Eastern Highlands. Dr. K. O. L. Burridge of the University of Malaya has mentioned a similar attitude among the Tangu of Madang District, and I have heard it referred to by Miss Chowning, from the University of Pennsylvania, among the Nakanai of New Britain. (Read 1955: 282.)

For the Tauade, then, behaviour is the product of particular situations, and of the emotions generated thereby, not the consequence of any adherence to abstract principles or obedience to group responsibilities and duties, and we must therefore analyse their values strictly in the context of social action and not on the plane of ideals which can be formulated separately. In this chapter I therefore consider the status of the passions; the relationship between love and hatred, especially within the context of the family; pride and shame;

and their attitudes to the heroic and the utilitarian, since these aspects of their society are crucial to their assessment of one another's behaviour, and to the practical application of their values.

I. THE STATUS OF THE PASSIONS

Consistent with their awareness of society as essentially composed of the interaction of forces between individuals and small groups of relatives, the passions have for the Tauade a very different status from that which they have in Aristotelian societies like the Konso.

For the Tauade the human passions are not socially dangerous forces to be carefully controlled and expressed only in customarily sanctioned ways. On the contrary, for them they are the normal basis of all behaviour. All actions are explained in terms of the condition of the *kimuv*, the insides: he did according to his will—*omei omene kimuv a*—'he his insides did', literally. He became angry—*omene kimuv kori la*—'his insides became bad'. When explaining to me why Aima Kamo used to kill people, they said *omene kimuv enam ae valele uopu*—'his insides were like fire'. Equally, to explain the frequently mediatory and pacific acts of his elder brother Kepe Maia they said *omene kimuv ip'ae valele uopu*—'his insides were like water', i.e. cool.

As we shall see, they have a capacity for deep affection, whose counterparts are grief in death and furious rage if the objects of this affection are injured or insulted, or if their expectations of affection are not reciprocated. They feel it right to compensate people for the sorrow which they feel and, in turn, acts of sympathy such as planting *elaivi* in memory of a dead friend, or killing a pig in his name, are themselves grounds for compensation in due course.

One of the most remarkable aspects of sympathy and grief, or suffering of any kind is that the victims can claim compensation for their emotions. Fastré gives a good example of this from Fuyughe behaviour:

They do not weep only at death, but at partings as well. On my return from my first trip back to France in 1926, the women came to find me.

'When you left for your country, we cried, and cried, and cried. What will you give us as the price[1] of our tears?'

'But here I am, back again. It's me. Cheer up!'

Obviously, it was a good argument, but a piece of pork, or some little present would have been much better. I think that they were pleased to

---

[1] *Prix.* I think Fastré would have meant 'compensation'.

see me again, but if, to my return, I had added a gift, it would have been perfect. (Fastré: 184.)

Precisely this belief that suffering or humiliation deserves compensation can be found in a modern development—the custom of a man having pigs killed for him by his relatives when he returns from jail, 'to wash the faeces from his hands'. This is a reference to the humiliation, as it is considered, by which prisoners are required to empty latrines when in prison.

I was told of a dance and pig-killing at Tokio in the Ivane which was held to celebrate the return of Maia Peeta, son of Ivoro Kimani. Ivoro told his guests to cut down a grove of pandanus trees. This was intended as *lok*, compensation, for the 'sore feet' of his son who had been far away in New Guinea on an educational course. It seems clear that the sore feet are an allegorical reference to his loneliness and homesickness while he was away. In another case, the pigs of Manua Tovana and Maia Laiam ravaged the garden of Oiabue Baro; all of them lived at Deribi. Oiabue in a rage punched Maia Laiam, and in revenge some of Maia's relatives came and beat up Oiabue— he and Maia are cross-cousins. The reconciliation involved Maia killing a pig for Oiabue, as *lok* for the humiliation which he suffered by being beaten up.

The payment of compensation to sufferers is one way in which their feelings are relieved; but the sufferer may himself relieve his feelings, especially if he is a man, by aggressive behaviour. A man whose friend or relative has died may place a taboo[1] on the gardens or pandanus palms of the dead man, even if he himself has no claim to utilize these resources himself. Especially if he is a chief, he may outlaw the use of a particular path, or declare that an area of the forest is out of bounds for collecting wood, pandanus leaves, and other products. In former days grief was assuaged in particular by violence directed in the general direction of that group most closely associated with the killer, but easily satisfied by the killing of men, women, or children who had even a tenuous connection with him. Women, however, in their grief tend to direct their violence against themselves, and it was very common for mothers especially to sever

---

[1] July 1945, C. R. James, P.O., Goilala S.-D.: 'Whilst in the Loloipa I found that it is quite common, following the death of a male native, to place a taboo on a grove of pandanus palm or the like. Until such time as the pigs for the death feast are killed, no one may cut the leaves of any palm (for house building) or interfere with the grove in any way. In this instance the breaking of the taboo led to an outbreak of pig killing.'

a finger-joint if a son or husband died. The mother of Apava Tulava, my namesake, proudly showed me one of her fingers whose joint was missing and which she said she had cut off when he died.

This kind of reaction to grief or anger is not peculiar to the Tauade. Sir Hubert Murray records the following examples of aggression following upon grief:

... I have known cases where a man, grieving over the loss of a relative or over some slight that has been put upon him, has set fire to his house, quite regardless of whether anyone was inside, with the result, occasionally, that a child is burnt to death, and I recently tried a case of murder which was the direct outcome of grief over the death of a pig. The prisoners were brothers, and their pig bore the pretty name of Mehboma; but Mehboma died, and the brothers in their unquenchable grief went forth and killed the first man they saw. The victim had nothing to do with Mehboma's death, but the mourning brothers did not care for that—somebody had got to be killed over it. The prisoners told me that it was the custom of their village to show their grief in this way, so that their neighbours must occasionally have suffered rather severely.

Again,

... to quote from my Report of 1908–9, 'one man, irritated because a baby would not stop crying, killed, not the baby, but his own mother; and I remember a case in which a man split open the head of another because he could not find his knife—the other man had never seen the knife, but that was immaterial. So cases happen of accidental wounding caused by the habit these people have of discharging arrows at random when they have a headache or feel otherwise out of sorts.' And a case is reported, also from the Western Division, where a man had a quarrel with his father and sought to relieve his feelings by committing a criminal assault upon the first woman he met; the woman, it may be added, was an absolute stranger and had nothing to do with the dispute. (Murray 1912: 214–15.)[1]

We saw earlier that the Tauade sometimes direct their rage not against others, but against themselves or their own possessions. F. E. Williams encountered the same kind of behaviour among the Oro-kaiva:

But the Orokaiva can on occasion be very sorry for himself, and it would seem that he wants others to be sorry for him, and particularly the man

[1] Murray later added, 'But, after all, we sometimes act in very much the same way ourselves . . . The same principle is illustrated by the story of the Anglo-Indian Colonel who, coming from the War Office after an unsatisfactory interview, relieved his feelings by administering a violent kick to a perfect stranger who was tying his boot lace in the street.' (Papuan Annual Report 1933–4, pp. 24–5.)

who has wronged him. His attitude is not so much 'I'll make you sorry for what you have done' as 'I'll make you sorry for me'; and so he takes 'the revenge of being injured'. According we find a person under a sense of wrong going to extraordinary lengths of self-castigation, from merely fasting or running away from home for a while, to delivering himself up to an enemy tribe or hanging himself from a tree. I have seen a dozen water-melons hacked into fragments and strewn upon the track. Their owner, finding them stolen, had demolished the whole crop and carried them to the path where the thief, whose identity he did not know, would pass and realize what he had done. Similarly I have seen a young man return home at evening and find one of his spears taken from his verandah; when his enquiries failed to trace his spear he took an axe and razed his house to the ground before the eyes of the whole village. Such an attitude of mind has a definite name, *sisira*, and is indeed often to be met with. Composed, I imagine, largely of anger and self-pity, it does not fail to excite a response in the impressionable heart of the man whose offence has caused it. He is affected with *meh*, that complex state of mind which, following the lead of pidgin English, I have elsewhere translated 'shame'. But whereas in the *meh* caused by public reprobation the predominant emotion is self-abasement, there is in the *meh* that results from the sense of having wronged a fellow man a definite admixture of pity. However, the culprit is very effectively 'put to shame', and very unpleasant he finds it. (Williams 1930: 332–3.)

However, a society which based itself entirely upon immediate and unrestrained response to emotional hurt would be a practical impossibility. We find therefore that the Tauade have evolved various methods of accommodating their behaviour to these inescapable facts of life. One is to don the mask of friendship, when inwardly seething with indignation. Especially in a society where violence can so easily break out, treachery and deceit are essential devices. One has only to study a few court cases, or the accounts of disputes which the people themselves give, to realize that they have a great capacity for harbouring grudges, until a favourable opportunity arises for discharging their accumulated venom.

C.N.M., April 1950.
A man, S—, of G—, kills a young boy of P—, adopted from a K— man.

K—, a step-brother of the defendant S—, from G—, states 'Some months ago [in September 1949] while a native named A— and I were working on a house at N—, the defendant came up to us and said "You know that your father was killed by the K— and that my uncle was killed a long time ago by Am— and others, and that only recently they killed my father by sorcery. Well, I have just killed Ke— and I want you both to come down and stand guard while I hide the body." A— and I then accompanied the

I

defendant to a place below G—. There, just in from the track, the defendant showed me the body of a small boy. I recognised the body. It was that of a boy named Ke—. I said to the defendant "Why did you kill this boy and put him here?" The defendant then said "I killed him because of our fathers." The defendant then said for us to take the body down to Raviri creek.' [There the corpse was cut to pieces with axes on a log and the bits thrown into the water, a traditional means of concealing bodies, though they were not usually dismembered first, as far as one can tell.]

S—'s evidence. 'My father [uncle, or step-father] was killed by the K— people. The P— people a long time ago killed my other father [uncle]. Am— and his brothers also killed my true father by sorcery. That is also why I killed Ke—. Because of all the deaths of my fathers I got Ke— and killed him.'

The evidence of M— K—, the adoptive father of Ke—. 'My name is M— K—, and I come from P—. Ke— was my adopted son. I adopted him from a man named O— some years ago. O— is a K— man. I looked after Ke— until he was about 11 or 12. Some months ago I was in the village with Ke—. All the other people had gone to work in the garden. During the day I watched my son playing. It got hot later on and I went inside to sleep leaving Ke— playing outside. I slept for a time and then went outside, Ke— was not there. I looked for him, but could not find him. I and other people looked for him that and the following days. He was not found.

Of course, compensation also exists as a socially recognized means of lowering emotional tension, and is frequently used in the settlement of disputes. But if more direct action is taken, it is, as we have seen, very often weak or insignificant people who are attacked, instead of the powerful principals.

The following case is a good example of the selection of a weak opponent as a substitute on whom rage could safely be discharged:

C.N.M., December 1955.

In a case from Ko—, the complainant, the father of the defendant's wife, says, 'A— B— [defendant] was angry because my daughter was cross with him for taking a second wife. He broke a saucepan belonging to me, my homicidal emblem, and two strings of dogs' teeth belonging to me. He then made as if to throw the broken saucepan at me. I walked away, I had done nothing to deserve this outburst.'

The defendant A— B— says 'I thought that if I hit my wife I would get into trouble [presumably with the administration] so I was angry with her father'.

When compensation is rejected, however, it may well not be in blind rage, but in order to savour the pleasure of more violent retribution, as the following case illustrates:

C.N.M., February 1954.

The defendant, P—, of M—, says 'Some time ago, M— killed a pig belonging to G— [of L—]. I and other natives ate it. Later G— and his friends came and got as compensation for this pig a pig belonging to me. My wife gave it to them. Because I had not killed the first pig, I claimed compensation from those who did kill it. They were M— and A—. They gave me two pigs [one from each man], I did not want two pigs, so I sent M—'s back to him. I kept thinking of my pig that was taken by G— and the others, so I killed a pig belonging to J— [of M—]. I ate it . . . J— killed one of my pigs before.'

2. LOVE AND HATRED

Hatred and violence and a fierce joy in humiliating and destroying one's enemies are constant themes in the lives of the Tauade, but one must also recognize their capacity for love and compassion, their easy tears at a reconciliation or a parting, and their genuine sentiments of hospitality and generosity to strangers. Indeed, their rage and venom cannot be understood without realizing that they are in some respects only the reverse of their capacity for affection. The bonds between close relatives are usually an intrinsic part of the process of conflict and revenge, and this is probably true of all atomistic societies.

I can still see the old man Avui Apava, his face alight with kindly pleasure when he greeted me at the mission airstrip on one occasion. He held my hand all the way along the road to the mission, stealing shy, affectionate glances at me all the way. Yet this same man had no hesitation in burning down his son's wife's house, with her and her lover inside it, when he caught them in adultery during the night (they escaped). Hides gives two graphic accounts of the sorrow of his prisoners' relatives when they saw their loved ones about to be taken away to the coast:

I then asked Gopa to tell his people that he was going away because he had committed a crime against a Government law; that his captors were not going to kill him but would return him safely one day to his people.

He understood; and with his hands manacled and his guards by his side, made his call note. When the wailing had ceased, he conveyed my message. But again the people did not understand, for the wailing increased and some of them began to call, in a pitiful note, the name of their chief. On Gopa's face I saw large tears, running down his wrinkled and ageing cheeks. He was a cannibal and a murderer, to be sure, but he was no criminal. Here was a man who loved and was loved.

He turned a sad face towards me, with traces of suppressed emotion.

'I want to speak again,' he said. And, when the interpreter told him he was quite at liberty to do so, he again called to his people, but this time in a voice broken with emotion. The interpreter told me what the message was. It was about his wives, his children, and his pigs, his gardens, his little treasures such as dogs' teeth, spears and cassowary plumes, and how all this was to be taken care of until his return. He concluded by asking the people not to fight the Government.

It was a pitiful scene, and I moved away from it as quickly as possible. I will always hear those women crying—their wails were piercing, long-drawnout—and see the tears streaming down that savage chief's face. (Hides 1935: 43-4.)

And again:

The Watagoipa were awake early to watch our departure and were quite friendly. Some of them, of course, were grief stricken at their men being taken away, and as we climbed up from the ravine, women came down the spurs to wail pitifully. At several places, farther along the track, some of them awaited us with baked potatoes for the prisoners; and, during one of these halts, a gentle old woman came up to me. She was old and wrinkled, and naked except for the usual perineal band. Tears streamed down her weather-beaten cheeks as she took hold of my arm, as though to detain me. Then with a significant gesture, she told me she was the mother of Giotame, the principal Watagoipa murderer; and through Interpreter Manumanu, she asked me to take care of her son.

My promise seemed to comfort her, for she then gave her attention to her son, whispering little words of comfort while she scraped the ashes from a baked potato that was for him. I realized the tender feelings she had for this magnificent savage who had once fed at her breast, and I felt like a criminal for having taken him away from her. (Hides 1935: 58-9.)

It is within the family that affection and, correspondingly, grief are most intense. The relationship between siblings is especially close. The younger brother is expected to help and assist the older brother, and there is the clear idea that the elder brother is superior in status to the younger brother. But it is precisely within the family, where the expectations of affection and trust are highest, that the disappointment of these expectations produces some of the most violent emotions.

The following story told about the culture heroes, the *agotevaun*, the non-human predecessors of the Tauade, illustrates this intensity of feeling within the family:

Ovelove and Kioitame were at Karom. When Ovelove was pregnant Kioitame went to Laitate. She gave birth first to Alili kato, then to Alili kori. [I omit here the circumstances of their birth.]

After they had grown up, Kioitame came to see his sons. When he saw them he said 'They are both my sons' and went back to Laitate. The boys became big, and went out to work in their gardens together, and built big houses. One day the rain fell very heavily, and the thunder roared, and the earth shook. The boys came out of their house and stood looking up at the sky. Then the lightning struck, and flung Alili kori to the ground, and the sky came down to the earth, and the earth rose up the sky, and they almost met. But Alili kato held up the sky over his younger brother on the ground, and pushed it up. He took a big piece of wood to prop up the sky, and the sky rose again, and the earth descended.

[Various adventures then befell them together, and at the end of these they both returned to Karom and slept at Puraita.]

The next day Alili kato was asleep in his house with the door shut. The house(s) of Ovelove and Alili kori was next door. Alili kori came back with food from the garden and gave some to his mother, but not to his elder brother. Ovelove said 'Take a sweet potato and give it to your brother; he is hungry!' So Alili kori took a sweet potato to his brother's house and opened the door and went inside to give it to him. 'Get up, Alili kato, and take your sweet potato!' he said. Alili kato jumped up and bit his younger brother. He was angry because he had not been given a sweet potato straight away, without Alili kori having to be told by his mother. Alili kato went and closed the door, and then came back and ate up his younger brother completely, and put the bones in a corner of the house. Then Ovelove called to Alili kori to come. Alili kato answered and said 'Your son has already gone': 'Did he come to you?' asked Ovelove. 'No' said Alili kato, 'He went away.' Alili kato came out of his house and closed the door. Ovelove said 'Where is your younger brother?' 'I didn't see him' said Alili kato. 'I told him to give you a potato' said Ovelove. 'No' said Alili kato, 'He didn't give it to me. He has gone.' Ovelove said 'Oh! where has my boy gone?' She looked everywhere for him. Then she saw blood under Alili kato's nails, and she took his hands and sniffed them. 'Ah!' she said 'You have killed him, you have killed my boy Alili kori,' and she wept. She took a piece of wood and hit Alili kato with it, saying 'You killed my boy!' She came to Alili kato's house to see what had happened to him, and found his bones. 'Oh! my son's bones' she cried and began to wail and weep. She cut off the end of her finger, and shook the blood about. She said to Alili kato 'You ate your brother; look here' showing him the bones. 'Yes' he said 'I killed him.' She cut a vine and hung the bones around her neck with it. In order to kill pigs, she told Kioitame at Laitate what had happened, and he came and killed pigs. 'Did you yourself kill and eat your brother?' he said. Alili kato replied 'I was hungry, and he didn't give me a potato, I was asleep for three days, and very hungry, so I bit him and killed him.'

Kioitame killed pigs, and he and Ovelove both mourned for Alili kori by giving away pork, and Kioitame said to Alili kato 'You will remain here with your mother, and take Alili kori's place, but I will go', and he returned to Laitate.

But Ovelove wept, and she was angry inside. She heated a very big stone in the fire, while Alili kato was away hunting animals in the bush. She dug a deep hole in the ground under her house. She took the stone out of the oven and put it in the hole. Then she put some boards over the hole, and sprinkled a little earth on them. Alili kato came home, and entered the house, and sat on the boards over the hole, and as he did so Ovelove kicked them away, so that he fell down the hole on to the hot stone. He was roasted to death. Ovelove got up and looked down the hole and saw that it was the end of him. She filled up the hole with earth, and stamped it down.

Then she took one of Alili kori's (the younger brother) bones, and put it in a little box, and his flesh came back on it, and made him again. She gave him some meat and he ate it. 'Say something' said Ovelove. 'I am Alili kori, I am your son' he said. She was overjoyed to see her son again, and gave him much food. Then he said 'Where has my elder brother gone?' 'He killed you' said Ovelove. 'Oh my brother, my brother! I did not give him food when he was hungry, so he killed and ate me. Did you see my bones, and kill him because of that?' he asked.[1] Then he said 'You have already come back to me, my mother, tell Kioitame to come here to see me alive' said Alili kori. So Ovelove went to Laitate to tell Kioitame what had happened, and he returned with her. He said to her 'Where has *my* son gone? *Yours* has already come back to you.' [Clearly implying that his favourite son is the elder, while hers is the younger.] Then Ovelove said 'I was very angry, and I put him in the ground because of Alili kori.' Kioitame went and saw the place. Ovelove drew the outline of the hole on the ground. Kioitame dug out all the earth and found the bones of Alili kato. Ovelove said 'They are Alili kato's bones.' Kioitame [?] cut bamboo and fetched water in it and poured it onto the bones in the grave. Alili kato's flesh began to come back on his bones, and he stood up and got out of the hole. Ovelove called her pig 'Etoro'—which was huge—to her, and Kioitame killed it over the hole so that the blood ran into it, and Kioitame smeared blood on Alili kato's feet and his fingers. [It is not clear if the pig's blood acted in conjunction with the water to revivify Alili kato.]

Kioitame made a speech about his two sons, 'My two sons were here originally [then he recounts the adventures omitted above]. Then they came back here. Alili kato was resting in his house, and killed and ate his brother. Ovelove was angry about her son and killed Alili kato, and buried him in the ground. Alili kori came back to life, and Ovelove came and told me, and I came back here, and Alili kato has now come back to life.'

Everyone [from the surrounding tribes] came to the feast, and was given pork and took it back to their village. [Further adventures follow again, which are not relevant here.]

[1] It is significant that he seems to bear his elder brother no ill will but rather to have forgiven him.

For our purposes, the most interesting features of this text are that Alili kato kills his younger brother, that their mother kills one of her sons as vengeance for the death of the other, and that the younger brother clearly forgives his older brother, in view of the provocation which he felt that he had been offered.

The Tauade have a deep sense of the obligations which they owe to their mothers and sisters especially; there is the recognized custom of giving a pig to a woman in payment for suckling a child, and in various legends the themes of the self-sacrifice of sisters and mothers are manifest, as in this legend, which tells of the compassion of a girl for her little brother:

A woman (*agoteve*) gave birth to two children, a boy called Luatsini, and a girl called Otelepe. [At the time of this story] the girl was about fifteen, and the boy about five.

The girl looked after her little brother, giving him food and so on. A rat came and made its nest under their house. The girl dug down to it with a stick, and while she was digging the boy saw her vulva; it was like raw meat. He cried for the meat, and wouldn't stop. She gave him the rat's babies to eat, but he did not want them, and threw them away, and still cried 'Give me some meat'. She gave him cucumbers, but he refused them too and threw them away. He would not take water, or sugar cane, or bananas, or sweet potato, or pandanus nut. 'What do you want, then?' she asked, and beat him with a stick. He cried and cried and said that he wanted the meat of her vulva. So she cut off her vulva, and gave it him to eat, raw. But Otelepe died [of loss of blood]. Her brother saw her lying there dead. Only her right eye still saw her brother. He cried because his sister was dead: 'Get up, get up!' he said. But she did not; her insides had become nothing.

A stranger, an *agoteve* called Koravili, came. 'Why is your sister dead?' he asked. 'I cried, and my sister cut off her vulva, and in doing so she died.' Koravili took Otelepe's leg and shook her. 'Get up' he said. Her eye saw him. He gave her water, she drank it, and her insides became alive. 'The boy saw my vulva, and cried for it, and I cut it off, and gave to him, and died.' Koravili asked 'How will I copulate with you?' Otelepe said 'Cut some pork and put it here' [between her legs]. Koravili took some pork, cut it and made another vulva, and put it on Otelepe. Then he copulated with her. All this happened at Alualanapu hamlet near the Aibala River, in Goilala territory.

Then all three went to Ameava, where there were some Iveyava trees. These are the *agoteve* of the areca nut palms, and are very tall. These were called Ivei kuta kuma, Ivei kavia lapoa, Ivei pana patiri, Ivei patiri kovetiri. The brother and sister, and Koravili made hand and foot ropes to climb these trees. Koravili climbed up his. It was much higher than a pandanus tree.

The boy also climbed up one, and so did his sister [women normally never climb trees]. They went right up into the sky. Koravili was high up when he cut the boy Luatsini's hand and foot ropes with his stone adze. The boy fell down to the ground and was killed, at the foot of the Iveyava. His sister was still high up when she looked down and saw her brother. 'You have killed my little brother' she said [and began to cry]. 'He was my enemy' said Koravili. One of Otelepe's tears fell on the boy's chest, and he then became alive again. He saw his sister up in the tree, and he became angry, and took an axe, and cut down Koravili's Iveyava; it fell down over a cliff, and Koravili had all his teeth knocked down his throat, and was killed. Otelepe came down her tree and rejoined her brother on the ground. 'Koravili cut your hand and foot ropes, and you fell down and were killed; my tears fell on your chest and brought you to life again. We will go.' Luatsini said 'He was an enemy, a useless man.'

Various further adventures befall the couple which are not relevant here. In another story, also about the culture heroes, a pig called Kurovepe gave birth to a boy, Kiala Emai, who was captured by some people and taken away by them. In time, Kiala Emai grew up and made a home, and grew sweet potatoes. He was host at a big dance, and one party of guests brought pigs to kill, including Kurovepe, his mother, who was pegged out in the dance yard, ready to be killed:

Kiala Emai knew his mother, and she saw her son, and she wept [and the tears rolled down her snout]. [When he had killed her] he went into the house and wept bitterly because he knew his mother. He put grass between the toes of his foot and wiped up his mother's blood with it. He wrapped this up and put it away in one of the houses. Then he sat on the verandah. The others skinned her, and he took the stomach and came to Tapini with it and cooked it in an oven, and ate it with other men. He had the grass with his mother's blood tied up with a piece of thread, called Kopala keegalete. He brought firewood and burnt the house which had contained her blood bundle. Then he took a log and put the blood bundle on it, and with *elaivi* in his mouth [because of his great grief] he smashed the bundle to pieces by battering it with a stone. As a result, everyone died, except Kiala Emai and two little children.

As we saw in discussing the disposal of bones, death is the principal focus of grief, and a woman would often cut off her husband's hands and dry them, and hang them round her neck. Widows also hung a variety of their husbands' bones on themselves, one of the most popular being the coccyx. A good photograph of this can be found in Baines's article (1953). Patrol Officer White described the custom as follows:

At Ororogaivara it was noticed that one of the old customs still persists. A recently bereaved widow had an arm bone, several rib bones and the complete hand of the late departed hanging on a string round her neck. She did not appear to mind the offensive odour. Fortunately the rest of the remains had been buried instead of being laid out on a platform in the village, as was the old practice. (C. H. White, P.O., Tapini, March 1945.)

It should be noted that the wearing of bones and/or the dried fragments of the dead seems to have been largely a female custom, though Neyland, A.R.M., refers to 'the men having their small children's hands around their necks' when passing through the Gane area (Kairuku, January 1919). The practice of severing the finger-joints was apparently entirely feminine. Widows also wore string bags over the upper parts of their bodies during their mourning. They wore these bones and net bags for about a year, until the first killing of pigs for the deceased. It seems that when a man married a widow, he might be the person who cut off these string bags.

3. PRIDE AND SHAME

I have been at pains to emphasize the affectionate side of the Tauade character as an essential basis of our understanding of them, but it would be wrong to describe it as playing a predominant part in their behaviour. Their demeanour among themselves is always tinged with reserve; anger is usually carefully repressed, and except with their children, or between close friends, their mien is dour. An attitude of competitive pride is their defence against a hostile world, always ready to undermine their prestige, frustrate their ambitions, and enjoy their discomfiture. Correspondingly, shame, *katet*, is felt when pride is humiliated. While shame is not often referred to as such in conversation, it is nevertheless a basic undercurrent of their lives.

They have a clearly defined sense of sexual shame, and public nudity, or, of course, copulation, would be considered highly disgraceful.[1] Anal intercourse is said not to occur, 'because only pigs and dogs copulate like that'. But a patrol officer told me that he had once observed, in a garden below the track he was following, a couple having intercourse in this way.

It is also considered shameful for parents to have intercourse in front of their children, so that they would only copulate when their children were asleep, but preferably would not use the houses at all, but go into the bush during the day. The genitals are covered because

[1] Egidi, however, records seeing a boy masturbating in public.

exposure suggests that the person concerned wishes to have sexual intercourse. Men put out their tongues if they see women's genitals.

The following anecdote conveys a vivid impression of their pride:

A prospector named Adamson[1] had established a camp in the Goilala district, among the spurs and lesser hills of the central range. The Goilala people, truculent and intractable in the past, had simmered down considerably under the steadying influence of a police camp established at Mondo some years ago.

The cost of transporting stores from the coast was prohibitive; a carrier would eat the greater part of his load on the way in, and what remained would not suffice to take him back to the coast for more. Adamson was dependent for supplies on the goodwill of the local chief, who proved quite friendly, and kept the small camp well stocked with native vegetables. All went well until a morning when the old chief paid a visit during Adamson's absence. He was received with gross inhospitality by Adamson's fox-terrier, who chased him out of the camp and into the river, where he took refuge on a boulder in mid-stream, and sat in growing indignation, with the terrier barking his hatred across ten yards of torrent.

Adamson returned to camp in the evening, called off the dog, and did his best to smooth matters over. But the old chief's dignity was too deeply wounded. He left the camp in resentful silence; supplies ceased abruptly, and Adamson was in serious difficulties when Patrol Officer Middleton arrived from Mondo. The position was explained to him, and he sent for the chief.

The dog was formally arrested, brought into court by a native constable, and prosecuted by Adamson on a charge of intimidation. The chief gave his evidence with point and dramatic enthusiasm, and, as there was no defence, the culprit was sentenced to six months' imprisonment at Mondo.

The chief was delighted, and jeered in unholy glee as the dog was led away by a constable, a chain attached to his collar. Honour was satisfied; produce flowed again into the camp, and the Government gained a strong adherent. (Lett 1935: 9–10.)

While I have not been able to discover the patrol report on which this story is presumably based, Lett is very scrupulous in his use of other patrol reports which I have seen. So, while one is always reluctant to use second-hand sources in this way, there is no reason to doubt the authenticity of this one.

Middleton himself wrote the following passage on the inordinate pride of the Tauade:

The desire for authority with the men of the Goilala districts amounts almost to a passion; the receipt of a piece of cloth of any kind from the

---

[1] C. J. Adamson, later a patrol officer.

hand of a government officer is considered to be an authority conferred upon the recipient, who forthwith commences to strut about giving orders and adopts the title of 'Sipi' (Chief). Consequently he is envied by the majority of his friends and neighbours, who do not hesitate to take every opportunity of reporting his misdeeds, imaginary or otherwise, to the officer (Patrol Report 30/5/32–7/6/32.)

Pride, then, is one of their dominant qualities, and it expresses itself in many small characteristics of their deportment. One notices, for example, that if one man gives, say, a piece of tobacco to another, both parties will take care to make as little movement towards one another as possible, each trying to force the other to come to him. Again, the Tauade are remarkable for an almost total lack of greetings or farewells. While they have adopted the European fashion of verbal greeting, such as 'Goos morning', 'Apternoon', 'Bye-bye', all used indiscriminately at any time of day, these are generally employed only in speaking to Europeans. A man joining a group will say nothing, nor will he when leaving, except that, if he is actually engaged in conversation with someone he is likely to end it by saying 'I am going now', or 'I will go', or 'I have already gone'. But if he is not actually speaking he simply picks up his axe and walks off. While they usually said 'Morning, Apava' to me, I was very struck, and never ceased to be disconcerted, by their habit in the evening, when I might be lighting my fire, of disappearing silently into the night, so that I would look up when the wood was well alight and find that a person with whom I had been speaking a few moments before was no longer there. Only if one meets them on the path is a type of greeting given, a gesture by the person whom one is passing, with the hand held palm down and flicked up repeatedly in the direction in which one is going, perhaps with a smile; the obvious meaning of this is 'I will not attack you, go in peace', but it is confined to meetings on paths outside hamlet areas.

It seems that it is their pride which inhibits formal salutations among them. For when we greet someone we make ourselves vulnerable, since the other person may ignore the greeting. To a people so conscious of their dignity and so motivated by pride as the Tauade a possibility of humiliation would be reason enough to refrain from giving anyone the chance of inflicting it—by remaining silent. We considered other aspects of their unwillingness to risk humiliation when discussing the nature of gift exchange in Chapter IV.

It seems that the Tauade propensity to lie is closely connected with a culture in which pride is a dominant characteristic. A European long resident in the area said to me 'The Tauade are not really liars, since they do not expect to be believed in the first place!' and this remark contains an important truth. For exactly the same could be said of diplomats. The practice of diplomacy depends, among other things, upon the ability of all parties to maintain 'face'. In the same way, the sensitive pride of the Tauade makes lying, and in general speaking to please rather than to satisfy some criterion of abstract truth, a perfectly comprehensible mode of behaviour, which is likely to be prevalent in atomistic, competitive societies, where the sensitivities of one's interlocutor must always be considered.

Again, consistent with all this, the Tauade are very sensitive to insult, which is an important factor in the aggravation of quarrels to the point of violence. The basic themes of insult are decrepitude and bodily feebleness, or what they conceive to be undignified and humiliating associations, such as the eating or drinking of faeces, urine, or semen, or sexual or other bodily relations with pigs or dogs. As the reader may imagine, there are many possible variations on these themes, upon which it would be tedious to dwell in detail, but I give some of the common insults here by way of illustration:

> You are bald-headed and broken-toothed.
> Your hair is white.
> Eat my/your faeces.
> Eat my/your pig's/dog's faeces.
> Lick my/your wife's vagina/anus.
> Drink my/your husband's semen/urine.
> Come and copulate with my/your pig.

People also react violently when they are ignored.

C.N.M., December 1964.

A case of rape between a man and woman both from K—. The defendant states 'Before, I was working on the road. I shovelled and threw away the ground. The woman K—'s pig was standing nearby and the dirt hit the pig. The pig cried out. Then K— came and wanted to know who threw the dirt on the pig. She said to me that the pig had a vagina and that if I wanted to I could have intercourse with it. I was angry about this talk about me having intercourse with a pig. I was very upset.' The defendant then raped the woman in question.

C.N.M., January 1961.

A witness in a case from L— states 'O— was missing looking for her child when the defendant called out to her. [She obviously did not answer, so] the defendant attacked her [on her return] with a stick striking her several times about the body. He then clawed her face, inflicting many lacerations.'

C.N.M., 1954.

'My name is Ke— and I am Village Councillor[1] of M—. On Saturday last the defendant [of M—] sent me some pig [pork] by two small boys. Later he called out to me to see if the boys had arrived at my village. I replied and said that they were staying with me for a little while. Shortly after this the defendant arrived at the village. He entered my house and without saying anything to anyone—I was in the house—he grabbed some fire and set fire to the house. The fire was put out. He went outside and so did I. I had a piece of wood and with it I frightened Ko— [the defendant] because he had come and set fire to my house. Ko— then swung his axe at me and hit me on the head with it, inflicting a wound . . . Ko— said he was angry with me because I had not replied to him, but I did when he called out. It is possible that he did not hear me.'

The Tauade are content to compete in terms of a 'negative-sum' game. That is, they are content to reduce what someone else has, by ridicule, rumour, theft, or violence, without actually gaining anything themselves. Now, where power in the form of virility, wealth, and social success is the dominant value of a society, it must follow that the possessor of a greater than normal amount of it will thereby become a threat to the self-esteem of others; it will therefore be rational for the inferiors of a man in these respects to try to remove the causes of his advantage or pre-eminence, and in consequence to treat an enemy's loss as a gain to themselves, as the following anecdote illustrates. Fr. Fridez told me that he was once asked to arbitrate in the matter of a pandanus tree whose ownership was disputed by two men. Each swore vehemently that the tree was his own property and that the other fellow had no possible claim to it. It seemed that there could be no escape from this dilemma, until, jokingly, Fr. Fridez suggested cutting down the tree. This proposal was immediately accepted as a perfect solution; he felled the tree, and both disputants went their ways thoroughly satisfied that the other had failed to get the tree.

4. HEROIC AND UTILITARIAN SOCIETIES

In the study of Tauade ceremonies in the last chapter it will have become obvious that the people have little interest in material wealth

---

[1] At this time a village councillor was a man recognized by the government as a spokesman for his tribe.

as such, but value it principally as a means of obtaining prestige and renown. They desire the white man's goods not for use but for ostentation; while men are expected to distribute their wealth the result is not an egalitarian society, but one with marked gradations of prestige based on generosity and meanness.

It should be noted, however, that their ecology is not well suited to the accumulation of wealth, since there is a general lack of storable commodities, and land itself has little value. Homesteads are impermanent, and the separation of men from their wives' homes in the men's houses has meant that there has been no incentive for men to express their status and ambitions in the adornment and magnificence of their dwellings.

The most significant aspect of their attitude to wealth is therefore not that they choose to convert what little material wealth they have into social status by giving it away, but that they seem to value display and destruction for their own sakes as manifestations of power.

For the Tauade, a great pig feast and dance is *kova karo namutu*, 'very great power', and destruction is one of the chief manifestations of power. Fr. Guichet once told me on his return from a trip to, I think, Omoritu, that he had met a chief of that place by the roadside. A big dance village had been built and festivities were in full swing. The chief was saying how his gardens had been completely destroyed by the guests. Fr. Guichet commiserated with him but the chief said, no, it was very good that his gardens should be destroyed, because he was a chief, a great man. Clearly, his acquiescence in the ravaging of his gardens was in some respects a form of generosity, the mark of a chief, but I believe that at a more fundamental level it manifested the Tauade enjoyment of destruction for its own sake.

Tauade respect for the frenzied, the manic, is nowhere more clearly displayed than in their treatment of madmen. For even violent, homicidal madmen are not killed, but are merely bound, to restrain them until their fits are over, when they are released. They explicitly state that they respect madmen because they are like the culture heroes, the *agotevaun*. They are vehicles of more than human power, in fact. The Konso had quite the opposite attitude to insanity, regarding it as highly dangerous and anti-social, and linked with the activities of evil spirits. Madmen were associated with the cosmological category of the Wild, and in most cases lived as outcasts feared and hated.

Enough has now been said about the Tauade and the Konso to show that Ruth Benedict's use of Nietzsche's distinction between Dionysian and Apollonian cultures applies rather well to these two peoples. Her definition of 'Apollonian' and 'Dionysian' is as follows:

The basic contrast between the Pueblos and the other cultures of North America is the contrast that is named and described by Nietzsche in his studies of Greek tragedy. He discusses two diametrically opposed ways of arriving at the values of existence. The Dionysian pursues them through 'the annihilation of the ordinary bounds and limits of existence', he seeks to attain in his most valued moments escape from the boundaries imposed upon him by his five senses, to break through into another order of experience. The desire of the Dionysian, in personal experience or in ritual, is to press through it towards a certain psychological state, to achieve excess. The closest analogy to the emotion he seeks is drunkenness, and he values the illuminations of frenzy. With Blake, he believes 'the path of excess leads to the palace of wisdom'. The Apollonian distrusts all this, and has often little idea of the nature of such experiences. He finds means to outlaw them from his conscious life. He 'knows but one law, measure in the Hellenic sense.' He keeps the middle of the road, stays within the known map, does not meddle with disruptive psychological states. In Nietzsche's fine phrase, even in the exaltation of the dance he 'remains what he is, and retains his civic name'. (Benedict 1961: 78–9.)

In their respective attitudes to the proper status of the passions, madness, and 'disruptive psychological states' generally, the Konso are clearly 'Apollonian', the Tauade equally clearly 'Dionysian'. But there is another aspect of the opposition between Konso and Tauade values which is relevant to many other societies, yet which is not necessarily contained in the distinction between Apollonian and Dionysian societies. It is a distinction between what one might call the Heroic and the Utilitarian.

I take it to be a mark of the heroic society that it disdains the calculation of the mundane consequences of acts in terms of their probable practical benefits, and that it exalts the will, especially of the powerful individual. Pagan Iceland would have been a good example of this type of society:

The Old Scandinavian poets exalt the brave and determined individual to a degree surpassing any other literature, and give him every opportunity to exhibit the strength of his character. What the Northmen desired above all else was fame and the poets gave the greatest fame to the man who stood fast against hopeless odds. Fate offered no odds at all, so the man who made his choice and then strove valiantly and unfalteringly against hopeless doom, attained the ultimate pinnacle of fame. (Wax 1969: 152.)

The Tauade, faced with hopeless odds, would certainly surrender or run away. Correspondingly, they have no conception of Fate or Destiny. But they are closely similar to the Norsemen in their contempt for consequences, measured in terms of material comfort and well-being, and in their thirst for renown and glory, and their disdain for manual labour as anything other than a tiresome necessity. Their lives have been dominated by a few ferocious men with a lust for combat, who dragged their fellows into frequent bloodshed with neighbouring tribes.

5. CONCLUSIONS

The traditional functionalist model of human society is hewn from the same timber as the dominant scientific conception of Man—both ignore the creative and the imaginative and both regard man and society as essentially robot mechanisms, bundles of stimulus-response reflexes, conditioned by education, regulated by the environment, and reflecting the properties of the gene-pool. Whatever the lip-service paid to the autonomy of culture, the prevalent anthropological model of Man is essentially that of a rather complicated animal. Yet one wonders how many open-minded persons could read, for example, the account of the warfare between the Sene and the Laitate and still believe that this kind of behaviour had any analogy in the animal kingdom. As von Bertalanffy, the biologist and founder of general system theory, expresses the point:

Natural science has to do with physical entities in time and space, particles, atoms and molecules, living systems at various levels, as the case may be. Social science has to do with human beings in their self-created universe of culture. The cultural universe is essentially a symbolic universe. Animals are surrounded by a *physical* universe with which they have to cope: physical environment, prey to catch, predators to avoid, and so forth. Man, in contrast, is surrounded by a universe of *symbols*. Starting from language which is the prerequisite of culture, to symbolic relationships with his fellows, social status, laws, science, art, morals, religion, and innumerable other things, human behaviour, except for the basic aspects of hunger and sex, is governed by symbolic entities.

We may say that man has values which are more than biological and transcend the sphere of the physical world. These cultural values may be biologically irrelevant or even deleterious: it is hard to see that music, say, has any adaptive or survival value; the values of nation and state become biologically nefarious when they lead to war and to the killing of innumerable human beings. (von Bertalanffy 1971: 208–9.)

Tauade pig-rearing, feasts and dances, fighting and vengeance are not biologically adaptive, or even socially useful in any objective sense. They form a complex of traits which is given coherence by the Heraclitean cognitive orientation and the value system of the society. The traditional life of the Tauade was a prolonged fantasy of power, a religion whose rites were burning villages; the cries of warriors and victims; feathers and blood; dying pigs; and the monstrous figures of dancers singing tumultuously in the darkness of the ranges. These were no sober agriculturalists, making narrow calculations of profit and loss to better their material circumstances, but savage men in the grip of a collective obsession with blood and death. For them, work in their gardens was a boring necessity, to be shifted on to the women as far as possible, valuable only as the foundation of the real business of life—the pursuit of glory.

VII
The Wild and the Tame

THE dialectical relationship between the Wild, *kariari*, and the Tame or domesticated, *vala*, is fundamental to the Tauade world-view. For them the Wild is not merely the destructive alternative to social order, but is the source of life and of creativity in general. The *agotevaun*, the culture heroes, are pre-eminently figures belonging to the Wild, but are also the sources of the Tauade's ceremonies, customs, and artefacts. Similarly, the primary forest is seen as the source of most of the domestic forms of plants. At the same time, the forest is contrasted with the life of the hamlet, just as in some legends male *agotevaun* are contrasted with female *agotevaun* in terms of an opposition between the animal and the human, the non-social and the social. In the legends there are no houses in the forest but nests of moss; people withdraw into the forest when they are angry and wish to shun human society, and culture heroes dwelling there have no knowledge of fire and the cooking of meat. In a Fuyughe legend the *agoteve* actually eats his fire-wood and burns his meat to warm himself. Again, the lack of sexual organs in some male *agotevaun*, referred to in Tauade and Fuyughe legends, is surely an example of the non-social life of the forest, since copulation is a relationship requiring two people. The theme of the isolation of the sexes, and the consequent deformation of behaviour, is emphasized by the theme of the women who masturbate, and the men who send their penises in the form of snakes to rape women. The ideal society is one composed of men who live with women for whom they have paid bridewealth, and have thereby established friendly relations with the women's men-folk.

A second aspect of this relationship between the Tame and the Wild is that women are portrayed in the legends as the inventors and sustainers of culture, while males are basically destructive. Alili kato and Alili kori, the two brothers, go off on a rampage through the Aibala Valley, but seem ashamed of telling their mother what they have been up to. Women are the source of fire, cooking and betel nuts, string bags, and the useful arts. This is quite consistent with the life of the Tauade as it is actually lived; the burden of maintaining the amenities of daily life falls upon the women, while the men are traditionally concerned with bloodshed and destruction.

This opposition between the Wild and the Tame rests upon two concepts of prime importance—these are *kovata*, power, and *ago*, which cannot be so succinctly defined. (I discuss a possible derivation of this word *ago* below, p. 270.)

Kovata has the meanings of physical energy, e.g. 'Give me salt, my *kovata* has gone, I cannot work in my garden'; of sorcery in general, and of mystical power, such that the killing of many pigs is *kova' karo namutu*, 'really big power'; *kovata* inheres in the blood especially.

Sorcery, *kovata*, is practised to make yams, taro, pandanus, sweet potatoes, children, pigs, and dogs to grow; to attract people sexually, to make rain—especially for spoiling other people's dances—to kill people, or make them sick; to make pigs run away from their owners into the bush, and so on. From all appearances, however, while sorcery embraces a wide range of activities and purposes, it is not a *very* important aspect of life, and, moreover, its techniques are neither complex nor confined to a knowledgeable élite of professionals, though there are men who are supposed to be especially proficient sorcerers, or who boast of being so. I have never heard it said that women engage in sorcery, apart from garden and love magic.

One of the commonest types of sorcery is that intended to kill an enemy. The sorcerer obtains some excretion from his victim—it may be his semen if he is seducing his wife—and puts it with a piece of tobacco, some chewed ginger, the root of some decorative plant, wraps them all in a leaf which is tied up with a vine, and smokes the whole in a fire. When the bundle is well smoked, it is taken down and smashed to pieces with a stone. The victim is then supposed to sicken and die. Other means of conveying sickness and death are also used. A man may climb to the top of a mountain and light a fire, into the smoke of which he says a spell. The smoke takes the spell and the victim's eyes begin running, and he sickens. This is said to be why the tops of some mountains are bare.

Sorcery does not frequently come before the courts; the commonest categories are those intended to kill people, and to entice women's affections. For the latter, one of the man's pubic hairs enclosed in a cigarette is said to be an infallible receipt for gaining her complete submission.

Magic to promote the growth of garden produce is not, of course, liable to appear before a court, but I do not think that, presently at least, it is very much practised.

The range of meanings comprehended by *ago* includes our notions of 'ancestor', 'proto-type', 'wild form', 'non-human', 'source of fertility', and 'immortal'. A very similar concept is clearly the basis of Fuyughe cosmology, under the name of *utam* which Fastré analyses at length. The Kunimaipa also seem to have the same idea, which McArthur (1971) translates as 'big big', but unfortunately she was unable to pursue any detailed researches in this direction.

I. THE CULTURE HEROES

Let us begin with the ancestral connotations of *ago*. The Tauade believe that long ago their country was inhabited by non-human beings of gigantic power who carved out the river valleys, established the traditional ceremonies, deposited sacred stones and the originals of animals and plants, and who were in some cases of immense fertility, often with penises 'like horses' ', or 'forty-gallon drums', to quote their standard similes, and who were also of extraordinary homicidal tendencies. These beings could burrow through the ground, or fly through the air like birds, and when the mood took them liked nothing better than to overturn a yard in a dance village as though it were a carpet and bury all the people underneath, and then call the river like a pig or dog to come and wash everything away. They roared over the country raping and pillaging, smearing people with faeces, and shoving lengths of wood up people's anuses or down their throats, and one of their favourite tricks was to fly up into trees from which vantage point they would urinate on the people. They are supposed in most stories to have been white, and to have had very long hair, and in some cases pigs' tusks or other animal characteristics. The Tauade refer to themselves, and other Papuans, as *vale namu(ma)*, meaning 'real people', or 'true human beings'. The culture heroes just described are *agotevaun* (*ago*+*tev(e)* (person)+*aun*— plural suffix), and they are of a basically different nature from the Tauade and the other Papuans.

The Tauade equate the white man with the *agotevaun*, not only on grounds of physical appearance, but because of his technological power and knowledge, and the ability to go where he pleases. The word for white man is *agoago*. It is said explicitly that he is 'like' the *agoteve*, and it seems that this basic resemblance is expressed in the word *agoago* which by its duplicative form nevertheless differs from that word which designates the culture heroes themselves. I recall an amusing conversation with Moise Apava in which he said that the *agotevaun* and the white men were not real people, but like pigs, or that maybe he was wrong and that it was the Tauade who were not real people, but like pigs. Whatever else might be the case, it was clear to him that both the white man and the Tauade could not be fitted into the category *vale namu*.

The impact of the white man on the Tauade has been strikingly similar to that described of the culture heroes—at once trampling on ordinary men, and offering them new artefacts and customs. To this extent the Tauade have correctly identified a basic ambivalence of power, which is that it is both creative and destructive, and that creation inherently involves destruction and the triumph of the will. (The possible objection that the legends of the culture heroes are an *ex post facto* version of the events of government pacification seems highly implausible when one considers their content and their aptness to the rest of their world-view, and society generally.)

While the *agotevaun* are the cultural ancestors of the Tauade they are not therefore thought of as their physical ancestors. These are referred to by the quite distinct terms *kava(ma)*, *opoma*, *otama*, or *iloma*. Thus one's great-grandfather, *kariovei*, may also be referred to as *neve kavateve*, 'my ancestor'. They believe that their *kavama*, and those of the Fuyughe and Kunimaipa, all came out of the same stone at a place called Kuvaleipi, on the other side of the Wharton Range, somewhere in the vicinity of Ioma.[1] They came first to Lova-Loleava, and then spread to Sopu, Iveyava, and the rest of the valley. According to the legends, the first Tauade and the *agotevaun* co-existed for some time, until the latter either turned into stones or went to live on the tops of the mountains.

The culture heroes are supposed to have originated the killing of pigs and the ceremonies surrounding it, together with burial rites and initiation, and the use of the bull-roarer. Unfortunately, legends describing these and other acts are too long to be included here.

Many natural features of the landscape, especially the river valleys, are also attributed to the culture heroes.

There were two *agotevaun* called Apava and Tapunia, who lived at Kuvaleoiava, on the New Guinea side of the range. It was a place like an

---

[1] They say 'Ioma', but this is only a rough direction, picked up from hearsay. Ioma is in Orokaiva country, but there seems little in Williams's account of the Orokaiva (1930) which is reminiscent of the Tauade.

airstrip. They left there and came to Piot Karama [Mt. Albert Edward] where there is still one of their foot-prints. They made their home in a cliff called Oropoiva. Then they went to Kuriti oiava, near Woitape, where the Ivane rises. The Ivane and Kosipe rivers did not go anywhere at that time; they were held back by a wall. [The Kosipe and Ivane rivers rise in the great swamp of Kosipe which has only one exit through a narrow gorge near the mission at Kosipe. At the opposite end of the swamp there is a natural wall of rock which acts as a dam above Woitape and the Vetapu Valley. Thus the topography of the area makes the actions described in this legend quite comprehensible.]

A woman called Katai lived there. She had made two pools, one called Kataia kamai kinaeara, and Ivale iva loi kinaeara. [It is not clear if these were the pools' names, or spells which she said when she made them, or both.] She put the water to sleep like a pig.

Apava and Tapunia came there to make gardens, and saw the pools. They said to Katai, 'Who are you?' 'I am Katai,' she replied. 'What is that which you have made?' 'They are my pools.'

Apava and Tapunia made a hole in the edge of one of the pools with a stick, and the water ran out in the direction of Woitape. The name of the river was Terenagepe. The Ivane and Kosipe were still asleep. An *agoteve* of Maini called Atovo dokile brought a cucumber runner and said 'Katai, Katai, I will call the Ivane', and he called the Ivane, like a pig, and it followed him to Uvapu, where he met Katai and Apava and Tapunia.

Katai's hair was very long and hung down to her feet. The name of the hair was Kopapa keutu; it was like a coat down her back. The Ivane went down to the coast. When they came to a mountain in the way, they all pushed it away with their hands, to let the water through. They came to Bavakapitai, near Tapini, a mountain where the Aibala and Lovo rivers joined the Ivane. [It appears that the rivers are thought of as retaining their separate existence even after their respective waters have intermingled.] Other *agotevaun* called the Aibala and Lovo. The Aibala, and Ivane came to a cliff called Etepoava poripoava. Apava and Atovo dokile made a hole in the cliff, while Katai put the rivers to sleep. Then when the hole was made, the water burst through. Then they all came to the sea. There was a mountain which stopped the water, called Kipuramaivi, and they pushed it aside. Where the river reached the sea, there was an oak *agoteve* which they put there, called Tseetakapiri. Tapunia meanwhile had gone with the river Terene agepe a different way and come out on the coast near Port Moresby [Brown River], through the country of the Koiari. He was joined by Apava and the others, and they all went back to Woitape, through the country of the Mekeo. They had no hair, and looked at the long hair of Katai, and so she took it off and gave it to them. (That is why the Mekeo have long hair to this day.) Then they all went on top of Piot Karama [Mt. Albert Edward], where they made some more lakes, and then went back to the New Guinea side.

A frequent characteristic of these beings is their despotic and exploitative relationship with humans, who violently resent this. The culture heroes commonly sit up in trees, where they devour men, or urinate on them as they stand below, and in retaliation the people bring axes and try to cut down the tree. It seems fairly clear that in many ways the power of the culture heroes and the subjection and resentment of their human victims have some allegorical reference to the relationship between the chiefs and ordinary folk.

The *agoteve* called Iburinaiburi lived in a tree called Orinidamana at Amiapa-Lavavai. He used to eat all the children from the places round about. He could fly like a bird, and flew down and carried them off shrieking. He put them in the fork of the tree while they were still alive. Then he ate them up, starting with the fingers and toes. He threw the bones down at the foot of the tree when he had eaten all the meat off them. He did not eat the bones. When he had eaten one child he started on another. He took the children from . . . [a large number of tribes] . . . The bones were a huge pile at the foot of the tree; they rose up the tree higher and higher . . . He took the parents' valuables with the children, the valuables under one arm and the child under the other, chewing on it as he flew . . .

So all the people were very angry because their children were being eaten, and said, 'We will go and cut down his tree'. When the children were all used up, Iburi started on the pigs. He only ate the guts, not the flesh or the bones, though he did eat the flesh of the children. He went everywhere eating all the pigs. So everyone got to work copulating to produce more children and they became many again. He finished off all the pigs, and then went back to the children again, throwing their bones at the foot of his tree. He came to Goilala and took the child of Kope Kaila, a true man, which was in Kaila's house. Kaila was ready with his spear, and hit him in the right eye, so that the spear came out of the back of his head. His head was destroyed. He fell to the ground. Kaila fetched his club, called Oiteve buriteve, and battered Iburi to death with it. His men, with the women, cut Iburi to pieces. His killing teeth were put on a stone, and bashed to powder, and then burned in the fire, a very big one. His bones, his skin, his ears, his hair, his teeth, were all burned to ashes. There was nothing left.

Kope Kaila boasted 'I am fierce. He came and took my son, and I killed him'. Everyone from all around came to see the remains, and he sang this song to them . . .

Another example, in some ways even more vicious and sadistic, of the contempt of the culture heroes for men, comes from the legend about Alili kato and Alili kori. They were two brothers, sons of

Kioitame and Ovelove, the principal culture-heroes of the Tauade, who also appear in Fuyughe legend.

After Alili kato and Alili kori had stuffed the wood down the throat of Kamaukau, the wood turned into a stone in the Aibala river. Ovelove went to the country of Oroipo (above Elava). Her boys Alili kato and Alili kori went and tore up the gardens of the Ilai people and flung their crops and the earth of their gardens into the Aibala. Then the boys went to Kiolivi country, cut spears and sharpened them. The people of Goilala, Kataipa, Tawuni, Oropoa went to Kovokupe [near the present mission] and danced there with spears. The people of Kiolivi were also away at this dance. The boys came and flung the men's houses, the pigs, the riches of the people of Kiolivi into the river. They collected all their soil into a heap and Alili kori defecated on it, then Alili kato put it up in a tree, and tied it there. The brothers then called to the Kiolivi people to come. When they saw the earth up in the tree they said 'What is that up there?' 'It is your pork', said Alili kato and Alili kori, lying. The people said to Alili kato and Alili kori, 'Bring the meat down for us to eat. You have thrown our houses, our gardens, our pigs and our riches into the river, so in return, give us the meat.' They all stood there under the tree with their mouths open. Then Alili kato and Alili kori pulled down the earth with the faeces in it all over the people, and it was in their hair, and all over them. They were all wiping themselves, and Alili kato and Alili kori went off, back to Ovelove's village. She said 'Where have you boys been?' They said 'We were at Kiolivi'. They did not tell her what they had done. They left their mother there, and came to Elava. They pulled up their pandanus trees, their gardens, their houses, and tied their pigs' legs together and poked out their eyes. They took little children and raped them, boys and girls. The parents came and said, 'Get off our children!' 'Who are you talking to?' said Alili kato and Alili kori. They took pieces of wood and beat the parents over the wrists and ankles. The people ran away into the bush with their children. Alili kato and Alili kori went to their village at Elava, and defecated in the ashes of their fires [to make the people think that the faeces were sweet potatoes cooking in the ashes]. Then they went back to their mother's village. She said 'Where have you been?' 'We were at Elava', is all they said. They did not say what they had done . . .

The legends make much of the great size of the culture heroes' penises, and in some tales the penis has the power of going off by itself to ravish women; sometimes such a penis is killed, and the owner dies simultaneously. In another tale, a cassowary eats a piece of a dead culture hero's penis and develops immense strength and ferocity.

As the first legend showed, however, the culture heroes were not invulnerable, in spite of their superhuman powers, and when killed were commonly dismembered and their bones burned and crushed to powder, upon which a great stone was often placed. The culture heroes had marvellous powers of putting themselves back together again, so these precautions were necessary, as well as being highly gratifying to those who had suffered from the victim's depredations.

Many of these legends' themes, such as the return to life and flying through the air, and their general character, are also reproduced in dreams, or more specifically, nightmares. Indeed, in one dream, my informant claims actually to have met two culture heroes, and it seems very likely that much of the legendary material is derived from dreams.

The word for 'dream' is *etalata*, and 'to dream' is *etalat ka*, to see a dream. To walk in one's sleep or to go mad is *etalat la*, to dream walk. They are well aware that what they see in their dreams is not experienced by their bodies, which is why they sometimes say *neve uvari*, my soul, did this or that, when describing dream experiences. They distinguish the ordinary dream from the nightmare, which they call *ovat ka*, to see sickness, and I give a number of examples here. (While they believe that dreams can foretell the future, the actual events have no symbolic significance—for them, in dreams everything is what it seems to be.)

I was asleep and had a nightmare. Many men come into the yard of the village, and kill pigs, and cook them. They take the meat out of the oven but it stinks, and they spit it out. Then the men and the women all begin copulating, without shame, and then they all attack me, and cut me to pieces, and leave me on the ground. My blood stinks horribly, and the people [*Uvarima*, spirits] fly away like birds. But I come to life again, and take my axe and spear, and chase the spirits. They kill me again, and roll me around and around, and throw me over a precipice into a pool. There is no way out, only cliffs, which I cannot climb. I shout to be rescued, and the spirits throw down a rope and I catch hold and am pulled out. Then the spirits fly off again like birds.

They light big fires over all the country that burn the grass. The fire roars all around me, burning me all over, then it goes out. The spirits come with weapons for war, and kill each other, and some of them beg for mercy. There is a spirit dog which bites the ankles and other parts of the body. A spirit pig comes along his path, and I put a spear in him, but he carries it, and bites me, so that I flee and climb up a tree. But the pig seizes my penis, so I put my knife down the pig's throat, and slash his face, and break his teeth, and kill the pig. Then I burn the pig to ashes.

Then a huge python goes along a path, as big a python as one with its tail in the Kataipa and its head at Moigili. I am going along and tread on the snake. It turns round and throws me to the ground.

There are several bodies buried in the ground. I am asleep, and I see a hand pushed out of the soil, a live hand which grabs me. I run away, but there is another hand on the path in the way. Wherever I run there is another hand outstretched. There were an old man and a woman there, and I told them, 'Some spirit hands are trying to grab me'. 'Where?' they asked. 'Look over there' I said, and woke with a start.

I was being carried along in a stream, and a bad spirit with a diseased skin [*tinea*] seized me and put his hand over my mouth. I bit his arm, so he bit me in return. So I hit him with my knife. I ran away and climbed up a tree and sat in the fork, and looked down to see if he was following. He was sniffing my tracks like a dog. He went away, and I went back to my place, but he followed me there, and I killed him with my axe. I chopped his body into pieces, and flung the bits into the bushes. His penis was the size of a horse's. There was a terrible stink. My bush knife stank. I wiped the knife in the ground to get rid of the blood and the smell.

My soul was at Dimanibi, and it [I] went up to Valubu [the hill above]. An *agoteve uvari* [the spirit of an *agoteve*, or an *agoteve* in dream form] was there with his wife. His face was jet black, and his wife's was white. Her teeth were huge, like a rat's. They both had put heaps of moss on their genitals, and were sitting with their legs apart. There was a big heap of moss beside them. My soul came and looked at them. 'Who are you?' I said. 'I am your grandfather' [*vapi*] the man said. Then I told them my name. Their house was made of moss. I was invited inside. I passed between them as they sat on the floor, and sat on the floor too. The woman gave me tobacco. A huge dog came and bit my buttocks, and I jumped up and sat somewhere else. The *agoteve* hit the dog with a lump of wood, and it went and sat outside. 'A guest has come, you will not bite him', said the *agoteve* to the dog. The woman was sitting on my right and I was by the door. They both had bare behinds. She got up and the moss fell from in front of her genitals. Her pubic hair was as long as the hair on your [author's] head. She took the hair and pulled it between her legs. Her husband had a gigantic erection. I was ashamed and looked away. Then we all went outside, and I left them and came home. They waved goodbye to me.

2. TOTEMS

The *agotevaun* also placed the prototypes of animals and plants all over the Tauade countryside, and these survive to this day. Some examples from Goilala are as follows:

Orapailovelove (f) and Povoipiomalale (m) are the *agotevaun* of an animal which has a long nose and eats ants. They do not die, but just breed. They live underground in a stone. They have two *piti*, or young, Poipoitai and Vatatautu, both *agotevaun*, but Vatatautu is blinded by the sun and stays underground. Orapai is too fast for men to catch, but if ever she were killed, the whole species would disappear. They live at Kavatubu.

Kavini tulapa (f) is the *agoteve* of a kind of squirrel, *davala*, or *lavara*. It lives underground at Kalava, and its fur is white. People shoot these animals with bows and arrows but if they try to shoot the *agoteve* it takes their bows and breaks them and throws them away. It has four tails and uses them to seize the bows. Its male companion is Kavini kaivala.

Kuruavu kotale (m) and Kuruavu Lītauvu (f) are the *agotevaun* of the *kuruavu*, or tree kangaroo. They live near Deribi.

The *agotevaun* of the rat are Oto togoke (m) and Laimapa (f). They live near Deribi.

The dog *agotevaun* are Kovela Poto (m) (*kovela* = dog) and Kovela Dave (f). They live in a stone in the ground at Perume. They are still breeding, and their offspring come out at night and howl.

The *doloiri* is apparently a kind of squirrel, like the *lavala*, and its male *agoteve* is Mumu doloiri.

The *tsitsi* is a smaller version of the *kuruavu* or tree kangaroo, and its *agotevaun* are Tsitsi keepilo (m) and Tsitsi doleve (f).

Kovela dīgu is like a dog, and eats toads and rats. Kovendīgu (m) is its *agoteve*. It digs up corpses and eats the eyes.

It will be noted that there is a strong association between the *agotevaun* and stones, recalling the stone from which the ancestors of the Goilala emanated. This stone was called Tsimala evipi, and was near Ioma. A man called Akuikui kila kuikui cut a hole in this stone—presumably from the inside, to let the people out. There was a big sacred oak beside this stone, called Eavopu kiririvoitana bītana, which the ancestors cut down. We shall see that such trees are also closely associated with the *agotevaun*.

Birds also have *agotevaun*, which are named individually, and are immortal, as are the various animal *agotevaun*. There are two basic bird 'totems'—the *kireago* and the *tuna ago*. *Kire* literally means 'bird', apart from specifically designated species such as *komai*, cassowary, and *tuna*, which is perhaps a harrier. The *kire* in the case of the *kireago*, however, is only of one species, the *kulolo*; this is a fairly large bird whose most striking habit is to sit in a tree in the morning or evening and emit piercing cries, and it is for this that it is chiefly remarkable in native eyes. A boy who is unusually talkative, for example, may be named 'Kulolo'.

Each man is associated with one of these *kireago*, by inheritance
from his father and respects it by not trying to shoot it. They fly
about just like real birds, even though they are immortal. They are
particularly associated with chiefs, however, so that when a particular chief is absent, it is said that his *kireago* has gone with him.
I have also been told that *kireago* is another word for 'chief'. This
special relationship between chiefs and so conspicuously noisy a bird
is surely not fortuitous, since oratory is one of the necessary ac-
complishments of a chief in Tauade society. The *tuna* also has *agotevaun*, in the same way as the *kulolo*.

Just as animals and birds have their *agotevaun*, so do trees. In the
small area of primary forest above the hamlets at Goilala there are
a number of sacred trees, mainly oaks and beeches, which are generally referred to as *varovete*.[1] The forest is divided into areas in which
one such tree is mystically dominant. I compared this with a hamlet,
with each of its areas under the control of a chief, and Amo agreed
that the comparison was just. He says that the roots of the chief tree
spread out under the earth in the area which it controls. I was shown
examples of the following *agotevaun*:

areca	Tiremui
ginger	Morouvutitiba, Apavukivalikivala
elaivi	Eetiko kovo vaikokova
vines	Damani, Dupapu, Tipotava
pandanus	Tamankeigeipi, Bulebulu, Kurupindiara
kovelapa	Tsienkovelaitsi

Each *agoteve* has its individual name, therefore, as well as its
generic name. These *agoteve* should not be cut or harmed. Some of
these *ago* trees seem to be larger and thicker than the normal speci-
mens (as in the case of ginger and the vines or creepers, which can be
as thick as a man's thigh), but in other cases they are actually more
spindly and more 'primitive' or 'archetypal' in appearance. No *ago*
is ever planted by man. Otherwise ordinary-looking trees will be
referred to as *ago* if they have seeded themselves. In the case of the
pandanus mentioned above, one *ago* was very old, but others were
apparently young. In their case I was told that they had seeded themselves. If the nuts of the old pandanus tree touched people they made

[1] *Varovete* is used particularly of such trees, but has the more general significance of 'spirit place'.

them sick. It was forbidden to put corpses in any of these trees, including the *damanata* or oak tree, if it was an *agoteve*.

There is one tree, an oak, called Ipurai damana, which has a hollow in the fork of its main branches. According to Amo a python called Umepaliava lives inside it. Like all spirit pythons, this one can turn itself into a *tuna*. These birds of prey and snakes are therefore very closely associated. At the base of the tree is a collection of dead leaves and branches, which are placed there out of respect for the python. (Similar offerings of grass or leaves are sometimes placed by sacred stones.) There is a pool (which was almost dried up at the time) which belongs to the python. Growing in this is the *kovelapa ago*. Just above this on the path above the forest are the *toneago* (see below).

This description of the *agotevaun* of trees and plants shows that the Tauade have a model according to which almost every plant has an archetype which is to be found in the wild, usually in the forest. There may be several of such individually named archetypes. (There are a few plants, however, which are said to have no wild archetypes or *agoteve*.) An interesting case of plant *agotevaun* concerns that of sweet potatoes. There is a small plant called *kupeago* (Lobelia) which grows especially on shaded banks of clay. Its leaves, although tiny, bear a close resemblance to the leaves of the sweet potato vine, hence its name—*kupe* = sweet potato. It is believed to be the *agoteve* of the sweet potato, and it is said that it is placed with the vine at the planting of the potatoes. Yet the people are perfectly aware that the sweet potato was introduced and is not aboriginal. While it may be the case that they are simply being inconsistent, which is not unlikely, it is also possible that they believe that a true connection can exist between an *agoteve* and something which is introduced into their country. I am thinking here of their identification of me as Apava Tulava, which is just one example of a general tendency to try to demonstrate that what appear to be novelties have really appeared among them because of a pre-existent relationship.

Besides plants and animals the concept of the *agoteve* also includes inanimate objects, both natural and man-made. The word *agoto* is used to describe these things, which is literally a contraction of the phrase *ape' agoto*, 'ancestral name'. Thus the word *agoto* refers to the *name* by which the thing is known, and the thing itself need not still exist to be a true *agoteve*.

For example, Ila Otauruma was the archetypal string bag (*ilata* =

string bag) which was made by Ovelove, the female *agoteve* who was the wife of Kioitame. But the string bag in question is not now an *agoteve* in the sense that it still exists, but simply was the archetype of all later string bags. Similarly, the first riches—shells, dogs' teeth, nose-bones, and other bodily decorations which first came to Goilala—are named. The ancestors who came to the hamlets of Poruamabitia and Oropokeliliva brought earth with them from their native lands—it was red and used for pig magic. Some red earth of this type is to be found in the patch of primary forest described earlier; it is called Amatupiti. Again, the stones from which adzes were made in the beginning fell down from the sky. The ancestors (*kava*) of the Goilala put them in the fire and split them up. Two of these first, or arche-typal adzes are called Mautatara and Ninimutara. The first drums' names are also recorded by each tribe. Casimiro told me that the first drums of Sene were called Lupivi doromeve, Tanava makiliaeve, and Ilau amunav. These have long since perished, but the drums made later have been given these names. At Sene there was, however, an actual *poloago*, a bull-roarer *agoteve* called Polo alumoto, which survived physically in the form of three bull-roarers which were carved from it—it was black like a coconut.

There are, however, some *agoto* which refer to existing *agoteve*—especially the names of types of rain and wind. Iguni laveguni is rain from the direction of Garipa, Kavatata kaviavi is rain from Mt. Kutumu, and rain from the direction of Sopu is Itura lavuru. These types of rain are *agoteve* because they frequently occur in the same way, and thus in a sense never die. Similarly, there are two strong winds, Tavai tatsiavai mānmai and Luaioreai mānmai, which blow houses down, and these are *agoteve*. The 'immortality' of the pheno-mena and their recurrence in the same form year after year makes their classification as *agoteve* quite understandable. In our culture we give what is almost *agoteve* status to winds, especially the mistral, the *Föhn*, and so on.

The sun, moon, and stars, are also *agotevaun*. 'Our ancestors grew up, begot and died, but the sun and the moon and the stars are the same, so they are *agotevaun*.' The only celestial bodies which have names, apart from the sun and moon, are the evening star, Lapoiri, and the morning star, Uruava. These are both *agoteve*, and when the people plant gardens under the influence of these stars, they will become big. This influence extends to pigs, children, and other valued objects as well. Traditionally, they held up a pig in the starlight of

Lapoiri and said *Neve poru ka, neve poru ka* 'Look at my pig, look at my pig'. Then, when Uruava rose, they made a big fire in the hamlet yard, took small children's hands, put them in the flames briefly, and showed them to the star. The purpose of putting the children's hands in the flames was probably to make them strong, as we shall see was done in the case of bows. When the morning star was shining they said spells, e.g. *Kino nain kopi, potsilo naini leiopu* or *Nev'ema kenea naini leiopu, Neve kupea loitsu naini leiopu* and planted their sweet potatoes, which would become big. They also put sweet potatoes in the *uru'enam* (the fire lit at the time when the morning star was shining) and fed them to their pigs, to make them big. These sweet potatoes are also called *kupe atuata*, 'the sweet potatoes of fierceness'. Men put their bows in the flames of this fire, and when the moon rose went hunting with their dogs and shot many animals.

If a man offers or shows his sweet potato to Uruava before going on a journey, it will sustain him all the way to his destination, and he will not go hungry.

The moon is an important *agoteve* for magical purposes, and spells are said to it:

> *one* (moon) *tomala*
> *one urita naurita uliuli*
> *one kaila papala*

People showed their bows to the moon when it was full, and said these spells before going hunting.

It is interesting that while the sun is said to be an *agoteve* it does not seem to be the focus of any magical esteem or attention, perhaps because it does not display the variability characteristic of the moon and the morning/evening star. It is possible that the sun only becomes the focus of religious attention in those latitudes where its yearly course can clearly be seen to fluctuate so that winter and summer solstices are evident. In such cases it will appropriately be the focus of ideas about growth, death, and rebirth. In latitudes close to the equator, such as those inhabited by the Konso and the Tauade, no solstices are evident and the sun is thus treated as like the sky, unchanging except for regular rising and setting. From a religious point of view patterned irregularities in the cosmos are more interesting than complete regularity. The Tauade believe that the sun travels under ground from its place of setting, *malaioroa*, to its place of rising, *orōtsua*. The terms for the places of sunrise and sunset are not used for the purpose of geographical orientation, analogous to east and west.

Names of the *agotevaun* are closely linked to spells. For example, someone who spoke the names of one of the winds would do so in order to become as swift as that wind in battle. Again, in a court case, a man is claimed to have threatened people by saying that the name of his axe was 'the old killer'. In at least two of the legends men with very large penises gave them the name of a rock in the Aibala River; the water here is apparently thrown into the air in a jet by this rock, giving the appearance of a permanent ejaculation. Particular spears, especially those which figure in the deeds of the *agotevaun*, are also given special names.

Perhaps the strangest *agoteve* are the corners of houses:

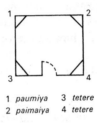

1 *paumiya*   3 *tetere*
2 *paimaiya*   4 *tetere*

It is said that these *unitago* (*uniti* = corner) are *agoteve*. One can see that as constructional forms they are changeless and undying elements of a particular form of house-building.

We must finally consider the words *porăgo*, *poruăgo*, and *toneăgo*. *ăgo* is said to be a stone, while *ăgo* is an ancestor. The *toneăgo* are long, thin stones which are probably phallic in significance, used by men for rubbing themselves before battle to give themselves courage and by boys to make themselves strong. *Toneăgo* could also be used for *aubu*, lethal sorcery. A fire was lit, the *toneăgo* heated in it, and then used to beat the body dirt, hair, etc., of the person whom one wished to kill. The *porăgo* is also a stone, but one which is rounder in shape. When I asked Casimiro why, if *ăgo* meant 'stone', and *ăgo* meant 'ancestor', *porăgo* was pronounced with a short 'ă', his explanation was that the -*ăgo* here referred to the *ăgoteve*—Kioitame, as it might be—with which the stone was associated. The ingenious parallel which he adduced was 'Jesu Christe', when someone was called a 'Christian' after baptism. The *porăgo* was a magical stone which may be used for a number of purposes. It can be used for removing sickness, and promoting the growth of pigs and sweet potatoes, but not of yams, taro, or cucumbers. With yams, *kopoiala* (Carpodeltus 687) is planted, as with taro and cucumbers.

A *porăgo* is inherited from father to son. In fact, from the list of *porăgo* and their owners which I obtained, it seems that they follow the same rules as the *kireăgo*, *tuna ăgo*, and so on, for inheritance.

Some *porăgo*, of which I obtained examples, are customarily kept in the possession of one man, and since individuals were able to sell me such stones it seems that in some cases they are individually owned. (It is always possible that they were not genuine *porăgo* at all, but simply any old rocks brought along to get money from the mad anthropologist, but the obvious signs of much handling, such as smoothness and a greasy patina, and in some cases, smoke stains, suggested that they had been the object of long and special attention, which substantiated the vendors' claims that they were *porăgo*.) Other *porăgo* are buried in the ground, and can be the stones inhabited by the *ăgoteve* of animals. For example, the *kene* (rat) *ăgo* called Ototoko laimapa, near Deribi, is the sacred stone in which lives the actual rat *ăgoteve*, which is alive and breeding, but the stone can be used for pig magic. (The actual stone is barely visible, being almost entirely buried in the earth.) The hair from the pig is placed on the end of a piece of cane and put on the stone; as a result, the pig from which the hair is taken grows big. In the case of a stone called Tupi amieve, upon which pig hair is also deposited for the same reasons, it is said that the *ăgoteve* put it there. It is a large rock near Poruamabītīa. When we passed it Amo Lume put some grass on it, as he did in the case of the *keneăgo* called Ototoko laimapa, as a gesture of respect. There is a stone at Poruamabītīa called Varitu, 'thief'. It is said that if a man sits on this someone will steal his pig, his riches, or his wife. Poruamabītīa is associated with the Karuai clan, since it is believed that their first ancestors lived there; the Karuai are also said to be thieves.

There is a big cliff close at hand called Keemala, from a crack in which runs a trickle of water, an *iăgopo*, called Dūrudoipi. *Iăgopo* means *ipi ăgo*, water 'ancestor'; I am not certain if this means simply a spring, or refers to this particular trickle of water, ascribing to it some special archetypal significance, perhaps because it runs out of a rock. This cliff is just above the bone cave Duruai orava, the name meaning 'the cave of Duru'.

Poruăgo means literally 'pigstone' and refers to stones used especially for magic associated with pigs.

It will be recalled that some of the culture heroes are supposed to have turned into rocks. They are also supposed to have been responsible for the well-carved stone artefacts, such as pestles, and mortars, and rock engravings that are found in the area. It thus seems possible that the original meaning of '*ăgoteve*' was 'stone person', for both the above reasons, the short '*ă*' being simply a modification of the long '*ā*' in '*āgo*.' In modern usage, the word for 'stone' is not '*āgo*' but '*evite*', though '*ăgotu*' means 'heavy'.

3. SPIRITS

Besides the *agotevaun*, there are two other kinds of supernatural beings; *uvari*, which has the sense of soul, ghost, and a being encountered in dreams; and *lume*, spirit akin to the pidgin *masalai*, 'the spirits thought to inhabit streams, rocks, trees, whirlpools, whirlwinds, eddies and such like' (Mihalic 1957: 82).

The Tauade notion of the constituent parts of the person thus seems confined to *kotsipe*, skin or flesh; *kovata*, energy or strength; and *uvari*, ghost or soul. They do not seem to believe that the ghosts or souls of the living or dead are seen by the living when awake, and any such manifestations would be considered as *lume*. It seems that one only encounters ghosts in dreams, but one can also have dream encounters with spirits not otherwise met with in the waking world.

As one might expect, given the general bias of Tauade culture, most spirits tend to be malevolent, but a few are well disposed to men and can affect the growth of crops. But the spirits have no significant relationship with the culture heroes and seem to be an independent element in the Tauade world-view. The following spirits are said to reside within Goilala territory:

Tsiapa and Valuvia

They live in a sacred tree, and strike men and send them mad, so that they pick up faeces and eat them, or smear them on other people. They (the people stricken) batter their hands on the ground, and bite wood until they break their teeth and their mouths are full of blood. They spit at people, make claws of their hands, and burn themselves with fire. The woman Aito Kotsipi had been to their place to get *omoriti* to make thread for her string bag. The spirits followed her back to the hamlet of Dululea maitsi, near Deribi, and killed her, so that blood came out of her ears, mouth, nose, and genitals.

Omoria and Poregia

They live in the earth near Deribi and come out and make a noise like an aeroplane. They used to come to women in the night and have intercourse with them. They no longer do this because the white men have come, and they have fled. They came once to the house of Kiani lavavai puleu, a chief of Oropo hamlet, whose daughter Leavai was living with him. The father and daughter both went to Deribi to cut wood for their house and the fire. They cut wood from the place where the spirits live, and the spirits followed them back to Oropo. They bit the girl on the forehead, and as a result she had a growth there (which was curved, like my pipe stem). Kiani invited the people to a pig-killing because of what had happened to his daughter, and said that he would no longer go to cut wood at the place of Omoria and Poregia.

Again, Evura Kavai's son, Tau Itoveama, came and took *elaivi* from this place, and the two spirits attacked him and he went mad and fell into the fire when he got home. The spirits put 'snakes' and centipedes[1] inside him, and when his relatives killed pigs the 'snakes' and centipedes smelled the odour, and came out of his penis and anus. Amo Lume says that he saw them. Tau died as a result, and is buried at Deribi.

Again, Kitai Komai and his wife Kamuni, and their little son Kulolo Kilemu, all came to this place and cut wood, which they brought back to their hamlet Kutupu, where they put it on the fire. While they were asleep that night, the spirits came and attacked the boy. His arms and legs turned black, and his hands were turned in, and his legs folded up, so that he could not walk. His head became elongated in front and behind. He had to lie on one side in order to defecate. But he did not go mad, and talked interminably. He died later, when still a small boy. He is buried at Dimanibi.

Again, a man called Etala Tapeegi came and took wood from this place. Poregia came to kill him, but he turned round in time and killed Poregia. [This is another puzzling case of a spirit being 'killed'; it seems likely that what Etala killed was an hallucination. Poregia apparently looked like an ordinary person.] But Omoria seized Etala and turned him mad, so that his tongue hung out like Kenepe's. He developed a hole in his thigh, from which much fluid came out; he lived a long time like this, and is buried at Punepe.

[Kenepe is a woman who lives at Kerau and who is supposed to have been turned mad by drinking the water from a pool in a rock belonging to a spirit. My first encounter with her was somewhat horrific. I was climbing Mt. Kutumu (Eyssautier), and with my guide came upon a small hamlet on the edge of the forest. A woman emerged from her house/pig-sty covered in scabs, with her right elbow bent back to front, her tongue hanging out with long threads of slime dripping from it, and mouthing insanely and wagging her head from side to side as she tottered towards us. There was an almost equally decrepit old man, picking his face, and covered only in a G-string and with scabs anointed with clay. He barked at us and then crawled back into his hovel.]

---

[1] Possibly maggots.

Again, Tau Omori and his wife Laupu came and took wood from this place, with their son Avui. The spirits attacked Avui, weakened his arms, and pulled his legs out of shape. [Avui is now a grown man, whom I saw quite often. He was stunted, with extremely bandy legs, and had difficulty in walking properly. He was blind in one eye, and had a prognathous lower jaw; he was clearly simple-minded, though perfectly amiable. After hearing all these accounts of people who persisted in getting their wood from this particular place, and the consequences that befell them, one is driven to the conclusion that the Goilala are singularly slow in taking a hint. Though it is likely that the symptoms declare themselves much more slowly than these accounts imply, and that the exact location of the place is also defined in retrospect.]

Keepiloli

He lives at Keepi, near Deribi, and makes the yams in the ground. He is a good spirit, and does not harm people.

Kamo Kalaluva

He is bad, and lives near the Aibala, at Pelatanitai. He seizes people on the path, like a big wind, knocking them over.

Varopo Laloipi

He is a good spirit; he makes yams and pigs, and gives water to sick people to make them well.

Kov Toniti

He is bad; he lives near the Aibala, and throws people into the river. He also throws pigs and dogs into the water.

Dura Notoapa

He comes and bites the toes of people asleep in their houses.

Amuna Avutolo

He kills people, pigs, dogs, and takes people's valuables.

Lume Koni

He is good, and pours water over sick people to make them recover from sickness.

Orin Komori

He lives at Tawuni, and comes and seduces women at night, and steals valuables, and bangs on the men's house. He goes to other places as well, such as Watagoipa and Kataipa. He comes and joins in the dances; people see him and flee.

Kipuvoiava

He lives at Ubulubu, near the Aibala. He digs up people's yams, sugar-cane, sweet potatoes, and cucumbers.

Topemamu

He lives at Komeaeve, near the place of the spirits Omoria and Poregia. He is a good spirit, and shouts out 'Take note of what I have seen in that place'. He shouts out this when he has seen thieves or adulterers at work, or when another tribe is coming to attack. He tells the names of thieves and adulterers. When people go to try and find him, there are only bones. Kopeiri chopped up these bones, and blood flowed out of them.

Kupupu Umuna

He lives at Toniava. He comes on people like a big wind, and destroys their houses and gardens as well.

Kerapa Viloli

He makes sword-grass in the bush. He also makes sap in the trees.

Ililiavupopetu

He makes bananas, which he gives to other spirits.

Amuna Avotoro

He makes water in the ground, and brings water to all springs.

Kate Kamune

When a sow has given birth to young, he comes to the nest and eats them. He eats the young of other animals as well.

Kamana Tsigatsiga

He makes taro, sugar-cane, and yams.

Ate Kogo

He lives at a big cliff called Tsitsiriava. He steals pandanus nuts and takes them home with him.

Kopu Konowa

He sends people mad. In the night he whistles, and comes and scatters the fire.

4. CONCLUSIONS

Creativity is therefore inherently linked with destructiveness in Tauade eyes, both being but the two faces of power, which in its highest manifestations is the property of the culture heroes, white men, and chiefs. Power never dies, but persists to invigorate and fertilize successive generations.

The cosmology is also quite consistent with the Heraclitean model of society, since it lends itself not to any concept of 'order', but to that of forces interacting. In this connection it is surely significant that the Tauade have paid little attention to time-reckoning. For an Aristotelian model of society and the world, change is the greatest of all threats to order and so must be controlled, primarily by reduction to cyclical form, but for a Heraclitean model change is integral to its operation. The closest such a cosmology can come to the notice of order is that of permanence, and it is clear that the *agotevaun*, in all their forms, are manifestations of a number of permanent and unchanging features in the Tauade world of flux and instability.

A Heraclitean cosmology such as this can have little or no place for a Supreme Being; according to Fastré the Fuyughe believe that a single being, Tsidibe, performed many of the acts attributed by the Tauade to the culture heroes as a whole, but even for the Fuyughe, Tsidibe, like the *agotevaun*, disappeared, and was essentially a Being of Power, not Order. (I am personally not convinced that Tsidibe is a single being at all, rather a generic term for 'culture heroes' as a whole.)

VIII

System[1] and Organism

THE purpose of this book has been to show how the basic organization of Tauade society leads inevitably to violence of considerable intensity. No single factor is responsible for this; as Fig. 17 shows, the degree of violence in the traditional society is the product of a complex interaction of factors, but four of these are of primary importance—the ecology, permitting mobility and leisure; the pigs, forming the basis of dance villages and networks of exchange; the Heraclitean mentality, according to which the Tauade see society in terms of personal interaction, inhibiting group formation, wherein the passions provide an entirely appropriate mode of conduct; and finally the ethos of aggression and destruction, which is independent of the other factors. This provides the really lethal component, but the social forms resulting from the ecology and the lack of group structures have allowed the Tauade propensity for violence to rage with a peculiar intensity.

It is therefore clear that violence is an integral part of their society, and not a pathological state; while some features of the society produce peace it can be seen from Fig. 18 that these are fewer and weaker than those making for violence. Tauade society is therefore a complex system from which bloodshed, warfare, and vengeance cannot be eradicated by internal processes.

The working of the society depicted in Fig. 17 is not, however, organismic, even though it has systemic properties. An organism has certain crucial variables like body temperature or blood-sugar level which must be maintained between certain values if the organism is to survive, and the feed-back processes by which these values are maintained have been evolved in the course of natural selection. They can thus be described as 'functional'.

[1] While this chapter is written from the perspective of general systems theory, there is no space here to consider systems theory in any detail. The application of systems theory in social anthropology will be the subject of subsequent publications.

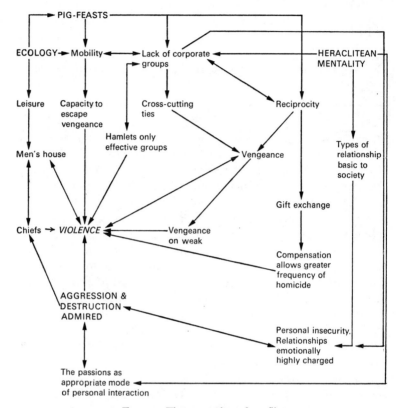

FIG. 17. The generation of conflict

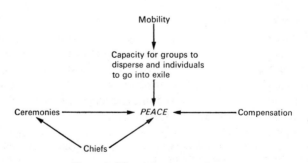

FIG. 18. The maintenance of peace

If one examines Fig. 17, however, one will see that there are no crucial variables which must be maintained at certain levels. If radical changes occurred in ecology, pig-raising, population pressure, or attitudes towards aggression, for example, the whole system would simply change, to a greater or lesser extent; it is not in such a critical state of adjustment to its environment that any other form of internal organization would be unviable, or produce contradictions within the society. Because organisms have crucial variables, they die—societies just change. Societies can and do try to maintain certain variables at particular levels, but these are decided by the value and belief system—there is no such thing as the 'health' of societies in the abstract.

An analogy may be drawn here between the working of this society and the atmospheric system. A complex series of interactions takes place constantly within the earth's atmosphere, and many of these interactions are themselves of a systemic type; that is, the variables go through a finite series of transformations and arrive at deter-minable states—the stages of a hurricane or a cold front are examples of this. But the atmosphere is not an organism produced by natural selection, and these processes are not 'functional', but merely systemic.

Given, therefore, the basic ecology, availability of pigs, demo-graphy, cognitive orientation, and values of the Tauade, one can show how these interact to produce, in this case, a high level of violence. But this violence is neither adaptive nor functional—it is merely a 'systems phenomenon' like inflation, urban decay, or the uncontrolled growth of bureaucracies.

There are, of course, certain social phenomena which have adap-tive characteristics, in the sense that they were designed to meet certain contingencies, and are modified according to changes in cir-cumstances. A good example is the location and design of the hamlet. Granted that the Tauade choose to live in hamlets, then their location and design can be shown to have been chiefly determined by the pro-perties of ridges, the need for defence, and the requirements of cere-monies, and consequently in modern conditions the stockade has vanished entirely, and the men's house only retains its traditional size and importance in dance villages (Fig. 19). But one cannot argue from such examples that every other institution in the society is also the product of an adaptive process.

It is sometimes falsely assumed by functionalists that because the milieu in which primitive societies commonly exist is physically arduous because of its lack of technology and medical facilities, it is therefore a rigorously selective environment, in which maladaptive institutions and customs will be swiftly weeded out. But our examination of the Tauade's natural environment has shown that it provides a wealth of raw materials that with the fertile soil and moderate

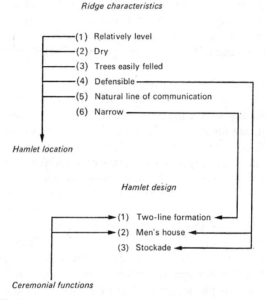

Ridge characteristics

(1) Relatively level
(2) Dry
(3) Trees easily felled
(4) Defensible
(5) Natural line of communication
(6) Narrow

Hamlet location

Hamlet design

(1) Two-line formation
(2) Men's house
(3) Stockade

Ceremonial functions

FIG. 19. Adaptive features of hamlet design and location

climate permit survival with relatively little physical effort; much of the labour of gardening is expended in the felling of trees and building of fences to keep the pigs out, which is a problem of the Tauade's own making. The cultivation of tubers is less arduous and time-consuming than that of cereal crops, and droughts of any real severity are almost unknown. In exactly the same environment it would be possible to fence the pigs, and so prevent their ravages of the gardens, to use their dung in combination with human faeces and vegetable compost as manure to allow more permanent gardens, to consume pigs in smaller numbers more frequently, and to preserve their meat by smoking to ensure a more regular and efficient use of protein, and to live in large settlements. This mode of livelihood

would require harder work, less leisure, more planning, and a different attitude to large feasts, but to describe it as more or less adaptive
than their present agricultural system would be mistaken; it would
simply be differently adaptive. Because the Tauade are able to maintain what to them is a satisfactory level of subsistence by their traditional methods of raising and consuming pigs and cultivating their
gardens, and because, objectively speaking, they do not suffer nutritional or other physically harmful effects, we should conclude that,
in relation to their physical environment, their mode of livelihood
is adaptively neutral, as opposed to optimal.

Again, in organizational terms, societies as inefficient as those of
the Tauade and neighbouring peoples are, for that reason, incapable
of organizing genuine competition between the component groups.
Violence itself is no evidence for competition which only exists in
a situation where definitive, permanent winners and losers are produced, whereas there are no clearly bounded groups among the
Tauade, and their warfare and violence leave the basic social organization and distribution of people unchanged. Because all those groups
with whom they came into contact were socially and economically
similar, and equally inefficient, no true competition existed, and this
allowed modes of behaviour and organization to flourish which
could not have survived in a more demanding natural and human
environment.

It seems, therefore, that in situations like New Guinea it is possible
to have a multiplicity of small groups, incredibly inefficient by our
standards of social organization, staggering along for century after
century, not really being able to do each other much harm, in a state
of minimal social change. The only significant social changes would
have been brought about by the peaceful diffusion of new commodities and skills. Only when faced with genuine competition in the form
of the Australian Administration, organized for true military and
social efficiency, do we have a situation resembling that posited as
normal by functional theorists, and in which native society was hope-
lessly inadequate to meet the challenge. I am not therefore saying
that competition between different societies does not take place—the
wars and conquests of the great nations of history, and especially
of the European colonial powers, are obvious examples of competing
societies—merely that in large areas of the world in the past social
inefficiency was so great and human populations so small that the
possibility of effective competition was very limited.

It might be argued, however, that some Tauade institutions such as the chiefs and the great feasts are the product of an internal process of adaptation within Tauade society. By this process of reasoning the chiefs, for example, would have been evolved as a means of social control in an acephalous society.

Up to a point one would at once concede that in atomistic societies the race will be to the swift and the battle to the strong, and where violence is an accepted means of imposing one's will, such societies will come to be dominated by men of the strongest personality. Moreover, there will be a tendency for the sons of such men, especially eldest sons, to derive a competitive advantage from their fathers' status, and for a large number of chiefs to be the sons or close relatives of chiefs. Processes of this kind occur in all societies, and for this reason we are able to discern clusters of traits by which types of society or social phenomena may be differentiated.

It would be fallacious to assume, however, that the chiefs have been evolved *as a means of* social control. They exist because the basic nature of the society allows no other effective form of power, not because of some innate tendency of society to evolve harmonious institutions.

Functionalist theory has been bedevilled by a conceptual confusion between stability and harmony. We know that in most societies where a disturbance occurs in some part of the organization it will tend to return to the same condition as existed before the disturbance. In Tauade terms, for example, an outrage is committed and violence follows: this violence is followed by retaliation, and finally the parties will be prepared to exchange compensation. But a propensity to stable equilibrium of this type has nothing to do with 'harmony' in the sense of 'absence of conflict'. Tauade social organization is highly stable in its basic forms, but thoroughly disharmonious. Thus the internal adaptation of a society over time will, in the absence of externally induced deviation, tend to result in stability, but not necessarily in harmony, which cannot in any case be satisfactorily defined.

In the same way, it would be fallacious to argue that the great feasts and dances contribute to the cohesion of the society by preventing permanent hostility between the tribes. Permanent hostility between tribes is organizationally possible, since this does not preclude marriage between them and the tribes are not effective corporate groups that can prevent private friendships even between members of traditionally hostile tribes. The dances do not occur as means of securing

social cohesion, but to further the various ambitions of their participants, and if they did not occur, there is no evidence that Tauade
society would be consumed by violence, or that any marked adjustment in their other institutions would result; indeed, just the opposite
conclusion should be drawn. Such concepts as 'social cohesion' are,
like 'harmony', incapable of precise definition or useful application,

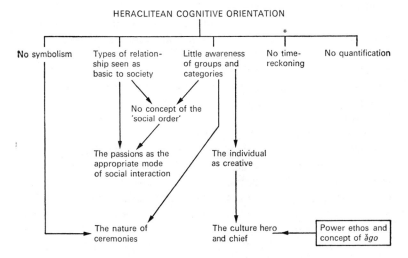

* Change is not a threat to a Heraclitean society,
  but on the contrary is integral to its operation

FIG. 20. Heraclitean cognitive orientation

yet without such concepts, that of 'function' itself becomes meaningless.

This brings me to another type of interdependence between institutions, and which also embraces the values and beliefs which compose
the society's world-view. There is clearly a basic integration of Tauade
modes of thought and their institutions, which is expressed in the
Heraclitean model set out in Chapter III, and in Fig. 20.

Maybury-Lewis suggests that a dualistic model is the most fruitful
for understanding Shavante society:

I think that a more useful concept of dual organisation is that it is an ideal
type corresponding to a theoretical society in which every aspect of the
social life of its members is ordered according to a single antithetical
formula. The discussion of whether or not a given society is a dual

organization or whether dual organizations exist then becomes irrelevant. Instead, anthropologists might consider how far a particular dyadic model was explanatory of a given society; or, to put it another way, what range of rules, ideas, and actions was rendered intelligible by the model and, equally significantly, what range was not. (Maybury-Lewis 1967: 298.)

I would defend the Heraclitean model as an 'explanation' of Tauade society in similar fashion, since it is the simplest yet most powerful model consistent with the facts.

But it does not of course explain *how* Tauade society, values, and cosmology reached their present form, and it is precisely the problem of how conceptual models can be reconciled with the processual nature of social evolution that leads many anthropologists to dismiss them as at best ingenious fictions. For surely, if one is proposing a certain model as basic to a society's institutions and beliefs, one is ascribing to it some primary causal virtue in determining that society's development? This is not so.

By way of illustration we may consider the case of liberalism in nineteenth-century industrial society. The concepts underlying this social philosophy can be reduced to a set of fundamental ideas about competition, utility, and rationality, which have found expression in legislation and a vast range of social institutions and attitudes. An ethnographer trying to understand the working of nineteenth-century industrial democracies would discover that a 'liberal' model would have considerable explanatory power. It would not have as much power as a dualistic model for Shavante society, or the Heraclitean model for Tauade society, because some societies are too complex to be reduced to models as simple as this, but its utility would be considerable none the less. The philosophy of liberalism was not evolved *a priori*, however, and then applied to society. As we all know, its evolution was a dialectical process in which social events were constantly evaluated in terms of a developing social philosophy which in turn was reapplied to society.

It seems that a basic propensity of the human mind and the necessities of social co-operation require the reduction of complex phenomena to a very limited set of ideas which are then developed richly in a way that still preserves their internal consistency. (The 'organic' model of society is a good example of this phenomenon in the realm of science.) But social institutions have their own developmental logic which may produce institutions that are incompatible with the cognitive system. It is in the interaction of the systemic properties of institutions with those of cognitive systems that we will find the principles governing the nature of societies, and not in crude analogies with organic evolution.

It does not seem to be accidental that such simple models as the Aristotelian, the dualistic, the Heraclitean, or Dumont's model of 'hierarchy' for the caste system, are so frequently relevant to traditional societies, but appear to have little obvious application to complex industrial societies like our own. The reason is not only the relative heterogeneity of belief and value systems in industrial societies, but also the simplicity of primitive modes of production, distribution, and exchange. It is evident that a society based on a subsistence economy of slash-and-burn agriculture can be arranged in a very wide variety of ways, but an industrial society has by its very nature to meet stringent requirements of organizational efficiency that are incompatible in many respects with elementary cognitive and value systems.

In the first place, institutions in an industrial society, such as business corporations, are self-adjusting to achieve efficiency, whereas those of traditional society usually have no clear purpose. Given the primary requirement of efficiency, none of the components of a business corporation has any absolute value, beyond its contribution to the success of the whole organization. But one frequently finds that groups and categories in traditional societies do have some absolute moral or symbolic value, irrespective of any putative contribution they may make to the efficiency of the whole society. Craftsmen in many societies of Ethiopia are despised, for example, in spite of their necessity for their host societies. This lack of absolute value by groups and categories is closely linked with another property of industrial organization, which is the substitutability of personnel, in accordance with the changing demands placed upon that organization. It would be impossible to run a large business efficiently if jobs were restricted to members of particular castes, descent groups, age-grades, or of one sex or class. As a consequence of this, tasks within the organization and categories of persons from whom the organization recruits its members must be entirely stripped of absolute value and symbolic or moral significance, yet it is this significance that allows traditional societies to be so thoroughly integrated by a single cognitive system.

Industrial societies are therefore organized very much more in terms of institutional logic than primitive or traditional societies, and it is for this reason that the materialist model of society as basically determined by the mode of production and use of resources is so frequently irrelevant to the societies studied by anthropologists. Engels made a basic error in assuming that because 'men must first of all eat, drink, dress, and find shelter before they can embrace politics, science, art, religion, and anything else . . .' that what they eat and how they grow it will determine their religion or their political institutions. It is not technology and the means of subsistence that of themselves govern social institutions, but the range and stringency of the conditions that must be satisfied before a particular technology can be operated successfully. One can see that industrial technology requires a very wide range of conditions to be satisfied before it can be operated successfully; these range from communications to education and the monetary system, whereas swidden agriculture is compatible with many different types of society—matrilineal or patrilineal, governed by chiefs or by age-grading systems, living in large settlements or scattered in hamlets, and so on. (Transhumant ecologies, however, are only compatible with a narrower range of organization.) It is a general law that the greater the complexity of any entity, the stricter and more comprehensive become its requirements for successful operation, and the freedom of choice in its operation is correspondingly reduced. For example, the constraints on the operation of a saw-mill are very much greater than they are for an axe. Our society is therefore dominated by its technology not because there is such a thing as 'technology' in the abstract that always 'dominates' or 'determines' society, but because our technology is a fragile hothouse plant which can only operate successfully when the society in which it flourishes can satisfy a rigid set of requirements for efficient operation, and is correspondingly less amenable to an ordering based on the type of simple model described in this book.

Appendices

I. Migration rates and hamlet populations

An examination of the migrations in and out of tribes in a particular Census District (Kataipa) over a number of years reveals that there are considerable fluctuations, and that these are reflected in the migrations of a single tribe—Goilala. Exactly why there should be this interconnectedness of population flow, and why there should be more in some years than in others are questions to which there are no obvious answers. But it is interesting that there seems to be little relation between migration levels within the Census District and migration levels out of the District to Port Moresby.

TABLE I. *Kataipa Census District*

Year	Migration (in and out)		Total	Total pop.	Per cent
	M	F			
1952–3	66	75	141	2,302	6·12
1958	78	99	177	1,783	9·92
1959	7	21	28	1,793	1·56
1960	68	83	151	1,864	8·1
1961	33	45	78	1,907	4·1
1962	18	44	62	1,925	3·22
1963	67	77	144	1,953	7·3
1964	129	154	283	1,964	14·4
1966	26	35	61	1,930	3·2
1969	5	11	16	1,767*	0·9
1970	36	35	71	1,903	3·7

* 1 tribe missing.

TABLE 2. *Goilala*

Year	Migration in		Migration out		Total	Total pop.	Per cent
	M	F	M	F			
1952	11	7	1	2	21	182	11·53
1958	1	5	6	7	19	164	11·58
1959	..	..	1	..	1	160	0·6
1960	2	4	..	..	6	171	3·5
1961	1	3	..	1	5	176	2·8
1962	1	3	..	1	5	180	2·77
1963	1	3	1	2	7	175	4·0
1964	2	5	6	12	25	162	15·4
1966	..	..	1	9	10	158	6·32
1969	..	..	..	..	0	176	0·0
1970	..	2	..	..	2	173	1·15

It is clear that there is a significantly higher migration rate for women than for men, as Table 3 shows.

TABLE 3. *Kataipa Census District*

Year	Migration			
	In		Out	
	M	F	M	F
1958	78	99	34	76
1959	7	21	10	19
1960	68	83	40	47
1961	33	45	20	45
1962	18	44	23	42
1963	67	77	52	78
1964	129	154	47	76
1966	18	22	13	40
1969	5	11	21	20
1970	17	21	28	48
	440	577	288	491
	43·3%	56·7%	37%	63%
	Men: 40·5%			
	Women: 59·5%			

TABLE 4. *Migration rates from the Goilala Sub-District*

Most migrants have gone to Port Moresby, but there has been some migration to other centres such as Lae.

Year	Total pop.	Absent	Per cent
Aiwara Census District			
1952	3,846	129	3·35
1955	3,872	291	7·51
1958	3,920	204	5·20
1959	4,007	165	4·1
1960	4,064	232	5·7
1961	4,185	397	9·49
1962	4,238	607	14·32
1963	4,279	540	12·62
1964	4,356	780	17·9
1965	4,208	614	14·59
1966	4,442	576	12·97
1969	4,086	819	20·0
1970	4,173	1,304	31·25
Kataipa Census District			
1952	1,673	42	2·5 (Lavavai not included)
1958	1,963	81	4·1
1960	1,864	106	5·7
1961	1,907	126	6·6
1962	1,905	133	6·98
1963	1,953	178	9·1
1964	1,914	223	11·65
1966	1,930	213	11·0
1969	1,947	217	11·14
1970	1,903	507	26·6
Ivane Census District			
1953–4	932	ǀ10	1·07
1955	943	25	2·65
1959	861	47	5·46
1960	1,024	48	4·69
1961	1,049	112	10·68
1962	1,052	69	6·56
1963	1,041	76	7·3
1965	940	100	10·64
1966	1,002	172	17·16
1968	1,166	173	14·84
1970–1	1,159	147	12·68

TABLE 4 (*cont.*)

Year	Total pop.	Absent	Per cent
Pilitu Census District			
1960	1,286	71	5·52
1961	1,379	45	3·26
1962	1,357	74	5·45
1963	1,400	120	8·57
1964	1,411	95	6·73
1965	1,432	87	6·07
1966	1,458	139	9·53
1968	1,523	80	5·25
1971	1,569	248	15·80
Cumulative totals			
1960	8,238	457	5·55
1961	8,520	680	7·98
1962	8,552	883	10·33
1963	8,673	914	10·54
1966	8,832	1,100	12·45
1968–9	8,722	1,289	14·78
1970–1	8,804	2,206	25·1
Migrations from particular tribes			
Goilala			
1952	182	14	7·69
1958	164	9	5·49
1960	171	13	7·6
1961	176	11	6·25
1962	180	10	5·5
1963	175	14	8·0
1964	162	37	22·84
1966	158	20	12·66
1969	176	11	6·25
1970	173	24	13·87

T A B L E 5. *House census from the Lowa Valley, 1945*

Name	Houses	Adults	Children	Total pop.	People per house
Sene	15	40	23	63	4·2
Koipa	9	24	9	33	3·6
Iveyava	30	60	30	90	3·0
Tamata	17	23	13	36	2·1
Tsiviro & Ivira	20	75	36	111*	2·7
Sopu	30	54	40	94	3·1
Peu & Tuili	15	50	25	75*	2·1
Lowa	12	23	16	39	3·3
Tori	14	22	14	36	2·6
Umu	14	25	8	33	2·4
Veile	13	28	10	38	2·9
Tuaruru	11	25	12	37	3·4
Noroava	16	44	15	59	3·7
Lamanaipa					
Wowe	9	12	9	21	2·3
Lumeiwa	14	20	3	23	1·6
Poviai	21	45	27	72	3·4
Kileipa					
Pulavi	12	29	17	46	3·8
Kato	9	30	13	43	4·8
Kuveiava	9	19	10	29	3·2
Malava					
Ilovepe	13	34	11	(absentees at Chirima)	
Peato	9	12	9	21	2·3
Gane					
Kautaupe	16				
Ketsioke	13	61	40	100*	2·9
Poroala	6				
Laitate	18	47	27	74*	2·7
Kamaiwa	9	(Kamaiwa included in Laitate total.)			

* Two or more hamlets.

Names *in italics* are those of tribes. Sometimes the name of a tribe and a hamlet are the same.

Average hamlet size: 14·4 houses
People per house: 3·0
Average pop. per hamlet: 45

TABLE 6. *Hamlet census of Kataipa Census District, 1956*

Name	Number of hamlets	Total pop.	Persons per hamlet
Tatupiti	8	131	16·4
Matsialavava	3	116	38·6
Eruma	3	103	34·3
Kariaritsi	3	110	36·6
Poruava	2	65	32·5
Kerau	3	67	22·3
Kulamutu	4	73	18·25
Karom	1	48	48
Lumioto	5	93	18·6
Goilala	11	171	15·54
Kunima	15	170	11·3
Oropoa	3	71	23·6
Kataipa	5	124	24·8
Kame	2	103	51·5
Tawuni	5	133	26·6
Bapiti	5	179	35·8

Average number of hamlets: 5
Average population of hamlet: 22·5

II. Sex ratios

Taken from 1960 Census.

Census District	Males		Females		
	age 10–16	16–45	10–16		16–45
Kataipa	114	595	91		550
	52·5%			47·5%	
Pilitu	105	355	79		295
	55·0%			45·0%	
Aiwara	301	1,126	227		1,013
	53·5%			46·5%	
Ivane	76	256	82		253
	49·7%			50·3%	
Totals	596	2,332	479		2,111
	53%			47%	

III. Kinship terminology

The kinship terminology, which is purely referential, and never used as a form of address, is as follows:

1.	*korovei*	MFF, MMF, FFF, FMF
2.	*korovepe*	MFM, MMM, FFM, FMM
3.	*vapi*	FF, MF, SS, DS
4.	*vapipi*	MM, FM, SD, DD
5.	*atsi*	F, FB
6.	*ini*	M, MZ, FZ
7.	*aga*	MB
8.	*ene*	eB, FeBS, MeZS
9.	*alu*	yB, FyBS, MyZS
10.	*ete*	eZ, FeBD, MeZD
11.	*alupu*	yZ, FyBD, MyBD
12.	*agopi*	MBS, MBD, FZS, FZD (ZS, ZD, but these can also be 13, 14)
13.	*lu*	S, BS, ZS (can also be 12)
14.	*epi*	D, BD, ZD (can also be 12)
15.	*alapi*	SS, DS (3 is commoner)
16.	*alapa*	SD, DD (4 is commoner)
17.	*epi ilini*	SW
18.	*ini ilini*	WM, HM
19.	*atsi imaepe*	WF, HF
20.	*lu imaepe*	DH
21.	(*neve*) *alupalai*	yBW (*neve* = my)
22.	(*neve*) *etaena*	eBW
23.	*iva kamaepe*	WZ

There are two features of this terminology which are not consistent with a cognatic descent system—the separate term for MB, and the distinction between cross-cousins and parallel cousins.

MB is perhaps given a distinctive term because so many men's mothers come from other tribes. This being so, the MB would be the male most closely related to the mother when her sons had grown up and wished to visit her tribe to make gardens there, and claim their share in her pandanus. Her father by such time would probably be dead, or too old to have much influence.

The distinction between parallel cousins (8–11) and cross-cousins (12) is consistent with the model of sister exchange, whereby FZS = MBS, MBD = FZD, although it should be noted that sister exchange only rarely occurs in practice.

In the figure below, because of sister exchange and marriage between AD and BC, 3 and 4 are both FZS, MBS, and FZD, MBD of 1 and 2, and vice versa.

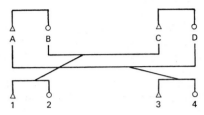

Sister exchange only rarely occurs, as remarked already, and is not in any case responsible for the lack of lineal distinction in the cousin terminology, since parallel cousins, between whose parents sister exchange should not take place, are not distinguished lineally either. The reason why two brothers do not marry two sisters is perhaps because the parents of the girls would be wasting the possibilities of spreading their alliances as widely as possible by marrying both girls into the same family.

IV. Homicide Statistics

While it is not my intention to claim any unique status for the Tauade within New Guinea, the statistics in this Appendix do reveal that the Goilala, and especially the Tauade, are more violent than most groups. Table 1 makes it clear that the Tauade speakers, in spite of their long history of government contact, remained the most prone to homicide of any group in the Sub-District even when violence in the area was on the wane.

TABLE 1. *Murders in the Goilala Sub-District for the years 1949–54*

Group	Murders	Population
Tauade	20	8,661
Kunimaipa	8	6,046
Fuyughe	8	14,053

Unidentified locations of murders: 4

The figures given in Table 2 are even more striking, showing the contrast in violent behaviour between the Goilala and a number of other groups in Port Moresby. While it should be noted that in New Guinea groups with little experience of urban life tend to be more prone to violence on their first introduction to it than more sophisticated groups, subsequent tables show that the Goilala have maintained a high level of violent and anti-social behaviour. Unfortunately, data from the latest Census do not give the Sub-District of origin of inhabitants of Port Moresby.

TABLE 2. *Arrests per 1,000 males residing in Port Moresby, by Districts and Sub-Districts, in 1961*

District or Sub-District	Total pop.	Male pop.	Arrests	Arrests per 1,000 males
1. Goilala	497	447	61	136·0
2. Gulf	4,926	3,249	128	39·4
3. Morobe	1,130	1,033	30	29·0
4. Kairuku	2,214	1,410	40	28·0
5. Abau	1,672	1,174	28	23·9
6. Rigo	2,260	1,450	28	19·3

Source: 'Drunkenness and Crime in Port Moresby', Report to the Commission on Alcoholic Drinking, by Mr. Nigel Oram, Dept. of Sociology and Anthropology, University of Papua and New Guinea, 1971, Tables 3 and 4. I am most grateful to Mr. Oram for supplying me with a copy of this report.

TABLE 3. *Types of offence for which arrests were made of the first four offending groups from July 1968 to June 1969*

I. Offences against property
II. Offences against the person[1]
III. Offensive behaviour
IV. 'Technical' offences, e.g. vagrancy, gambling

District or Sub-District	I %	II %	III %	IV %	Total offences
1. Goilala	28·61	33·76	6·7	30·9	388
2. Gulf	34·74	35·71	5·52	24·0	308
3. E.H.D.*	21·13	46·03	10·19	22·64	265
4. Morobe	22·96	44·02	14·83	18·18	209

* Eastern Highlands District.   I+II+III+IV = 100%

Source: 'Ethnic Crime Statistics', prepared by the Criminal Investigation Branch, Royal Papua and New Guinea Constabulary.

[1] When it comes to murder and attempted murder, however, the figures show a very different picture, viz.:

TABLE 4. *Arrests for murder and attempted murder for the period July 1968 to November 1971*

District or Sub-District	Arrests	Per cent
Port Moresby	1	3·1
Rigo	2	6·25
Gulf	6	18·75
Goilala	19	59·38
Chimbu	4	12·5
	32	100%

TABLE 5. *The percentage of total arrests of the five leading groups of offenders in Port Moresby July–November 1969; whole of 1970 except November, and all 1971 except July and December*

District or Sub-District of origin	1969 %	1970 %	1971 %
1. Gulf	17·03	14·47	16·03
2. Goilala	15·07	12·4	12·68
3. E.H.D.*	11·46	12·09	10·51
4. Chimbu	6·91	9·75	7·20
5. Morobe	6·19	6·24	6·84

* Eastern Highlands District.

Source: Same as Tables 3 and 4.

V. Medical statistics

TABLE 1

R. Hill, P.O., 30/7/60–21/8/60
Medical report sent to the P.H.D. by Mr. Tinnion, E.M.A.
Total number of people seen: 2,401

Disease	Per cent
Tropical ulcers	10·4
Scabies	12·7
Tinea	4·5
Elephantiasis	0·04
Conjunctival diseases	0·6
Other eye conditions	0·7
T.B. glands	0·33
Congenital abnormalities	1·1
Dental caries	25·1
Deformities	0·2
Nutritional disease	0·3
Enlarged livers	1·2
Fever	0·8

Spleens examined: 501
Palpable: 0·1% [1·0%?]

TABLE 2

Clements, F. W., 1935, Medical report, p. 453
Incidence of disease:
out of 588 natives at Goilala (Aporota)

Yaws	0
Tinea	8
Misc. Surg.	1
Misc. Med.	1
Chest lesions	0
No. of children with enl. spleens	0
Goitre	2

VI. Meteorological statistics

TABLE 1. *Average rainfall at seven stations in the Goilala Sub-District*

Fane	117·17
Guari	105·88
Kerau	88·07
Kamulai	108·6
Ononghe	80·65
Tapini	77·01
Woitape	125·02

TABLE 2. *Temperatures at Goilala* (*Fahrenheit*)

	1970		1971		1972	
	Max.	Min.	Max.	Min.	Max.	Min.*
January					63·5	51·8
February			69·0	52·5	66·6	52·2
March			64·9	52·9	65·6	52·2
April			67·8	53·4	65·8	52·1
May			68·2	53·1		
June	67·3	51·4	68·1	52·1		
July	66·5	51·6	67·0	51·6		
August	66·9	50·3	69·1	51·5		
September	67·6	52·4	69·3	52·4		
October	66·3	52·8	70·2	51·7		
November	67·6	52·0	68·9	51·8		
December	66·2	53·1	67·4	51·6		
Average max.	67·3					
Average min.	52·1					
Highest max.	75·0					
Lowest min.	44·0					

*These temperatures are all monthly averages.

VII. Soil samples

Goilala soils

No.	pH	Per cent Nitrogen	Exchange capacity m.e. %	Exchangeable Cations—m.e. %				Per cent base saturation
				Na	K	Ca	Mg	
1	4·2	0·59	20·3	0·31	0·49	8·2	13·2	100
2	4·9	0·41	24·6	0·29	0·47	5·7	7·4	56
3	5·2	0·28	27·6	0·33	0·30	6·3	8·2	55
4	5·0	0·29	39·0	0·11	0·16	3·3	5·8	24
5	5·3	0·36	31·2	0·17	0·36	6·0	16·5	74
6	4·1	0·16	27·5	0·26	0·34	10·6	18·9	100

Legend
1. Primary forest about 8,500 ft.
2. Old garden, about 7,200 ft, fifteen years fallow.
3. Recently abandoned garden, about 7,000 ft.
4. Garden in mid-production.
5. Newly planted garden.
6. Grasslands, about 6,000 ft, burnt off for decades.

Bibliography

I. ITEMS IN THIS SECTION ARE RELEVANT TO THE ETHNOGRAPHY OF WHAT IS NOW THE GOILALA SUB-DISTRICT. MOST OF THEM ALSO SPECIFICALLY MENTION THE TAUADE.

Baines, Charles 1953 'Bone wearers of Papua', *Walkabout*, vol. 19 (11), pp. 16–17.

Bottrell, A. M. 1954 'The distance between the government and the governed', *South Pacific*, vol. 7, pp. 901–3.

Capell, A. 1969 *A Survey of New Guinea Languages*, Sydney University Press.

Clements, F. W. 1936 A medical survey in Papua. Report of the first expedition by the School of Public Health and Tropical Medicine to Papua, 1935. *Medical Journal of Australia*, vol. 1 (of 1936), pp. 451–63.

Dubuy, J., M.S.C. 1931 'The relations between religion and morality among the Ononghe tribes of British New Guinea', *Primitive Man*, vol. 4, pp. 29–31.

Dupeyrat, A., M.S.C.
1935 *Papouasie. Histoire de la mission (1885–1935)*, Éditions Dillen, Paris.
1948 *Papuan Conquest*, Araluen Publishing Company, Melbourne. (Contains much translated and edited material from Dupeyrat 1935.)
1954 *Mitsinari*, trans. Erik and Denise de Mauny, Staples Press, London. First published in French as *Vingt et un ans chez les Papous*, A. Fayard, Paris, 1952.
1955 *Festive Papua*, trans. Erik de Mauny, Staples Press, London. First published in French as *Jours de fête chez les Papous*, La Colombe, Paris, 1953.
1963 *Papua. Beasts and Men*, trans. Michael Heron, McGibbon & Kee, London. First published in French as *La Bête et le Papou*, Éditions Albin Michel, Paris, 1962.

Egerton, W. S. 1954 'An account of state of health and problems of medical interest in Goilala, Papua', *The Medical Journal of Australia*, Sept. 1954, pp. 444–7.

Egidi, V. M., D.D., M.S.C. 1907
'La tribù di Tauata', *Anthropos*, vol. 2, pp. 675–81, and pp. 1009–21. (Second part grammatical and lexical.)

Fastré, P., M.S.C. 1937–9
Mœurs et coutumes foujoughèses, unpublished MS. The pagination given is that of Bishop Sorin's copy.

Gore, R. T. 1965
Justice versus Sorcery, Jacaranda Press, Brisbane.

Hallpike, C. R. 1973
'Functionalist interpretations of primitive warfare', *MAN* (N.S.), vol. 8, no. 3, September.

1974
'Aristotelian and Heraclitean societies', *Ethos*, vol. 2, Spring.

1975
'Two types of reciprocity', *Comparative Studies in Society and History*, vol. 17, no. 1.

Hides, J. G. 1935
Through Wildest Papua, Blackie & Sons, London and Glasgow.

1938
Savages in Serge, Angus & Robertson, Sydney and London.

Kariks, J. *et al.* 1958/9
'A study of the heights, weights, haemoglobin values and blood groups of the natives of the Goilala Sub-District, Papua', *Oceania*, vol. 29, pp. 117–22.

Klieneberger, H. R. 1957
'Bibliography of oceanic linguistics', *London Oriental Bibliographies*, vol. 1, pp. 26–69, Oxford University Press, London.

Lambert, S. M. 1942
A Doctor in Paradise, J. M. Dent & Sons, London.

Lett, Lewis 1935
Knights Errant of Papua, William Blackwood & Sons, Edinburgh and London.

McArthur, A. M. 1961
The Kunimaipa. The Social Structure of a Papuan People, doctoral dissertation (unpublished), Australian National University.

1971
'Men and spirits in the Kunimaipa Valley', in *Anthropology in Oceania. Essays presented to Ian Hogbin*, eds. L. R. Hiatt and C. Jayawardena, Angus & Robertson, Sydney.

Monckton, C. A. W. 1922
Last Days in New Guinea, John Lane, The Bodley Head, London.

Murray, J. H. P. 1925
Papua of Today, or an Australian Colony in the Making, King & Son, London.

Papuan Administration
Papuan Annual Reports
1914–15   p. 57.
1917–18   pp. 61–2, 94, Appendix E 14.
1918–19   pp. 50, 61–2.

1920	p. 116.
1920–1	p. 126, Appendix II, and Plates.
1921–2	pp. 63–4.
1925–6	pp. 107–115, Appendix III.
1926–7	pp. 39–40.
1927–8	pp. 3–4.
1928–9	p. 9.
1931–2	p. 20.
1932–3	pp. 18–20.
1933–4	pp. 21–3.
1934–5	pp. 28–9.
1935–6	pp. 15–16.
1936–7	p. 26.
1937–8	pp. 29, 33–5.
1938–9	pp. 24–5.

Early Patrol Reports

Keelan, J. F.	Ioma, 23/10/11–22/1/12.
Pettitt, F.	Ioma, 7/2/17–7/3/17.
Wilson, L. J.	Ioma, 13/11/17–7/12/17.
Grist, Storry, and Wilson	Ioma, 19/1/18–6/8/18.
Neyland, J. W.	Kairuku, 2/5/18–10/7/18.
Neyland, J. W.	Kairuku, 10/1/19–?/1/19.
McCleland, K. C.	Kairuku, 14/1/22–10/2/22.
Karius, C. H., and Thompson	Kairuku, 6/2/24–13/4/24.
Karius, C. H., and Champion, I.	Kambisi, 31/5/25–20/6/25.
Champion, I., and Smith, S.E.	Kambisi, 6/12/28–16/1/29.
Champion, I., and Smith, S. E.	Mondo, 4/8/29–7/9/29.
Faithorn, B. W., and Smith, S. E.	Mondo, 5/2/30–27/2/30.
Faithorn, B. W.	Mondo, 1/7/30–31/7/30.
Faithorn, B. W., and Smith, S. E.	Mondo, 28/8/30–15/9/30.
Middleton, S. G.	Kambisi, 1931.
Middleton, S. G.	Kambisi, 15/2/32–5/3/32.
Middleton, S. G.	Kambisi, 30/5/32–7/6/32.
Middleton, S. G.	Kambisi, 1/12/32–15/12/32.
Middleton, S. G.	Mondo, 3/6/33–13/6/33.

Later Patrol Reports

White, C. H.	Tapini, Mar. 1945.
James, C. R.	Goilala, July 1945.
Driver, F. G.	Tapini, Aug. 1947.

Bottrell, A. M.	Tapini, Aug. 1950.
Purdy, W. M.	Tapini, Mar.–Apr. 1951.
Purdy, W. M.	Tapini, Apr. 1951.
Wilson, B. G.	Tapini, Jan. 1952.
Hearne, R. F.	Tapini, Nov. 1953.
Wadsworth, C.	Tapini, 19/8/58–7/10/58.
Hill, R.	Tapini, Patrol 3/58–9.
Flowers, A. N.	Pilitu, 23/11/61–29/11/61.
Hunter, P. R.	Loloipa, 18/4/63–9/5/63.
Briggs, P.	Aiwara, 23/8/66–9/9/66.
Graham, W. J. S.	Tapini, 16/6/69–27/6/69.

Peters, W. *et al.* 1958   'Malaria in the highlands of Papua and New Guinea', *Medical Journal of Australia*, vol. 2 of 1958, pp. 409–16.

Pratt, A. E. 1906   *Two Years among New Guinea Cannibals: a Naturalist's Sojourn among the Aborigines of Unexplored New Guinea*, Seeley & Co., London.

Ray, S. H. 1912   'Notes on the Papuan languages spoken about the headwaters of the St. Joseph River, Central Papua', in R. W. Williamson, *The Mafulu* (see below).

1929   'Languages of the Central Division of Papua', *J.R.A.I.*, vol. 59, pp. 65–96.

Sacred Heart Mission   Publications by the Sacred Heart Mission, Yule Island, in the Tauade language.

1936   Fr. Norin, *Illustrated Bible History*, 319 pp. Referred to by Steinkraus and Pence 1964, but unknown to the author at the time of field-work.

1949   Fr. C. Gallina, *Biblia Ninipi*, Part One, *Testamento Opo* (*Little Bible*, Part One, *Old Testament*), 258 pp. A simple restatement of basic bible stories, not a direct translation. Mimeographed.

1950   Fr. A. Benedetti, *Nanene Ami Iesu Christe ae Tsinata, picture voiete* (*The Story of Our Lord Jesus Christ, in pictures*), 45 pp. Contains an English translation under each paragraph of Tauade.

An elementary exegesis of Christian doctrine in three parts was planned, on the basis of the Persons of the Trinity, under the general heading of *Manapo e Kani* (*The Road to Heaven*). Only the first two parts were in fact written.

1952   Author? *Jesu Christe nane mi akil enaieteve, Deov ae Lu* (*Jesus Christ our Saviour, the Son of God*) 41 pp. Mimeographed.

1953	Fr. J. Fridez, *Deov atsi oi-gupari-araun toviena-eteve* (*God the Father, Creator of All Things*), 48 pp.
1954	Fr. C. Guichet, *Catechism of Christian Doctrine* (no vernacular title), 95 pp.
1958	Fr. J. Fridez, *Menamena Malama Book* (Hymn Book), 87 pp.
n.d.	Dictionary of the Tauade language, 203 pp. typescript. Compiled at Kerau, unedited, and of uneven quality. Never published by the Mission.

Scragg, R. F. R. 1971   *The Eyes of the Crocodile*, inaugural lecture at University of Papua New Guinea, Dept. of Social and Preventive Medicine, 14 October 1971.

Sinclair, J. P. 1969   *The Outside Man: Jack Hides of Papua*, Angus & Robertson, London.

Steinkraus, W., and Pence, A. 1964   *Languages of the Goilala Sub-District*, D.I.E.S. Government Printer, Port Moresby. For Summer Institute of Linguistics.

Taylor, M. M. 1924   *Where Cannibals Roam*, Geoffrey Bles, London.

White, J. P. *et al.* 1970   'Kosipe: a late Pleistocene site in the Papuan Highlands', *Proceedings of the Prehistoric Society*, vol. xxxvi, December.

Williams, M. 1964   *Stone Age Island. Seven Years in New Guinea*, Collins, London.

Williamson, R. W. 1912   *The Mafulu Mountain People of British New Guinea*, Macmillan & Co. Ltd.

II. OTHER WORKS REFERRED TO IN THIS BOOK

Armstrong, A. H. 1965   *An Introduction to Ancient Philosophy*, University Paperbacks.

Barnes, J. A. 1962   'African models in the New Guinea Highlands', *Man*, Jan. pp. 5–9.

Benedict, R. 1961   *Patterns of Culture*, Routledge & Kegan Paul.

von Bertalanffy 1971   *General System Theory. Foundations, Developments, Applications*, Allen Lane, The Penguin Press.

Blackwood, B. M. 1950   *The Technology of a Modern Stone Age People in New Guinea*, Occasional Papers in Technology, no. 3, Pitt Rivers Museum, Oxford.

Campbell, J. K. 1964   *Honour, Family and Patronage*, Clarendon Press, Oxford.

Fox, J. J. 1971   'A Rotinese Dynastic Genealogy. Structure and Event', in *The Translation of Culture*, ed. T. O. Beidelman, Tavistock Press.

Gluckman, M. 1965 *Politics, Law and Ritual in Tribal Society*, Basil Blackwell, Oxford.

Hallpike, C. R. 1972 *The Konso of Ethiopia. A Study of the Values of a Cushitic People*, Clarendon Press, Oxford.

Hides, J. G. 1936 *Papuan Wonderland*, Blackie & Sons, London.

Hogbin, I., and Wedg- 'Local groupings in Melanesia', *Oceania*, vol. 23, wood, C. 1953 no. 4, pp. 241–76.

Kaplan 1954 Discussion in *Language and Culture*, ed. H. Hoijer, University of Chicago Press. Memoir no. 79 of the American Anthropological Association, p. 207.

de Lepervanche, Marie Social structure, in *Anthropology in Papua New* 1973 *Guinea* ed. Ian Hogbin, Melbourne University Press.

Malynicz, G. L. n.d. 'Pig keeping by the subsistence agriculturalist of the New Guinea highlands', *Tropical Pig Breeding and Research Centre, D.A.S.F. Goroka.*

Maybury-Lewis, D. *Akwe-Shavante Society*, Clarendon Press, Oxford. 1967

Mead, M. 1968 *The Mountain Arapesh*, Natural History Press.

Meggitt, M. 1965 *The Lineage System of the Mae-Enga of New Guinea*, Oliver & Boyd, Edinburgh and London.

Mihalic, Francis Fr. *Grammar and Dictionary of Neo-Melanesian*, 1957 Techny (Illinois) Mission Press, S.V.D. (Society of the Divine Word).

Munch, P. A. 1971 *Crisis in Utopia: The Ordeal of Tristan da Cunha*, Longmans, London.

  1974 'Anarchy and *anomie* in an atomistic society', *MAN* (N.S.), vol. 9, no. 2, June, pp. 243–62.

Murray, J. H. P. 1912 *Papua, or British New Guinea*, T. Fisher Unwin, London.

Oram, N. 1971 'Drunkenness and crime in Port Moresby', in *Report to the Commission on Alcoholic Drinking*.

Prebble, J. 1967 *Culloden*, Penguin Books.

Rappaport, R. 1968 *Pigs for the Ancestors. Ritual in the Ecology of a New Guinea People*, Yale University Press, New Haven and London.

Read, K. E. 1955 'Morality and the concept of the person among the Gahuku-Gama', *Oceania*, vol. 25, no. 4, pp. 233–82.

Royal Anthropological *Notes and Queries on Anthropology*, 6th edition. Institute

Sorenson, E. R. 1972   'Socio-Ecological change among the Fore of New Guinea', *Current Anthropology*, vol. 13, no. 3–4, June–October.

Sinclair, J. 1966   *Behind the Ranges. Patrolling in New Guinea*, Melbourne University Press.

Stauder, J. 1972   'Anarchy and ecology: political society among the Majangir', *Southwestern Journal of Anthropology*, vol. 28, pp. 153–68.

Strathern, A. 1971   *The Rope of Moka. Big-men and ceremonial exchange in Mount Hagen*, Cambridge Studies in Social Anthropology, no. 4, Cambridge University Press.

1972   *One Father, One Blood. Descent and group structure among the Melpa people*, A.N.U. Press, Canberra.

Wax, R. H. 1969   *Magic, Fate and History. The changing ethos of the Vikings*, Coronado Press, Kansas.

Williams, F. E. 1930   *Orokaiva Society*, Clarendon Press, Oxford.

Index

abortion, 72, 122

Adamson, C. J., 51, 246

Administration, first contacts with Tauade, 4–5, 27: patrols of, 3, 4–8, 18, 27, 52, 239–40; strong patrol officers admired, 12–13; capital punishment demanded by Tauade, 13–14; causes of fighting with Tauade, 5–9, 214; number of Tauade killed by, 9, 214; arrest of criminals regarded as government vengeance by Tauade, 7–8, 11–12; fraudulent use of courts in vengeance, 36; rapid turnover of staff prevents good understanding of people, 15; failure of Tauade to comprehend policies of, 7–10, 21, 24–5; opposition to dances, 20, 173; orders building of rest houses, 9; sanitary policies of, 10; recruitment of carriers, 9, 227; censuses, 4–5, 9, 27, 45, 184; encourages economic development, 20–3, 29

adoption of children, 122, 184, 187

adultery, 10, 17, 34, 35; categories of person between whom it occurs, 117, 133, 134; frequency of, 117; occasioned by dances, 20, 171; women as initiators of, 34, 134, 216; compensation for, 10, 74, 132, 133, 189; violent reaction to, 128, 132, 133, 154–5, 171, 230, 239; and sorcery, 255

age, lack of respect for, 137, 248; announcement of old age, 174; failure to conceptualise distinction between generations, 138

agnates, lack of patrilineal principle of descent, 84, 85, 91, 95; co-operation between, 84, 97, 117, 122, 180; residential distribution of, 90–1, 112–14; marriages of, 124, 125; inheritance of pandanus trees, 104–8;

inheritance of bird totems, 264; inheritance of magic stones, 269

ago, definition of, 156, 255, 256

agoteve, agotevaun, definition of, 254; and totems, 262–70 *passim*; and stones, 263, 268, 269, 270; and trees, 264–5; and sun and moon, 266–8; and the Wild, 254–5; as representing principles of power and permanence, 142, 254–5; as corners of houses, 268; as forms of wind and rain, 266; *see also* 'culture-heroes', '*ago*', 'totem', 'stones', 'Wild'

Aibala river, 10, 16, 40, 43, 68, 108, 118, 177, 203, 215, 219, 220, 228, 258, 260, 272, 273

Aima Kamo, 104, 114, 115, 117, 118, 149–50, 151, 152, 153–4, 180, 185–6, 199–201, 204–5, 210, 211–14, 218, 219, 232, 234

Aiwara, *see* 'Aibala'

Akwe-Shavante, 281–2

Albert Edward, Mt., 39, 157, 258

allegory, use of in speeches, 146–8, 155

altruism, incomprehensible to Tauade, 12, 19

Ambo, 15

ami, etymology of word, 143; *see* 'chief'

Amiapa tribe, 46, 57, 123, 125, 202, 228, 229

Amo Lume, 29, 35, 36, 37, 72, 73, 86, 89, 106, 107, 111, 112, 122, 132, 141, 144, 153, 160, 181, 182, 188, 201, 203, 204, 207, 210, 214, 264, 269

Amuganiawa tribe, 45, 65, 123, 124, 126, 153, 176, 177, 196, 202, 203, 204, 213, 216, 219, 222, 229

Apava Tulava, identification of author with, 30, 31–2, 183, 236, 265

Aporota, 3, 9, 14, 27, 48, 150, 183, 196, 198, 199, 200, 201, 297

Aristotle, 77, 78
'Aristotelian' society, characteristics of, v, 77–83
Armstrong, A. H., 77
arson and incendiarism, 14, 68, 119, 196, 204–5, 220–1, 249
artistic skills, lack of, 1, 27, 63
atomism, 24, 81, 82, 115–16, 135–6, 233, 275–7; see also 'Heraclitean' society
Auga valley, 45
Avui Apava, 31, 32, 101, 183, 184, 185, 200, 206
Avui Maia, 73, 101–4, 141, 148, 184–5

Bachelier, Fr. M.S.C., 15
bachelors, 65, 72–3, 129, 144
Baines, C., 244
Bakoiudu C.M., 47
bananas, 1, 64, 65, 226, 243
bark cloth, 63, 153
Barnes, J. A., v, 77
Benedict, R., 251
von Bertalanffy, L., 252
Besson, Fr. M.S.C., 199
'big-man', inappropriateness of model in Tauade society, 139–43; see 'chief'
birds, exterminated with shot-guns, 75; associated with chiefs, 156, 263–4; as totems, 263–4; associated with culture-heroes, 166, 256, 259
births, distribution of pork to celebrate, 174, 177, 181–6; see 'names'
Blackwood, B., 63, 67
Blake, William, 251
blood, as principle of descent, 84, 85; in conferring rights of land use, 100; loss of regarded as serious, 35
de Boismenu, Bishop, 3, 6
bones, 10, 89, 96, 157–8, 162, 242, 245; see also 'corpses', 'mortuary customs'
Bottrell, A. M., 51, 174, 206–7
Brett, M., 3
Briggs, P., 25, 141
bull-roarer, 257, 266; use of at initiations, 146, 158, 159, 160; enclosures built for, 146, 153–4, 192, 212, 213, 228
Burridge, K. O. L., 233

calling, ability to communicate over long distances by, 52–3

Campbell, J. K., 78
cannibalism, 239; Tauade shame of admitting to, 209–10; motives for, 208–9; occasions when practised, 86, 208–10, 213, 216; see also 'homicide', 'warfare'
Capell, A., 78
cargo beliefs, 26, 29, 32
Casimiro Kog, 35, 37, 63, 126, 146, 156, 158, 160, 161, 207, 210, 227, 266, 268
cassowaries, 260, 263
ceremonies, 81, 137; basic forms of, 57, 162–4, 174–88; small, 163, 174–88; large, 163, 164–74; antagonism between participants, 163, 185–6; lack of elaboration of, 81; see also 'dances', 'pig killing', 'speeches'
Chabot, Fr. M.S.C., 27, 71
Champion, I., 47, 56, 197
chiefs, definition of, 141–3; ambiguities in status, 138, 139; characteristics of, 135, 138; and 'big-men', 139–40; class solidarity of, 149, 150–1, 152–4; frequency of marriage between children of, 127, 149, 150–1; as leaders of hamlets, 115; and men's houses, 115, 224; appointment as village constables, 141, 150; clan leaders, 89, 90, 94–6, 101–4, 155; guardians of the land, 89, 138, 223; polygyny of, 138, 148, 149; size of pig herds, 71–3, 148–9: hereditary aspects of status, 80, 141–3, 155; cosmological status of, 138, 156, 158–62; associated with birds, 156, 263; disposal of bodies of, 157–62, 212, 213; conventional dignity of, 138, 154–5, 190, 246; assaults on highly resented, 154–5, 190; not mutilated in battle, 210, 215, 216; vengeance taken for death of greater than for ordinary men, 148, 151–2, 221, 225; reasons for emergence of, 280; despotism of, 137, 138–9, 149, 154–5, 210, 223, 259; ability to kill low status men with impunity, 138, 148, 149–51, 191; assassinations arranged by, 146, 223; war leaders, 138, 210, 212–29 passim, 232, 252; good fighters, 199; speechmakers, 55,

75, 138, 146–7, 163, 167–9, 170, 179, 181–5, 187; peacemakers, 115, 138, 145, 163, 169, 205, 210–11, 213 n., 214, 219, 226; give and receive compensation gracefully, 190, 197; organisers of ceremonies, 138, 145, 146, 163, 165, 167, 168, 169, 179, 210, 250; generosity of, 250; control over paths, 148, 191, 199, 235; ability to travel freely, 138, 146, 148, 199; mobility of status, 148 n.
Chirima Valley, 43, 63
Chowning, A., 233
clans, principles of membership, 80, 86–98; names of, 86; history of, 96–8, 184; genealogical structure of, 89–95; and chiefs, 89, 90, 94–6, 101–4, 155; no homicides within, 91, 93; hamlets of, 86–9; land of, 80, 86–7, 96, 100–4; bone caves of, 89, 96; pandanus trees of, 96, 105; lack of significance of, 80, 84, 96, 124; dispersed among hamlets, 80, 90–1, 92, 93; ability to change membership of, 80, 91, 95; inter-marriage of members, 123
Clements, F. W., 49–50, 297
climate, 1, 39; seasons, 40; tempera-tures, 41, 43, 298; rainfall, 40, 41–3, 266, 298; winds, 40–1, 266, 272, 273; humidity, 43
cognitive orientations, vi, 77–83, 281–4; of 'Aristotelian' societies, 274; of 'Heraclitean' societies, 273–4, 281–4
compensation, 169, 174, 188–92; forms of, 118, 191; not paid, 200, 217 n., 224; and ethos of reciprocity generally, 189; social pressure on men to give, 117, 118, 119, 130 n., 150, 190, 192, 229; offering and acceptance a mark of a chief, 190, 197; occasions for acceptance in warfare, 211; emotional reasons for, 189, 234–5, 238; violence sometimes preferred, 137, 189, 190, 238–9; as factor in aggravating level of vio-lence, 154, 230; for insult, 188; for grief, 234–5; for theft, 117, 118, 119, 189, 239; for adultery, 10, 74, 133, 189; to women for suckling children, 182, 243; for murder, 150–

1, 153, 191, 201, 205, 224; for deaths in warfare, 225
corpses, exposure of, 10, 138, 154, 158–62, 212, 265; mutilation of, 150, 205, 208, 213, 215, 217, 218, 225, 227; see also 'bones', 'cannibalism', 'mortuary customs'
cross-cutting ties, as factor in magni-fying hostilities, vi, 136, 154, 229
culture heroes, origin of name (agote-vaun), 270; non-human aspects, 254, 256–7, 259–62; long hair of, 256, 258; association with birds, 166, 256, 259; association with trees, 256, 259; gigantic size of penises, 256, 260; power of their penises to travel independently like snakes, 260; homicidal be-haviour of, 26, 256, 259; associated with madmen, 250; delight in humiliating ordinary men, 26, 256, 259, 260; creativity, 254, 256–8, 273–4; cutting of river beds, 256, 258; able to put themselves back together again when killed, 261; providers of prototypes of all species of animals and plants, 262; asso-ciated with stone, 63, 257, 266, 270; makers of stone pestles and mortars, 63, 270; associated with white men, 21, 256–7; legends referring to, 26, 134–5, 223, 240–4, 257–60

dances, duration of, 164; frequency of, at present time, 173; in past, 172; held to honour bones of dead, 164; displays of food by hosts, 64, 164, 228; emotional significance of, 63, 97, 164, 171, 253; most important held during the night, 163, 165–6; means of humiliating enemies, 147–8, 169–70; sexual display involved in, 163, 171, 228; adultery caused by, 134, 171; hostility between hosts and guests, 147–8, 163, 169–70, 215, 222, 228; licensed destruction by guests, 163, 169, 250; facilitated by ecology, 75, 97; adaptive functions of, 171, 172, 280–1; epideictic func-tions of, 172; frequency of affected by warfare, 19, 172; harmful conse-quences of, 20, 134; opposition to by mission, 17, 20; restrictions on by

dances (*cont.*):
  administration, 20, 173; *see* 'ceremonies', 'pig-killing'
dance villages, size of, 58; not built by each hamlet, 58, 172; allowed to decay after dance, 1, 60, 97; cause disruption of existing settlement pattern, vi, 54, 97
dance-yard, in centre of hamlet, 57, 163
Dilava Valley, 43
dogs, 75, 148, 160, 170, 228, 229, 246, 248, 262, 263, 272
dogs' teeth, 23, 63, 150, 205, 212, 225; *see* 'compensation'
dreams, as sources of legendary material, 261–2; and madness, 261; as paranormal evidence of distant events, 133, 261
Driver, F. G., 164–6
Dubuy, J., Fr. M.S.C., 15, 30–1, 209
Duffey, C., Fr. M.S.C., 199
Dupeyrat, A., Fr. M.S.C., 6, 15, 19, 25, 28, 71, 74

ears, piercing of, 174
earth ovens, 178, 208
east and west, lack of conception of, 267–8
ecology, 1, 41, 63–75, 193, 275–9; and population mobility, 50–3, 76, 97, 229; and hamlet location, 60–2; and political relations between tribes, 50–3, 204–7; and leisure, 75–6, 275; as contributing factor to conflict and warfare, 76; facilitates holding of dances, 75, 97; *see* 'land tenure', 'leisure', 'pigs', 'pandanus', 'warfare'
economic development, encouraged by administration, 21–2, 23, 29; encouraged by Sacred Heart Mission, 23, 24; failure of, 21–3; Tauade attitudes towards, 21–4; reasons for failure, 21–4
Egerton, W. S., 130
Egidi, V. M., Fr. M.S.C., 27, 46–7, 58, 62–3, 245
elaivi, (*Cordyline terminalis*) 271; planted as boundary marker, 70, 105; as windbreak, 31, 41; sent to allies in war, 210, 212, 214, 217,

221; ceremonial uses of, 158; in mourning, 200, 213, 234
envy, 24, 81, 246, 247, 249
evening star, 266–7
Eyssautier, Mt., *see* 'Kutumu'

faeces, 10, 131, 132, 151, 186, 235, 248, 256, 260
Faithorn, B. W., 7
family, emotions generated within, 240–5
Fane, C.M., 41, 298
Fastré, P., Fr. M.S.C., 25, 28, 35, 43, 59, 63, 72, 74, 134, 147, 148, 156, 160, 166–8, 169–70, 171, 172, 173–4, 207, 209, 234–5, 256, 274
fingers, mutilation of, 235–6, 245
Flowers, A. N., 11
Fore, 7
forest, felling of for gardens and fences, 67, 110, 112; significance of as scarce resource, 68, 75; place of in cosmology, 254, 264
Fox, J. J., 37
Fridez, J., Fr. M.S.C., 249
Froden, D., 157
Fuyughe, 3, 6, 7, 19, 27, 28, 43, 44, 45, 46, 47, 48, 49, 52, 56, 58, 59, 63, 90, 95, 97, 147–8, 156, 160, 161, 164, 166–8, 171, 172, 173–4, 209, 221, 226, 234–5, 254, 256, 257, 274

Gahuku-Gama, 233
Gane tribe, 14, 15, 27, 45, 54, 123, 126, 153, 176, 186, 199, 200, 202, 213, 214, 217, 222, 229, 245, 289
gardens, preferred sites, 60, 66–7; size of, 66; fallow period, 66, 100; preparation of, 65, 266; fences as major source of demand for timber, 67–8; location of in relation to hamlets, 60, 62, 64, 109; cultivation of by members of different hamlets, 62, 116; destruction of by pigs, 64, 67, 72, 75, 97, 174, 203, 204, 235; ravaging of in warfare, 71, 138–9, 172, 211
Garipa tribe, 45, 123, 176, 196
generosity, 75, 144, 250; *see* 'chiefs', 'malavi'
ghosts, 270
gift-exchange, as weakening social solidarity, vi, 97, 136; cuts across

hamlet and clan membership, 155, 156; absence of, in Konso society, 192–5; reasons for prevalence of in Tauade society, 192–5; there are too many instances of gift exchange for them to be indexed individually.

Giumu, 4–5, 47, 48, 51, 138–9, 197

Giumu Valley, 2, 50

Gluckman, M., 136

Goilala, Big, 47, 138–9

Goilala Police Camp, *see* Aporota

Goilala, Small, *see* Giumu

Goilala Sub-District, previous ethnography of, 27–8; location and area of, 1–2; physical geography of, 39–43; languages and peoples of, 2, 27, 43–9; relations between languages of, 43–4; population of different groups, 45; bloodgroups, 49; origin of name, 1 n., 47–9; incidence of disease, 1, 297; natural obstacles to economic development, 21; isolation from coast, 21, 49; untouched by World War II, 14; established as Sub-District, 48; migrant labour in Port Moresby encouraged by administration, 2, 14, 27; responsible for lowering crime rate in Sub-District, 15; nature and rate of crimes committed by Goilala in Port Moresby, 15, 294–6; bad reputation of Goilala in Port Moresby, 2, 15, 48

Goilala tribe, 18, 45; location of, 47; population of, 29, 54, 65; population density of, 65; area of, 65; gardens of, 65–6; distinguished from Sub-District of same name, 18, 29; first visit of administration to, 27; all other aspects of this tribe are indexed under the appropriate headings, e.g. 'chiefs', 'gardens', 'hamlets', etc.

goodness, Tauade definition of, 232, 254

Graham, W. J. S., 36

grassland, 108, 109, 110; burning of, 68, 75; fertility of, 23, 67, 68

greetings, absence of, 247

grief, 186, 189, 192, 208, 222, 224, 225, 228, 234–7, 239–40, 241–2, 244–5

Guari, 41, 298

Guichet, C., Fr. M.S.C., 23, 32, 101, 205, 250

Guivarc'h, Fr. M.S.C., 15, 27, 183

hamlets, location of, 55, 60, 108, 109, 112; traditional plan of, 55, 57, 277–8; defensive protection of, 55–6, 62, 207; duration of occupation, 80, 84, 109, 110, 112, 117; dispersal within the tribe, 54, 60; proximity of to one another, 62, 108; rights of residence in, 115; population of, 54, 57–60, 109, 289, 290; composition of population, 80, 84, 93, 111, 113–15; inability of social organization to control large hamlet populations, 60, 115–16; diminution of population as result of pacification, 59, 60; dispersed by building of dance villages, 97, 109; mobility of population, 60, 80, 84, 112; original clan basis of, 97; and chiefs, 104, 115; solidarity of, 115–19, 122; prevent effective unification of tribe, 84, 135–6, 230; *see* 'ceremonies', 'dances', 'gardens', 'homicide', 'land tenure', 'warfare'

Hearne, R. F., 51

height, symbolic significance of, 157, 162–3

'Heraclitean' society, characteristics of, i, ii, 77–83, 97, 253, 274, 275, 281–4

Heraclitus, xix, 77, 78

Hides, J., 12–13, 20–1, 74, 148, 160, 161, 168–9, 208–9, 239–40

Hill, R., 128, 297

Hogbin, I., 53

Hoijer, H., 79

homicide, enjoyed for own sake, vii, 7, 253; cases of, 93, 121, 128, 131–2, 149–52, 153–4, 191–2, 197–201, 205, 206, 209, 211–27, 236, 237–8; within hamlets, 117, 131–2, 149–51; within tribe, 93, 109, 117, 119, 120, 121, 128, 131–2, 149–52, 153–4, 191–2, 206, 207, 236; between tribes, 119, 120, 196–202, 204–5, 211–27, 237–8; secret disposal of corpses, 151, 199, 201; accidental homicide not recognized, 153, 191–2; statistics of Goilala homicide in

homicide (*cont.*):
Port Moresby, 295; in Goilala Sub-District, 294; rate of in relation to population, 120; *see* 'compensation', 'vengeance', 'warfare'
homosexuality, *see* 'vice, unnatural'
House of Assembly, 25, 27; irrelevance to Tauade, 25
houses, materials used in, 69; ease of construction, 75; design of, 69; number of inhabitants, 289
houses, men's, 1, 55, 56, 58, 69, 115, 145, 174, 220, 224, 230, 277, 278
humility, contempt for, 12, 13, 18–19
Humphries, W. R., 160
Hunter, P. R., 25
hunting, 75, 223

Iceland, 251
Ilai tribe, 14, 54, 123, 217, 229
informants, recruitment of, 29, 35; *see also* Amo Lume, Casimiro Kog, Moise Apava
initiation, 146, 153–4, 157, 158–62, 192, 213
insult, 131, 137, 147, 151, 169–70, 186, 187–8, 200, 248–9
Ioma, 4, 5, 27, 56, 197, 199, 257
Ivane, 15, 43, 45, 46, 50, 51, 63, 168–9, 258

Jacob, T., Fr. M.S.C. 186
James, C. R., 235

Kairuku, 4, 30, 56, 57, 64, 201, 210, 245
Kambisi Police Camp, 4, 56
Kamulai, C.M., 22, 28, 35, 41, 43, 298
Kaplan, A., 78–9
Kariks, J., 2, 49
Karoava tribe, *see* Sopu
Karuama Valley, 43, 45
Kataipa tribe, 16, 41, 45, 46, 65, 123, 125, 126, 153, 154, 174, 176, 177, 180, 187, 202, 203, 204, 213, 219, 222, 228, 290
Katé, *see* 'Kunimaipa'
katoro, *see* 'pandanus'
Keelan, J. F., 4–5, 27
Kerau tribe, 45, 86, 123, 124, 125, 126, 176, 177, 186, 197, 203, 212, 229, 290

kiava, *see* 'dance-yard'
kinship terminology, 84, 292
Kiolivi tribe, 32, 164, 203–4
Koiari, 2
Konso, v, vi, vii, 33, 77, 78, 79, 80, 81, 82, 192–3, 233, 250, 251, 267
Kosipi, C.M., 28, 35, 41, 43, 50, 67, 74, 210, 258
kovata, (power) definition of, 255, 270; *see also* 'sorcery'
Kubuna, C.M., 30
Kukukuku, 2, 63, 67
Kuni, 47, 52, 72
Kunima tribe, 16, 45, 54, 123, 153, 176, 177, 180, 186, 202, 203, 204, 211, 212, 213, 214, 216, 217–19, 222, 229, 290
Kunimaipa, 27, 28, 43, 44, 45, 46, 48, 51, 52, 60, 67, 71, 99, 120, 122, 130, 136, 160, 161, 170, 172, 173, 189, 201, 209, 220, 256, 257
Kuputaivi tribe, 19, 42, 43, 45, 60, 174, 229
Kutumu, Mt., 40, 41, 45, 266, 271

Laitate tribe, 118, 123, 126, 153, 176, 196, 202, 203, 215, 216, 289; warfare with Sene tribe, 37, 204, 206, 220–7, 252; migration due to shortage of timber, 68, 75, 85
Lamington, Mt., eruption of, 26
land, intensity of cultivation, 65–7, 75; lack of population pressure on, 1, 65–7, 75, 230; not a factor responsible for warfare, 205–6, 230; principles of tenure, 99–104; obscurity of claims to, 34–5; clan ownership of, 80, 86–7, 89, 96, 100–4; chiefs as guardians of, 89, 138, 223
leisure, opportunities for, 75; as factor generating violence and warfare, 75, 230, 275
Lett, L., 5, 6, 246
lineal descent, absence of idea, 142; absence of terminology, 80, 84, 292
Local Government Council, 4, 27, 141, 173; failure of Tauade to understand, 24–5
Loini creek, 58, 225
Loloipa, 22, 25, 43, 45, 170, 208–9, 235

Lova-Loleava tribe, 5–7, 8, 27, 45, 47, 48, 54, 55, 56, 57, 123, 125, 138–9, 197, 222–4, 257
love, Tauade capacity for, 239–45
Lutheran mission, 19, 60
lying, Tauade propensity for, 16, 33, 34, 35, 36, 248

McArthur, M., 28, 35, 43, 51–2, 67, 71, 99, 120, 122, 130, 136, 172, 173, 189, 220 n., 256
McCleland, K. C., 55, 56, 57, 64, 210
madmen, respect for, 250; and spirit possession, 270–3
Maini tribe, 45, 50, 57, 65, 123, 124, 126, 176, 177, 182, 196, 198, 199, 202, 203, 215, 216, 221, 222, 258
Majangir, 82
malavi (rubbish-man), 19, 118, 149–50, 151, 159, 191, 210; connotations of word, 143; poverty of, 143; feebleness of, 144, 151; meanness of, 75, 144; aggressiveness of, 144; greed and dishonesty of, 144
Malynicz, G. L., 173
manari tsinat, see 'allegory'
marriage, frequency of between tribes, 122–4, 203–4; marriage with other tribes condemned, 185; between enemy tribes 202–3; frequency of between clans, 123; between children of chiefs, 127; negotiations for, 126–8; bridewealth, 127; role of mother's brother in, 127; sister exchange, 128, 292–3; polygamy, serial, 129; polygamy, simultaneous, 129, 138, 148, 149; instability of polygamous unions, 130–1; friction between co-wives, 130–2, 199–200; freedom of women to leave husbands, 130, 134; reasons for divorce, 130
Martin, J., 22, 148, 162, 185
Maybury-Lewis, D., 281–2
Mead, M., 33
mediation, absence of, 188
Meggitt, M., 78
Mekeo, 2, 141, 258
men, work conventionally performed by, 64, 65, 70; attempts to control women, 122, 126–8, 132–5; *see also* 'women', 'sex', 'marriage'

Middleton, S. G., 48, 56, 109, 196, 214, 246–7
migration, traditional, 50–3, 96–8, 285–9; of Goilala labourers to Port Moresby, 2, 3, 14, 27, 287–8
Mihalic, F., 270
Moise Apava, 32, 73, 86, 101, 144, 183, 215
Monckton, C. A. W., 157
Mondo Police Camp, 4, 7, 196, 197, 216, 246
moon, 34, 266–7
morning star, 266–7
mortuary customs, 10, 17, 138, 153–4, 157–62, 179–81, 212, 244–5, 265
mother's brother, social role of, 127, 292
Motu, 34, 130, 145, 155
Murray, Sir Hubert, 6, 9, 11, 160, 196, 236

Nakanai, 233
names, at birth ceremonies, 183, 184; giving of names an honour to donor, 184; magical power of, 268; unsystematic nature of traditional personal names, 37, 106
Neo-Melanesian, absurdity of term, 37 n.; *see* 'Pidgin'
Neyland, J. W., 57, 245
Nietzsche, xix, 251
nose, piercing of, 160, 174

oaks, sacred, 258, 263, 265; *see* 'trees'
Oldham, E. R., 4 n.
Ononghe, C.M., 28, 30–1, 35, 41, 44, 50, 209, 298
oral history, value of, 36–7
Oram, N., 294 n.
Orokaiva, 2, 236, 257
Oropoa tribe, 41, 45, 46, 121, 123, 125, 126, 153, 176, 177, 202, 203, 206, 229, 290
Owen Stanley Range, 39 n.

pandanus nuts, 1, 65, 243; collecting of, 65, 69, 70, 207, 218; smoking of, 70, 71; ceremonial use of, 70, 71, 179, 182, 183; emergency rations in times of war, 71; theft of, 189, 190, 191; harvesting of, 65, 69, 70, 207, 218; people killed by falling nuts, 70, 192 pandanus trees, varieties and uses of, 69; ownership and inheritance of, 70, 100, 104–8, 249; ownership of as definition of tribal membership, 84, 85, 86; felling of in malice, 189, 212, 228; friction over ownership, 50, 206; and *agoteve*, 264–5; climbing of, 65; falls from, 70; taboo on, 235

parish, inappropriateness of term to New Guinea society, 53 n.; *see* 'tribe'

passions, seen as foundation of all behaviour, 77, 234; restraint of, 237–8, 245; place of in Tauade society, 77, 80–1, 82, 234–53 *passim*; legitimate basis for violence, 81, 234; *see also* 'envy' 'love', 'power', 'grief', 'sentimentality', 'homicide', 'vengeance'

pay-back, as principle of Tauade society, 17, 189, 199; *see* 'reciprocity', 'vengeance'

peace, absence of word for in Tauade language, 81, 145; maintained by balance of force, v, 81, 188, 227

peace-making, necessary for dances, 137; function of chiefs, 115, 138, 145, 163, 169, 205, 210–11, 213 n., 214, 219, 226

Pence, A., 44

Pidgin, 37, 270

pigs, size of herds, 72–3, 173, 174, 175; changes in genetic characteristics, 64, 67, 71, 172–3; as source of prestige, 23, 71, 75, 168; ceremonial killing of, 57, 64, 72, 74, 75, 146, 164, 166–9, 174–5, 212, 215, 217, 257; ferocity of slaughter, 74, 166–9; mass killing of seen as manifestation of power, 26, 250, 253, 255; periodic killing of large numbers a necessary feature of exchange system, 178; affection for, and taboo on eating by owners, 71, 72, 74, 136; mourning for when killed, 72, 167; killing of once accompanied by magical rites, 162; magic employed to ensure growth of, 267, 268, 269; ritual use of pigs' blood, 212; and spirits, 272, 273; suckling of by women, 71–2; strain on women of rearing, 75, 97, 173–4; ownership and rearing of, 71–2, 173–4; parasitical role of in Tauade society, 75, 97, 173–4, 253; social conflict caused by, 75, 97, 203, 204, 206, 230, 235, 275; destroyers of gardens, 64, 67, 75, 97, 174, 203, 204, 235; *see also* 'pork'

poliomyelitis, 50

polo, see 'bull-roarer'

polygamy, polygyny, *see* 'marriage'

Popole (Mafulu), 28, 31, 72, 171, 209

population mobility, 50–3, 65–6, 76, 97, 112, 219, 229; *see also* 'hamlets', 'migration', 'residence'

pork, pattern of distribution, 175–8; given to allies 211, 214; formal distribution of, 74–5, 146, 179; rotten pork sometimes eaten, 74; *see also* 'pigs'

Port Moresby, 2, 3, 14, 15, 24, 30, 48, 49, 70, 98, 183, 185, 198, 199, 258, 285, 287, 294, 295, 296

power, basic Tauade value, vii, 26, 156, 157, 158, 161, 232–3, 249, 250–3; displayed in destruction, 26, 250–2; displayed in killing of pigs, 26, 253, 255

Pratt, A. E., 27, 43, 52–3, 59–60, 209

Prebble, J., 217

pride, basic Tauade value, 80, 82, 135, 170, 245–9

Purdy, W. M., 14

quantification, rudimentary powers of, 22, 34, 81

Rappaport, R., 171, 172, 173

Read, K. E., 233

reciprocity, basic Tauade value, 80, 188–9, 192, 230, 232–3; exact notions of, 189, 212 n., 216, 246; distinction between reciprocity of goods and services, 192–5; and Heraclitean society, 80; *see also* 'bride-wealth', 'compensation', 'gift exchange', 'ceremonies', 'pork', 'vengeance'

residence, 85, 86, 95, 97, 98, 108–17 *passim*, 124–6; *see also* 'hamlets', 'migration', 'population mobility'

Ridgeway, R., 128

ritual, general lack of, 162; *see* 'ceremonies', 'mortuary customs', 'initiation'

Roro, 2, 49, 141
Rotinese, 37
rubbish-man, see '*malavi*'

Sacred Heart Mission, 141, 146; arrival in Tauade area, 14–16; early work in Goiala Sub-District, 3, 28; road-building 3, 9–10, 16; school, 3, 16, 17, 27; moral teachings of, 17–19; percentage of conversions, 18; forbids dances to Christians, 17, 20; use of catechists, 16, 17, 186, 203; influence of, 15–19 *passim*, 60; Kerau station, 3, 10, 14, 15, 24, 27, 28, 34, 35, 41, 42, 166, 183, 184, 199, 205, 207, 298; all other stations of the Mission are indexed separately
St. Mary, Mt., 39, 52
Sene tribe, 15, 16, 27, 35, 45, 123, 125, 157, 202, 266, 289; warfare with Laitate, 15, 204, 206, 220–7, 252
sentimentality, 81, 239–45; see 'love', 'grief'
settlement pattern, see 'hamlets', 'migration', 'population mobility', 'residence'
sex, occasions of sexual intercourse, 57, 245–6; sexual intercourse and menstruation, 220; and shame, 245–6, 248, 262; see also 'adultery'
sex ratios, 130, 291
sexes, lack of formal antagonism between, 81, 134–5; lack of clear roles, 65; conventional relations between, 254; see also 'men', 'women'
shame, 33–4, 74–5, 146, 153, 170, 190, 237, 245–9, 262; see 'insult', 'pride'
Sicot, Fr. M.S.C., 74
Smith, S. E., 56, 197
snakes, 260, 265, 269
social order, lack of idea among Tauade, 137
soil, fertility of, 1, 64, 299; see 'land', 'gardens'
Sopu tribe, 4, 6, 17, 27, 45, 50, 51, 54, 55, 58, 64, 123, 125, 138, 164, 176, 182, 197, 202, 210, 221, 222, 257, 266
sorcery, 10, 17, 162, 237–8, 255–6, 267; see also '*kovata*'

Sorenson, E. R., 7
Sorin, Bishop, M.S.C., 15
speeches, at ceremonies, 57, 75, 163, 167–9, 170, 179, 181–5, 187; and chiefs, 55, 75, 163, 167–9, 170, 179, 181–5, 187; inherent boastfulness of, 146; allegory in, 146–8
Speedie, P.O., 9, 149, 150, 183, 200, 201
spirits, 270–3
Stauder, J., 82
steel tools, 62–3, 207
Steinkraus, W., 44
stone, quarrying of by Fuyughe, 63; as symbol of permanence, 270; and totemic beings, 262–3, 269; legend that Tauade emerged from, 257, 263; associated with culture heroes, 63, 256, 257, 266, 270; pestles and mortars believed to have been made by culture heroes, 63, 270; source of power, 268–70; magical stones, 225, 268–70
stone adzes, replaced by steel, 62–3, 207; making of, 63; trees felled by, 63
Strathern, A. J., 77, 78, 90, 142
strength, displayed in dancing, 165, 166; regarded as ultimate arbiter, 8, 12–13; see 'power'
string bags, invented by culture heroes, 265–6
sugar cane, 64, 65, 226, 243, 273
sun, 266, 267–8
Swadesh's word list, 44
sweet potatoes, 1, 64, 65, 66, 67, 179, 181, 226, 243, 265, 267, 268–9, 273; see 'gardens'
symbolism, as dormant possibility of Tauade thought, 77, 81, 162, 261; see also 'height', 'stone'
systems theory, 252, 275

taboo, 214, 235; on property of deceased, 182–3; on paths, 148
Tame, cosmological category of, 232, 254–74 *passim*
Tangu, 233
Tapini, 2, 4, 9, 10, 13, 14, 15, 21, 22, 24, 27, 28, 30, 36, 41, 42, 49, 51, 130, 131, 141, 154, 157, 169, 173, 174, 184, 187, 198, 199, 201, 206, 214, 228, 245, 258, 298
taro, 1, 64, 65, 226, 273

Tatupiti tribe, 43, 46, 56, 85, 198, 290

Tauade area, location of, 2, 44; population of, 45; origin of name, 1 n., 46–8; language, 37, 43–4; dialect groups, 27, 43–8; similarity of language to those of Fuyughe and Kunimaipa, 43–4

Tauade people, first reaction to white men, 4–5, 16, 21; reasons for failure of economic development, 21–4; physical characteristics of, 2–3, 9; deceitfulness of, 16, 33, 34–5, 248; general unpleasantness of, 27, 33

Tawuni tribe, 45, 46, 112, 123, 124, 125, 126, 133, 152, 153, 154, 157, 170–1, 176, 177, 180, 182, 201, 202, 203, 204, 213, 222, 290

theft, 16, 34, 75, 100, 117, 118, 119, 144, 189, 190, 203, 204, 212, 214, 217, 269

time-reckoning, absence of, 34, 81, 274

tobacco, 23, 29, 65, 75, 144, 183, 184, 247, 255

totems, 262–70

tracks, native, 10, 55, 148, 199, 235; graded, 3, 9–10, 16, 71; see also 'chiefs, and their control of tracks'

trade routes, 50, 231

travel, danger of, 52, 199–201; see also 'chiefs'

tree kangaroo, 263

trees, planting of, 68, 70; felling of, 67; sacred, 157, 158, 169, 264–5, 270; see also 'chiefs', 'culture-heroes', 'forest', 'oaks', 'pandanus'

tribe, definition of, 53; criteria of membership, 83–6; boundaries, 53, 64, 80, 84, 206; areas of, 65; land of, 64, populations of, 65; population densities of, 65; stability of membership, 80, 98; strangers in, 187; homicide within, 93, 109, 117, 119, 120, 121, 131–2, 149–51, 153–4, 191–2, 206, 207, 236; conflict between hamlets, 117, 119, 120, 206, 207, 220–7; see also under names of individual tribes.

truthfulness, not regarded as virtue, 16, 33, 34, 35–6, 248

tseetsi (burial platform), 17, 154, 157, 158, 159; see 'mortuary customs'

Ungabunga River (St. Joseph), 31, 60

United Nations, ineptitude of policies, 4, 24–5

values, as principles integrating institutions and modes of behaviour, vi; changes in over time, vii; unwillingness of Tauade to make absolute value judgements of behaviour, 233; see 'power', 'pride', 'shame', 'reciprocity', 'wealth', 'vengeance'

Vanapa Valley, 43

vengeance, 211–31; averted by flight or dispersal of population, 191, 211; not taken against guilty party himself, 11–12, 197–201, 211; taken against weak, 33, 191, 192, 197, 199–201, 205, 229, 237–8; taken by fraudulent court cases, 36; as preliminary to acceptance of compensation, 189; see also 'reciprocity'

Vetapu Valley, 258

vice, unnatural, unknown in Tauade society, 36

village constable, 4, 8, 25, 141, 150

Wadsworth, P.O., 154

warfare, frequency of, 14, 196; causes of, 196, 206, 210, 211–28 passim, 229–31; generated by internal friction within tribes, 52, 220–7; in relation to geographical proximity of tribes, 202–4, 206; ecological factors involved in, 52, 203–4, 206, 230, 275–7; irrelevance of population pressure on land as causal factor, 205–6, 230; no conquest of land, 206; role of chiefs as peacemakers, 115, 138, 145, 163, 169, 205, 210–11, 213 n., 214, 219, 226; as warleaders, 138, 199, 210, 212–29 passim, 232, 252; halted by dispersal of one of the parties, 206, 211, 219; generosity of other tribes in offering refuge, 206, 221, 222–3, 226–7; role of leading warriors, 210, 211–19 passim, 252; recruitment of allies, 210–11, 212–27 passim, absence of clear patterns of alliance and enmity, 202; pork given to allies, 211, 214; human flesh given to allies, 208; inhibited frequency of dances, 172; inhibits marriage between tribes, 202–3; weapons used, 205, 207; tactics of ambush, 207, 214, 216, 218, 221–2, 226; no formal challenges, 207; treachery in, 7, 200, 207, 215, 221–2, 223, 224; cannibalism and mutilation, 86, 205, 208–10, 213, 215, 216, 217; destruction of pandanus trees, 217; destruction of gardens, 71, 138–9, 172, 211; lack of adaptive value, 230–1, 252–3, 275–7

Watagoipa tribe, 45, 65, 123, 126, 153, 176, 177, 186, 196, 202, 203, 204, 213, 216, 221, 222, 228, 229, 240, 273

Watson, J. B., 233

Wax, R., 251

weakness, contempt for, 12–13, 33, 232

wealth, desire for, 21–5, 33, 233, 240, 249–50

Wedgwood, C., 53

Wendling, Fr. M.S.C., 15, 27

Wharton Range, 2, 39, 257

White, C. H., 244–5

white man, first reactions to, 4–5; identified with culture heroes, 21, 256–7

widows, conventionally defenceless state of, 143, 220; mourning customs of, 245

Wild, cosmological category of, 232, 254–6, 262–74

Williams, F. E., 236, 257

Williamson, R. W., 27–8, 35, 43, 56, 58, 71–2, 90, 95, 97, 164, 172, 207, 209

Wilson, B. G., 157, 169

Wilson, L. J., 5–6, 56, 138, 139

Woitape, 31, 41, 43, 50, 123, 258, 298

women, work conventionally done by, 65, 70, 71–2, 166, 244; sexual aggressiveness of, 36, 134–5, 216; incite men to violence, 130; partiality to violent men, 144; men's desire to control them as cause of violence, 126–8, 132–5; violent assaults on and murder of by men, 119, 120, 121, 128, 132, 134, 187, 192, 197, 198, 199, 200, 201, 205, 215, 216, 219, 248–9; seen as sustainers of culture, 135, 253, 254–5; see also 'marriage', 'sex', 'widows'

Wynne-Edwards, V. C., 171, 172

yams, 1, 64, 65, 203, 204, 205, 269, 272, 273

yam houses, 64

yaws, 49

Yule Island, 4, 19, 30, 49, 201

Yule, Mt., 43, 161